MW00779986

SAVAGE SKIES, EMERALD HELL

THE U.S., AUSTRALIA, JAPAN, AND THE FEROCIOUS AIR BATTLE FOR NEW GUINEA IN WORLD WAR II

JAY A. STOUT

STACKPOLE
BOOKS

Essex, Connecticut
Blue Ridge Summit, Pennsylvania

STACKPOLE BOOKS

An imprint of The Globe Pequot Publishing Group, Inc.
64 South Main Street
Essex, CT 06426
www.globepequot.com

Distributed by NATIONAL BOOK NETWORK

British Library Cataloguing in Publication Information available

Library of Congress Cataloging-in-Publication Data

Names: Stout, Jay A., 1959– author.
Title: Savage skies, emerald hell : the U.S., Australia, Japan, and the ferocious air
   battle for New Guinea in World War II / Jay A. Stout.
Other titles: U.S., Australia, Japan, and the ferocious air battle for New Guinea in
   World War II
Description: Essex, Connecticut : Stackpole Books, 2025. | Includes
   bibliographical references and index.
Identifiers: LCCN 2024027779 (print) | LCCN 2024027780 (ebook) | ISBN
   9780811775632 (cloth) | ISBN 9780811775649 (ebook)
Subjects: LCSH: United States. Army Air Forces—History. | World War,
   1939–1945—Campaigns—New Guinea. | World War, 1939–1945—Aerial
   operations, American. | World War, 1939–1945—Aerial operations,
   British. | Australia. Royal Australian Air Force—History—World War,
   1939–1945.
Classification: LCC D767.95 .S768 2025 (print) | LCC D767.95 (ebook) |
   DDC 940.54/265—dc23/eng/20240723
LC record available at https://lccn.loc.gov/2024027779
LC ebook record available at https://lccn.loc.gov/2024027780

∞™ The paper used in this publication meets the minimum requirements of
American National Standard for Information Sciences—Permanence of Paper for
Printed Library Materials, ANSI/NISO Z39.48-1992.

My wife is Monica. She has never read a single word of the very many books I've written because . . . well, I don't know. Still, I love her mightily. And even though she'll never know it, I dedicate this book—and every good thing I've ever done—to her. And to dogs. I love dogs. This book is also dedicated to dogs even though, like Monica, they'll never know it.

CONTENTS

Acknowledgments   vii

Preface   ix

Prelude   xi

1   "It Was Trickling Down My Legs"   1

2   "He Never Said a Word"   23

3   "I Decided to Go to Horn Island"   31

4   "A Very Attractive and Polished Gentleman"   49

5   "He Had Avoided Combat Often"   55

6   "He Had No Parachute"   61

7   "Father, Don't Try to Persuade Them"   67

8   "I Would Be Loyal to Him"   75

9   "We Pray for Absolute Victory"   85

10   "One's Head Lying on Another's Chest"   97

11   "Most of Us Went Away Shaking Our Heads"   107

12   "Send Troops Immediately"   121

13   "It Was More Than I Could Stand"   133

14   "What We Didn't Get, the Sharks Got"   153

15   "The Zero Exploded Just Before Hitting the Water"   161

16 "We Never Did See Them"   *171*

17 "Sell the P-47 or Go Back Home"   *177*

18 "Making Fool of the Jap Man"   *181*

19 "My God, What a Sight!"   *191*

20 "But He Was Always Cheerful"   *207*

21 "Great Gushing Gouts of Fuel Ignited"   *213*

22 "Tickling a Giant's Throat with a Feather"   *219*

23 "He Was Lying"   *233*

24 "We Tended to Black Out"   *247*

25 "I Don't Remember a Lot Being Made of It"   *261*

26 "Everyone Except MacArthur Looked Skeptical"   *271*

27 "Part of a Burned Body Slipped from the B-25"   *281*

28 "We Had Hoped to Catch a Few Jap Planes in the Air"   *291*

29 "He Cursed and Shouted"   *299*

Epilogue   303

Notes   307

Bibliography   321

Index   323

ACKNOWLEDGMENTS

I knew the day would come when I would not be able to interview veterans for my World War II work. That day is here. Thankfully, many other organizations had the foresight to record and archive the recollections of a great many men. Among those organizations were the Australian War Memorial, the American Fighter Aces Association, and the Australians at War Film Archive.

Many writers before me created excellent work about specific aspects of the air campaign over New Guinea. Among these experts are Michael Veitch, Lex McAulay, Eric Bergerud, Michael Claringbould, and the late Henry Sakaida. I am indebted to them.

I thank my friends at Globe Pequot, particularly Dave Reisch and Stephanie Otto, for helping to ensure this book is as good as it is.

And finally, thank you to my wife, Monica.

PREFACE

"Really? I didn't know we fought the Japanese in Africa." This was my friend's response upon learning that my most recent book was about the Allied air campaign against the Japanese over New Guinea during World War II.

My shoulders sank as I briefly considered the truth that a comprehensive knowledge of world geography—or World War II history—was not imperative for a person to succeed in life. And to be fair, among its many nations, the African continent does include a Guinea, a Guinea-Bissau, a Gambia, and a Ghana. Although my friend's familiarity with the world map was disappointing, I was heartened by the obvious fact that my subject matter was not overexposed.

The site of the fiercest fighting in the Southwest Pacific, New Guinea ranks among the absolute worst places in the world to fight a major conflict. Its interior is an inhospitable hell, largely inaccessible even today. Cloaked by smothering jungles and stinking swamps—and spiked by cloud-shrouded mountains—it hosts myriad diseases and is populated by indigenous peoples who might or might not be friendly. It simply swallowed fighting men from both sides. Many thousands of them remain missing.

The seas surrounding the island are equally merciless. An accurate count cannot be known, but many downed airmen were eaten by sharks. Men who weren't eaten often drifted away and died of exposure. Weather, especially in the form of violent thunderstorms, could make life on the island miserable. Those same storms made flying deadly.

The Allies, mostly Australians and Americans, endured all of this as they battled a deadly, determined, and unforgiving foe. The Japanese were many things—including breathtakingly cruel—but they were never described as pushovers. Fighting them in the infernal perdition that was New Guinea could only be understood by those who had to do it.

No one wanted to fight in New Guinea—neither the Japanese nor the Allies. But each side was compelled to do so. Japan needed bases there from which it could isolate Australia. The Allies needed bases there to keep them from doing so. New Guinea was simply too big and too strategically situated not to be contested. And contesting it by air was critical to success.

The fighting in New Guinea featured prominently in the nation's public consciousness during the early part of the war. But the grind there continued until the end of the war, and even though it was still killing men, it was eventually overshadowed to a certain degree as more campaigns—North Africa, Italy, the Solomons, and others—got underway. By the time Europe was invaded, it had become almost a backwater, thanks to Allied successes.

Since the war, for many reasons, the fighting that happened elsewhere during World War II has attracted more attention from academics and readers of military history. And, as indicated by my friend's surprise, it remains largely unknown to perhaps the majority of Americans. This is regrettable, as the story of the New Guinea campaign highlights the best and worst of the participants and includes remarkable examples of brilliance, buffoonery, and bravery. Moreover, the lives of the men lost there were just as dear to their wives and mothers as were the lives of the men lost elsewhere.

My goal for this book is to create more awareness about the fight for New Guinea by describing it in the context of the air actions that made the Allied victory possible. While it is necessarily a wide-ranging overview that cannot possibly include every unit or engagement, I hope that the many stories, vignettes, and anecdotes underscore the hardship and terror endured by these very real men who fought a unique war during a hard and terrible time.

PRELUDE

The sun had burned most of the fog from the Nadzab fighter strip, although everything—the ground, the grass, and the runway—was still wet. Water dripped from the wings and fuselages of the aircraft. And skeins of low clouds still clung to the distant hills, but the sky had already turned from gray to blue.

The month had been a slow one for the men of the 35th Fighter Group. They were transitioning from the indifferent P-39 Airacobra to the P-47 Thunderbolt, a powerful monster of an aircraft, but not a lovely one. Lovely or not, it didn't matter. The P-47 was the aircraft they had been assigned, and the P-47 was the aircraft they would fly.

Jeeps and trucks bumped along the ground to the different revetments where they delivered pilots and ground crews and tools and material. Mechanics banged panels into place and buttoned them tight. That and everything else done, they wiped what was left of the fog from windscreens and canopies. Pilots—many of them not convinced of the P-47's worth— walked around their aircraft, poking here and pulling there. Satisfied, or not, they donned their gear and got ready to fly.

The noise was just a faint whine at first, little more than a ringing in the ears. And yet, it persisted. Indeed, it didn't just persist, it grew louder. Men stopped what they were doing and scanned the horizon.

And there they were. Eight black dots in a line-abreast formation dropped from the sky toward the 35th's flight line. Some of the men shaded their eyes with their hands and scrutinized the dots more carefully.

The dots turned into aircraft. Bright flashes—gunfire—winked from their wings and noses. And the 35th's men ran. Some of them ran for trenches and some of them ran behind revetments and some of them simply ran for distance and kept running. Others crouched behind aircraft.

"We could hear the bullets whistling by as they strafed," said Joe Potts. "They really did whistle, just like in the movies! They were sleek-looking planes with that inline engine."[1] Bullets and cannon rounds spattered across the ground and into aircraft.

The enemy fighters ripped overhead seconds later, just high enough to keep from flying into the P-47s which sat fat and still and unperturbed and still dripping wet. The strafers were painted dark, their fuselages and wings splashed with the blood-red roundels of Japan. They were Kawasaki Ki-61s—code-named Tony. And, as Potts noted, they were fast and streamlined and deadly beautiful.

And then they were gone.

The 35th's narrative for that day, January 15, 1944, noted, "Some of the boys at the line really had ringside seats. Although no one was hurt, and only four P-47s were hit, three of which were put out of commission."

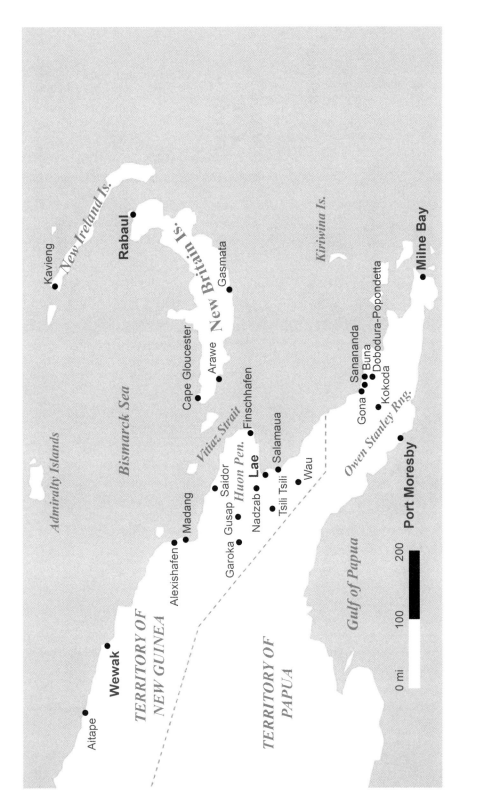

Kavieng

New Ireland Is.

Rabaul

New Britain Is.

Gasmata

Kiriwina Is.

Admiralty Islands

Bismarck Sea

Cape Gloucester

Arawe

New Britain

Milne Bay

Sanananda

Buna

Dobodura-Popondetta

Gona

Kokoda

Finschhafen

Vitiaz Strait

Huon Pen.

Salamaua

Owen Stanley Rng.

Madang

Saidor

Lae

Wau

Alexishafen

Garoka

Gusap

Nadzab

Tsili Tsili

Gulf of Papua

Port Moresby

Wewak

TERRITORY OF
NEW GUINEA

TERRITORY OF
PAPUA

200

100

0 mi

Aitape

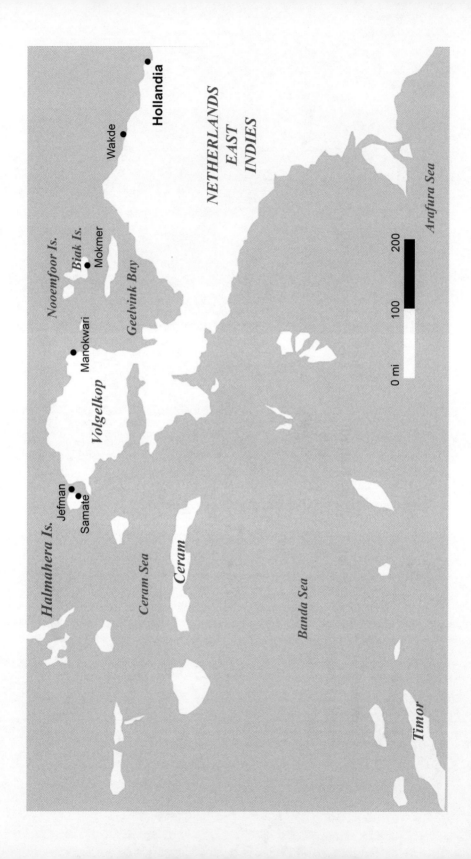

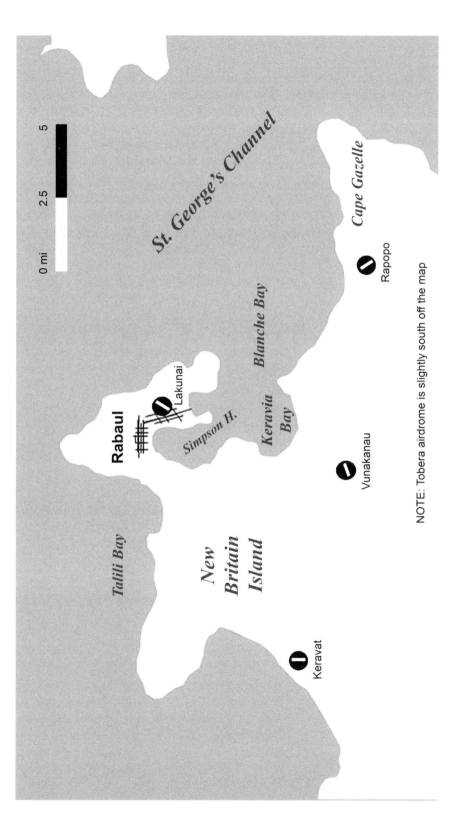

St. George's Channel

Cape Gazelle

Rapopo

Blanche Bay

Lakunai

Rabaul

Keravia Bay

Simpson H.

Vunakanau

New Britain Island

Talili Bay

Keravat

0 mi   2.5   5

NOTE: Tobera airdrome is slightly south off the map

1

"IT WAS TRICKLING DOWN MY LEGS"

"I've got 'shits' entered in my logbook with my first combat," said Arthur Tucker, a P-40 pilot with the Royal Australian Air Force's, or RAAF's, 75 Squadron. "That wasn't fear. That was the fact that it was trickling down my legs because I had gastroenteritis."[1] Such was life at Port Moresby, New Guinea, for the Allied men fighting there in early 1942.

★★★

The second-largest island in the world, New Guinea was vast, unexplored, and dangerous when it was first spied by the Portuguese in 1526. That was still true to a great degree at the outbreak of World War II more than four centuries later. It wasn't until 1938, just before the war, that a highland valley inhabited by tens of thousands of natives was discovered from the air. When they were reached by foot, it was the first time they had encountered anyone from outside their world.

Spanning roughly 1,600 miles from east to west, and 450 miles from north to south at its deepest, New Guinea sits less than a hundred miles from the northernmost point of Australia's Cape York Peninsula. Mountain ranges rise across much of it, reaching heights greater than 16,000 feet at points. The majority of the island is covered by near-impenetrable jungle while much of the rest is swamp. Dry scrub and grasslands are only occasionally encountered. Ridges and peaks and canyons and rivers and jagged escarpments make roads nearly impossible, and foot travel a misery. Snakes and insects and leeches and diseases and mean-spirited plants—spiny and poisonous—make it worse. Compounding the wretchedness of it all are regular, often severe, thunderstorms. The saying goes: "It rains nine months out of the year, and then the monsoon season starts."

It wasn't until nearly a century after it was discovered by the Portuguese that New Guinea was proved to be an island. It was inhabited by tribes of dark-skinned, fuzzy-haired people, Papuans, who lived in a state of near-continuous conflict with those who weren't from the same village or area. Many of the tribes took heads as trophies and sometimes ate each other. Primarily hunter-gatherers, they also practiced subsistence agriculture. Their civilization was not advanced in the traditional sense, but they thrived in an ecosystem that regularly killed or ejected white colonizers, traders, and missionaries.

Partly because there were easier and more lucrative places in the world to seize or colonize, and partly because it was literally on the other side of the world, Europeans took time to pay serious attention to New Guinea. It wasn't until the 19th century that they established themselves in the region and began to divvy up the islands. The Dutch took the western half of the island, which was called Netherlands New Guinea, or more commonly, Dutch New Guinea. The Germans helped themselves to the northeastern part of the island and nearby archipelagos, which they sensibly named German New Guinea. The British and Australians took the southeastern part, which they christened British New Guinea.

Assessing that it didn't offer much value, Great Britain passed control of British New Guinea to Australia in 1906. Because the different parts of the island couldn't be named and renamed often enough, the Australians called it the Territory of Papua New Guinea. A few years later, during World War I, Australian forces captured German New Guinea, and it was subsequently awarded to the British following the cessation of hostilities. But the British weren't particularly taken with their new prize and gifted Australia with the responsibility for its administration. Australia subsequently renamed it the Territory of New Guinea. Ultimately, at the start of World War II, Australia called the two different parts of the island for which it was responsible the territories of Papua and New Guinea.

★★★

Following their sneak attack on Pearl Harbor on December 7, 1941, the Japanese advanced rapidly through Asia and across the Pacific. The American forces at Guam were defeated within a couple of days, and Wake Island was seized later that month. The British were defeated at Hong Kong at the same time while their supposedly indomitable fortress at Singapore—to the great shock and embarrassment of the entire empire—fell with barely a whimper in February 1942. The Japanese raced down the Malay Peninsula from there and thence to the Netherlands East Indies. America mourned when the last of its defenders in the Philippines surrendered in May 1942. In the central Pacific, the Japanese built bases in the Marshall, Caroline, and Gilbert Islands, and elsewhere.

What the Japanese accomplished in early 1942 was remarkable. But New Guinea seemed to confound them. They had little trouble ousting the Australian garrison at Rabaul on New Britain Island, or chasing the Australians out of other outposts. However, the main island and its peripheral islands were a vast territory of little value to them other than as points from which to isolate Australia from the United States. It seemed simple enough.

It turned into a nightmare that killed men and destroyed equipment on a scale the Japanese could not afford.

★★★

The city of Port Moresby was the Allied center of gravity in New Guinea at the start of World War II. It sat on the southern coast of the tail of land that extended east from the central part of the island. Discovered and named in 1873, it wasn't developed until late in the 19th century but grew steadily to become the region's largest city and trading center. It had a deep natural harbor ringed by protective mountains and consequently became a center for shipping that serviced commercial enterprises both on the coast and in the interior. Wharves and warehouses were developed, as was an airport and the sorts of infrastructures typical of a modern city. This included water and electrical services, roads, hospitals, and government buildings, not to mention residential areas.

In short, it was the most important city in New Guinea. Its location, just more than 300 miles northeast of Australia's extreme northern limits, together with its other attributes, made it strategically important. This fact was not lost on Australia, and work to expand Port Moresby's capacity as a wartime base began even before the Japanese attack on Pearl Harbor. By early 1942 it hosted a hodgepodge of military organizations, including engineering, artillery, antiaircraft, and anti-tank units.

But there were no RAAF fighter squadrons to protect it. On the heels of Australia's defeat and ejection from Rabaul on New Britain Island at the end of January 1942, the Japanese sent their first air raid against Port Moresby on February 3, 1942. There was nothing to oppose it. There were no defending fighters, and the enemy aircraft flew higher than most of the antiaircraft guns could reach.

If the defenders at Port Moresby were not literally sitting ducks, they were certainly defenseless, and able to do little more than take cover from the Japanese bombs. They did occasionally fire their rifles and machineguns when enemy fighters—namely the Mitsubishi A6M Zero—dropped down to the deck to strafe whatever their pilots felt might be worth a burst of machinegun or cannon fire. Simply put, the Japanese operated however and whenever they pleased over Port Moresby.

There were rumors that a squadron of Curtiss P-40 fighters would arrive soon. Named Kittyhawks by Britain's Royal Air Force and the Commonwealth nations, these fighters would, at a minimum, snatch away the free rein that the Japanese enjoyed. Indeed, there were hopes that the Kittyhawks—frontline American-made fighters—would be a real deterrent.

But they didn't arrive. And they continued to not arrive. Day after long day, suffering through regular air raids, the men at Port Moresby waited. They started referring to the Kittyhawks as Tomorrow-Hawks, Never-Hawks, and other derogatory names. Were it not for the increased level of activity in the harbor, the defenders might have justifiably felt abandoned.

In truth, the RAAF was moving as fast as it could to get a unit of capable fighter aircraft up to Port Moresby. However, except for a few problematic and much-maligned Brewster Buffalos, Australia had no modern fighters, and its aircraft industry was not capable of producing anything of that sort in the near term. Aside from a few license-built Bristol Beaufort torpedo aircraft, the most modern indigenously produced aircraft was the Wirraway, built by the Commonwealth Aircraft Corporation, or CAC. But it was little more than a derivative of the North American NA-16, an American training aircraft.

But good things came from bad things. Shipments of Curtiss P-40s that were destined for American units in the Philippines were ordered to Australia instead. The Japanese had established a strong blockade around the Philippines, and the odds of beating it were small.

As the aircraft crates were unloaded in Australia, the recently cobbled-together U.S. Army Air Forces, or USAAF, headquarters in Melbourne allocated the aircraft to its own newly arrived units and also set some aside for the RAAF. Americans and Australians together assembled and trained on them. By March 1942, up to 300 aircraft had been put ashore. The USAAF sent some of them to Java in an attempt to stem the Japanese advance there, but that abortive effort achieved virtually nothing. In truth, it was a disaster as too many pilots were killed, and too many aircraft were destroyed or left behind during the rush to escape back to Australia.

All this occurred during an exceedingly desperate period for the Allies. There was no indication whatsoever that the Japanese could be stopped. The Allies had won no meaningful victories, and the Japanese had swept unchecked across Asia and the Pacific. Arthur Tucker, a pilot with the

RAAF's 75 Squadron declared, "Australia was in a state of absolute panic, and defeatism, and lack of leadership." This, he believed, was mirrored in the RAAF. "I believe that there was incredible defeatism in all levels of our community."

The nonstop defeats and failures were a despairing backdrop for how and where the RAAF ought to use its exceptionally meager resources. Where the defense of New Guinea was concerned, its leadership was caught in a dilemma. The longer it took to train pilots to fly the P-40, the more at risk were the forces being bombed at Port Moresby. But should the pilots be sent to Port Moresby without the training they needed, disaster was sure to follow.

There was no good answer, and pilots from different units were given orders to the base at RAAF Townsville in northeastern Queensland, Australia, where 75 Squadron was formed on March 4, 1942. The unit was to be assigned 24 P-40Es, the first of which was received on March 8. Flight training began on March 11, and pilots, ground crews, and aircraft continued to arrive during the next couple of weeks. There was a bare handful of pilots with experience from fighting alongside Britain's Royal Air Force, or RAF, in the Middle East, but most of the rest had no combat time, many fewer flying hours, and no experience at the controls of the P-40.

That lack of training was made apparent by a handful of minor mishaps and two more serious accidents that left the aircraft involved very badly damaged. The P-40 was a bigger, heavier, more complex, and higher-performance aircraft than the Wirraway, and it was understandable that it wasn't immediately mastered. Arthur Tucker recalled that simply climbing into the P-40 made an impression. "To get into a Kittyhawk you had to climb up onto the wing and then clamber up in the cockpit," he said, "and there, sticking in front of you, was this great 12-cylinder V-engine with an air scoop on the top. And it sort of went up almost at forty-five degrees, and you couldn't see anything ahead of you. You had to look out to about forty degrees to the side to see, with your tail down."

John Pettett arrived at Townsville from Brisbane on March 14—the same day his son was born. "My feeling," he said, "was one of longing to be with my wife, of course." He had been flying less than a year, and like Tucker and Crawford, had very little experience with the P-40. He made a unique observation about the aircraft. "I remember more than anything else the smell, and I can still smell it. Sometimes you get the smell in a ship [aircraft] and I don't know what it is, whether it is cables or what, or metal, or whatever they treat the metal with, but there is a certain smell about it—particularly American airplanes."[2]

Despite its weight, size, performance, and complexity, none of the Australian pilots described the P-40 as a particularly difficult aircraft to fly—it was simply different and new. Arthur Tucker said, "If you'd flown a Wirraway, you could fly a Kittyhawk right from the beginning, and it was simple and smooth and easy." Still, there was much to learn about it, and had the Australian pilots been given more time to fly it, they would have become more proficient. But they were not. "I flew it three times," said Arthur Tucker. Fellow pilot Robert Crawford's experience was the same. "I had six hours on the type," he declared.[3]

That level of P-40 experience was fairly common for the pilots of the newly formed 75 Squadron. It could not have been otherwise. The unit was formed on March 4, 1942, and received its first P-40s on March 8. It flew its first training sorties with the Kittyhawk on March 11, and the squadron's first aircraft left for Port Moresby and the war eight days later on March 19. The situation was that desperate.

★★★

The day that seemed as if it would never arrive finally did. Men squinted into the late morning sky at the four fighters approaching 7-Mile Drome at Port Moresby. After weeks of being hammered by the Japanese, most of them thought it was another enemy raid. "One machine-gunner thought it was the usual enemy visitation," noted a newspaper report. "He opened fire. Others followed suit until the valley resounded with a fusillade. Intensive fire continued until the first machine touched down."[4]

The aircraft were P-40 Kittyhawks of the RAAF's 75 Squadron. These fighters at which the men at Port Moresby were shooting were the fighters for which they had waited so long. And they didn't realize it.

William Bellairs remembered, "And so our boys gave them, with their rifles and their light machineguns, a bit of a welcome, which didn't endear us very much to them, I can assure you of that. But it was not our fault really, because no one was informed, and then the order come through, 'Stop firing, stop firing, they're ours, they're ours.'"[5]

But if there was a bright side to the incident, it was that the skills of the defending gunners were reasonably good. 75 Squadron recorded that all four aircraft were hit and that one bullet missed the lead pilot, Peter Jeffrey, by half an inch. It slammed into his headrest. Unfortunately, one of the other aircraft was no longer flyable.

The confusion and shouting and finger-pointing eventually subsided, and the two aircraft that had been least damaged were refueled. An unescorted enemy reconnaissance aircraft was reported inbound, and two pilots, Wilbur Wackett and Barry Cox, took the two P-40s airborne. They spotted a Mitsubishi G4M twin-engine bomber—code-named Betty—and made several attacks as it dived away. The Japanese aircraft was unable to escape the two Australians, and it exploded before falling into the sea. It was perhaps the easiest victory 75 Squadron would score over Port Moresby.

The destruction of the Japanese bomber and its crew occurred in full view of the units that garrisoned Port Moresby. The men erupted with spontaneous cheers and backslaps and jigs. Trucks full of cheering men—almost giddy at the spectacle—bumped up and down the rough roads. The men of the antiaircraft units recalled the event.

> How every one was cheered and what a beautiful sight to see two of our chaps get that Jap recco plane way out over the reef. The little planes dashed around searching for the Jap in a big cloud bank. And what a cheer when the Jap was seen to crash in flames and a large column of black smoke reached up to, and flattened itself against, the low cloud bank![6]

These were men who had been bombed by the Japanese for six weeks and who had been able to do nothing but endure it. Certainly, they would be bombed many more times, but no longer would they be undefended.

Later that day, a Lockheed Hudson from the RAAF's 32 Squadron led 13 more P-40s from 75 Squadron to 7-Mile Drome. Happily, they were not fired upon. They were followed by a handful of other fighters and pilots during the next couple of weeks to help buttress the squadron's strength. Continuous losses kept the unit from ever reaching its authorized strength of 24 aircraft. But overall, March 21, 1942, was a good day for the Australians at Port Moresby. It would stand in contrast to the many dark days the men would endure in the coming months.

Peter Jeffrey, who had nearly caught a friendly bullet in his head when he landed at 7-Mile Drome, had passed command of the squadron to John F. Jackson two days earlier on March 19. Jackson was tall and balding, and his ears stuck out a bit. In appearance, he certainly was not the movie star cliché of a fighter pilot. And at 34 years of age, he was quite old when compared to his comrades. John Jackson was referred to as "Old John."

A veteran of the fighting in the Middle East with the RAAF's 3 Squadron during 1941, he was already an ace, having been credited with downing four German, and two Vichy French aircraft. He was not an ebullient sort but instead was quiet and businesslike and nice—he moved with confident ease. Moreover, he led by example and flew more than his share of missions.

As they grew to know him, Jackson's men embraced his "do as I do" leadership. Arthur Tucker recalled, "He was a magnificent fellow, middle thirties, ex-estate agent, and he was that sort of wonderful, solid, Australian countryman that we all like to think most Australians are, but few ever reach that sort of stature." Tucker had more to say. "He was the only bright spot of it. And I would say that had John F. Jackson not existed, the squadron would not have been effective in that defense role for as long as it was."

William Whetters, another of Jackson's pilots, recalled him as "a most outstanding man, and with great consideration for the pilots under him. . . . He would have duties that he could give to others but preferred to do them himself."[7]

Not everyone, however, was convinced of Jackson's suitability for the role. Peter Jeffrey, the recently promoted wing commander who passed command of 75 Squadron to Jackson, had been Jackson's commanding officer in the Middle East. "He was a bit hard of hearing and his eyes weren't all that good," Jeffrey said. "He shouldn't have been in fighters because he was a bit old." Jeffrey also mentioned that flying close formation with Jackson was a bit dicey, as "when he turned his head, he also turned his aircraft."

Jackson also tended toward being too aggressive and was not inclined to "wait to fight another day" when the odds were stacked against him. When Jeffrey expressed his doubts to Jackson, Jackson replied, "I've got a wife and kids back there in Australia and no Jap bastard's going to get anywhere near them except over my dead body."[8]

Despite his misgivings, and his belief that Jackson would press himself and his men too hard, Jeffrey passed command of 75 Squadron to Jackson. "And that would be his only fault as far as I'm concerned," Jeffrey said. "But he had extraordinary courage, extraordinary courage."[9]

Jeffrey was not mistaken. Press hard is exactly what Jackson did. Ground crews armed and fueled and otherwise readied 10 aircraft for an early morning strike against the Japanese airfield at Lae. At 0630 on March 22, the day after 75 Squadron arrived at 7-Mile Drome, Jackson advanced the throttle of his aircraft and rolled down the runway to lead the formation 190 miles almost straight north across the Owen Stanley Range to where Lae sat on New Guinea's northern coast.

One of Jackson's pilots, John Le Gay Brereton, swerved to dodge a Lockheed Hudson that had taxied onto the runway. Brereton avoided smashing into the other aircraft, but his wing struck a small hillock and his aircraft's landing gear was torn away. The wrecked aircraft skidded to a stop and caught fire. Brereton was pulled from the burning P-40 and survived, albeit with injuries.

Jackson led the remaining aircraft across the island and out over the sea to set up for a strafing attack on Lae from the north. The Japanese had seized the town only two weeks earlier on March 8, 1942, and immediately started using its airfield. But Jackson's group was not to be the first to hit the enemy there.

Two U.S. Navy aircraft carriers, the *Lexington* and *Yorktown*, had sent more than 100 aircraft against the Japanese on March 10, two days after they came ashore at Lae. Launching from the Gulf of Papua, the Navy flyers crossed the island from the south, crested the Owen Stanley Range, and caught the Japanese completely by surprise, sinking three transports at the cost of one aircraft. Satisfied with the day's work, the Navy sailed away.

After arriving overhead Lae, Jackson led five Kittyhawks in a diving line astern to shoot up Japanese aircraft parked around the airfield. The enemy fighters were lined up on one side of the airfield, and the bombers were arranged in a row on the other side. It made them easy targets, and the six .50 caliber machineguns carried by each P-40 made a raucous rumble as they sent streams of bullets into the Japanese aircraft. Above them, four other P-40 pilots flew high cover in the event that enemy fighters tried to disrupt the attack.

Flames and smoke spiraled up into the sky. The Australian pilots, buoyed by the spectacle of destruction they had created, wheeled around and made another attack from the opposite direction. The enemy defenses were either caught by surprise or were incompetent, for there was little antiaircraft fire.

The P-40 pilots continued their attacks. John Piper fired his guns at a line of bombers but fixated too intently on his last target. "I got too low and hit the propeller of the aircraft," he said. "It made a good bit of a clang and I hadn't realized it then, but a gun had fallen out." The impact had also severed a wing spar—a critical structural component. "But it kept on going alright," Piper said.

A patrol of three Japanese Zeroes finally dived on the Australians while the four high-cover Australian pilots also roared into the fight. At the same time, John Piper raced to escape with his damaged aircraft, but the enemy pilots were determined to make certain he didn't. "We were being chased out at that time," he remembered, and the 20-millimeter cannon fire from the Zeroes impressed him mightily—they looked like gasoline-dipped cricket balls that had been set afire. "And all of a sudden," he said, "Zip! They go past you like that!"[10]

During the ensuing fracas, the Australians claimed two Zeroes downed in air combat. Peter Turnbull and his wingman, John Pettett, made claims for one apiece. Pettett recalled seeing a Zero attack a Kittyhawk as it was strafing. Finished with its firing pass, the Japanese fighter zoomed into a high climbing turn, "more or less in front of me," Pettett said, "and all I instinctively did was pull back on the stick and pull the trigger and allowing what I thought was enough deflection and that aircraft went down."

A pair of Lockheed Hudson light bombers from the RAAF's 32 Squadron was scheduled to bomb and photograph Lae following 75 Squadron's strafing attack. Jackson and his men were tasked with escorting them over the target and taking them back to Port Moresby. As planned, the two Hudsons motored over Lae and dropped their bombs. The Kittyhawks raced to their aid, but a single Zero outpaced them and attacked both aircraft. Two crewmen were wounded, but the gunners aboard the Hudsons shot the Japanese aircraft down.

The many fires burning on the airfield indicated the raid's success. But it didn't come without cost as two P-40s were missing. Wilbur Wackett and Bruce Anderson failed to return, and none of the other pilots were certain what happened to them, although it was presumed that they were shot down by the enemy fighters.

That presumption was correct in the case of Wilbur Wackett. He was part of the high-cover flight and dived on the Zeroes which were attacking the strafers. During the dive, the light in his gunsight failed, but he nevertheless maneuvered to take a shot at one of the enemy fighters. However, when he pulled the trigger, only one of his six guns fired. Still, he scored strikes on the Zero's left wing.

"I then dove away," he said, "and the next thing I knew was that my engine was hit by a burst of fire." Wackett never saw his attacker. He ducked into a bank of clouds and tried to bring his engine back to life by switching fuel tanks and activating the emergency fuel pump. It didn't work. The engine failed as he descended out of the clouds at 1,000 feet. In the distance, he saw two burning Zeroes smash into the mouth of the Bwong River. When he put his dead aircraft into the water, he was eight miles from the coast.[11]

Jackson led 75 Squadron and the two Hudsons back to Port Moresby. Analysis of photographs from one of the Hudsons confirmed that nine Zeroes and three twin-engine bombers were destroyed on the ground. Added to this number were the two Zeroes destroyed in aerial combat by Turnbull and Pettett and the Zero shot down by the Hudsons.

But the single day's action had claimed nearly a quarter of 75 Squadron's 17 aircraft. Brereton's takeoff accident, combined with the loss of Anderson and Wackett over Lae, totaled three aircraft. But later in the day, John Piper wrecked another of the precious P-40s when he landed after spending two hours over Port Moresby, waiting to intercept an enemy raid that never materialized. Piper was uninjured, but if 75 Squadron kept losing aircraft at the same rate, it wouldn't last but a few more days.

★★★

Although Jackson and his men almost certainly didn't care, it is interesting that the P-40 went by three different names for no rational reason whatsoever. The USAAF settled on Warhawk for all variants, whereas the RAF named the early models—P-40Bs and P-40Cs—Tomahawks. The P-40D and later models were called Kittyhawks, or Kittys, by the RAF and the Commonwealth nations. 75 Squadron flew P-40Es at that point in the war.

Whatever they were called, the aircraft were fine fighters. Curtiss had modified its radial engine-powered P-36 in 1938 with the inline, 12-cylinder, Allison V-1710 engine. After refinements, the new design, the P-40, demonstrated top speeds in excess of 350 miles per hour. Although it lacked the turbo-supercharger necessary for high-altitude operations, it was a very good fighter at medium and low altitudes. Compared to the German Me-109s it encountered over North Africa, it was just as fast in level flight. In a dive, it was faster. It also turned better and had considerably greater range and endurance. Built exceedingly tough, it endured harsh operating conditions worldwide.

However, all was not rosy for 75 Squadron as the P-40s were new not only to most of the pilots who flew them but also to most of the mechanics who maintained them. And replacement parts were virtually nonexistent as the supply line from Port Moresby to the Curtiss factory in Buffalo, New York, measured nearly 9,000 miles. And in light of everything else happening across the globe, 75 Squadron was not at the top of the priority list.

But the squadron's pilots were happy with the aircraft. It was as fast or faster in level flight than the Zero. In fact, its liquid-cooled engine produced approximately 1,200 horsepower—as much or more than most other fighters at that time of the war. One pilot recalled how it accelerated: "Not as sensitive as a Wirraway but has tons of power. Boy, do they give you a push in the back!"[12]

In fact, it could dive away from the Zero if a pilot got into trouble. And it was much more rugged and carried better armament. But it was not nearly as maneuverable as its Japanese counterpart, nor could it climb as fast or high, or fly as far. In practice, this meant that the Zeroes could fly so high that the P-40s, equipped with only a single supercharger, could not reach them. This made it possible for the Japanese pilots to choose when and how to start a fight. And because it wasn't as maneuverable, if the P-40 pilots chose to engage the Zeroes in a turning fight they stood a good chance of getting dead.

John Pettett recalled that "the Kittyhawk was beautiful" in appearance. And he appreciated its speed in a dive. "If you got into trouble at high altitude," he said, "you could just put the nose down and it streaked away, and it was strong enough to come out of a high-speed dive." Pettett especially liked the P-40's armament. "Its best feature was its guns," he said. "It had tremendous striking power. As you can imagine with six, half-inch [.50 caliber] guns, three in each wing, and the damage they did was incredible."

That it had good armor protection also gave its pilots comfort. Pettett recalled other pilots describing how they could hear and feel Japanese machinegun rounds rattling off the cockpit armor. This was protection the Zero pilots did not have. Pettett's friend Alan Whetters was flying over Port Moresby on one occasion when he was attacked from behind by a Zero he never saw. Rather, it was the reverberating shock of the enemy aircraft's rounds hitting the armor plate behind his seat that alerted him. "Like piano notes without the music," he said.

Another protective feature was the P-40's self-sealing fuel tanks. These became standard on American combat aircraft. When hit by a bullet or cannon round, the material inside the self-sealing tanks—typically two layers of rubber or rubber-like material—would expand to seal or minimize the hole. The P-40 often came home with its fuel tanks riddled by bullets, whereas its Japanese counterparts were transformed into flying torches when their fuel tanks were hit by just a few machinegun rounds.

Pettett was saved by the P-40's sheer ruggedness on April 6, 1942, during an attack on a formation of Betty bombers. In a steep climb, almost at stalling speed, he fired his guns. At the same instant, the rear of his aircraft was hit by a 20-millimeter cannon shell fired by the bomber's tail gunner. His aircraft was knocked out of control.

"I just spun straight out of it," he said. "I just went in all directions and finished up pointing straight down at the ground . . . I pulled out of it. It was no problem really . . . But when I looked back, I could see this great . . . it was like a can opener had been through the leading edge of the tailplane on the starboard side."

Pettett was uncertain what effect the damage might have on the aircraft's flyability, and he put the aircraft through some gentle maneuvers. "I couldn't say that it made any difference actually," he said. Confident in the aircraft's structural integrity, Pettett landed back at 7-Mile Drome with no problems.

An issue with the P-40 that especially vexed the Australian pilots was that the light bulb that reflected the aiming reticle onto the gunsight's glass failed too often and easily. And there were no replacements except for what could be cannibalized from wrecked aircraft. Inasmuch as shooting down enemy aircraft with its guns was the primary mission of the P-40, the means by which to aim them was of critical importance.

No ready solution was at hand, and the pilots were forced to shoot their guns by guesswork, or to fly so close to the enemy aircraft that they could not miss. With no good options, the resourceful ground crewmen crafted fixed sights from water pipes and wiring. They might have been better than nothing, but the point was debated.

For all its faults, flown correctly and properly maintained, the P-40 was a fighter with which 75 Squadron could make things difficult for the Japanese over Port Moresby. But that was not possible if the unit's men were sick. Even though the development of 7-Mile Drome had been underway for months, there was little emphasis placed on health, hygiene, or comfort.

In fact, there were no provisions for the pilots or ground crews to relieve themselves. Rather, they grabbed a communal shovel and a page of old newspaper before stepping a few feet into the tall kunai grass. There, they dug a small hole and defecated. Many of the men, suffering from the effects of gastroenteritis or dysentery or similar maladies, made several trips a day. The grass grew trampled and spotted with little mounds marking the locations where the men had done their business. Indeed, 75 Squadron moved their camp on one occasion because the health of the men was so poor.

But still, the men worked, and the pilots flew. The cockpits, which baked in the humid heat, were rife with infectious microbes as the bowels of many men simply let go, and there was no good way to get the residue out of the many nooks and crannies. One man had malaria so badly that he vomited on the windscreen and was unable to see well enough to continue the mission. This was perhaps just as well as he lost consciousness immediately after he got the aircraft back on the ground. He had to be lifted from the cockpit.

The problem with the diseases against which the pilots struggled wasn't just that being sick degraded their performance. Rather, that poor performance also caused accidents that damaged or destroyed aircraft. And those aircraft were just as damaged or destroyed as if they had been shot up by the Japanese. For example, Flying Officer P. Scandrett blacked out during takeoff and crashed on April 17. Although he survived with injuries, the aircraft was so badly wrecked that it was written off.

When 75 Squadron's pilots weren't too sick to fly, they sat alert close to their aircraft in a tent where they read, or talked, or played cards, or wrote letters. Or they squatted in the Kunai grass outside. Or just sat. A telephone was attached to a pole in the tent, and when it rang with information that a raid was inbound, the call went up: "It's on!" Or, "Pilots!" The men raced to their aircraft and, helped by their ground crews, hurried to strap into their seats, and to don their helmets and throat microphones and other flying gear. They started their engines, taxied to the end of the airfield, advanced their throttles, and rattled down the runway in clouds of dust or sprays of mud.

These were the most anxious moments for many of the men. While idling away their time on the ground or trying to sleep, they regularly imagined all manner of awful fates. Too-real nightmares sometimes braced them upright out of already fitful slumber. Conversely, when they were airborne in actual combat, they didn't have time to ruminate on what horrible things might happen to them—they were too busy trying to kill and trying not to be killed. But the in-between time, as they rushed to get airborne and were vulnerable to strafing or bombing attacks, was desperately unsettling. "That was the worst time of all," said John Piper.

Once airborne, the leader typically started a turn to give the other pilots an opportunity to cut the corner and join him. They clawed for altitude at the same time, desperate to intercept the Japanese bombers before they reached Port Moresby. In the event they reached an advantageous position and altitude, they flung themselves pell-mell at the enemy aircraft.

Such an aggressive spirit was laudable, but it was unorganized and degraded the effectiveness of the squadron. The men were not trained in tactics, nor did their leadership maximize their effectiveness with relevant training. That such was the case is curious because their leadership was John Jackson.

Jackson was 75 Squadron's commanding officer, but he was powerless to fix much of what was wrong at Port Moresby. He could do little about the diseases that wracked the ranks of the men, and he couldn't get adequate replacement aircraft and parts—there simply weren't enough available. And he didn't have the resources available to launch training sorties.

However, one thing he could have done was gather his pilots to discuss the best tactics and techniques for engaging the Japanese. He was smart, he was experienced, and he was certainly motivated to kill as many Japanese as he could. And he was empathetic toward his men.

But the fact that 75 Squadron had no established tactics for engaging the enemy is certain. "This was one of the unusual conditions of the squadron," said William Whetters. "I cannot recall any information whatsoever on the tactics to be employed. All that we did was take off together, meet the enemy, and then operated as individuals." Arthur Tucker's recollections were virtually identical. "With regard to flying organization, there was none," he said. "The leader would take off and you scrambled to follow him. We didn't have any tactics at all, except that we tried to stay together and tried to stay alive."

One exception was an admonition rather than a tactic. Jackson repeatedly warned his pilots against dogfighting with the Japanese aircraft—doing so was a virtual death sentence as the P-40 simply was not maneuverable enough. Rather, they were to make a firing pass, then dive away. When they had created enough separation, they could reverse direction and reengage.

The failure to create a meaningful set of squadron tactics no doubt cost lives, and just as certainly kept the men from shooting down as many Japanese as they could have. Still, Jackson's men followed him without reservation, and he maintained positive and confident, as indicated in a letter to his wife. "I think we'll hold the yellow bastards here," he said. "We've already given them a few decent cracks."[13]

In such primitive conditions, there were no pretenses at Port Moresby regarding uniforms or military courtesies, or even hygiene. Indeed, John Piper once flew a mission to Lae while wearing his pajama top. "Our dress didn't conform to any regulation," said pilot Robert Crawford. "[It] was just shorts and no rank, no nothing, and a hat. . . . I doubt if I ever washed in Moresby because there was nowhere to wash."

Crawford also recalled that he didn't wear socks with his boots until another pilot told him that if he went down in the water and his boots came off, the white soles of his feet would flash as he swam and attract sharks. Likewise, Crawford didn't wear gloves until it was pointed out to him that if he bailed out from a burning aircraft, his hands might be so badly injured that he would not be able to pull his parachute's ripcord.

★★★

A lone Japanese aircraft was reported inbound from the northwest in the early afternoon of March 31. It turned southwest, then northwest. "And when about 4-to-5 miles distant," observed the 75 Squadron operations record book, "enemy aircraft observed to be diving to earth. One wing came adrift, and the aircraft crashed to the ground, and a huge cloud of black smoke arose. No antiaircraft burst seen or heard; obviously a case of aircraft 'made in Japan.'"[14]

John Pettett, 75 Squadron pilot, had watched the enemy aircraft from the ground alongside his friend and fellow pilot Peter Turnbull. Turnbull had spent a great deal of time in the rough interior of Australia and had a reputation as a jokester. He threw himself into a made-up version of an Aboriginal dance. As he finished, he pretended to fling a curse at the Japanese twin-engine bomber, a Mitsubishi G3M, code-named Nell. It was nearly exactly at that time that the enemy aircraft shed its wing. Turnbull turned to Pettett and flashed a smile. "Got the bugger," he said.

★★★

Ground crews in 75 Squadron worked tirelessly to keep their unit's Kittyhawks flyable. It was miserable work in awful conditions, but it was necessary. The more aircraft that 75 Squadron could put airborne, the more difficult it was for the Japanese to bomb Port Moresby. But much of the good work performed by the mechanics was squandered by false alarms.

Although radar was being rushed into service around the world and had already proved its value in Europe, there was no such capability yet at Port Moresby. Instead, the defenders relied on men with radios who lived in isolated jungle outposts, or often on the run. Situated close to Japanese bases or along the routes that the Japanese flew, these men—coastwatchers—counted the number and types of enemy aircraft, estimated their altitude and heading, and then radioed the information so that Allied units could react in time.

However, a review of 75 Squadron's records shows that the aircraft that scrambled out of Port Moresby encountered empty sky more often than they encountered the enemy. For example, all available aircraft were hurriedly launched on the afternoon of April 9 at two different times. They found nothing. This happened for several reasons. At times the enemy formation went to a different target, or was turned back by weather, or was recalled, or simply never existed.

The service the coastwatchers provided was no doubt valuable, and it was much better to have a rudimentary and imperfect warning system than to have nothing at all. But the false alarms did exact a cost. They put unneeded wear and tear and strain on the engines and airframes. This increased the need for maintenance that would otherwise not be required. Moreover, scrambles were opportunities for the tired and sick men of 75

Squadron to get into accidents that might kill or injure them, and damage or destroy their aircraft.

★★★

The Australians at Port Moresby were soon joined by new American friends. These were the men of the 3rd Attack Group's 8th Bomb Squadron who flew the Douglas A-24 Banshee dive bomber, the USAAF's version of the Navy's SBD Dauntless.

With an eye on developments in Europe, the Army Air Corps had dabbled in dive bombing during the 1930s but never committed to it to the same degree as the Navy. However, recognizing the workhorse nature of the SBD, and the investment being made by its sister service, the Army piggybacked on the Navy's procurements and placed an order for a small number of aircraft in 1940. Its variant, the A-24, differed little from the Dauntless—the main changes being the replacement of the Navy radios, and the removal of equipment related to operations aboard the aircraft carrier, namely the heavy arresting hook.

Initially, three squadrons of the 27th Bombardment Group (Light) in Georgia were equipped with the type. These units participated extensively in various wargames during the latter half of 1941. During November, the aircraft were hurriedly disassembled, crated, and dispatched to the Philippines along with the group's men. The United States was rushing to buttress its forces in the Philippines, and the 27th Bomb Group and its A-24s were part of that rush.

The men arrived before the machines, and after the Japanese sneak attack on Pearl Harbor, the aircraft, still aboard ship, were diverted to Australia. Although some of the men were evacuated from the Philippines, several hundred were left behind and compelled to fight as infantrymen with the specially created 1st Provisional Air Corps Regiment. Many were part of the Bataan Death March following the collapse, defeat, and surrender of the American forces. Fewer than half survived the war.

The A-24s, 52 of them, reached Brisbane, Australia, in mid-December and were uncrated and readied for assembly. The men putting them back together were stunned at their poor condition. They had been flown hard and minimally maintained during the months preceding their shipment. Most of the engines needed an overhaul. Moreover, many components were caked with dried mud, and others were worn out or completely missing.

The commanding officer of the 27th Bomb Group, John Davies, declared that the organization responsible for preparing and packing the aircraft "should be charged with criminal negligence."[15] Nevertheless,

Australian and American mechanics worked side-by-side to get a number of the aircraft fully assembled and ready for action by January 1942.

Aside from the dire situation in the Philippines and elsewhere, the Allies were also being beaten by the Japanese in Java. Consequently, 15 of the newly assembled A-24s were sent there during the early part of February to support the badly battered and retreating Allied forces. It was a long and difficult multiday trip across Australia and most of Java. Ultimately, only 12 aircraft arrived, and of those, just a handful were fit to fight. They were committed to the fight, mostly in twos and threes, and were badly handled by enemy fighters and antiaircraft fire. Although the desperate A-24 crews fought bravely and with ingenuity—and did score a handful of successes—the battle was already lost, and the men were withdrawn back to Australia at the end of the month. There remained only three aircraft, and those were abandoned and subsequently destroyed by Dutch forces as the Japanese advanced.

Most of the A-24s remaining in Australia were assembled and reassigned to the 3rd Attack Group's 8th Bomb Squadron. Going with the aircraft were the men of the 27th Bomb Group which—with most of its men trapped in the Philippines—was subsumed by the 8th Bomb Squadron. Although experience with the A-24 up to that point had not been particularly encouraging, the 8th was nonetheless ordered to Port Moresby at the end of March 1942. The situation in New Guinea was considered desperate enough to put the type back into the fight.

When escorted by fighters, the newly arrived A-24s established a record that was, if not outstanding, at least passable. After flying into Port Moresby on March 31, 1942, the 8th flew its first combat mission the next day. Escorted by RAAF P-40s from 75 Squadron, five of the 8th's A-24s hit Japanese installations at Salamaua—not far from Lae—on New Guinea's northern coast. No aircraft were lost.

On April 6, eight A-24s and an escort of six Australian P-40s from 75 Squadron headed for Lae. Approaching the enemy airfield, they dived from an altitude of 13,000 feet. Japanese on the ground ran for cover at the same time they looked fearfully skyward at the plummeting aircraft. They were not only unused to being attacked by dive bombers but were also unfamiliar with the sight of the olive-green painted A-24s.

Unmolested by enemy fighters, the American A-24 pilots let go of their bombs and continued down across the beach and toward the water. They leveled out just above the wavetops while, behind them, smoke and fire leaped skyward from the burning wrecks of five Zeroes and seven bombers. The pilots reconstituted their formation as they turned for home, but Ed Chudoba brought with him an unwelcome extra aircraft—a Zero, whose pilot was intent on revenge. Having holed Chudoba's aircraft with gunfire, the Japanese pilot made two passes at the rest of the formation and no doubt would have continued had he not been shot down by the rear gunners. One A-24 was lost during the attack, probably downed by antiaircraft fire.

★★★

Just as Port Moresby was the primary target for the Japanese, the Japanese base at Lae on New Guinea's northern coast was the primary target for the RAAF's Port Moresby–based 75 Squadron. When directed by higher head-quarters, the unit's commander, John Jackson, regularly flew his P-40 over the Owen Stanley Range to assess the disposition of the Japanese at Lae and elsewhere. These solo missions were dangerous, but a reconnaissance in force would have left fewer of the too few aircraft at Port Moresby to defend against Japanese raiders. And because they were dangerous, Jackson usually flew them rather than order someone else to do so.

The risks finally caught up to him on April 10, 1942. On that day his route took him past Nadzab, Salamaua, and Lae. A deck of clouds forced him down to 600 feet near Lae where he was jumped by three Zeroes over the sea. Although he jettisoned his belly tank, the particular P-40 he flew that day was not fast enough to escape the enemy fighters.

Jackson's aircraft was quickly riddled with holes, and his windscreen was shot away. Wind howled into the cockpit and whipped bits of glass around his face as it tore at his helmet and clothing. Although he knew it was a losing move, he felt he had no choice but to turn hard into the more maneuverable Zeroes. He hoped to be able to get off a burst of gunfire, or at least confuse or scatter the enemy pilots.

Remarkably, he was able to maneuver behind one of the enemy fight-ers, but his aircraft had been so badly shot up that his guns would not fire. Outnumbered, Jackson was shot into the sea. His Kittyhawk skipped atop the waves and sent a towering plume of spray into the sky before coming to a sudden stop. "My plane sank in a few seconds," he said. Stunned and likely suffering some degree of shock, Jackson pushed clear of the sinking aircraft and struck for shore, fearful that the enemy pilots might strafe him. His fears were for nothing. Perhaps the Japanese had no interest in killing him, or maybe they lost sight of him as his aircraft disappeared below the surface.

Regardless, Jackson kicked away his boots and continued for the coast, almost a mile distant. His heart skipped a beat when a deadly maneater—a saltwater crocodile—poked its head out of the waves. But for whatever reason, the reptile left him alone. Nor was Jackson bothered by sharks.

Nearing land, he was spotted by two young native men—Papuans—Arthur and Edmond. They helped him from the water and took him a short distance to the village of Busama. The village elders didn't seem particularly eager to help Jackson, and he grew nervous as they held a confab that did not include him. While they argued, the two young men appeared again and hurried him down the coast.

"Hadn't gone far before we sighted Japanese boats," Jackson wrote in a letter to his wife. "So, we went into the jungle, swimming creeks in my clothes, and struggling through swamp and jungle, going down to [my] waist in slime and mud." Jackson struggled to keep pace with the two youngsters; he wasn't as fit, and he lacked their lifelong familiarity with the terrain. Moreover, and perhaps most importantly, he was barefoot.

However, the sound of a Japanese search party, assisted by some of the villagers, compelled him to move faster than he might have done otherwise. Arthur and Edmond spirited Jackson deeper into the jungle until the shouts of his pursuers faded away. Still, they went on as fast as Jackson could go on his bruised and cut and swollen feet, which grew worse with each step. "When we came to a stony river crossing," Jackson said, "my feet wouldn't work, and they had to carry me across."

Although Jackson had escaped the Japanese, he had not escaped the suffocating terror that was New Guinea's jungle. There followed much misery that grew in intensity each day. Stinging plants and leeches and insects and snakes and mud and grasping branches and roots all took their toll on the Australian airman, who was most likely already sick with gastroenteritis even before he climbed into his Kittyhawk on the day he was shot down. So badly did his condition deteriorate as the days passed that the young natives made him a pair of crutches and took turns physically pushing him up the steeper slopes.

Notwithstanding all the horrors the jungle visited upon him—and the lack of food and clean water—it was his unprotected feet that tortured Jackson the most. "They felt like two pulps," he said, "and I could hardly stand to touch them with my hands, let alone stand." He did his best to keep from becoming dispirited, despite the slow going. "You can walk all day in New Guinea," he said, "and in the afternoon seem no distance away from the place you left in the morning."

Jackson rested with Arthur and Edmond all of April 13. The two young men were kind to him and helped to wash and care for his feet. They also made him a rudimentary pair of sandals. He took heart when the noise of an air attack on Lae reached up to where he sat at the top of a mountain. "Heard our boys bomb Lae," he said, "and saw four of our fighters but didn't see the bombers. My two boys here cheered as the bombs were falling."[16]

The trio reached the village of Mapos on the following day where they were treated well by the chief and the other villagers. Since April 10, they had traveled a straight-line distance of just less than 30 miles. On April 16 a pair of soldiers from the New Guinea Volunteer Rifles arrived to take custody of Jackson.

The two Australians—who gave Jackson a pair of boots—shepherded him a dozen miles south to Wau where there was a rudimentary airstrip hacked out of the brush. It had been used before the war to service mining operations in the region. There was also a radio, and on April 18 the men of 75 Squadron were overjoyed upon learning that their unflappable leader would soon be back among them. Arrangements were made for one of the newly arrived USAAF A-24s, escorted by a trio of 75 Squadron Kittyhawks, to fly to Wau without a rear gunner and bring Jackson back to Moresby. The flight took off from Port Moresby on April 21 with 300 pounds of supplies and equipment for the New Guinea Volunteer Rifles, but the weather was poor and Wau could not be located.

Another attempt was made two days later, April 23, with Virgil Schwab at the controls of the A-24. He was escorted by John Piper in a Kittyhawk. This time, the flight was able to locate the strip at Wau, and Jackson was hastily loaded aboard. Schwab got airborne, and the flight back to Port Moresby was uneventful.

Feeling frisky, Schwab roared by 75 Squadron's camp as low and fast as his aircraft would go. Jackson waved from where he sat in the gunner's position. The Japanese rudely cut the celebration short when a flight of three Zeroes dived seemingly out of nowhere and attacked the hapless A-24.

Schwab wrenched his aircraft into a violent turn and nearly scraped the ground with a wingtip as he tried to shake the enemy fighters. A hare pursued by hounds, the A-24 banked violently in one direction and then the other. The Zero pilots took turns firing at the American aircraft while the machinegun crews on the ground blasted volleys of bullets into the sky as the Japanese flashed past. Piper, in his P-40, harried the enemy pilots as best he could but failed to score. On the other hand, Schwab's aircraft was hit in the fuselage by a 20-millimeter cannon round and several machine-gun bullets.

The Japanese finally gave up and flew away. The A-24 held together despite having been damaged, and Schwab put the aircraft on the ground with little trouble. For his part, Jackson was thrilled to be back at Port Moresby with his squadron even although the tip of his right index finger was shot away.

Notwithstanding his poor physical condition, Jackson put himself back into operations almost immediately. No one else in the squadron could match his experience and leadership. "He was in a bad way, but he wouldn't think of not flying again," said Robert Crawford.

One of the squadron's other downed flyers had returned the day prior, on April 22. Wilbur Wackett had been shot down a month earlier on March 22, during the squadron's first mission to Lae. After swimming to shore he was helped by natives and taken to men from the New Guinea Volunteer Rifles. During the next four weeks Wackett crossed the whole of New Guinea from north to south by foot, canoe, and the occasional truck. Like Jackson, his feet suffered mightily. Unlike Jackson, Wackett contracted malaria, and rather than returning to the cockpit, he was sent to Australia to recover.

2

"HE NEVER SAID A WORD"

The USAAF's 22nd Bomb Group introduced its B-26 crews to combat at the same time that 75 Squadron was doing its best to defend Port Moresby, and while the 3rd Attack Group's A-24 crews were making their first tentative strikes. Based at Garbutt Field, Townsville, in northeastern Queensland, Australia, the 22nd typically loaded bombs aboard its aircraft and sent them north to Port Moresby. There, at 7-Mile Drome, the B-26s were topped off with fuel while the crews caught what sleep they could on cots underneath their aircraft before departing on their missions in the early morning darkness. Once the mission was flown, the aircraft recovered back to Port Moresby where they were refueled and readied for a mission the following day or sent directly back to Garbutt Field.

The group's very first mission followed this template. As might be expected for a first mission, the greenness of the crews and of the supporting units and infrastructure was apparent. For instance, of the 11 aircraft which taxied for takeoff at Garbutt on April 5, 1942, one hit an obstacle and was too damaged to take off.

The 10 remaining aircraft got airborne with no issues and set course for Port Moresby. However, one of them developed engine issues and was compelled to return to Garbutt. At Port Moresby, one of the nine remaining aircraft blew a tire and was not ready in time for the mission.

The 22nd's crews were briefed and got a few hours of sleep before being wakened in time for the eight aircraft to make an 0330 takeoff in rain and fog on April 6. The miserable weather made it difficult for the crews to rendezvous. After flailing in and out of the clouds, and unable to join the main formation, two of them returned to Port Moresby.

Those six B-26s continued to Rabaul where they made medium-altitude attacks against shipping in Simpson Harbor. Although a claim was made for one freighter sunk, Japanese records indicate that no damage was done. A handful of near-obsolescent A5M fighters—with fixed landing gear—tried unsuccessfully to intercept the faster B-26s. Likewise, antiaircraft fire from both ship and shore did not deter the 22nd's crews.

Michael Bauman, an enlisted bombardier, described his experience during this, the 22nd Bomb Group's first combat mission. It underscored the poor state of training that existed during this early part of the war, a product of the rush to get men and machines into the fight as quickly as possible. "Our first mission was to Rabaul, which was on New Britain Island—it was a long way over there," Bauman said. As they neared the target, the crew spotted a large ship in the open sea, presumably a freighter of some sort, as it didn't fire on them. "We had four 500-pound bombs," Bauman said. "I was going to drop two. If I missed with them, I'd have one more chance."

As his pilot closed on the ship, Bauman was frustrated as he couldn't get his bombsight to perform properly. "I looked over," he said, "and here we were going downhill about 300 miles per hour and 1,000 feet per minute." The bombsight was designed to work while in straight and level flight. For whatever reason, Bauman's pilot was diving on the ship. Bauman was furious.

"I just reached over," he said, "and closed the bomb bay doors." Confusion followed. "I can't drop when you are dive-bombing," Bauman told his pilot. "If you can't fly this dang thing, we'll just take it back. I didn't come over here to see how many fish I could kill. I came over to see what we could do, and do it right."

The pilot climbed back to altitude and set up for a proper, straight, and level bomb run. For all the damage done, he might just as well have never left Australia. "I was so mad I was shaking," Bauman said. He released all four of the bombs which fell short. The enemy ship continued undamaged. "I got on the mike and chewed him out for about an hour on the way back," Bauman said. "He never said a word."[1]

One of the six B-26s was captained by Albert Moye. Due either to a mechanical malfunction or antiaircraft fire, his fuel transfer system was not working properly and one of its engines failed and would not restart. Moye turned south for Kiriwina Island and had nearly made it when the second engine failed. The aircraft went into the water, and all but one of the crew was rescued by friendly Papuans. So then, of the 11 aircraft originally scheduled for the mission, only six actually participated, and one of those was lost.

★★★

During much of April 1942, the RAAF's 75 Squadron kept at least two aircraft on standing patrol over Port Moresby to guard against surprise attacks. These were typically listed in the squadron records as security patrols. In the event that the rest of the squadron was scrambled to meet an incoming raid, the two aircraft often joined them as they climbed for altitude or stayed low to disrupt strafing attacks. But depending on the timing, the security patrol could be caught short on fuel, without enough to climb with the rest of the squadron or enough to fight low over the airfield.

Robert Crawford was flying security patrol on April 24 with Lester Jackson when a Japanese raid caught them low on fuel. They ducked into the little airstrip at Kila Kila rather than 7-Mile Drome—their base and the usual target. At Kila Kila the two P-40s were quickly refueled and took off again. They accelerated and turned over the harbor where they spotted an American B-26 at about 500 feet. The B-26 was chased by five or six Zeroes.

Crawford and Jackson threw themselves at the Japanese fighters and were soon caught in a wheeling fight over the water. Crawford's throat microphone was shot away, and his neck sustained a wound. Outperformed by the Zeroes, and unable to dive away, Crawford's aircraft was shot up so badly that he was forced to put it into the sea.

"I survived the ditching, and I thought I was going to be strafed in the water," he said. However, the enemy pilots were more interested in shooting up a pair of Consolidated PBY flying boats moored close to the beach, and Crawford was left to soak.

Crawford was only one of the Japanese victories that day. Not so lucky was Oswald Channon who was shot down over the jungle near Porebada village and killed. Mick Butler's P-40 was so shot up that he put down in a controlled crash. On the other hand, the B-26 that Crawford and Jackson tried to save did escape.

The loss of Oswald Channon and other pilots—comrades and friends—affected the survivors, but in a way, or ways, that are impossible to measure. "Ah, it's a bit hard to explain," said Robert Crawford. "You're with a bloke one minute and the next minute he's not there. And I think, the morale of the pilots was such that you'd feel greatly sorry in your heart and whatnot. But if you dwelled upon the problem it would get to you."

Although its condition unraveled as April drew to a close, 75 Squadron lurched on while the Japanese continued to bomb Port Moresby. Alan Whetters was caught too far away from 7-Mile Drome during the morning of April 26 while chasing after a formation of enemy fighters and bombers. Unsure that he had enough fuel to make it back to Port Moresby, and not certain he could find a good place to put the aircraft down if he continued on his route and did run short of fuel, he decided to land on a level stretch of ground covered with kunai grass. He slowed, dropped his landing gear and flaps, turned, and lowered the Kittyhawk's nose toward the promising patch. As it settled to the ground, the propeller scythed swaths of the grass into the sky, and his aircraft made a rushing rumble as the tall, heavy grass scrubbed its underside and dragged it quickly to a stop.

"This particular kunai grass was over six feet tall," he said, "and I was indeed fortunate that I had in actual fact, landed without hitting any obstacles." Whetters crawled down from his undamaged P-40 and oriented himself. A short time later, he parted the tall grass and struck for the coast, intent on making it to the sea, or at least to someplace where he could get help.

He made it only a short distance through the suffocating scrub. It was not long after he started that he realized he was lost. Thinking that he might die before he found help, he found his way back to his fighter and crawled back into the cockpit.

"Whilst I was sitting in the cockpit, just wondering what my next move would be," Whetters said, "I noticed some natives stealthily creeping through the kunai. I stood on the wing, to let them see that I was still there." Happily, the men were part of a New Guinea Volunteer Rifles unit and had seen him land. Their commanding officer, an Australian, showed up and spoke with Whetters. He learned that he was not far from the village of Rarona, about 30 miles northwest of Port Moresby.

Whetters checked his fuel gauge and second-guessed his decision to put his fighter down in the kunai grass. After some consideration he thought that perhaps he might be able to make it back to Port Moresby after all. The volunteers were willing to help him on his way and went to work cutting the kunai grass. After an astonishingly short time, there was a clear strip where before there had been an impenetrable sward of thick, tall grass.

Whetters shook hands with his rescuers, crawled into his aircraft, started it, and was soon bouncing down the ad hoc strip and airborne. He checked his fuel gauge as he climbed for altitude and, after some carefully considered calculations, decided that his initial decision to land in the kunai grass had not been a rash one. Almost embarrassed, he lowered his landing gear and flaps and rejoined his new friends in the kunai grass. This particular unit of the New Guinea Volunteer Rifles was one that got things done. Arrangements were made for fuel to be hauled overland, and Whetters returned to 7-Mile Drome the following day.

He arrived to very little fanfare after his abortive adventure in the kunai grass. The squadron had sent an aircraft to look for him without success on the day he had gone down. Notwithstanding the failed search, word was received by other means that he was safe. "I can't recall that anybody was really interested," Whetters recalled. "There was no discussion." The squadron had lost so many men and aircraft in such a short time that none of his comrades had the interest or energy to expend in celebration of his return. The official squadron record simply noted that Whetters "forced landed owing [to] lack of fuel at Rororna but obtained fuel and returned to base safely [the] next day."

★★★

John Jackson was directed to report to his superiors on April 27 and was upbraided for the performance of his men. There was a belief that some of them were cowards—that they were shirking their responsibilities and avoiding combat. The slang term for them was dingoes—after Australia's feral dogs. In particular, they cited the fact that 75 Squadron's pilots weren't aggressively engaging the Japanese Zeroes in dogfights.

This was true. The pilots were not fighting with the enemy fighters in close-quarter, twisting, turning air combat. And they didn't do so because it was almost impossible to win, regardless of a pilot's skill. It was an excellent way to die—a virtual guarantee of getting shot down. No Allied fighter in service at that time could outfly the Zero in a dogfight. The P-40 pilots could fight the Zero successfully only by employing high-speed diving attacks, and then using their superior airspeed to run away. Once safely out of range, they might climb back up to altitude and set up for another attack if the Japanese were still in the area.

In short, Jackson's superiors were ignorant of what the men of 75 Squadron were up against. Jackson was a skilled pilot, an ace who had downed German, Vichy French, and Japanese pilots. There were few, if any, combat-experienced pilots in the RAAF who had as much credibility as he did. But he somehow let himself be bullied. His humiliation was apparent when he returned to the squadron and shared the news that his commanders lacked confidence not only in him but in the unit.

They would from that point, he declared, start dogfighting the enemy fighters. Jaws dropped and eyes popped as the meeting erupted with howls of disbelief. After all, it was Jackson who had admonished them over and over again against turning with the Zeroes. Arthur Tucker recalled how he and his squadron mates protested, "But, you know we can't dogfight them! You told us not to!" Jackson's reply was, "Tomorrow, I'm going to show you how."

But there was no "how" to show them. Jackson had not experienced a sudden air combat epiphany and the P-40 had not somehow grown more capable. Nor had the Zero's attributes been degraded. It was just as formidable as it had always been.

The record book of 75 Squadron's operations noted that Jackson got airborne at the head of six Kittyhawks late during the morning of April 28, 1942, to intercept a flight of eight Japanese bombers, escorted by Zeroes. No detailed description of the complete encounter exists, but it can only be supposed that Jackson made good on his declared intent to turn and fight with the enemy fighters. A Zero was shot down, and credit is often given to Jackson. But that victory came at a cost. Both Jackson and his friend Barry Cox were shot down and killed. Jackson's aircraft was seen streaming smoke in a steep dive. It smashed into Mount Lawes, and Jackson's remains were recovered a few days later.

Jackson's brother, Les Jackson, had been with the squadron since before Port Moresby and was put in command following his brother's death. He was a skilled pilot, but he didn't inspire the men as his brother had. He did less than inspire fellow pilot, Arthur Tucker. "He should never have been let out of his cage," said Tucker. "He was a, well, a nasty bastard, in the kindest words I could put to him. He was a divisive, degenerate, drunken lout, without any sense of responsibility whatsoever."

Disease, accidents, and the Japanese had beaten 75 Squadron down to the point that it was essentially ineffective as April drew to a close. Its ground crewmen struggled daily—and nightly—to get just a bare handful of aircraft ready for operations each morning. Only a very few Kittyhawks had been brought up from Australia to replace the unit's losses, and parts were in short supply. Wrecked aircraft, and aircraft that weren't wrecked, were cannibalized to keep others flying.

And many of those that were flying shouldn't have been. Poor access to spare parts, poorly trained personnel, poor working conditions, and poor leadership combined to produce poorly maintained aircraft. Arthur Tucker recalled that pilots who aborted missions with broken aircraft, or who simply pointed out mechanical issues, were often accused of what can only be defined as spinelessness. "Every time a pilot reported a misfunctioning aircraft," he said, "it was put down to pilot trouble and very loudly, and various individuals were loudly talked about. One was singled out and it led eventually to his suicide back in Australia. Another one who was an absolute gentleman, and I believe a very valiant and proper pilot, for years afterwards was spoken of by the then-CO [probably Les Jackson] in most defamatory terms, and it was totally untrue."

And the squadron's few remaining pilots, usually outnumbered in the near-daily air battles that raged over Port Moresby, were shrinking in number. It was a losing fight, and what was left of the unit should have been stood down and sent back to Australia for rest and refit. Essentially, although no one had given up, the unit had been destroyed. There were virtually no aircraft left to fight with, and few men left to fly them.

3

"I DECIDED TO GO TO
HORN ISLAND"

The initial deployment of the first American fighter units to New Guinea was a disaster. The 8th Fighter Group, having spent less than two months training at various camps and airfields after arriving in Australia on March 5, 1942, sent 15 P-39 Airacobras from its 35th Pursuit Squadron on a multi-leg flight to Port Moresby on April 26.[1]

Commanded by George Greene, the pilots took off in two formations from the airfield at Woodstock, just south of Townsville, near Australia's northeastern coast. They followed the coast northward which eased their navigation. After a short flight of only about 200 miles, all pilots landed safely at Cairns.

After a brief respite to refuel, the two formations were airborne again. The weather en route was forecast as satisfactory with a scattered-to-broken layer of clouds at about 3,000 feet and occasional rain showers. Greene, leading nine of the 15 P-39s, climbed to 10,000 feet and continued north along the coast. The next stop was planned for Horn Island, just north of the tip of the Cape York Peninsula at the top of the Australian continent. It was a distance of more than 500 miles.

The low layer of clouds developed into a line of towering cumulus that climbed past to 20,000 feet. Leery of punching into them and losing sight of the ground, Greene led his flight down through a hole in the weather and leveled off at about 2,000 feet. "The visibility was not more than two miles," he said, "and then we ran into a solid front of rain."

Not able to see much of anything by which he could navigate, Greene reversed course, hoping to get clear of the storm so that he might find a break in the rain and resume his route back to the north. A short time later, the other formation of six P-39s rocketed past, still headed north and into the heavy precipitation.

Greene tried to contact Charles Campbell who led the other flight, but he received no response. "I turned to follow," said Greene, "as I thought they had seen an opening in the rain." It was for naught. Greene lost sight of the other P-39s and failed to find a way through the weather. "It seemed to be getting darker and raining harder," he said.

Once more, with the rain pummeling his aircraft so hard that it nearly drowned the sound of his engine, Greene turned back south and considered his situation. He called his flight over the radio and declared that he was going to take them to the airfield at Cooktown, which they had passed on their way north. He estimated that it was approximately 270 miles down the coast. "At this time, we had a gasoline check," he said, "and I heard one or two pilots state that they had about 45 gallons of gas. This was not enough gasoline to reach Cooktown."

Greene, as the flight leader, was responsible for the safe execution of the mission. Accordingly, he had difficult decisions to make. All the pilots in his flight still had enough fuel to make it to Horn Island, but he had already encountered severe weather on that route and was uncertain that he could get the flight there safely. Based on his experience to that point, he might not have been able to find it in the driving rain, and he ran the risk of getting lost and dropping his pilots into the sea as they ran out of fuel.

On the other hand, Cooktown's weather had been reasonable when the flight passed earlier, but at least two members of the flight did not have enough fuel to reach it. Southwest of his position, the airfield at Coen was another option, but Greene had never been there. It was 20 miles inland from the coast, and he had little confidence that his rudimentary charts were accurate enough for him to find it.

"I decided to go to Horn Island," Greene said. Although the decision presented risk, Horn Island was the only airfield that all the aircraft in his formation could reach. He declared his intentions over the radio and directed the flight to jettison their empty drop tanks and ease back on their throttles. However, the rain beat down so noisily that he wasn't sure he was understood.

Nevertheless, he turned north once again and set a course for Horn Island, descending as he did so. Leveling off at 500 feet, he followed the bare ghost of an outline that was the coast. To his side and slightly behind, he saw his wingman, John Casey, but no one else. "I could not see behind me," he recalled, "because my clothing bag was in the glass canopy. I thought the [rest of the] formation was behind me."

Over Cape York at the tip of Australia, the rain stopped, the clouds began to clear, and Greene continued toward Horn Island with Casey on his wing. During the few remaining miles, Greene looked in vain for the rest of his flight. It was nowhere to be seen. On the other hand, the weather was clear, and he landed without trouble with only 35 gallons of fuel remaining. Casey touched down with a mere 15 gallons. No other aircraft from the flight arrived, and it soon became apparent that they had put down elsewhere or crashed, out of fuel.

None of the other seven aircraft in Green's flight made it to an airfield. Three of the pilots put down and abandoned their aircraft at Cape Grenville, a polyp-like peninsula on the coast, about 120 miles short of Horn Island. One pilot landed on the beach at Princess Charlotte Bay trying to get back to Cooktown. His aircraft nosed hard over in the sand. Another pilot also made for Cooktown but landed 35 miles north of Port Stewart, landing gear up, not wanting to risk his wheels digging into the soft sand and somersaulting the aircraft. Two pilots, John Long and Jack Hall, were never found and were presumed lost in the vicinity of Cape Grenville.

The other six aircraft led by Charles Campbell fared better. Campbell reversed course to the south after entering the heavy weather and made for Cooktown where four of the P-39s landed safely. The other two pilots failed to reach the airfield and were forced down north of Cooktown by lack of fuel. Both of the pilots were safely rescued.

The loss of so many aircraft when so few were available was nothing short of a catastrophe, although at least a couple of the P-39s were salvaged for parts or recovered and put back in service. Greene sent messages to multiple points to mobilize a rescue effort, and during the next few days, the surviving pilots were recovered by land, sea, and air.

But those activities also met with heartbreak. Montague David Ellerton was a P-40 pilot with the RAAF's 75 Squadron who was ferrying an aircraft to New Guinea. He had been alerted to search for, and render assistance to, the downed American pilots. On April 28, he spotted William McGovern and his P-39 on a beach north of Cooktown.[2] McGovern had been part of Campbell's second flight of six aircraft.

Beach landings were hazardous, and although McGovern tried to wave Ellerton away, the Australian P-40 pilot persisted. He descended, dropped his wheels and flaps, and touched down. Almost immediately his wingtip struck the sand, and the aircraft twisted onto its back and skidded to a stop in a great spray of water and wet sand, trapping Ellerton inside. McGovern's attempts to free the Australian pilot were futile and he was able to do nothing but watch in sickening terror as the incoming tide slowly covered and drowned Ellerton.

Fellow Australian Arthur Tucker recalled his conversation with Ellerton in their tent at Port Moresby only a week or so earlier. They were two of the few 75 Squadron pilots remaining to fly the unit's even fewer remaining P-40s. Virtually all the other pilots who had arrived with the squadron less than two months earlier were dead, sick, or evacuated home.

The mood was one of resignation as pilots were being killed at an approximate rate of a couple each week. Ellerton was reading letters from his wife. Tucker recalled that they were written on blue stationery. Ellerton looked up at Tucker and asked morosely, "I wonder which of us it'll be tomorrow, you or I?"

"It seemed a logical sort of question," Tucker said. "I don't know that I answered it." A short time later, Ellerton was told that he was being sent to Australia to pick up a replacement P-40, and that once he had brought it back, he would be relieved of combat duty for a spell. Instead, a few days later, he drowned on a desolate beach in an overturned aircraft.

★★★

George Greene obviously failed in his duty to safely lead the 35th Pursuit Squadron's 15 P-39s to Port Moresby. Hindsight makes it easy to criticize him, but any censure should be tempered by the context of the time and by consideration of his experience, or lack of experience. First, he was only a first lieutenant with perhaps a few hundred flight hours and little operational background. And he was charged with leading 14 other first lieutenants who likewise did not have a great deal of experience. Moreover, he and the other pilots were flying primitive aircraft with primitive radios and primitive navigational instruments across primitively mapped geography and informed by primitive weather services. Another consideration was the operational pressure he was under to get the aircraft to the beleaguered forces at Port Moresby as quickly as possible.

Greene's chief failing was his lack of decisiveness in a scenario in which fuel was a critical factor. Although he cannot be faulted for his initial course reversal away from Horn Island in the face of the poor weather, he should have continued south to a safe landing area while his pilots had adequate fuel to do so. Or, he could have bet on decent weather at Horn Island and continued there without delay. In the end, his vacillation and multiple course reversals cost nine aircraft and two lives.

Sadly, his failure was not unique, and, incredibly, the disaster was essentially mirrored only two days later on April 28, 1942. The 8th Fighter Group's 36th Pursuit Squadron, sister squadron to the 35th, sent six P-39s north with the final destination being Port Moresby. Led by Charles

Falletta, they didn't get there. The weather once more proved to be an overwhelmingly powerful foe, and the six pilots lost their way, ran out of fuel, and crashed. One pilot was killed.

So then, of the 17 aircraft the 8th Fighter Group sent to Port Moresby on April 26 and April 28, 15 were lost. It was a loss rate of 88 percent. The losses the Japanese would inflict in the coming months would never come close to matching the destructive power of the region's weather, and the ineptitude of the pilots on those two days.

The 8th Fighter Group's ground crews began arriving by C-47 transport aircraft at Port Moresby during the last few days of April 1942. The group was assigned to operate out of 7-Mile Drome from where the RAAF's much-beleaguered 75 Squadron flew the small handful of hard-worn P-40s it had remaining. The newly arrived Americans were billeted and messed a short distance away at John's Gully, a miserable, fly-infested, sweltering shithole of a place made worse by a dearth of tents, food, potable water, and other essentials.

"A herd of cattle roamed the camp," recalled the 36th Pursuit Squadron's historian, "and the open sores on their sides and their flanks were covered with flies. A few were so far gone with infection that blood from the open sores would form a pool on the road, wherever they chose to rest." When the Americans protested the presence of the sick animals, the Australians made the strange assertion that the sick cows somehow acted as camouflage against Japanese bombers. Sanity and the American medicos won the day, and the cattle were moved to a better location a few days later, but not before the pestering flies sickened many of the men with fevers.

Indeed, the newly arrived Americans quickly made improvements in a number of areas, as noted by 75 Squadron pilot John Piper. "[Of] course the Americans, the very first thing they did was [set up] their latrine and they had a proper collection system, and they were very superior to us in hygiene. I think Australians rather consider[ed] them sissy in the extreme." Sissies or not, Piper marveled at the energy of his American friends. "The first [thing] they did in any of the places, they put up a sawmill and they started pounding out lumber. So, you had floors in the tents, and doors, and as it turned out, it meant their casualty rate was a fraction of ours from that point."

The morning of April 30, 1942, saw the arrival of 26 8th Fighter Group P-39s, an event that was cheered by one and all. The Australians, who had been holding the line for so long with just a small number of aircraft, were heartened by the sudden appearance of so many new fighters. The sleek, olive-green little aircraft touched down one by one and taxied past the burned-out husks of aircraft that had not survived the bombing raids of the previous weeks.

The Americans were happy to finally be in the fight and anxious to put their training and machines to the test. And they were ready to do so immediately. Not just during the coming weeks, or even the next few days, but rather on that very day. While the ground crews serviced the aircraft, Lieutenant Colonel Boyd "Buzz" Wagner assembled and briefed a group of 13 pilots—half of the newly arrived force—for an offensive raid across the Owen Stanley Range against Lae and nearby Salamaua.

The 25-year-old Wagner was only temporarily assigned to the 8th Fighter Group. He was a veteran combat pilot and somewhat of a celebrity as he was the first and leading ace not only of the Army Air Forces but of the United States. He had been credited with shooting down five enemy aircraft while flying P-40s over the Philippines during the weeks following the Japanese sneak attack on Pearl Harbor. Since that time, he had escaped the Philippines and made his way to Australia where he was put in charge of training and reconstituting various USAAF fighter units. During this period of considerable confusion as well as limited resources and personnel, it was very much a "learn as you go" process that required a substantial degree of leadership, ingenuity, and audacity.

And now, in the early afternoon of April 30, 1942, Wagner was exercising all those attributes. At 1300 he took off at the head of 13 P-39Ds from the 35th and 36th Pursuit Squadrons and climbed for altitude to clear the Owen Stanley Range. The formation became smaller by two aircraft when their pilots were compelled to turn back due to mechanical difficulties.

Once clear of the mountains, Wagner dropped the formation to low altitude and crossed the coast some distance from the enemy bases. He led the other pilots approximately 50 miles out to sea before arcing back toward the Japanese airfield at Lae at only a hundred feet above the wavetops. On Wagner's direction, four of the P-39s climbed and accelerated ahead to engage any aircraft that might be patrolling overhead.

Head-on, the diminutive, little fighters were almost invisible until they approached within a mile of Lae. The surprise was virtually complete, and the P-39s blasted parked aircraft, floatplanes, supply dumps, and enemy troops without sustaining any hurt despite curtains of light antiaircraft and machinegun fire. Immediately afterward, as a unit, they turned toward the airfield at Salamaua intending to repeat their success.

But over Salamaua they were met by a defending force of about a dozen Zeroes. The P-39 pilots released their drop tanks, and a wheeling dogfight followed. During the twisting, turning melee, Wagner was credited with downing three enemy aircraft, and George Greene, who had failed in leading so many of his squadron mates from Australia to Port Moresby, was credited with knocking down another.

But the scoring was hardly one-sided. Edward Durand was set upon by a Zero and badly mauled. "The Zeros were waiting for us," recalled Arthur Andres, "sitting right above and hit us way hard. One Zero was on Ed Durand's tail and I turned around to give the Zero a taste of American bullets but I'm afraid Ed was on his way down."[3] No trace of Durand has ever been found.

Andres himself was chased by a Zero until he ran short of fuel. He crash-landed his aircraft about 20 miles southeast of Buna and was rescued by natives. He returned to Port Moresby nearly a month later. James Bevlock followed his flight leader, Louis Meng, away from the Zeroes and into some cloud cover, but they were headed in the wrong direction. Meng eventually turned them south, back toward Port Moresby, but Bevlock lost sight of him over the Owen Stanley Range and eventually ran out of fuel, landing on the beach at Iokea, about 80 miles west of Port Moresby. He made it back to 7-Mile Drome a couple of days later on May 2.

The Zeroes shot up Paul Brown's P-39, but he managed to make it to the south shore of New Guinea where he crash-landed, out of fuel, near Point Hood, 60 miles southeast of Port Moresby. He was met and rescued by Australian forces who had also captured a Japanese pilot, Yoshimitsu Maeda, who had gone down a couple of days earlier. The two of them were returned to Port Moresby a few days later.[4]

The Japanese pilot, Maeda, with his flight leader, Yoshisuke Arita, had attacked a B-25 a couple of days earlier on April 28 and claimed it as destroyed, although it had only been damaged. Maeda ended up on his own and crossed the Owen Stanley Range and continued south to the coast where he spotted an Australian freighter. Descending to strafe it, the careless—or incompetent—Maeda struck a palm tree along the beach and crashed into the ground where he was subsequently captured.[5]

Once back at Port Moresby's 7-Mile Drome, the 8th Fighter Group pilots congratulated each other for their successes against the Japanese at Lae and Salamaua. But in fact, they were celebrating an air combat during which they and the Japanese lost equal numbers of aircraft—and that was only true if the number of victories claimed over the Zeroes was correct. The four aircraft the 8th Fighter Group lost that day, when added to the 15 lost during the ferry flights from Australia only a few days earlier, totaled 19. And this, after they had been in combat for a grand total of just one afternoon. It was a waste—an indifferent performance at best.

★★★

A standing patrol of P-39s was established beginning the morning of May 1. Early morning fog and low clouds delayed the launch of the first six aircraft, but once the visibility permitted, the P-39s roared down the runway at 7-Mile Drome and clawed skyward. But a few minutes later, there came the sound of an aircraft feeling its way back toward the field with a sick engine. The pilot managed to find his way through the murk but botched the landing and broke off the nose gear. The olive-green fighter skidded to a stop and blocked the runway. The pilot was unhurt.

The maintenance men rushed to the wrecked aircraft and, with the aid of an Australian truck, winched it clear of the runway and into the Kunai grass. It was just then that a flight of Zeroes—their pilots perhaps intent on avenging the previous day's raid against Lae and Salamaua—dropped out of the clouds, guns firing, and sent the men to ground. Happily, the aircraft revetments were more attractive to the enemy pilots than were the scurrying ground crews, and it was against these that they directed their attention before climbing once more into the gray.

It was then that the P-39 patrol caught up with them. Several of the pilots reported scoring good hits against a few of the Zeroes, but Donald McGhee of the 36th Pursuit Squadron actually bagged one of the enemy fighters. He was shot up for his trouble, but not so badly that the aircraft wasn't repaired and back in service the next day. Stating that the aircraft was simply repaired does a disservice to the work actually done by the maintenance men.

They went directly to work on the aircraft that had crash-landed just before the Zeroes attacked and, as the squadron reported, "stripped it of every available, removable part. The guns came out, the ignition harnesses, the plugs, the carburetor, the flap motors, the radio, the dynamotor, and the wiring. The engineers, armorers, and radiomen worked there until the nerves and the muscles of the ship had been removed, ready for transfer to another plane."

That plane was McGhee's aircraft, which was cobbled back together in record time. The work paid dividends because the Japanese fighters were back in force the following day, May 2. The 8th Pursuit Group's P-39s, a total of 11 from both the 35th and 36th Pursuit Squadrons, wrangled with 15 Zeroes. Louis Meng threw himself head-on at a flight of four of the enemy aircraft, knocking one of them into the jungle with his gunfire. Joseph Lovett attacked a group of three Zeroes and claimed one of them, while John Mainwaring caught an enemy pilot unawares from the rear. The hapless fighter went down east of the field.

This engagement proved to be an unequivocal fighter-versus-fighter victory for the 8th Fighter Group's P-39 squadrons, a fight that vindicated advocates of the little aircraft. A greater test came the very next day, May 3, 1942, when six Mitsubishi G3M, twin-engine bombers, code-named Nell, arrived overhead at 23,000 feet in two flights of three. The bombers were escorted by seven Zeroes.

At this altitude, the patrol of four P-39s struggled to get into position as a turn of any degree caused them to lose altitude. Nevertheless, the American pilots were able to attack the first three silvery bombers. Charles Chapman hit the lefthand Nell, setting its left engine and wing afire. Charles Schwimmer fired his guns at the righthand aircraft, which fell out of formation and "was seen to crash," as reported by the 36th Pursuit Squadron. John Barley was given credit for shooting down the lead bomber.

It wasn't until then that the Zero pilots—whose entire job was to protect the bombers—arrived to engage the Americans. Joseph Lovett, who had claimed a Zero the previous day, was shot up and likely killed in his cockpit. His P-39 was last seen in a high-speed, vertical dive streaming a thin trail of coolant. It plunged into a layer of clouds before smashing into the ground.

The next day, May 4, the 35th and 36th Pursuit Squadrons put up 10 aircraft to strafe Lae in a repeat of the Wagner-led attack of April 30. Low, rain-sodden clouds rolled over Port Moresby following their departure, and the weather en route and at the target was likewise dismal. The pilots that did reach Lae—the exact number was never determined—shot up a handful of bombers on the ground while meeting no aerial opposition. Hours after the mission was complete, the number of P-39s that had returned to 7-Mile Drome was six. What happened to the missing four aircraft is unknown as none of the surviving pilots could provide any relevant information. In all likelihood, the missing pilots ran out of fuel over the jungle or the sea and were simply swallowed up.

Following these first few days of combat operations with the P-39, Boyd Wagner compiled a report on the aircraft's effectiveness as a frontline fighter. In particular, he focused on its performance relative to the Mitsubishi A6M Zero, as well as its mechanical suitability for operations in New Guinea. "The Zero outperformed the P-39s very markedly in maneuverability and climb," he said. "The P-39, however, with no belly tank could pull away from the Zero."[6]

He commented further on the differences in performance between the two types in the context of airspeed. "At 325 [miles per hour] indicated,

just above the water, the P-39 pulled slowly away out of range. In accelera-
tion, the Zero was markedly better than the P-39, attaining a high speed
from cruising in a very few seconds while the P-39 was much slower. As a
result, from a cruising start, the Zero could actually pull ahead of the P-39
for a few seconds and then the P-39 slowly drew away at full throttle and
high RPM."

Wagner noted that the teamwork between the enemy pilots was
"excellent," and that they appeared to fly in flights of three in a weaving
line astern. He was not so impressed by their marksmanship. "First one
and then another would place his plane behind the P-39, firing intermit-
tent bursts for about ten seconds, then zooming up to either side to be
replaced by the most forward plane on that side. Accuracy of fire was not
very high especially at long range while P-39 was making himself a poor
target by roughly slipping and skidding violently." Wagner also made the
point that the Zero did not have self-sealing fuel tanks and caught fire
easily when hit.

So overall, the Zero was rightly recognized as more maneuverable,
better climbing, faster accelerating, and nearly as fast. Moreover, it had
much better high-altitude performance. Its armament was good, although
it lacked armor protection for the pilot and self-sealing fuel tanks. Wagner
declared, "All were impressed with a thorough respect and admiration of
the flying qualities of the Zero fighters."

The nation's first ace also had plenty to say about the P-39s shortcomings. First, it was absurd that the pilots had to activate the emergency
fuel pump or operate the hand wobble pump to keep the engine operating
above 18,000 feet where it was already badly outperformed because it had
only a single-stage supercharger. He also felt that the engine needed armor
protection as it seemed that all the aircraft that had been shot down had
been hit in the engine. Additionally, he rightly believed that the single-
channel radio was inadequate.

Although he liked the effects of the single, 37-millimeter cannon
which fired directly through the propeller hub, it frequently failed to fire,
jammed too often, and didn't have enough ammunition. Moreover, it had
to be manually charged, which was physically demanding. Wagner also
identified the firing solenoids for the .50 caliber guns as very unreliable.

Routine airfield operations were not necessarily so in New Guinea.
Taxiing the aircraft in the rough conditions—including sticky mud and
uneven surfaces—was often problematic as the narrow tires on the main
landing gear often sank into the ground, and the nose strut sometimes
simply broke under the loads imposed by the less-than-ideal surfaces. The

variable-pitch propeller also caused issues as it leaked hydraulic fluid that frequently coated the pilot's windscreen. Since it was critical for a fighter pilot to be able to see to accurately fire his guns, this was an obvious problem.

The reality was that many of the fixes that Wagner desired—more armor protection, hydraulic charging for the guns, beefier tires and landing gear, a better radio, and more ammunition for the cannon—would have added considerable weight to a small aircraft that was already overloaded and underpowered. The P-39 was not the right aircraft for the fight, but it was the aircraft that the men had, and they continued to fly it and score some successes.

Perhaps it was a reflection of the notion that men sometimes develop unreasonable loyalties to the machines with which they work, but one of the closing statements Wagner made in his report is not only untrue but seems demonstrably silly: "Comparatively speaking, in performance," he wrote, "the P-39 airplane is believed to be about ten percent better in every respect than the P-40 airplane, except in maneuverability in which case the P-40 is slightly better." It was a declaration with which few men who had flown both types would have agreed.

Indeed, Frank Adkins had flown P-40s against the Japanese with the 24th Pursuit Group in Java during the very early days of the war. After his first combat experience with the 35th Pursuit Group's 39th Pursuit Squadron—at the controls of a P-39—he made it clear that he was less than impressed with the little fighter. "Could have done better with a truck," he said. "It's more maneuverable and will go higher."[7]

Truly, the P-39 was not a well-loved aircraft—at least not within the USAAF, and the story of its creation explains why. It had been designed and manufactured by Bell Aircraft in response to an Army Air Corps requirement for a high-altitude interceptor. Ironically, it suffered from poor high-altitude performance its entire career. This significantly detracted from its useability in virtually every theater of war, including the Pacific.

A modern and progressive concept, the design was influenced by the Army Air Corps requirement to carry a 37-millimeter cannon measuring more than seven feet in length. A weapon of such size had to be carried in the aircraft's nose, but its length and bulk left no room for an engine. Consequently, the P-39's liquid-cooled V-1710 Allison engine was mounted *behind* the pilot with a shaft that passed underneath the cockpit and into the nose where it drove a gearbox that was connected to the propeller via a much shorter shaft. This arrangement made it possible to accommodate the cannon but with only 30 rounds of ammunition.

Another unusual arrangement was a fixed glass hood or roof above the cockpit. Unlike virtually every other fighter of the day, the P-39 featured automobile-type doors on both sides. Its pilots entered the cockpit from the side rather than from the top through an open canopy. This made it difficult to exit the aircraft during an emergency. On the other hand, the tricycle landing gear arrangement made the P-39 easy to taxi.

It was a small, streamlined aircraft with very little internal volume available to incorporate improvements. There was no room in the fuselage for a fuel tank. The only fuel it carried internally was in the wings, and it consequently had a relatively short operational range. Originally intended to be equipped with a turbo-supercharger for high-altitude operations, the aircraft could not accommodate it without a significant redesign. However, it was determined that a redesign might impose aerodynamic drag penalties that would cancel the benefits of the turbo-supercharger.

Neither Bell nor the Army wanted to spend the time and money to fix the issue, and the decision was made to minimize drag as much as practicable and produce the P-39 with a single-stage, single-speed supercharger. The result was an aircraft that was speedy enough, well-armed, and reasonably maneuverable at altitudes below 12,000 feet. Above that, performance dropped off significantly, and the type was outperformed by virtually all its adversaries.

This only became apparent to the RAF after it received the first of several hundred export variants—designated P-400—that it had ordered. The RAF had essentially been duped into believing the aircraft was much more capable than was actually the case. Only one squadron was equipped with the type, and it saw no real combat. Deciding that the P-400 was wholly unsuited for combat over Western Europe, the RAF declined further deliveries. However, they did give the little aircraft a name—Airacobra.

Many of the remaining aircraft produced for the RAF were delivered to USAAF units in the Pacific, including the 8th and 35th Fighter Groups. The primary difference between the P-400s and the American P-39s was that the P-400s carried a single 20-millimeter cannon in place of the much larger 37-millimeter cannon. It was a more reliable weapon with a higher rate of fire, and the P-39 could carry much more of its smaller ammunition. (Note that P-400s are described as P-39s in this work to reduce confusion and improve readability.)

So then, the aircraft that reached the 8th and 35th Fighter Groups were reasonably capable fighters, so long as they were used to fight at low-to-medium altitudes. The type was as fast as its contemporaries with a top speed that exceeded 350 miles per hour, it had self-sealing fuel tanks and armor protection, adequate radios, and relatively heavy armament. If flown intelligently, especially as part of a mutually supportive formation, it could hold its own with the Japanese fighters, so long as its pilot didn't make the mistake of dogfighting.

The P-39's potential was demonstrated by Soviet pilots who used it with great success against the vaunted Luftwaffe over the Eastern Front, where the fighting generally took place at lower altitudes. Several of the Red Air Force's highest-scoring aces—five of the top 10—enjoyed their greatest successes while flying the P-39. Indeed, two of them scored more aerial victories with the P-39 than any American scored in any aircraft.

But at high altitudes the P-39 cannot be characterized as anything other than a failure. Without a turbo-supercharger, the engine simply couldn't get enough air to generate the power it needed. Japanese bomber pilots soon learned, much to the frustration of the Americans, that they could stay out of reach by simply flying above the P-39's service ceiling.

★★★

The last few days of 75 Squadron's time at 7-Mile Drome were a misery. On May 2, two aircraft that couldn't be made combat-capable in the field took off for Australia. There remained only three operational Kittyhawks. They took off in the early morning together with seven American P-39s to intercept an inbound raid. One of the Kittyhawks landed with a bad engine, and another was shot down. Its pilot, Stuart Munro, was killed.

On the following morning, May 3, 1942, 75 Squadron had only one operational aircraft available. It was the same Kittyhawk that Bill Whetters had put down in the kunai grass the previous week. Arthur Tucker took it airborne in company with eight P-39s. The engine, its air coolers probably clogged with scraps of kunai grass, overheated. Tucker subsequently parted company with the Americans and landed safely. With that last sortie, 75 Squadron's operations at Port Moresby came to an ignominious, wheezing finish after 44 remarkable days of hard-fought air combat.

An after action report sent to the air board secretary in Melbourne acknowledged the hurried manner by which 75 Squadron had been rushed into combat. "It will be recalled that this squadron was brought into being, equipped, trained and sent into its first battle in Papua within fourteen days."[8] Another report noted that while, "on the whole, the standard of flying in 75 Squadron was high," there were signs of "under confidence" in those pilots who had logged less than 100 hours on the Wirraway.

These undertrained pilots were, in bureaucratically benign language, declared to be "not up to operational standard." Worse, there were no aircraft available at Port Moresby which could have been used to increase their experience. Indeed, these pilots, numbering approximately 10, had less than 10 hours of flight time in the P-40, and were noted for having "great difficulty in the carrying out of their job efficiently."

Pilot casualties for 75 Squadron were noted by RAAF officialdom as being "rather high," as 10 pilots were killed in combat during the five weeks the unit flew out of Port Moresby. Moreover, on any given day, five pilots were unable to fly due to illness, and almost that number were unavailable because of other duties. This left approximately 10 to 12 pilots available each day on average. A report declared that due to the miserable living conditions, the long hours of standing duty, and the stress of combat, the remaining pilots "showed signs of tiredness and *lost interest* [emphasis added]." It was additionally noted that if steps were not immediately taken, "It is obvious the enemy will take complete control of the air over Port Moresby."[9]

Ultimately, 75 Squadron was operational at Port Moresby from March 21 to May 3, 1942. During that period, it flew every day but one, March 29, for a total of 436 combat sorties. Its pilots claimed a total of 18 enemy aircraft destroyed in air combat and 17 destroyed on the ground. The squadron actually lost 12 pilots and nearly all of its 24 aircraft—both to the enemy and to accidents. But more important than these numbers was the fact that the Japanese, because of 75 Squadron, were unable to establish air supremacy over Port Moresby. It was the first time since the start of the war that they had failed to achieve such an objective.[10]

In the context of that bleak time, it is telling that the USAAF's 3rd Attack Group's 8th Bomb Squadron included a special note about 75 Squadron in its official narrative. The Australians had escorted the 8th's A-24 crews multiple times—and done it effectively. "It is the desire of every member of the 8th Squadron," the unit declared, "who ever knew and flew with the men in the RAAF's 75 Squadron, that these boys get the commendation and attention they deserve. At times, toward the end of April when they were having great difficulty in getting airplanes and parts, they could only get four into the air, yet these four unhesitatingly attacked sixteen Zeroes in one formation. Despite being the only fighter squadron at Moresby, they were always eager to have a crack at the Japs, either over his airdrome or ours." The admiration of 75 Squadron's American friends was obvious and well-deserved.

To be sure, the cooperation between the Australian flyers and their American counterparts was generally outstanding. At the very highest levels, although the relationship was never perfect, the leadership of the Americans was accepted by the Australians. They recognized and appreciated not only the commonalities between the two nations but also the very practical matter that it was the United States that was, and would be, contributing so many men and so much material and equipment to the war effort.

Robert Crawford recalled his experience as a 75 Squadron pilot when the unit escorted the 8th Bomb Squadron's A-24 dive bombers against Japanese targets. He noted that the generally gregarious nature of his American counterparts was evident even during combat. "In the air," he said, "they were always chattering over the radio . . . Yanks. You know it was like a telephone conversation with them sometimes. But they did a wonderful job."

He also noted that the volume and variety of the Australian flying kit improved when the Americans showed up in strength. The life raft, or dinghy, was an example. Initially, the RAAF's Kittyhawk pilots didn't have them available. That changed as the USAAF's P-40 units began operating in strength and brought with them—and shared—their much more extensive material resources.

★★★

Although they might have guessed at it while they were fighting their first air battles over New Guinea, none of the men of the RAAF's 75 Squadron knew for certain that the Japanese had a concrete plan, code-named Operation Mo, to take Port Moresby. Beginning in March 1942, the U.S. Navy intercepted reports of a Japanese plan that had as its objective, the seizure of Tulagi in the Solomon Islands, as well as Port Moresby. Certainly, the Japanese raids on Port Moresby were intended, in part, to grind down the defenses there, including 75 Squadron. Considering the condition of 75 Squadron at the start of May, there could be no arguing against the fact that the objective had been achieved.

The two fleet carriers and one light carrier that the Japanese sortied to support Operation Mo were more than enough to deal with the recently arrived American P-39 units. Combined, the aircraft carriers embarked nearly 140 aircraft. As it developed, Tulagi was successfully taken on May 3. Port Moresby was scheduled to be secured by May 10.

The U.S. Navy intervened. In a cat-and-mouse clash that took place in the Coral Sea east of New Guinea, the United States won its first meaningful victory in the Pacific from May 4 to May 8, 1942. Although the Japanese sank the *Lexington*—a desperately precious fleet carrier—the Americans destroyed the Japanese light aircraft carrier, *Shōhō*. Both sides lost other minor combatant vessels. Importantly, the battle ushered in a new type of naval warfare as it was fought entirely from the air. Indeed, it was the first naval engagement in which the surface combatants never came within sight of each other.

In terms of tonnage sunk and damage inflicted, the Japanese scored a tactical victory as the loss of the *Lexington* created a hole in the Navy's fleet carrier force that was difficult to fill. However, because the Japanese retreated and canceled the invasion of Port Moresby, the Allies won the more important strategic contest. Port Moresby was safe, for the moment.

★★★

Meanwhile, back in Australia, except for the 8th Bomb Squadron's A-24s, the 3rd Attack Group was still without aircraft. An improbable figure was about to fix that.

Part pirate, part pilot, part engineering genius, and part just-about-everything-else-that-is-interesting, Paul "Pappy" Gunn's exploits and irascible personality made him a legend—almost a comic book hero—in the Southwest Pacific. Born and educated in the Arkansas hinterlands, he spoke with a high-pitched, almost whiney twang that did not make a good first impression.

However, one needed to spend only a short time with the man to realize that, accent or not, Gunn was a man of enormous intelligence and capabilities. Direct, even caustic, he was the sort who knew what he wanted and had little patience for anyone who denied it to him. Moreover, his capacity for hard work and resourcefulness put most men to shame.

Born in 1899, he enlisted in the Navy as an aircraft mechanic shortly after World War I and eventually became an accomplished Navy pilot, serving in fighter, transport, and seaplane units before retiring in 1939. Despite not having a formal engineering education, he showed a savant-like intellect for developing effective solutions to mechanical issues of all sorts. The Navy recognized this and put him to work on all manner of projects; he lost his front teeth while refining a crane recovery system for ship-launched seaplanes.

Gunn moved his family to the Philippines shortly after he retired from the Navy and was managing a small airline when the war started. After hiding his wife and children in Manila, he put the airline's three small Beechcraft D-18S transports into service for the USAAF. He flew tirelessly—and survived being shot down twice—as he delivered men, material, and equipment around the islands and as far as Australia.

Lewis Brereton, the commander of the Far East Air Forces, commissioned him as a captain in the USAAF and put him in charge of whatever transport aircraft he could locate and press into service. The eclectic assortment of aircraft that Gunn scraped together formed the nucleus of what eventually became the Fifth Air Force's Air Transport Command. It was grinding, exhausting, but undeniably heroic service, especially as Gunn's family was trapped in Manila and he fretted every day at not being able to get them out of the Philippines.

When Gunn wasn't flying aircraft, he was working on them. He maintained his company's transports and pitched in to help keep flying whatever USAAF aircraft hadn't been destroyed. Working shoulder-to-shoulder with men less than half his age, he was tagged with an enduring nickname at age 42—Pappy.

Pappy was in Australia when the first shipment of P-40s and A-24s arrived in crates in late December 1941. It was due in part to his expertise that they were put together as quickly as they were. And when a batch of assembled P-40s was flown north to Java, it was Pappy in one of his Beech-craft transports who navigated the way for the pilots.

It was late March 1942 when Gunn overflew an airfield in Australia and spotted several medium bombers parked in neat rows. Curious, he deviated from his planned route and landed to see what he might find out about the aircraft. As it developed, they were B-25s waiting to be delivered to the Netherlands East Indies Air Force. But as there were no Dutch air-men to fly them, they were sitting idle.

The story of these aircraft has been mythologized, and the facts have been lost to time. These include the airfield, the number of aircraft, and the exact dates—as well as the truth about how the B-25s came to equip the 3rd Attack Group. One probably exaggerated account has Pappy waving a Thompson submachinegun at the officer who had official custody of the aircraft. Other accounts suggest a more civilized exchange of paperwork generated on the basis of convenient half-truths, deceptions, omissions, and lies. Ultimately, a cadre of 3rd Attack Group pilots ferried the B-25s to their base in early April 1942. They were flying combat soon after.

The North American B-25 Mitchell—built in two separate factories in the United States—would become one of the hardest-hitting weapons of the war. Its origins were barely prewar. Betting that the United States would be drawn into the growing global conflict, the Army Air Corps placed orders for the type in 1939. And it continued to place orders until 1945.

A twin-engine medium bomber with a nominal crew of five, the type had good range and payload capacity, was easy to fly and straightforward to maintain. Exceedingly rugged, it offered good performance and could exceed 200 miles per hour at low altitudes. But perhaps the most valuable characteristic of the type was that its heavy construction and size made it readily adaptable for all sorts of modifications. Guns and gun turrets were added and removed, additional fuel tanks were incorporated, noses were glazed or not, and specialized equipment such as cameras and special radio suites were readily accommodated. Ultimately, it was a combat jack-of-all-trades that served the USAAF well throughout the war.

4

"A VERY ATTRACTIVE AND POLISHED GENTLEMAN"

On May 15, 1942, the USAAF redesignated all of its pursuit units as fighter units. The new word fit the role of the aircraft type better. Pursuit was an anachronistic label left over from World War I and seemed less relevant to the many roles that the aircraft type fulfilled in the new war. As a practical matter, it made essentially no difference to the men who flew and maintained them. Otherwise, the matter was an administrative one that involved the admittedly tiresome tasks of changing letterheads, addresses, signage, and other trivialities.

★★★

The commander of the air forces in Australia and New Guinea was Lieutenant General George Brett. He had served in various capacities during the previous several months since arriving at Rangoon, Burma, immediately after the attack on Pearl Harbor. There followed many weeks of shuttling from Burma to China to Java and Australia and back in several different capacities as the most senior American officer in that part of the world. Allied forces, disjointed, ill-equipped, badly trained, and poorly led, crumbled everywhere in the face of the aggressive Japanese offensives. No man, competent or not, could have staunched the disaster.

Finally, during the debacle that was the barely battle for Java, Brett was ordered to Melbourne, Australia, in February 1942. There, during the confusion that characterized that part of the world at that time, he was made Commander Allied Air Forces, Southwest Pacific Area. A lieutenant general, Brett was not unqualified for the job. Having been trained as a pilot during World War I, he had served in—and commanded—many units between the world wars. In particular, he was a material and supply expert.

What there was for him to command upon his arrival in Australia was a mixed bag. There were ragtag elements of units that had survived the fighting in the Philippines, Java, and elsewhere before reaching refuge in Australia. An example was the 19th Bomb Group, which flew B-17s. It was in tatters after weeks of combat while on the run.

At the same time, other aircraft dribbled in from the States in small groups. Still other units arrived in their entirety via ship. The 8th, 35th, and 49th Fighter Groups arrived with their aircraft in crates, while the 3rd Attack Group also arrived, but without aircraft.

Still, as bleak as the disposition of the American organizations seemed, the RAAF units under Brett's command were even more dreadfully under-equipped. There were no domestically produced modern combat aircraft except a small number of license-built Bristol Beaufort torpedo bombers. The RAAF's 75 Squadron, which had fought so desperately to save Port Moresby, had done so with P-40s that Brett had given it. The Australians were willing, ready, and able to fly and fight, but they had little with which to do so. Consequently, they weren't doing Brett much good at all.

On the other hand, the aircraft coming from the States during the first few months of 1942 were being made operational. Men, material, and equipment continued to arrive, and the Australians—government, military, and industry—contributed with their own resources. Assembly and repair depots were busy making ready to fight the few aircraft that Brett had in his possession.

So, the truth was that although the material situation was desperate, it wasn't hopeless. And it was getting better as shipping from the United States continued to arrive. Indeed, Brett had an air force of several hundred aircraft as the halfway mark of 1942 approached. Of course, many of those were still in crates, or in various states of repair or rework, but they were his to disposition as best he could. And although it was true that the vast majority of his men were green, it was also true that they were enthusiastic and learning fast.

Brett's biggest problem was Douglas MacArthur, his boss and the Supreme Commander of the Southwest Pacific Area. MacArthur had flown into Australia on March 22 with his wife, child, staff, and various hangers-on. The effort to fly him out of the Philippines had not gone well, not necessarily because of anything Brett had done or failed to do, but MacArthur was nevertheless displeased. Exacerbating Brett's problem was MacArthur's chief of staff, Major General Richard Sutherland. Characterized as a self-important, autocratic, back-stabbing hatchet man, he was loathed by virtually everyone. All this was made worse by the fact that Sutherland was exceedingly smart.

Sutherland was a senator's son, a Yale graduate, and, like MacArthur, an infantry officer who had seen service in World War I. His chief attribute—if it could be called such—was his loyalty to MacArthur, with whom he had served since the late 1930s. As chief of staff, Sutherland allowed very few people to get through to MacArthur. That included Brett, the man in charge of MacArthur's air force.

Almost as bad as blocking Brett's access to MacArthur was the fact that Sutherland got into Brett's business to a preposterous degree. An infantry officer, Sutherland nevertheless fancied himself a combat aviation expert and regularly issued orders that should have come from Brett or his staff. Sutherland went so far as to specify mission routes, altitudes, airspeeds, and other details. These were particulars that should have been determined at the squadrons by the pilots.

One pilot recalled that a memo came from Sutherland which declared that the ratio of ammunition fired per enemy aircraft shot down by the P-39 pilots was too high. It further directed that each round fired was to be individually aimed. Such a thing was not just stupid but impossible. That Brett tolerated this sort of interference from Sutherland was not just unfathomable, it was dereliction of duty.

MacArthur's acceptance of such a poisonous relationship is curious. He had left his army behind in the Philippines, and Brett's men and aircraft were virtually the only means by which he could strike at the Japanese. He did order Brett to formulate a miniature pseudo-campaign against the Japanese in the Philippines to relieve pressure on the units still fighting at Corregidor. Brett resisted, reasonably arguing that his aircraft were beat up, his men were tired, and nothing they could do would do the situation in the Philippines any lasting good. MacArthur pressed, and Brett sluffed the effort onto his deputy, Ralph Royce.

Royce and his men pulled off a small series of daring raids during mid-April 1942 that became known as the Royce Mission. But the flights, although audacious, had little material impact and pulled resources from the air force that Brett was trying to assemble. In truth, they were little more than a stunt.

It is generally true that the competence of a military organization is a reflection of the competence and leadership skills of its commander. Clues as to what sort of commander Brett might become were noted by a senior officer early in his career. He wrote a scathing evaluation of Brett's performance during the latter part of World War I: "This officer is not physically fit for service in the U.S. Army under War conditions either in the field or bureau work. . . . Major Brett was, in my opinion, headstrong and difficult to handle. His desires seemed to be more in securing leave of absence than to be helpful to the Washington office and the winning of the War." However, the reporting officer did note, "Personally Major Brett is a very attractive and polished gentleman."[1] Subsequent reports varied in their assessments, but it is undeniable that Brett performed well enough to reach the rank of lieutenant general.

Overall, Brett's leadership in Australia seemed misdirected, especially as a Japanese invasion of Australia was feared imminent. Frederick Smith, the commander of the 8th Pursuit Group, came to see Brett soon after he arrived in Australia. He looked for guidance and for help finding the equipment he needed to get his aircraft out of their crates and put back together. Brett's reception was less than inspiring.

> I got down to Melbourne and went immediately to General Brett's headquarters, and he received me right away. I started to tell him about my heavy equipment missing, and this that and the other, when he said, "Now, I am going to talk first, see," he said. "There will be no training accidents, and I mean none, zero!" I said, "General Brett, I can't make a commitment like that. I have got 80 pilots I don't even know. I'm just picking them up and I have got to train them, and there will be an accident or two."[2]

Brett doubled down and told Smith that if his group experienced any accidents, he would be relieved of command. Such an attitude was an absurdity and highlighted not only Brett's arrogance but an acute lack of awareness about the conditions under which his men were operating. Most of the 8th's pilots hadn't been at the controls of an aircraft for weeks, if not months. And there was no guarantee that the aircraft, once they were reassembled, would be mechanically sound, "straight-out-of-the-box."

In fact, Brett had little firsthand knowledge of what was going on with his men mostly because he didn't make much of an effort to gain that firsthand knowledge. An observer remarked on Brett's seeming lack of interest in his units fighting in New Guinea:

> He didn't get up there very often; I think he was up there maybe twice. They didn't have much equipment and weren't getting any more equipment; they weren't getting spare parts when their airplanes began falling apart. Brett didn't get them up to them, and he didn't check and find out what they needed and see that they got it. Their food was terrible stuff, and he wouldn't do anything about that. They were getting malaria pretty badly, and there was nothing done about that.[3]

But Brett did make time to participate in Melbourne's social scene. In and of itself, this wasn't frowned upon, and it was necessary to a certain degree to cultivate and maintain goodwill with the Australians. But some held opinions that he aligned himself too closely with the wrong elements of Australia's political sphere. They entertained him, and he entertained them in return. This did little to advance the effectiveness of his air force, which bumped along in ineffectual fits and starts and showed little promise of being able to defeat the Japanese.

An issue that vexed the Allies during Brett's tenure and beyond was the fact that the Japanese regularly sent air attacks against the Australian mainland. This, even though the Japanese high command had decided against an invasion. Japan's forces were already stretched too thin, and Australia was too big, and beyond their capacity to take and hold. Nevertheless, four aircraft carriers launched a total of nearly 250 aircraft on two separate strikes against Darwin on February 19, 1942. Darwin had no proper defenses, and the Japanese sank 11 vessels and destroyed 30 aircraft.

The fledgling 49th Fighter Group was sent to the region for several months before being relieved by other units. The strikes continued until November 12, 1943, by which time more than 100 had been launched. Except for the first raid against Darwin, they never presented a severe threat but were still a menace against which precious resources had to be allocated.

5

"HE HAD AVOIDED
COMBAT OFTEN"

American bomber operations over New Guinea were still in their infancy during the spring of 1942. Typically, the B-17s, B-26s, and B-25s flew from their bases in Australia to stage out of Port Moresby before heading to their targets, usually the following day. After returning to Port Moresby, they often spent the night before heading back to Australia. This practice reduced their exposure to Japanese bombing attacks. Another consideration was the fact that Port Moresby did not yet have all the infrastructure in place to accommodate the thousands of men required to maintain and sustain the big bombers. On the other hand, it did put wear and tear on the aircraft, and essentially required three days to execute a single mission.

★★★

Wesley Dickinson of the 3rd Attack Group's 89th Bomb Squadron was about to climb into his B-25 on May 23, 1942, when a ground crewman, Earl Sevene, approached and asked if he might be allowed to fly as an observer on that day's mission. Dickinson considered the other man's request. Permitting such riders was not uncommon, but it could be risky to everyone on the aircraft if the enemy was encountered in force. The observers were generally untrained and often got in the way. And they were sometimes killed, which consequently robbed the ground effort of a skilled worker and a family of a beloved man. Still, it wasn't guaranteed that they would see heavy action that day, and Dickinson agreed to Sevene's request.[1]

The 89th Bomb Squadron was putting up six aircraft that day for an attack on the Japanese airfield at Lae—a regular target. The formation, led by Herman Lowery, got airborne, and shortly afterward one of the other B-25 pilots aborted. Dickinson knew the other pilot and was not surprised.

He was certain that the man would invent a mechanical malfunction of some sort to explain his failure to continue. "He had avoided combat often," Dickinson said. "A few pilots had gone to their commanders and said they would not fly combat anymore. I don't know what happened to those guys. They just disappeared."

The remaining five bombers flew across the Owen Stanley Range and took a route that set them up for an attack on Lae from over the sea. Dickinson's copilot, Theodore Wuerpel, was a Mexican American who recently returned to flying duty after being grounded for a bad ear infection. Before the flight he had told Dickinson that he was happy to be flying with him again. Now, quickly approaching Lae at 6,000 feet and just more than 200 miles per hour, they readied to release their bombs. Sevene, the ground crewman, leaned forward between them to see everything as best he could.

Immediately after the formation released its bombs a Zero attacked from directly ahead and put rounds into the right engine of Henry Keel's aircraft. Keel was Lowery's wingman. Lowery throttled back and lowered the nose of his aircraft so that Keel might trade altitude for airspeed and stay with the rest of the formation with his one good engine. But Keel's aircraft was still unable to keep up, and he waved the other crews ahead. Wuerpel leaned back from where he sat to the right of Dickinson and kept an eye on the damaged B-25. A short time later he reported that Keel had put his aircraft down in the water.

A short time later, as Lowery climbed to turn the rest of the flight back to Port Moresby, another Zero—or perhaps the same one that had hit Keel—made a second head-on attack against the remaining four aircraft. There was a booming crash. "A shell exploded in the cockpit," Dickinson said. "White smoke blinded me, and I smelled burnt gunpowder." A swirling, roaring, storm of wind drowned the sound of the engines. It also cleared the smoke enough for Dickinson to see that Lowery and the other two aircraft were outpacing him. "I was on my own," he said. "I turned to speak to Wuerpel, but what I saw turned me away." The cannon shell had literally blown Wuerpel apart.

Dickinson wrestled to control his aircraft. The right engine was shot out and the propeller blades failed to feather, which created a great deal of drag. The bombardier, James Webb, crawled into the cockpit from his position in the nose of the aircraft. Dickinson turned and shouted at Webb to parachute from the doomed aircraft. At the same time, he threw the switch for the bailout bell to signal the two gunners in the back of the aircraft. It was then that he saw Sevene, dead, atop the escape hatch in the navigator's compartment. His head had been shattered by the Zero's gunfire.

And his body blocked the way out for both Dickinson and Webb. While Dickinson struggled to keep the B-25 upright, Webb pushed and pulled at Sevene's body with little success. Finally, using his legs, he shoved the dead man out of the way and into the bombardier's tunnel. That done, Webb released the escape hatch, dropped through the opening, and was gone.

Dickinson fussed with the controls as long as he dared, trimming the aircraft so that it would stay in level flight long enough for him to escape. "When satisfied with my trim settings," he said, "I unfastened my safety belt, climbed down into the navigator's compartment and without hesitation slipped through the opening." Once clear of the aircraft he deployed his parachute, which jerked him to a sudden stop. He almost marveled at the silence, and at the carpet-like appearance of the landscape below him.

He did not marvel when he spotted his pilotless aircraft in the distance. It was in a gentle left turn back toward where he was descending. As the seconds passed it became clear that the B-25—with his dead comrades aboard—might very well chop him out of the sky. Dickinson desperately considered how he might tug on the lines of his parachute to alter his rate of descent, or somehow turn it out of the path of the oncoming bomber.

And then, when it had almost completed its turn, the B-25 rolled, and its nose dropped, and it dived at high speed into the jungle and exploded. Dickinson had little time to consider his good fortune as the ground rushed up at him. Seconds later he crashed through a tangle of tree branches and splashed uninjured into a swamp.

★★★

In the meantime, Henry Keel's crew was fighting to survive. Louis Murphy, a gunner, recounted what happened.

> Lieutenant Keel decided to chance a landing on the water. The landing was accomplished smoothly, and we abandoned the ship and immediately launched the life raft. We began grouping around the life raft and the four Zeros began strafing us. This making such a large target, we were ordered by the pilot [Keel] to separate. At this time, we were all safe and intact. I began swimming in the opposite direction from the rest and this was the last I saw of my crew.[2]

Ultimately, Murphy made it back to his unit. Keel was captured and died in a camp in Rabaul. The fates of the rest of the men remain unknown.

★★★

After collecting his wits and pulling a compass and a large Bowie-type knife from his survival kit, Dickinson headed southwest toward where he had seen a native village. After less than an hour he stepped out of the sucking mud and water and onto a well-used path. He followed it and spotted a handful of natives some distance ahead of him. He raised his hand and shouted at them in a friendly manner.

They considered him warily. He continued toward them until he was close enough to extend his hand in a gesture of friendship. The man to whom he offered it, Hangiri, took it hesitantly. Dickinson smiled. The smile Hangiri returned took Dickinson aback. A lifetime of chewing betel nut had turned the Papuan man's teeth shiny and black. Indeed, all the natives had black teeth.

They led Dickinson to their village, Fufuda, where he was welcomed like a celebrity. "About fifty men, women and children came out and lined up to greet me," he said. "I shook each of their hands, while they chattered and giggled as I followed Hungery [Hangiri] into their village."

There followed much excitement as Dickinson shared his story as best he could. Hangiri had once worked as a houseboy for an Australian in Port Moresby and understood some English. The village boys retrieved Dickinson's parachute and harness, and they delighted in trying it on and pantomiming dropping from the sky. Dickinson enjoyed the kindness of the natives and the care and food they shared with him—carefully cleaning a wound they discovered on his arm.

The following day, Hangiri and a handful of other natives escorted him down the coast by canoe and on foot until they reached the Anglican mission at Gona. There, he met Reverend James Benson; the mission nurse, May Hayman; and Mavis Parkinson, the mission's schoolteacher. Dickinson thanked his native friends, who were continuing to the Australian outpost at Buna to make them aware of the American pilot's disposition. Hangiri was much pleased when Dickinson gifted him his knife.

The mission was not grand, but it was well-sited and comfortable, consisting of the main house of native construction and several outbuildings. It was surrounded by a well-groomed lawn and sat just off the tree-shaded beach where it caught cooling sea breezes. It was an idyllic setting, seemingly far from the carnage and wreckage of war.

Benson and the two women, like the natives, welcomed Dickinson and treated him kindly. "I felt more relaxed and at peace than I had since before the war began," Dickinson said. As the days passed, he grew close to the three missionaries as he waited for the boat which periodically serviced the various outposts in that part of New Guinea.

He was especially fond of Mavis Parkinson, the schoolteacher. The two of them relaxed on the beach on many evenings listening to her Gilbert and Sullivan records on a wind-up phonograph, often singing along. They shared stories of their very different lives, he from the United States, she from Australia. "Waves lapped a slow rhythm against the shore," he said. "Stars eaves dropped through the palm trees and a flowery fragrance filled the air. We wormed our toes in the sand, lay back and sang along with her scratchy records."

Dickinson enjoyed lolling in the sand with Parkinson but stayed clear of the waves. "I often walked along the beach," he said, "but I never went into the water. I had seen too many sharks swimming along the New Guinea coast when I was flying."

Dickinson pressed Parkinson to leave New Guinea—to get out of the war's way. To go somewhere safe. To go home to Australia. He recalled her reply: "What is there to be afraid of Wes? I know God won't let the Japanese bother our little mission."

James Webb, Dickinson's bombardier, arrived at Gona, having survived his parachute jump and the journey along the coast. The two of them were the crew's only survivors. When they were finally retrieved and returned to their unit, the three missionaries remained resolutely behind, determined to continue caring for their community.

★★★

The 3rd Attack Group's 8th Bomb Squadron continued to fly the A-24 with indifferent results. After standing an uneventful alert during the Battle of the Coral Sea, most of the aircraft were sent back to Australia with just a handful remaining to perform submarine patrols and other types of utility duties. An unusual mission on May 31 highlighted not only the desperation of the military situation in New Guinea but also the naiveté of the American leadership. It especially underscored the difficulty of conducting operations in the mountainous jungle and scrub that made up virtually the entire island.

The 8th Bomb Squadron was ordered to fly three A-24s to where a tiny clearing had been hacked out of the brush about 50 miles west of Lae. "Captain Rogers," declared the squadron, "against his better judgement, was ordered to land three A-24s and pick up several pilots who had survived a B-25 crash." Floyd Rogers did as he was ordered, leading three aircraft without their gunners to the ad hoc landing strip. He and James Holcombe were able to get their aircraft down unscathed, but the third pilot, Claude Dean, nosed over on the treacherous little landing ground. His A-24 was unflyable.

A short time later, Rogers, as the squadron commander, led by example and took off first. His engine, a variant of the A-24's engine that was salvaged from a B-17, got him airborne only barely in time. And then, it quit. The aircraft smashed into a tree-covered hillside, breaking Rogers's nose and injuring his leg.

Rogers was pulled from the wreck and loaded into the back of Holcombe's A-24. The ground proved too rough, and Holcombe flipped the aircraft onto its back during takeoff and was killed. Rogers survived his second plane crash of the day. All the aircraft had been destroyed at this point, and the men were eventually evacuated several weeks later by other means.

6

"HE HAD NO PARACHUTE"

Although the USAAF's cast of players was thin during mid-1942, a combined strike of B-25s, B-26s, and B-17s—with an escort of eight P-39s—was launched from Port Moresby on June 9. The group hit Lae and was in turn attacked by a formation of defending Zeroes. The B-26s dived to wavetop level and sped away from the Japanese fighters at top speed.

The P-39s were late to rendezvous with the bombers and only arrived as the B-26s were fleeing. "We could hear them squalling, going on, calling for Charlie," said Curran "Jack" Jones, who led the second flight of four P-39s. "Our call sign was Charlie, and it was, 'Come on, Charlie!' and 'We need help!' and this sort of thing."

"So, I luckily spotted a glint that you always got—you never did see an airplane," said Jones. "You just saw a small glint of sun off of something, just a little flash."[1] Jones called for his flight leader to cover him as he dived after the enemy aircraft. The flight leader replied that his propeller pitch control had failed and that he was out of the fight. Jones continued anyway. He recalled that the Japanese fighters were "scattered like flies." It took almost no time for him to pick a target.

"I knew my flight was with me," said Jones, "so I pressed home my attack. We all four fired at one aircraft which did the usual steep climb followed by a kind of hammerhead stall. As we came around in trail formation my flight was strung out."

There followed a bit of confusion as Jones and his flight tried to determine how how they had grown from four aircraft to five. Shortly afterward his number four man called out, "Uh-oh." The fifth aircraft was a Zero.

Jones wracked his P-39 into a very tight right-hand turn and passed the second, third, and fourth members of his flight head-on as he closed the distance on the enemy fighter. "I still had a good bit of speed," he said, "and was running wide open when the Zero started his usual vertical climb so that I was able to go up a good distance with him. I started firing short bursts. I realized my speed was getting low but was too busy to be concerned. Most fortunately, I saw what I think to be one of my 20-millimeter shells explode in front of the cockpit."

Jones's aircraft slowed quickly as it reached the top of its climb. He needed to destroy the enemy fighter immediately or risk being outmaneuvered and shot down himself. As it developed, he had already won the fight.

> There was a movement of the pilot as I approached, and I realized that he was climbing out of the cockpit. I tried to pull in a little tighter in order to shoot him off the wing but would have stalled out as I was down, I believe, to around 140 miles per hour with wide open throttle. As I passed behind his crate, he was holding on to the cockpit and looking back at me, and the nose of the Zero was just beginning to drop. He had no parachute. There were two red diagonal stripes just after the cockpit around the fuselage.[2]

Jones saw the enemy pilot's clothes flapping in the windstream. He later recalled to his squadron mates "that he looked at me as though I was the last man he would see alive." Jones watched the enemy fighter smash into the sea, its pilot still clinging tightly to the cockpit.

The doomed man was one of five victories claimed by the 39th Fighter Squadron that day. However, Japanese documents record only one loss. This was almost certainly the Zero that Jones shot down. The Japanese pilot was Satoshi Yoshino who had been flying since 1936 and was variously credited with shooting down from 7 to 25 Allied aircraft. On the other hand, this was the first time that Jones had encountered enemy fighters.

The 22nd Bomb Group sent 11 B-26s to Lae that day. Spread out between them were five VIP observers—part of a fact-finding mission from the States. They were tasked with gathering information on the condition and disposition of American forces in Australia and New Guinea. The little party had already met with MacArthur and his staff and had toured several installations. Eager to "see some action," they had secured permission to ride along with the 22nd Bomb Group.

They were late flying into Port Moresby from Townsville, Australia, on the morning of the mission, and the takeoff was delayed for an hour. Among the VIPs was Navy Lieutenant Commander Lyndon Johnson. He boarded one of the B-26s, *Wabash Cannonball*, but climbed back down either to retrieve his camera or to relieve his bladder. Accounts differ.

When he returned to the aircraft Johnson found his place taken by another of the VIPs. As far as he was concerned, one B-26 was much the same as any other, and he climbed into a different one, which carried the name *Heckling Hare*. After takeoff, the flight to Lae was fairly uneventful until reaching a point approximately 80 miles south of the target. The generator on one of *Heckling Hare*'s engines failed. It was a serious enough malfunction that the aircraft's pilot jettisoned the bombs and turned back for Port Moresby, landing at about the same time that the rest of the formation was bombing Lae. Heavily engaged by a force of up to 20 Zeroes, the 22nd lost one aircraft that day. Everyone aboard *Wabash Cannonball*, including the officer who had taken Johnson's seat, was killed when the aircraft was shot down.

Johnson met with MacArthur after the mission. MacArthur recognized an opportunity when he saw one. And Johnson, who was on a leave of absence from his seat in Congress, was an opportunity. When he returned to the States later that month, it was with a Silver Star Medal, the nation's third-highest decoration for valor in combat.

Johnson, who had gone on the mission as little more than baggage, did nothing whatsoever to earn the award. *Heckling Hare* had not been attacked, and the crew never saw Lae or a Japanese aircraft. Later accounts that described a ferocious battle against eight enemy aircraft were pure fabrications.

But MacArthur saw Johnson as a potential ally who could not only champion his goals in the Southwest Pacific but also advocate on his behalf after the war when he might seek political office—perhaps even the presidency. MacArthur was a man whose principles frequently pivoted around whatever was best for MacArthur. Accordingly, giving the Silver Star to Johnson without justification was a trifling nothing.

The fact that the Silver Star was not awarded to anyone else on the aircraft or to anyone who actually attacked Lae underscored the truth that its award to Johnson was a political favor—nothing more than base bribery. Moreover, the citation justifying the award was mostly based on lies. Ultimately, the entire episode denigrated the award and those who actually earned it. Yet Johnson wore it proudly throughout his political career, including his time as the nation's president.[3]

★★★

The Mitsubishi Type 0 fighter, or "Zero," that the Allied pilots encountered over New Guinea had been in service since 1940. It was flown by pilots of the Imperial Japanese Navy and its official designation was A6M. The "A" was assigned to carrier-based fighters, the "6" acknowledged it as the sixth carrier fighter design to be developed for the Japanese Navy, and the "M" came from the fact that it was designed by Mitsubishi. Later, the Allies gave it a code name of Zeke, with some variants dubbed Hap, or Hamp.

It was powered by a reasonably reliable radial engine, and its two 20-millimeter cannon and two rifle-caliber machineguns were adequate. And it was about as speedy as most of the fighters of its day. But its performance—particularly its range and maneuverability—was astounding. Many observers were incredulous that the Japanese could have created such an aircraft on their own and believed they had stolen from American and British designs and technologies. Other than the fact that all aircraft manufacturers kept a keen eye on developments across the industry, there is little basis to support the assertion that the Zero's design was not original. Rather, it was the product of innovative engineering and an overriding emphasis on lightness of construction.

As nimble and long-ranged as the Mitsubishi Zero was, it had aspects that frustrated its pilots. Its radio was next to worthless, and the Japanese high command had little interest in improving it. "After all," the higher-ups asked, "how many enemy aircraft can a radio shoot down?" Sadamu Komachi was a Japanese Navy pilot whose career spanned the entire war and included several months of combat over Rabaul. Decades later, he still felt strongly about the stupidity of the higher-ups. "Even now," he said, "when I think about it, I want to stamp my feet in frustration!"[4]

Indeed, Japanese leaders very much believed that courage and skill should overcome shortcomings in equipment, and they valued individual lives virtually not at all. This was evidenced by the fact that the Zero and its contemporaries were built with very little protection. For instance, Japanese aircraft typically erupted into fireballs when their unprotected fuel tanks were hit by gunfire. Zero pilot Kazuo Tsunoda recalled exactly this when a formation of Zeroes scrambled to takeoff at Buna in 1942. "[Australian] P-40s appeared out of nowhere. The strip was narrow so only one plane at a time could take off. Our first three Zeros off the ground were immediately shot down, two becoming fireballs when barely a few metres up."[5]

American-built fighters typically did not catch fire like this. "No matter how much we hit them," said Sadamu Komachi, "we got the impression that there was never any fuel leakage. Now, while we very much wanted the same sort of protection fitted to our own aircraft, in the eyes of the military general staff this was cowardice, and so quite out of the question."

The same was true of armor protection. "Frankly speaking," said Komachi, "while enemy aircraft had armour in many places around the cockpit, the Reisen [Zero] had as good as no such protection." Again, this reflected the attitude of the Japanese leadership in the context of individual lives.

To be sure, the incorporation of armor and self-sealing fuel tanks came at the cost of performance. The outstanding maneuverability of the Zero would have suffered noticeably were it equipped with the safety and protection features found on its American counterparts. And although many American pilots lamented the shortcomings of their aircraft against the Zero early in the war, they were especially appreciative of the ruggedness of those same aircraft when, badly shot up, they flew safely home.

And of course, because the United States invested heavily in technology and development, those same American pilots enjoyed the best of both worlds—performance and protection—when newer aircraft were introduced later during the war. Examples included the Army's later models of the P-38, the P-47, and the P-51, and the Navy's F4U and F6F. Later Japanese aircraft, including the ultimate models of the Zero, were also equipped with some of the protection features they lacked early in the war, but these were thin gruel compared to the robust equipment the Americans fielded.

★★★

The Imperial Japanese Army Air Service equivalent to the Zero was the Nakajima Ki-43 Hayabusa, which the Allies assigned the code name of Oscar. It entered service in 1941, a year later than the Zero. Although the two types were distinctly different in detail, they resembled each other to a very great degree and were often confused for each other during the freewheeling confusion of air combat. That confusion was exacerbated when the two types were present during the same engagements as sometimes happened.

Just as the Oscar resembled the Zero, its performance was very similar in terms of speed, operating altitude, range, and, especially, maneuverability. Marginally smaller than the Zero, the Ki-43 had a slightly higher wing loading, but also a slightly greater power-to-weight ratio. Although, like the Zero, it was very light and a delight to fly, it was poorly armed and carried only two cowl-mounted machineguns and no cannon. On the other hand, the Oscar had armor-plating protection for the pilot, and primitive self-sealing fuel tanks, which proved to be fairly ineffective.

Ultimately, the Allied pilots cared little about the distinctions between the Zero and the Ki-43. Both were worthy adversaries.

7

"FATHER, DON'T TRY TO PERSUADE THEM"

The Kokoda Track could kill a man in a hundred different ways. Malaria was the most effective, although it was hardly the only disease that waited along the route. Dysentery, scrub typhus, and a great gamut of rashes and fungal infections were endemic. A tangled trail, or set of trails, it started on the northern coast of the island between Buna and Sanananda. From there it wound through thick jungle as it climbed, then crested, the Owen Stanley Range at its namesake village of Kokoda. Thereafter it continued south before descending toward Port Moresby. Too rugged for vehicles along most of its length, it was trafficked on foot by Papuans, or by the occasional white man, usually aided by Papuans.

Following their defeat at the hands of the American Navy at the Battle of the Coral Sea in May 1942, the Japanese contrived a plan to seize Port Moresby by coming overland, across the Owen Stanley Range, via the Kokoda Track. They began executing that plan on July 21, 1942, with a shore bombardment by naval vessels. Immediately afterward, they landed troops at Gona and at a point a couple of miles northwest of Buna.

James Benson at the Gona mission, together with May Hayman and Mavis Parkinson, were alarmed at the sound of the naval guns. These were the three missionaries who had treated Wesley Dickinson so kindly when his B-25 had been shot down a few months earlier. They had rejected his entreaties to evacuate to safety during that time. And now, as they watched Japanese soldiers moving ashore, they scooped up what they could carry and fled into the jungle.

The landings were unopposed, and beachheads were quickly established as infantry units moved inland. The Japanese planned to establish a substantial logistics node to support the overland push to Port Moresby. It was a straight-line distance of almost exactly 100 miles. But straight lines didn't exist when traversing New Guinea on foot. Up and down, and side to side, and around and around through some of the most inhospitable terrain in the world was what the Japanese—and the Allies who fought them—were about to encounter. And they would do it while hungry, sick, and with disease-ridden bowels that defied control.

The Allies immediately tried to dislodge the Japanese with air attacks but simply could not muster the forces necessary to do so. Handfuls of air-craft flew raids during the next several days, but with little success except for the sinking of a single transport, *Ayatosan Maru*. The situation in the Buna-Gona area was so desperate that the 3rd Attack Group's 8th Bomb Squad-ron's A-24s were ordered back from Australia to Port Moresby. They were used in various attacks in the Buna-Gona area with unremarkable results.

The 3rd Attack Group also sent B-25s to bomb the enemy lodgments from medium altitude on July 24 and July 25. The results were indifferent but came at a high price. The attack on July 24 included eight B-25s sent to strike the Gona Mission area. The bombs were dropped in the jungle with unobserved results. Immediately afterward, the formation was attacked by eight Zeroes. The mission report noted that "the fighter cover of 6 P-39s did not intercept these Zeroes and [the] pursuit lasted for 15 minutes." Although none of the bombers were lost, they were "badly shot up by cannon and machinegun fire."

Such was not the case the following morning as five of the 3rd's B-25s approached Gona and were jumped by 15 enemy fighters. "Bombs were jettisoned, and coal was poured on in a run for home in close formation," noted the group's mission narrative. The aircrews were surprised at the performance of the Japanese aircraft: "25s indicated 280 miles per hour at 10,000 feet and Zeroes stayed with them easily."

The Japanese chased the B-25s from the top of New Guinea to the bottom, shooting down two of the bombers along the way. One of the doomed aircraft "was seen burning fiercely from nose-to-tail with [the] copilot halfway out of [the] top hatch." The other B-25 was set afire and broke in half before likewise falling into the jungle.

The three surviving aircraft were badly shot up. Wings, fuselages, and engines were riddled with holes. The top turret of one was simply shot away. The enemy pilots were so persistent that their machinegun fire ricocheted from the runway at 7-Mile Drome as the American bomber crews landed.

A few days later a convoy of eight Japanese vessels carrying men and material was spotted en route to the Buna-Gona area. Those cargoes were critical to the success of the enemy advance up the Kokoda Track. The

Japanese had already reached the village of Kokoda, and the Allies were consequently very keen to destroy the convoy and what it carried.

But only keen enough, on July 29, 1942, to send a formation of eight A-24s. It was led by the 8th Bomb Squadron's commander, Floyd Rogers, who had survived two crashes in one day just a couple of months earlier. The formation climbed the Owen Stanley Range and made its way toward the enemy vessels as a flight of seven; one aircraft had turned back with mechanical issues. A total of 20 P-39s—10 as close escort and 10 as high cover—were assigned to protect Rogers and his little group, but they lost contact with the A-24s at some point before reaching Buna.

Continuing the mission without the fighter escort was dangerous, and Rogers could have aborted the mission without fear of censure or reprisal. It is not possible to know why, but he continued north up the coast past Buna. It was at about this point that the 500-pound bomb carried by one of the other aircraft simply fell away. Unaware, unfazed, or in a show of solidarity, the pilot stayed with Rogers and the rest of the formation. Counting the aircraft that had turned back, and the one continuing without its bomb, Rogers's little flight had already lost 25 percent of its bombs—and it had yet to engage the enemy.

Rogers finally sighted the Japanese ships about 20 miles north of Gona where they sat just a mile or two off the coast. He put himself at the head of the first three aircraft, followed by a second flight of three, and then a single. From an altitude of 10,000 feet, he started his dive and was soon rocketing down through a thin overcast. John Hill, who followed immediately behind Rogers, saw three transports in a line astern flanked by a destroyer on each side.

Rogers and Hill released their bombs. Both scored near misses on a pair of transports, while one of the following aircraft scored a direct hit on the *Kotoku Maru*. Hill strafed one of the transports and leveled off just above the water, while a short distance away the stricken Japanese transport belched smoke as its crew hurried to control the damage. Hill looked to his right and saw Rogers in a left-hand turn toward him with two Zeroes in hot pursuit. Seconds later, the enemy fighters shot Rogers into the water, killing both him and his gunner.

Hill turned away from the enemy fighters and climbed, hoping to escape into a bank of clouds before the Zero pilots saw him. But he was only able to reach about 2,000 feet before one of them latched onto his tail. Just before the enemy pilot closed to firing range, Hill dived away toward the coast and maneuvered wildly, doing his best to spoil the Japanese pilot's aim.

Hill's gunner, Ralph Sam, traded machinegun fire with the Zero pilot who, apparently full of bravado, rolled upside down on occasion to shoot at the fleeing A-24. For his part, Sam found it difficult to aim his twin .30 caliber machineguns as Hill crossed the beach and aggressively wracked the aircraft left and right and up and down. The enemy pilot, despite Hill's violent airmanship, put accurate gunfire bursts into Hill's aircraft two separate times. One of those bursts nearly tore Ralph Sam's right hand from his arm and also broke his thigh bone. Sam refused to give up and continued to fire his guns using his left hand. Finally, out of ammunition, he pulled his .45 caliber pistol from its holster and emptied it at the Zero.

Hill spotted another A-24 a few miles ahead of him. It was flown by Raymond Wilkins, who was flogging his aircraft as fast as it would go. Although neither knew it at the time, they were the only two crews who weren't shot down during the attack.

The enemy fighter pilot also saw Wilkins and, for whatever reason, winged away from Hill and Sam to chase after him. The Zero pilot closed the distance in short order but received a dose of machinegun fire from Wilkins's gunner and turned away. Perhaps his aircraft was damaged, or he was wounded or low on fuel or out of ammunition. Regardless, the Japanese pilot flew out of sight, leaving the Americans unmolested.

Wilkins continued to Port Moresby and landed uneventfully. Hill, his aircraft damaged, decided to continue southeast down the coast rather than risk climbing the Owen Stanley Range. Should the aircraft fail, his and Sam's chances of surviving in the mountainous jungles were slim, even if they weren't killed in the crash. And of course, Sam was badly wounded and desperately needed medical aid. Hill set a course for the airfield at Milne Bay at the eastern end of New Guinea and landed there low on fuel.

Hill helped pull Sam from the rear of the aircraft and saw him safely to the hospital. He returned to the aircraft where Australian mechanics were doing what they could to patch his aircraft, in fact using a length of salvaged gingham cloth to replace the shot-up fabric of his rudder. Returning to the hospital, Hill found Sam to be in good spirits and chatty. Indeed, his prospects for recovery seemed good.

The following day a B-17 put the *Kotoku Maru* out of its misery with a pair of bombs, while Ralph Sam was evacuated to Australia aboard a flying boat. Meanwhile, Hill flew his A-24 back to 7-Mile Dome at Port Moresby. There, the 8th Bomb Squadron's remaining A-24s were already being prepared for the long flight back to Australia, as the decision had been made to completely remove them from active operations in New Guinea.

Tough and heroic Ralph Sam died of gangrene on August 2.

Not dead, however, were four other A-24 crewmen who had been shot down during the July 29 mission. On July 30, 3rd Bomb Group headquarters was informed that a radio message had been received from the Ambasi signal station. The message declared that pilot Joseph Parker and his gunner, Franklyn Hoppe were safe, as were pilot Claude Dean and his gunner, Allan La Rocque. The details are unknown, but the fliers were recovered by Lieutenant Arthur Smith of the Australian Army who was scouting the region around Gona. The radio message additionally stated that Japanese patrols were operating in the area. No further communications were ever received.

Smith was afield a bit more than a week later on August 8 with the four A-24 crewmen, plus another American flyer, four other Australian soldiers, and five Papuans. That evening they encountered a small party from the Anglican mission and hospital at Gona. That party included Reverend James Benson, May Hayman, and Mavis Parkinson. They had been fleeing inland since July 21, when the Japanese started bombarding Gona preparatory to coming ashore. Since then, they had experienced close calls and endured considerable hardships.

Benson planned to trek farther into the interior where he and the two women might join with other missionaries and sit out the war unbothered by the Japanese, who had little interest in that part of the island. Smith, on the other hand, was keen to cross the whole of New Guinea to the southern coast, and thence to Port Moresby. It was an extraordinarily ambitious objective.

Benson hesitated at committing himself and the two women to such a hazardous undertaking, especially as they were poorly provisioned, their clothes were threadbare, and they were wearing remnants of shoes patched together with bark. He recalled that May Hayman said, "Father, don't try to persuade them. This is a soldier's war, and we should leave the decision to them."[1] Benson reluctantly agreed.

The mixed group moved carefully but steadily during the next few days, even though Joseph Parker was wounded and compelled to use a crutch. His gunner, Franklyn Hoppe, also traveled well and cheerfully although his hands had been shot up so badly that he needed help with the simplest tasks. The group was led by various Papuan guides who came and went at different times. Some fled out of fear of the Japanese. One of them, the other guides warned, intended to betray them.

The group reached the vicinity of Popondetta on August 15 and grew especially wary of the Japanese presence there. One of the guides spotted a Japanese patrol and everyone scattered, per plan, and waited breathlessly in the jungle until the danger was ascertained to have passed. Once regrouped, they pushed on for another 10 minutes, then stopped to catch their breath and celebrate their good fortune. Benson was heartened by the "happy smiles of the sisters."

"Then came the stutter of rifle fire," recalled Benson. "We spun round and before I dived headlong into the bush my mind registered the scene in exact detail; the eighteen or twenty Japanese, with rifles to their shoulders, ranged along the edge of a clearing less than fifty yards away. I remember Miss Hayman crying out; I remember her starting to run, then she seemed to spin round and fall. I dived into the bush . . . I was very much afraid."

Lieutenant Arthur Smith's direction to the group in the event of an ambush was to scatter, and this is what they did. The American airmen, who had pistols and a single Thompson submachine gun, engaged the Japanese in a running battle until they finally escaped the area. One or more of them might have been killed. The two missionary women, Hayman and Parkinson, fled into the brush and found each other. Benson stayed undiscovered. Smith escaped, but all his Australian comrades were killed.

Ultimately though, no one but Benson—who never again saw anyone from the group—survived. The missionary women were found by a native and turned over to the Japanese. The Japanese locked them in an outbuilding at Ururu coffee plantation for a short time. There, they were baited and teased with food which was snatched away as they reached for it. Finally, a pair of graves was dug. The two women, May Hayman and Mavis Parkinson—who had assured a love-struck Wesley Dickinson that no harm could befall her—were prodded from their enclosure by Japanese soldiers.

> One of the soldiers approached Mavis Parkinson and attempted to embrace her. She resisted and he stepped backward and plunged his bayonet into her side. She fell to the ground. Sister Hayman moaned and lifted a towel or cloth to her face, and her [Japanese] escort plunged his bayonet with an upward plunge into her throat.[2]

Moments later their bodies were dumped into the already-dug graves. The following year, on May 17, 1943, *The Times*, of London, described the fates of the others:

> The Australian officer [Smith], meanwhile, combed the jungle for the women, but after two days and nights dropped exhausted. Three natives found him and took him away, and it is believed that he was killed. The three Americans were lost in the bush when some natives accosted them. One American fired a shot and was speared, and all were then

bludgeoned to death. Mr. Benson was last seen in Sanananda, whither he had gone to seek a safe-conduct for the women. It is feared that he, too, was murdered.

In fact, physically and mentally exhausted after being lost in the brush for days, Benson found a Japanese unit and tried to give himself up. One of the soldiers punched him and pushed him about for a bit of sport, but otherwise they ignored him. Out of his wits, he tried to get the enemy soldiers to behead him. Both amused and bemused, they waved him off and left him behind.

Although Benson did not know it at the time, many of the Japanese soldiers that he encountered were destined to die on the Kokoda Track along which they were already traveling. But that was weeks or months in the future. By the time he was being kicked and shoved by the Japanese in late August, the village of Kokoda and its rudimentary airfield had already changed hands three different times.

★★★

During June 1942 the Navy's SBDs—its version of the Army's A-24—sank four Japanese aircraft carriers at the Battle of Midway, one of history's greatest naval victories. And as the Japanese advanced south across New Guinea during the coming weeks, Marine Corps and Navy pilots started flying their SBDs with great success in the fierce fighting around Guadalcanal and the rest of the Solomon Islands. And they continued to do so elsewhere until the end of the war. But the USAAF, for various reasons, essentially gave up on its A-24s. Although it would later use the type on a small scale in the Gilbert Islands where there was little aerial opposition, it was by and large relegated to training and utility duties back in the States.

Interestingly, John Davies, the commander of the 3rd Attack Group, felt that the simple little aircraft had merit, especially for attacking shipping. Rather than using big expensive bombers with big crews, he was an advocate of dive bombing. "We could have done it all easier with dive bombers," he said. "You wouldn't need such highly trained personnel as a bombardier—you can't train them overnight. You can train a dive bomber pilot in no time at all. I think it [dive bombing] is really the dope for that business where you are against surface craft."[3]

8

"I WOULD BE LOYAL TO HIM"

Lieutenant General George Brett, the commander of MacArthur's air forces, was going to be fired. Although his resources were thin, they did exist but were not achieving much. He, his commanders, and his men were viewed as preening prima donnas who talked more than they fought. Brett's clashes with MacArthur's staff, particularly Richard Sutherland, had become worse than a distraction—the acrimony was keeping necessary tasks from being accomplished.

MacArthur finally had enough, and asked his boss in Washington, D.C., George Marshall, for a replacement. MacArthur acknowledged that Brett was "unquestionably highly qualified as an air technician and in air administrative duties of a productive or supply character." He additionally observed that Brett was "an unusually hard worker" but that he tended to focus on unimportant nothings at the expense of critical matters. Without explicitly saying so, MacArthur also damned Brett as a mendacious schemer, more interested in politics and parties than in getting the job done. "He is naturally inclined toward more or less harmless intrigue," MacArthur said, "and has a bent, perhaps due to his delightful personality, for social entertainment and the easy way of life." Although MacArthur didn't want to destroy Brett, he wanted him gone.[1]

There wasn't much pushback. Secretary of War Henry Stimson recalled that, among those who knew Brett, no one felt "that he was good for very much."[2] MacArthur was given two candidates to consider, George Kenney and James Doolittle. Doolittle was famous as an air racer and for leading the daring raid against Tokyo, which bore his name. MacArthur, perhaps concerned that Doolittle might siphon away some of the publicity he so craved, chose Kenney.

He couldn't have picked better. The dichotomy between Kenney and Brett was stark. Kenney was energetic and smart and a man who got things done. He was an open book, not particularly interested in politics and intrigue, and he knew how to operate within the established system. However, if the system failed him, he didn't hesitate to blow it apart, steamroll whoever and whatever was left, and accomplish what needed accomplishing in his own way. Moreover, not only was he operationally savvy and an expert pilot, but he was also a trained engineer—he understood what made combat aviation possible.

Kenney had owned a civil engineering firm but enlisted in the Army as a flying cadet when the United States entered World War I. He flew with the 91st Aero Squadron and was credited with shooting down two German aircraft. Moreover, he was awarded the Distinguished Service Cross—second only to the Medal of Honor—as well as the Silver Star for his service and bravery in combat operations.

During the interwar years he attended various schools, including the Army War College where he worked with Richard Sutherland. He was also a test pilot and pioneered the integration of machineguns into the wings of aircraft. At the outbreak of World War II in Europe, Kenney was sent as an observer to France from where he sent alarming reports of the German Air Force's capabilities. As was the case with many career men, he was promoted quickly as hostilities reached the boiling point, and had reached the rank of major general within three months of the Japanese attack on Pearl Harbor.

Kenney's boss was Henry "Hap" Arnold, the chief of the U.S. Army Air Forces, or USAAF. Longtime friends, both were strongminded and often butted heads over professional issues, but they maintained their mutual respect. "He called me almost daily about a multitude of matters, some big, some little, and sometimes, I suspected, just to blow off a little excess steam," said Kenney of Arnold. "Hap lived with the throttle well open most of the time." During the coming years, Arnold's patience with Kenney would be tested many times as the latter did the difficult balancing necessary to keep MacArthur pleased while also being careful not to blow to pieces his relationship with Arnold.[3]

Kenney arrived in Australia on July 28 at the same time that James Benson and the two missionary women were thrashing through the hills above Gona, and the day before Floyd Rogers led his desperate A-24 mission against Japanese shipping. He had dinner that night with Richard Sutherland, who wasted no time vilifying Brett and virtually everyone associated with the air effort. "According to Sutherland," Kenney said, "none of Brett's staff or senior commanders was any good, the pilots didn't know much about flying, the bombers couldn't hit anything and knew nothing about proper maintenance of their equipment or how to handle their supplies."

Sutherland spared no one. "He also thought," Kenney said, "there was some questions about the kids having much stomach for fighting. He thought the Australians were about as undisciplined, untrained, over-advertised, and generally useless as the air force. In fact, I heard just about everyone hauled over the coals except Douglas MacArthur and Richard K. Sutherland."

Kenney met the following day with George Brett, and then with MacArthur. MacArthur's assessment of the air component in Australia did not differ substantially from Sutherland's. He spent half an hour detailing its shortcomings and declared that its, "contribution to the war effort was practically nil." He additionally questioned Brett's loyalty and that of his staff.

Finally, Kenney interrupted what had become a barely veiled diatribe. "I knew how to run an air force as well or better than anyone else," he told MacArthur, "And, while there were undoubtedly a lot of things wrong with his show, I intended to correct them and do a real job."

Kenney also addressed the lack of fealty that MacArthur believed he received from Brett and his staff. "As far as the business of loyalty was concerned, I added that, while I had been in hot water in the Army on numerous occasions, there had never been any question of my loyalty to the one I was working for. I would be loyal to him, and I would demand of everyone under me that they be loyal, too. If at any time this could not be maintained, I would come and tell him so and at that time I would be packed up and ready for the orders sending me back home."

Kenney noted an immediate change in MacArthur's demeanor. Gone was the tight angry look. MacArthur got up, put his arm around Kenney's shoulder, and observed that it seemed they were "going to get along together all right."[4] There followed considerably more discussion. This time it shifted to topics that were more substantive and useful. When Kenney finally took his leave, he was confident that he would be able to satisfy his new boss.

Having been a frontline combat pilot himself, Kenney had a special affinity for his pilots and support personnel. He was gregarious and enjoyed celebrating their accomplishments with them. He loved a good story and had no issues with making a good one even better. And he personally directed practical changes to enhance the conditions in which his men worked and fought. For example, startled at how poor the food rations were in New Guinea, and at how badly the men suffered from malaria and other diseases, he ordered measures that immediately improved the food and reduced sickness.

Kenney was an empathetic leader but didn't hesitate to replace men who were incapable of performing their jobs, be they inept, sick, lazy, or worn out. He valued performance above all else and promoted men who, like him, got the job done. In short, he was a man who led from the front, and he earned the respect and loyalty of his men from the start. He was just what MacArthur needed.

★★★

The task of defending the Kokoda Track fell almost entirely to the Australians and Papuans. Committed but poorly trained and equipped, they were compelled to march up the Kokoda Track from the Port Moresby area. All too often, they were sick and exhausted before they even reached the fighting—the terrain was so rough in places that they were forced to move on hands and knees.

A fighting force required adequate provisions to fight effectively. On the Kokoda Track, rugged terrain, disease, and combat made the logistics effort particularly difficult. Both sides recognized the challenges. The Australians—aided by the Americans—took measures to meet their requirements, although those measures were sometimes inadequate. On the other hand, the Japanese recognized the problems but seemed disinclined to do anything about them.

The Japanese brought about 2,000 carriers, or laborers, with them from Rabaul, and additionally pressed natives from the Buna-Gona area into service. They also used a small number of horses. Combined, these resources were still drastically short of what was needed to transport the needed material. The Japanese made matters worse by mistreating—and even murdering—the carriers. This caused desertions, which only exacerbated an issue for which they had no solution. And ironically, as the Japanese succeeded in driving the Australians back along the Kokoda Track, their supply lines grew longer. Consequently, the ability to sustain them became even more strained.

The Australians relied primarily on nearly 3,000 native carriers but were also able to use American jeeps in places as well as mules and brumbies. These were tough bush horses from the mainland. Although there were issues with desertion, the Papuans were the linchpin around which the Australian supply effort revolved. Tough and stoic, their sure-footedness, endurance, and strength kept the Australians in the fight. They were renowned for bringing the sick and wounded back down the track, showing a remarkable degree of devotion and care.

An Australian report noted: "To watch them descend steep slippery spurs into a mountain stream, along the bed and up the steep ascent, was an object lesson in stretcher bearing. They carry stretchers over seemingly impassable barriers, with the patient reasonably comfortable. The care which they show to the patient is magnificent."[5]

The Australians also leveraged American air transport to keep their units supplied—something that the Japanese never really attempted. It wasn't a panacea, but it was valuable despite many difficulties. The biggest issue was that there were not a great many aircraft available—they were a hodge-podge of military and impressed civilian types, in ones and twos, including DC-5s, DC-2s, B-18s, a B-17, and several DC-3 or C-47 variants.

Maintaining and operating such a jumble of aircraft was a challenge, as was getting crews trained on the different types and keeping them current. Weather was always an issue, and as the aircraft carried no defensive armament, they required fighter escorts. This added a coordination burden and pulled precious fighters away from other duties. Finally, dropping supplies directly to units in the field was problematic as there were no reliable maps, and the jungle made it difficult to see anything below the tree canopy. And nothing happened at all if the weather was poor.

When possible, as at Kokoda when the airstrip was under Australian control, the aircraft landed to deliver their goods. When that wasn't an option, the material and equipment were dropped on a pair of dry lakes, Myola #1 and Myola #2, and then it was pulled and stockpiled. At times it was flung from the aircraft directly atop the supported units.

Parachutes were hard to come by, so the supplies were typically put into a bag, which was in turn put into a second, or even a third bag. These were additionally stuffed with blankets to provide cushioning. Once the transport aircraft were over friendly units, they slowed and descended as low as they dared, and then the crew simply tossed the packages overboard. Breakage was common, as were losses, and occasionally the supplies were mistakenly delivered directly to the Japanese.

For all its faults, this rudimentary means of supply worked. Although it was costly and sometimes wasteful, it was responsive so long as the weather cooperated. And the material that was delivered by air was material that didn't have to be carried by the Papuans. On the other hand, the Kokoda Track was not always the top priority, and there was never enough air transport to meet demand.

Air support in the form of firepower was an advantage the Australians enjoyed to a much greater degree than did the Japanese. Strikes against the beachhead at Buna-Gona continued, and although there were few spectacular successes, the regular grind of them was effective. Ships and barges were destroyed, supplies were ruined, and men were killed, not to mention the confusion and clamor that was created.

Weather permitting, air strikes were also delivered along the track. All manner of aircraft—P-39s, P-40s, B-26s, and B-25s, even Wirraways—were sent against the Japanese. But striking accurately was exceedingly difficult as the enemy positions, hidden by the jungle canopy, were rarely visible from the air. Rather, the supported units had to talk the aircrews onto the target via radio. Sometimes the enemy locations were marked by smoke from artillery or mortar fire. And occasionally the fliers got lucky and actually got their eyes on the enemy.

But the conditions were difficult, and the majority of bombs and machinegun fire never found their marks. Neither the pilots nor the men they supported had trained together, and in fact, most of them had no training whatsoever in those sorts of operations. Ground units were sometimes stunned to see aircraft mistakenly bombing the jungle a mile or more from the target.

Still, some missions were effective. The 35th Fighter Group was especially proud of its efforts, the effects of which it might have overstated: "It was the daily strafing," it declared, "of the Kokoda-Moresby trail by planes of the 35th Fighter Group between August and October 1942 which subsequently came to light as being one of the contributing factors in the Allied recapture of Kokoda. The trail was piled high with Japanese dead which were not seen from the air."

The RAAF's Bristol Beaufighters—with their batteries of cannons and machineguns—were especially effective. One Japanese officer complained of being encircled by Australian units supported by Beaufighters: "All morning their planes have bombed and strafed us." But it was dangerous flying and one of the robust Beaufighters was lost when it smashed into a hill.[6]

Although the operations did have effects, George Kenney didn't believe that interdicting the Japanese after they had melted into the vegetation on the Kokoda Track was the best use of his aircraft and crews. He believed, rightly, that the best way to starve the enemy was to sink its shipping before it reached Buna. "We were bombing along a trail that we could only see in spots," he told MacArthur. "Maybe we could scare away the native bearers and make the Jap carry his own supplies, but the surer way was to sink his ships and shoot down his planes. Even the Jap couldn't fight long without food and there was nothing to eat along that trail."[7] MacArthur gave Kenney free rein to kill the enemy however he wanted—in the jungle or on the sea. Ultimately, Kenney did both.

Although the fight along the Kokoda Track was a series of advances and retreats, the Australians gradually fell back toward Port Moresby. It was to their advantage to some degree as it shortened their supply lines at the same time it essentially stretched, then snapped, those of the Japanese. The closer the enemy got to Port Moresby, the more exhausted and starved he was.

That was the optimist's view. Outside the Kokoda Track there was concern—edging on panic—that the Japanese would push the Australian units aside and reach Port Moresby. The low point came in mid-September 1942. By September 17 the Japanese had advanced to Ioribaiwa, less than 30 miles from the prize that was Port Moresby. "The Japanese were advancing so fast," Kenney told MacArthur, "that the Australians had had no opportunity to organize any resistance, and their withdrawal had been so fast that they had abandoned the food dumps at Kokoda, Efogi, and Myola Lake that we had put so much effort into building up by air drop during the previous two weeks."[8]

Kenney likewise noted that the Australian morale at Port Moresby was on the rocks. The men were exhausted, and the continuous column of sick and wounded coming off the track darkened the spirits of the men being staged to replace them. There were those, he said, "who had no hesitancy in saying that they wanted no part of fighting up on the trail. There was a definite lack of inspiration and a 'don't care' attitude that looked as though they were already reconciled to being forced out of New Guinea."[9]

While his fighters and light bombers were beating up the Japanese on the Kokoda Track, Kenney did everything but badger MacArthur to let him fly American troops from Australia into Port Moresby. Doing so would not only help buttress the Allied defensive position but also help to motivate the Australians. He also understood the public relations disaster that would result should Port Moresby fall while American troops were living the comparative good life in Australia.

MacArthur was reluctant but let Kenney move a company of the 32nd Division. When that succeeded, he agreed to let him move a regiment. Kenney cobbled together a force of transports—some borrowed from Australian civil carriers—and moved the regiment well before the rest of the division arrived by ship. It was an accomplishment that raised Kenney's stock with MacArthur to the highest levels.

And then, late in September, with the great grassy expanse of the Port Moresby area—and the sea—in sight, the Japanese gave up. Near starvation and short on ammunition, they considered a last desperate attack. Should they succeed, they would find food and respite. Should they fail, they would die. Retreat was the other option, but retreat was failure and failure was dishonor and dishonor was worse than death. Yet this is what they chose.

In fact, the Japanese commander, Tomitarō Horii, had already been ordered to retreat. The fight for Guadalcanal in the Solomons was going poorly, and the Japanese leadership felt they did not have the means to fight both there and on the Kokoda Track. They had been stunned at the resistance they had encountered from the Australians.

Okado Seizo, a Japanese correspondent, recounted one of the many gruesome scenes that unfolded as he traveled back to Buna with what was left of the Japanese forces on the track. He spied large numbers of bodies, "here and there," and noted that "a nasty stifling smell, like that of burning old cloth, filled the air, giving us a stifling sensation of nausea. It was the smell of dead bodies, rotting human bodies, lying in all possible postures." He was perplexed by what appeared to be black masses that grew, "glittering and wriggling," from each body's abdomen. "I approached one of the bodies," he said, "and found that it was a heap of maggots bred in the belly, where the rotting process seemed to set in before any other part of the body."[10]

The Australian units that chased the Japanese back up the track were likewise horrified by what they found. The retreating enemy—literally starving—tried to eat everything but the dirt on which he walked. Particularly gruesome to the Australians were bodies of their fallen comrades, stripped of flesh and eaten. It justifiably hardened their already hard hatred for the Japanese.

Although the Japanese were retreating along the Kokoda Track, the fighting lasted many more months and culminated in the Allied capture of Buna and Gona at the start of 1943. Meanwhile, Kenney and his Fifth Air Force were already planning for the culmination of that campaign and the many more that would follow.

★★★

Plans were all well and good, but they were worthless without aircraft to execute them. Although new aircraft continued to arrive from the States, there were never enough of them during this early period, and it was imperative that those already on hand be kept operational. And to be kept operational they needed spare parts, which were often not available via the traditional supply system.

But there were stocks of used spare parts that had been pushed off the ends of runways, or left rotting at the edges of airfields or in the jungles, or in disused hulks here and there that would never fly again. Indeed, every wrecked or unserviceable aircraft, even if it sat miles away on a jungled hillside, became a parts bin. They were dragged—often in pieces—to salvage yards to be picked apart so that other aircraft might fly. Ugly and sundered and seemingly worthless, their true value defied calculation.

In one instance several B-25s were unflyable for lack of wheel bearings. Kenney dispatched a C-47 to carry a young sergeant with a small working party to the northern side of the Owen Stanley Range. There, they salvaged wheel bearings from a B-25 crash. A bonus find was a P-40 wreck over which they stumbled and from which they also pulled much-needed parts.

This sort of dogged and artful cannibalism made Kenney's air force more capable than it otherwise would have been. Wing skins torn from a P-40 might be cut and shaped to repair a P-39 cowling, or a hydraulic pump might be pulled from the wreck of one fighter and installed in another. The possibilities were virtually unbounded, limited only by the imaginations of the Depression-era men who performed this much-needed work.

★★★

In discussions of the air war over New Guinea, aircraft units are often described as having been based at, or taking off from and landing at, Port Moresby. Actually, there was no single airbase named Port Moresby, but rather a complex of airfields, some larger than others and some better suited for smaller aircraft such as fighters rather than bombers. The runways of some were made of pierced steel planking, or PSP, laid over prepared gravel and dirt, while others were surfaced with bitumen or asphalt. Regardless, hard use and the weather kept the engineers who built and maintained them constantly busy.

The original airfield was Kila, or Kila Kila, which was built by the Australians during the early 1930s. The Australians used the British term, airdrome, often shortened to drome, and Kila was also known as 3-Mile Drome, presumably based on its distance from the town of Port Moresby.

Larger was nearby 7-Mile Drome, which was also constructed before the war. It had two parallel runways, and later, following the arrival of the Americans, three. It was mostly from there that the RAAF's 75 Squadron flew their P-40s during the early desperate days of March and April 1942. Also called Jackson Field following the death of 75 Squadron's commanding officer John Jackson, it was used by aircraft of all types through much of the war. It was improved with revetments and support infrastructure of various types and survives today as Port Moresby's commercial airport.

Connected by a taxiway to 7-Mile Drome was 5-Mile Drome, or Ward Field. It was named after an Australian Army officer who was killed on the Kokoda Track. Built after the arrival of the Americans, and featuring two long, parallel runways, it hosted bomber, fighter, and transport units and was perpetually busy.

The convention of naming the airfields, or airdromes, based on their distances from Port Moresby is curious, especially as the straight-line distances were wrong. For instance, 3-Mile Drome was less than two miles from the town. Similarly, 7-Mile Drome was less than three miles away, as was 5-Mile Drome. These inconsistencies were consistent.

Berry Field, or 12-Mile Drome, sat just more than six miles northeast of Port Moresby and served primarily as a fighter field. It was from there that the RAAF's 75 Squadron fought during late April and early May. It was named after P-39 pilot Jack Berry, the commanding officer of the 39th Fighter Squadron, who was killed in a training accident on August 4, 1942. No one wanted any of the airfields named in their honor.

Schwimmer Field, or 14-Mile Drome, located seven miles from Port Moresby, was named after another dead P-39 pilot. Charles Schwimmer was killed in combat on November 10, 1942. The field was also sometimes known as Laloki. Edward Durand was killed in combat while flying a P-39 during the Boyd Wagner mission on April 30, 1942. His name was given to 17-Mile Drome, also known as Waigani, which sat six miles north of Port Moresby.

Finally, Rogers Field was named after Floyd "Buck" Rogers, the commanding officer of the 8th Bomb Squadron, who had been killed in his A-24 during the strike at Buna on July 29, 1942. Also called 30-Mile Drome, it was located 35 miles northwest of Port Moresby.

9

"WE PRAY FOR ABSOLUTE VICTORY"

George Kenney, the new head of the air forces in the Southwest Pacific, was already moving at full speed. One of his first orders of business upon officially taking command on August 4, 1942, was confronting Richard Sutherland, MacArthur's chief of staff. Sutherland had issued detailed instructions for a set of impending air operations that very day. This was a blatant and overt trespass on Kenney's domain, and Kenney, infuriated, went directly to Sutherland's office and challenged him.

When Sutherland grew confrontational, Kenney invited him to step into MacArthur's office. "I want to find out who is supposed to run this Air Force," he said. Sutherland backed down, knowing the fight was unwinnable. Kenney grabbed a piece of paper and drew a dot on it. "The dot represents what you know about air operations," he told Sutherland. "The entire rest of the paper is what I know."[1] Sutherland never again seriously challenged Kenney's authority.

Kenney visited virtually every installation where he had men in Australia and New Guinea. At Charters Towers, a large and growing repair and supply depot, the colonel in charge denied badly needed parts and equipment to combat units if the paperwork was improperly completed. "It was about time these combat units learned how to do their paperwork properly," he declared.[2] Kenney sent him back to the States the next day and ordered that all future requests—verbal or written—were to be fulfilled. He further directed the depot to fly the parts to the requesting units to shorten repair times.

Brian "Blackjack" Walker, an RAAF commander, recalled the immediate effects of Kenney's new orders. "If you wanted something in the squadron you simply got on the blower and you got it. That was the way that Kenney operated. Get it, and get it fast, and get that aeroplane into the air. That was his main thought was to get that aircraft back in the air and it was a war winner."[3]

Kenney's firing of the colonel in charge at Charters Towers was not an isolated case. He scythed through his staff and sent home several brigadier generals and more than forty colonels. "I decided to have a real housecleaning right away," he said. "Those who were not pulling their weight could go home and the rest would move north to take their turns eating canned food and living in grass huts on the edge of the jungle."[4]

Kenney also set about untangling Australian personnel from his various staffs. Brett had mixed both nationalities during the earliest days in Australia, and although the arrangement worked to a certain degree, it became confusing and less efficient as more American units arrived. Moreover, lines of communication and loyalties became strained. Kenney reorganized his units along more traditional lines.

And, importantly, he codified the name of his organization. Although it had officially been formed in 1941, its various names had been confusing and too long. "On the 7th [of August 1942] I had sent a wire to Washington," he said, "asking for authority to organize a numbered air force. I said that if they were not using the number five, I'd like to call it the 5th Air Force."[5] George Marshall, Chief of Staff of the Army, granted his approval.

Kenney also improved morale with awards that recognized outstanding performance, and he ensured his commanders did the same. When a plan in the States was advanced to issue ribbons in place of actual medals to save material, he advocated against it. "If you could see the pride in the faces of these youngsters as they steal a look down at the medals after they get back in ranks, I believe you would feel as I do about this business of substituting ribbons for the real thing."

Best of all, Kenney and MacArthur were proving to be a great team. Unlike Brett, Kenney saw MacArthur virtually every day—both socially and professionally. And MacArthur's confidence in Kenney became unwavering as Kenney and his men delivered results. "I had carte blanche to do anything that I wanted to," Kenney noted. "He [MacArthur] said he didn't care how my gang was handled, how they looked, how they dressed, how they behaved, or what they did do, as long as they would fight, shoot down Japs, and put bombs on the targets."[6] Indeed, as time passed, Kenney and MacArthur developed a strong and trusting relationship that was founded partly on Kenney's recognition that MacArthur was, in effect, his customer. And if his customer wasn't happy, he could not be happy.

Kenney was not blind to MacArthur's character flaws. He knew that his commander was vain, self-interested, a publicity hog, that he hated failure, and that he hated the fact that the Japanese had run him out of the Philippines and captured his army. But Kenney also recognized MacArthur's considerable intelligence and generalship. And, like so many others, he was taken in by the man's magnetism and the indomitable aura he projected. Kenney recalled visiting one of his fighter units with MacArthur. "As usual, anyone that saw him and talked with him or listened to him for fifteen minutes was sold on Douglas MacArthur."[7]

But Kenney's men were more sold on him than they were on Mac-Arthur, as recalled by Robert McMahon, a young fighter pilot who later became an ace. McMahon was visiting a young, well-connected American woman in Brisbane when Kenney and Ennis Whitehead arrived for a surprise visit. After recovering from his initial shock, MacMahon—a second lieutenant—enjoyed the opportunity to chat with the two general officers. "He seemed to be a real savvy airman and a very sharp general officer," said MacMahon. "And I think he was probably the guy who was instrumental in selling MacArthur in the proper use of airpower, and did much toward really winning the initial battle of the Pacific. . . . And I think that this, probably more than anything, made MacArthur realize that he had to use airpower and use it properly."[8]

As he familiarized himself with his new command, Kenney was pleased to finally meet Pappy Gunn. Gunn was frustrated and angry that his family had been seized and interned by the Japanese. Unable to do anything about it, he focused his energy on two things—killing Japanese and creating ways to kill more Japanese. Where his family was concerned, Pappy carried a grudge.

He was already working on one of his Japanese-killing concepts when Kenney met him. The disassembled A-20 Havocs that arrived in Australia in early 1942 were lightly armed, short-range bombers that were ill-suited for combat over New Guinea. Specifically, they couldn't carry enough fuel—with necessary reserves—to reach the Japanese airfield at Lae, much less more distant targets. Moreover, the A-20 was designed to bomb from formation at medium altitude against more traditional foes over more conventional battlefields. In short, the A-20 was designed for a European war and consequently wasn't suited to hit moving ships and barges, or targets hidden by jungle foliage.

Designed and built in response to a set of Army Air Corps requirements for an attack bomber, the A-20 first flew in 1938. Designated by Douglas as the DB-7, the Army Air Corps initially didn't seem particularly impressed. On the other hand, it was of particular interest to the French as they scrambled to get ready for the coming war with Germany.

The first of the DB-7s reached France just after the start of the war and saw action against the Germans in very small numbers but really never had a chance to develop a reputation. Following the fall of France, the remainder of the aircraft it had on order were divided between the United States Army Air Corps and the RAF, who put them into service as the Boston—consistent with their convention of naming bombers after cities. Many other nations, notably the Soviets, ordered the type and put it into frontline service.

The Army Air Corps finally got interested in the little bomber, and they designated it as the A-20. Most notably the engines were upgraded from the 1,100 horsepower Pratt & Whitney R1830, to the 1,600 horsepower Wright R2600. With its crew of three—pilot, bombardier, and gunner— the aircraft's top speed was well more than 300 miles per hour—not much slower than the Japanese fighters it would encounter over New Guinea.

As a flying machine it was well-liked by its pilots for many reasons, one of which was that it flew almost like a fighter. It was fast, powerful, and light on the controls. It was also reliable, readily maintained, and easy to fly. And important to those who eventually flew it over New Guinea, the A-20 was tough and lent itself to modifications and upgrades.

And that was what Pappy was doing during mid-1942. The A-20's range problem was satisfied by the installation of extra fuel tanks in one of the aircraft's two bomb bays. And it occurred to Gunn that removing the bombardier and packing the nose of the A-20 with four .50 caliber machineguns would give it the firepower necessary not only to make it an effective strafer but also to spray the decks of enemy vessels with gunfire, thereby compelling the defending gunners to take cover. That done, the A-20 could get in close enough to make low-altitude skip bombing attacks, which were much more effective than bombing from medium altitude.

Gunn didn't do it alone but rather worked with a team that included engineers and experienced aircraft mechanics to develop, test, and field the A-20 modifications. Happily, there were plenty of .50 caliber machineguns available, scavenged from the wrecks of P-40s and P-39s. The results were encouraging as the concentrated fire of the four guns packed a powerful punch. The modified aircraft were finished in August 1942 and delivered to the 3rd Attack Group's 89th Bomb Squadron, which took them to Port Moresby and started combat operations in September.

★★★

The A-20 also played a role when Kenney, who described Gunn as "a super-experimental gadgeteer and all-around fixer," wanted to give his flyers a new weapon. Before the war, Kenney had pioneered the development of parachute-suspended fragmentation bombs, or "parafrags." He recalled that development:

> Back in 1928, in order to drop bombs in a low-altitude attack without having the fragments hit the airplane, I had put parachutes on the bombs; the parachutes opened as the bombs were released from the airplane. The parachute not only stopped the forward travel of the bomb, but slowly lowered it down to the ground while the airplane got out of range of the fragments by the time the bomb hit the ground and detonated. With a supersensitive fuze, which kicked the thing off instantaneously on contact with anything—even the leaf of a bush, the bomb was a wicked little weapon.[9]

Kenney wanted Gunn to design and build custom bomb bay racks so that the A-20s could carry his parafrags. "I told him I wanted sixteen of them ready in two weeks," he said. "Pappy said he would have them."[10] Indeed, they were done in time for a raid against the airfield at Buna on September 12, 1942. The 89th Bomb Squadron's pilots roared over the ground at 70 feet and dropped 300 of the 23-pound parafrags, claiming 17 Zero fighters destroyed.

And just like that, Kenney had made the Fifth Air Force more deadly.

But the parafrags could be vexatious. When they exploded as designed, the steel casings shattered into several hundred or more sharp pieces that sliced into soft targets such as aircraft, vehicles, and people. However, they were prone to dud, that is, fail to explode, which was actually a double-edged sword. A bomb that didn't explode did no damage, but it still had to be cleared. And during that clearing it might blow up and kill the clearers—ultimately contributing to the effort.

Moreover, the parachutes were sometimes snagged by trees or buildings or other structures and did not detonate. But as the wind twisted them one way or another, they often dropped free and subsequently exploded. Effectively, a bombing raid that included parafrags wasn't over until hours after the attacking aircraft were gone.

Of course, the parafrags were not the answer to every problem. They were small and essentially useless against runways or ships or other hard targets. Larger, general-purpose demolition bombs up to 2,000 pounds were used when something big needed to be broken. If necessary, the smaller of these bombs—100-, 200-, and 300-pounders—were dropped with parachutes so that they could be used in low-altitude attacks in the same manner as parafrags. These were called parademolition bombs and were sometimes wrapped with heavy gauge wire, which fragmented into whistling scythes when the bombs detonated, further adding to their lethality.

★★★

One of the good surprises—among the many bad ones—that Kenney found when he reached Australia was Ennis Whitehead. Contemporaries, the two had known each other since serving together in France during World War I. Similar in temperament, Kenney and Whitehead were like-minded about what needed to be done to turn back the Japanese—namely, organizing the resources they had, getting rid of the deadwood, improving morale and actually fighting.

Kenney knew that he had to keep his headquarters close to MacArthur's in Brisbane not only for leading the air effort but also for political considerations. As much as he might have wanted to do so, he could not stay in Port Moresby to oversee daily operations. Fortunately, aside from being smart and loyal, "Whitey" Whitehead was as much or more a man-of-action than Kenney. Kenney made him his deputy, as well as commander of the Fifth's Advanced Echelon, or ADVON, in Port Moresby. Whitehead, under Kenney's direction, was responsible for executing the air campaign over New Guinea. Ultimately, he was one of the best things to happen to Kenney and the Fifth Air Force.

★★★

During the summer of 1942 the Australians and the Japanese were back-and-forthing on the Kokoda Track, the Japanese were raiding Port Moresby, and the Australians and Americans were hitting Lae and Salamaua and the shipping that reinforced the Japanese in New Guinea, especially at Buna and Gona. At the same time, the Americans were desperately trying to cobble together an air force out of the dribs and drabs of aircraft, men, and material that had survived the retreat from the Philippines, and the trickle of new resources that came into Australia from the United States.

But during much of that desperate and dangerous period, neither side attempted to secure the eastern tip of New Guinea. This was even though both the Japanese and the Allies recognized the importance of that particular bit of geography. Specifically, Milne Bay was critical to controlling the maritime approaches that led to the south side of New Guinea as well as Australia.

As time and resources permitted, the Allies moved first and came ashore in June. Work on a fighter strip began immediately as did the construction of defensive positions. By the middle of August 1942, the RAAF's

75 and 76 Squadrons, both P-40 units, were operating out of Fall River, a few miles inland from the bay. By the end of August, nearly 9,000 troops—mostly Australian, but also more than a thousand American engineers and antiaircraft personnel—had been moved into the area. Moreover, two bomber airstrips were completed.

Conditions at Port Moresby had been harsh, but the airfield at Milne Bay sat on water-soaked ground with all its attendant miseries. In comparison, Port Moresby seemed quite satisfactory. Milne Bay was notable for rain that was not only extraordinarily heavy but seemingly continuous. P-40 pilot Robert Crawford recalled that the runway "used to have a lot of mud and water over it. And, so much so, that with you landing and even taking off, the mud and water, especially on landing, used to damage the flaps." Blackjack Walker noted that conditions were so bad that landing aircraft disappeared in sprays of black mud that rocketed up through the holes in the runway's pierced steel planking.

Indeed, the undersides of the aircraft were often so covered with mud that they were unsafe to fly until the ground crews washed them clean. Moreover, the mud was so pervasive that it penetrated voids and creases and joints where it was never expected, and where it caused electrical problems, engine issues, balky flight controls, and corrosion.

The Japanese, although distracted by the American landings at Guadalcanal which began on August 7, moved to seize Milne Bay at the end of the month. On August 24, 1942, they put nearly 400 troops ashore on Goodenough Island, about 65 miles to the north. These were roughly handled that same day by Australian P-40s, which strafed and sank the landing barges and killed many of the newly arrived men.

The following day, August 25, the main Japanese landing force was caught 60 miles east of Milne Bay by another formation of P-40s—24 of them—armed with 300-pound demolition bombs. Ill-trained for the mission, the Australian pilots nevertheless did sink one small vessel at a cost of one of their own. Still, this was hardly enough to turn the Japanese back. The convoy pressed on and disembarked its troops on the northern shore of Milne Bay late that night.

Those troops numbered only about 1,100. It was a number that the Japanese high command—badly informed by its intelligence apparatus—believed was adequate to overcome what they were told was a defending force of only a few hundred Australians. And so, outnumbered nearly 10 to 1, they were doomed from the start.

Nevertheless, the next day, reinforced with two light tanks, the Japanese pressed toward the Allied positions. The air cover they had been promised failed to materialize as those aircraft were engaged over Buna and suffered significant losses. Other aircraft from Rabaul were turned back by poor weather. Meanwhile, American B-17s, B-25s, and B-26s—together with RAAF P-40s and Hudsons—bombed and strafed the Japanese throughout the day. Landing barges were destroyed as were supply dumps, not to mention many men killed and wounded.

There followed nearly two weeks of savage fighting in a series of give-and-take battles that frequently devolved into slogging skirmishes and even hand-to-hand combat through the mud and swamps and jungle. The Australians performed heroically, making multiple stands against waves of frantically fanatical Japanese attacks. The smaller American contingent of engineers and antiaircraft personnel—the first of their countrymen to see ground combat in New Guinea—also fought well.

For their part, the Japanese were vicious and tenacious, often feigning death only to spring up and attack Allied troops as they passed through hard-won ground. It didn't take long before the Australians bayonetted or shot Japanese bodies, no matter their condition. An Australian infantryman recalled: "Our policy was to watch any apparent dead, shoot at the slightest sign of life and stab with bayonet even the ones who appeared to be rotten."[11]

The RAAF's 75 and 76 Squadrons flew their P-40s almost continuously, strafing the Japanese whenever they could find them under the smothering cover of the jungle. Peter Turnbull was the commander of 76 Squadron and a veteran of the early fighting in the Middle East where he was credited with downing four German and five Vichy French aircraft. Upon being transferred back to Australia he was sent to Port Moresby where he shot down three Zeroes.

Turnbull was especially aggressive and was noted for leading by example. He was true to form at Milne Bay. On August 27, he dove to attack a suspected Japanese position. His P-40 rolled inverted at an altitude of only 200 feet and subsequently slammed into the ground, killing him. The cause was never determined. He could have been hit by enemy ground fire, or could have clipped a tree, or dried mud could have compromised his flight controls. Regardless, he was much mourned not only by his flying comrades but also by the men on the ground whom he had so doggedly supported.

The situation on the ground at Milne Bay was far from certain on August 29 as Japanese troops approached the airfield. The RAAF's leadership was anxious to preserve the pilots and aircraft of the two squadrons there—75 and 76—and ordered them to evacuate to Port Moresby. This was done, although much of the ground staff was left behind as there simply was not enough air transport to move them.

One of the P-40s had mechanical difficulties and was not able to leave Milne Bay with the main body of aircraft. It was late afternoon before it was repaired and its pilot, William Cowie, took off. He arrived over Port Moresby after nightfall with his navigation lights on, and the other pilots watched as he set up to land.

Cowie lowered his landing gear, which, in the P-40, created aerodynamic forces that caused the nose to drop. This was typically corrected by applying backstick pressure while rolling in nose-up trim. "And we think that he didn't realize that the nose was going down," recalled Crawford. "And in the ensuing turn [to] crosswind, and with the undercarriage going down, he clipped the top of a high ridge and the aircraft exploded and he was killed instantly."

As it developed, the Japanese made a frenzied attack against the airfield at Milne Bay that same night but were repulsed with devastating losses. The airfield was saved, and the two squadrons were ordered back to Milne Bay the following day. Once back, they resumed support to the ground forces as they mopped up the remaining Japanese invaders.

The Japanese were reinforced with another 800 men on the south side of Milne Bay on the night of August 29. However, despite these reinforcements, and notwithstanding the naval gunfire support provided by a variety of warships, the Japanese effort faltered. Outnumbered, outfought, and battered by Allied airpower, it soon became apparent to the Japanese that they could not win. The commander sent a radio message to higher headquarters on September 2: "We will together calmly defend our position to the death. We pray for absolute victory for the empire and for long-lasting fortune in battle for you all."[12]

But rather than fighting "to the death," the Japanese were much more pragmatic. Evacuations began on September 5 and continued for some weeks. The fight for Milne Bay was over, and after losing roughly 600 men, the Japanese never again mounted a serious attempt to take control of the area.

But they did persist in trying to retrieve their soldiers. Two destroyers were dispatched from Rabaul on September 10 to bring back the men who were stranded on Goodenough Island on August 24. Tipped off by Allied intelligence, a flight of nine B-17s from the 19th Bomb Group launched from Port Moresby on September 11, 1942, to intercept the enemy vessels.

William Crawford Jr. was a copilot aboard one of the big bombers, and his excitement upon sighting the enemy warships sent his nerves jangling. His pilot, Jack Thompson, alerted the crew for action as the formation closed on the two destroyers, one of which was misidentified as a cruiser. "Our attack was planned and executed at varying altitudes," Crawford said, "and with split-second timing to avoid [the] possibility of collision or being hit by our own bombs."[13]

The lead flight of three aircraft flew directly at the two ships at 1,500 feet. The three aircraft on the left banked away and took up a course 45 degrees from the destroyers as they climbed to 1,600 feet. The three aircraft on the right, including Crawford's, mirrored the aircraft on the left, turning in the opposite direction and descending to 1,400 feet. After 90 seconds both sides turned directly toward the two destroyers while the three leading aircraft readied to release their bombs. Essentially, the nine B-17s formed a three-pronged attack formation. Meanwhile, the crews of both ships, intent on surviving, fired torrents of antiaircraft shells at the approaching bombers.

The lead aircraft scored near misses on the larger of the two destroyers but failed to score any hits. On the other hand, the three aircraft on the left dropped their bombs with devastating effect. "Tiny specks of men," Crawford said, "could be seen swarming over the cruiser's decks, over the sides in lifeboats, sliding down ropes into the churning water."

Thompson and Crawford changed course to attack the other destroyer. An antiaircraft shell detonated on the right side of the aircraft and sent a chunk of shrapnel through the Plexiglas next to Crawford's head. It narrowly missed him and rocketed across the cockpit and out the other side, only barely missing Thompson. Nearing the enemy ships, Crawford heard and felt a booming rattle as the ball turret gunner on the bottom of the aircraft showered the destroyer with .50 caliber machinegun rounds. And then, the bombardier released the bombs.

A few seconds later, the B-17 was wracked by a mighty blast that lifted it off kilter and knocked many of the crewmen out of their positions. Fragments of flying metal punched holes into the aircraft through which the wind howled. There followed much confusion as the crew tried to determine the cause of the blast and, more importantly, make certain that the aircraft was still flyable.

Finally, out of the confusion, the ball turret gunner reported that his rounds had struck one of the bombs as it fell away from the aircraft. The bullet struck it in such a way and location that—against all odds—it detonated and nearly blew them from the sky. But only nearly. Below and behind them they saw that at least one of their other bombs had hit the destroyer and that it was down in the water.

The ship was the veteran destroyer *Yayoi*, which had served in most of the major campaigns to that point. The crew was forced to abandon ship at a cost of 68 of its 151-man complement. The remaining 83 men were later rescued from nearby Normanby Island where they had sailed their lifeboats. The other destroyer was the *Isokaze*. Although badly damaged, it limped back to Rabaul where it underwent extensive repairs and was returned to service, surviving until being sunk near the end of the war.

10

"ONE'S HEAD LYING ON
ANOTHER'S CHEST"

The 90th Bomb Group, equipped with B-24s, began arriving in Australia in late October 1942. They were immediately grounded as B-24s across the globe were experiencing cracks in their nosewheel anti-shimmy collars. Should a collar fail during takeoff or landing, an aircraft could vibrate badly enough to damage itself, or even go out of control. New ones were ordered from the States, but Kenney also directed the local fabrication of replacements from scratch. He wanted "all the tool shops in Brisbane busy making some out of steel. The cracked ones were not steel, but we didn't know what they were made of, so we played safe and made them strong enough."[1]

Finally, fitted with the new parts, the 90th launched its first mission on November 15, 1942. It was a raid from the three-airstrip Iron Range complex, in northern Queensland, Australia, to Bougainville. Kenney was unhappy with the effort.

> Eight B-24s took off to bomb the shipping in the Buin-Faisi anchorage at the south end of Bougainville Island. They got there but made no hits. On the way back they got separated in a rainstorm. Two landed in the water off New Guinea. Both crews were saved. The others landed at four different airdromes in northeast Australia.[2]

Actually, all except two crewmen aboard one of the bombers was killed. So then, at the cost of two desperately needed heavy bombers and eight men, the 90th's green crews accomplished absolutely nothing and got lost while doing it.

But that miserable performance was almost forgotten in the wake of the disaster which followed the next night. The 90th was tasked to make a morning raid against Rabaul on November 17. As Rabaul sat nearly 900 miles northeast of Iron Range, the 15 B-24s—loaded with six 500-pound bombs each—were scheduled to take off just before midnight on November 16.[3]

The crews, likely mindful of and demoralized by the group's poor performance earlier that day, climbed aboard their aircraft in the dark. Their flashlights cast dull, yellow-white beams that were only barely adequate for them to see well enough to prepare their positions. This was to be the first mission for most of them, and it promised to be not only long but also dangerous. Rabaul was the most heavily defended Japanese base in that part of the Pacific, and if the crews were anxious, or even fearful, it was for many good reasons.

Blue flames, not normally seen during the day, burst momentarily from the engines as they spun to life. Conversely, the blue-gray smoke that was so evident in daylight was almost invisible. The racket of the first engines was joined by that of many more until the entire airfield pulsed with a dull, harmonized thrum. Dimly illuminated by cockpit lighting, the faces of the pilots appeared as shadowy apparitions to the ground crews who stood by and waited for the big bombers to move toward the runway.

The three airfields at Iron Range were primitive, little more than landing strips with the barest of essentials. They were cut out of mature rainforest with little room for dispersing, or even parking, large numbers of aircraft. There were no control towers or any other means of controlling traffic either on the ground or airborne. Consequently, in the dark, the movement of the B-24s to the runway was confused and not according to the briefed order as the pilots had difficulty discerning one aircraft from another. Adding to the confusion was the fact that some crews were not ready on time due to mechanical issues.

The first aircraft carried the 90th's commander, Arthur Meehan. It rumbled airborne at 2300, roiling a cloud of dust into the air as it did so. The second aircraft, for undetermined reasons, did not start its takeoff roll for almost another 15 minutes. Another nine aircraft took off at tighter intervals. Dust made visibility difficult. The lights which lined the sides of the runway were of little help as they were too dim and spaced too far apart. Each pilot peered intently into the darkness to ensure his aircraft tracked down the center of the runway.

Paul Larson, the pilot of *Bombs to Nip On*, advanced the throttles of his bomber and felt it roll slowly forward and then pick up speed. His feet danced instinctively on the rudder pedals, keeping the B-24 in the middle of the runway as best he could. Behind him, his crew likewise felt the aircraft accelerate but could see very little.

Larson somehow lost control of the big, heavily ladened aircraft. It careened off the runway and headed to where another B-24 was parked, surrounded by its ground crew. The men scattered. One of them ran into a small tree with such force that it was literally lifted from the soil, its roots intact.

But the parked B-24 could not run, and *Bombs to Nip On* clipped its nose section with a wing and tore it away. The out-of-control bomber subsequently spun around and smashed into another B-24 and a B-17 before skidding into some nearby trees and erupting into a massive fuel-fed fireball. A short time later, its bombs detonated with a roar that reverberated across the surrounding area.

John Klausner, a doctor, was asleep more than three miles away when the explosion woke him. He recalled the sky as "blood red" and suspected a Japanese air raid. Soon after, he learned the truth and raced in an ambulance toward the airstrip. There, he found fire and chaos as machinegun rounds from Larson's bomber cooked off and nearby fuel stores were set alight. Klausner's men sprinted after a man who was stumbling about, afire, but were knocked down by a detonating bomb.[4]

The accident killed 11 men. Once the fires allowed, Klausner and his men set to the grim task of recovering the bodies. Or rather, the pieces of bodies. "Recovered a dead bombardier in nose of first plane struck and shoveled pieces of burned bodies," he said. "Legs–arms–hands–heads from 10 other men."

Larsen and his copilot were found more than 100 feet away from the wreckage of *Bombs to Nip On*. "Still together strapped to their seats," Klausner said. "One's head lying on the other's chest and a piece of fiery shrapnel sticking out of his chest. One's abdomen was blown open and the other had both feet blown off and one arm."

Once he returned to his quarters, Klausen thanked God for his blessings and the safety of the ones he loved. He also prayed for the families of the men who had just suffered such violent deaths. Finally, he noted that he had lost much of his interest in flying.

Another medical officer, Frederick Knight, vented his anger at the tragedy.

> I am sick of such unnecessary waste. Why have we never had a traffic manager on the airdrome? Vehicles and planes come and go as they please. Why were planes allowed to be lined up down the runway for permanent parking, especially when loaded bombers were taking off on a mission? The brass hats will protect their fannies by condemning the field as no good . . . but no fear, someone's neck must be saved.[5]

The final insult was that the first aircraft to take off that night disappeared. And disappearing with it was the 90th's commander, Arthur Meehan. As badly as he needed the B-24s to fly operations, Kenney ordered the 90th taken off combat duty until it received the training it needed to perform effectively.

★★★

It was at about this time that Kenney directed Pappy Gunn to proceed with modifying the B-25 in a way that Gunn had already been investigating for several months. "I sent word to Major Pappy Gunn at Brisbane," said Kenney, "to pull the bombardier and everything else out of the nose of a B-25 medium bomber and fill it full of fifty-caliber guns, with 500 rounds of ammunition per gun. I told him I wanted him then to strap some more on the sides of the fuselage to give all the forward firepower possible. If, when he had made the installation, the airplane still flew and the guns would shoot, I figured I'd have a skip-bomber that could overwhelm the deck defenses of a Jap vessel."

Indeed, should Gunn's modifications work, Kenney's B-25 units would be able to choke off any Japanese base that was reliant on resupply from the sea. This was essentially all of them. "With a commerce destroyer as effective as I believed this would be," Kenney said, "I'd be able to maintain an air blockade on the Japs anywhere within the radius of action of the airplane." Ship killing aside, the modified B-25s would be able to successfully execute virtually any low-level attack mission.[6]

Ever malleable, the B-25s were readily adapted with Gunn's modifications. The initial configuration removed the glazing, or glass, in the nose so that it could better accommodate four .50 caliber machineguns. An additional two—four total—were scabbed to both sides of the fuselage below the cockpit. Consequently, the combined rate of fire available to the pilot from the eight machineguns was nearly 100 rounds per second. After some trepidation, the B-25's manufacturer, North American Aircraft, embraced the concept, and the aircraft eventually accommodated eight .50 caliber machineguns in the nose together with the four fuselage guns. The firepower available to its crews—especially when teamed with bombs or parafrags—was breathtaking.

So modified, the B-25 was just the weapon Kenney needed to destroy Japanese shipping. An aircrew that attacked at low level and at close range could successfully skip a bomb into a ship at least once in every two attempts. Compared to traditional attacks from medium altitude, this success rate was an extraordinary improvement. This was highlighted by a Fifth Air Force study which despaired at the poor bombing results achieved by traditional attacks.

> The results were pitiful. During the month of August [1942], 19 hits were achieved by dropping 434 bombs resulting in a 4.4% probability of hit. Only one transport and one cargo ship was sunk. September was worse. Out of 425 bombs dropped, only nine ships were hit and only one cargo ship was sunk resulting in a dismal 2.1% probability of hit.[7]

Many other modifications were made to the Fifth's B-25s, as well as to later models produced in stateside factories. In particular, the lower turret was removed. It was a balky arrangement and proved unnecessary for missions flown at low level. A fuel tank designed and created by the Fifth's engineers in Australia replaced it, thereby extending its range. Various tail gun arrangements were also tried until they came standard from the factory. Later, there was a variant which carried a 75-millimeter cannon in the nose. In practice, it proved to be balky and was eventually removed.

Regardless, as the strafer-modified B-25s began to enter service in early 1943, they proved to be as effective for Kenney and his men as they were terrifying to the Japanese.

★★★

There was no denying that the men flying combat missions against the Japanese endured terrible stresses—both mental and physical—that over time had real and detrimental effects on their performance. There was nowhere in New Guinea where the men could be sent to recover. Consequently, they were sent to Australia.

If it wasn't heaven, it was close. Brisbane, Sydney, Melbourne, and other towns and cities welcomed the Americans with open arms. There was good food, clean lodging, booze, entertainment, and especially women. Many of the Fifth Air Force units rented flats or entire houses on an informal basis. They held onto them through the duration of the war as the men rotated in and out during their periods of rest and relaxation. The men also hired housekeepers, many of them live-in. These Australian women cleaned, cooked, and did other favors for the men. Moreover, they were handy dates, and many of them became brides.

But the relationships formed between the American servicemen and the Australian women weren't always smooth—especially in the context of Australian men. Earnest Ford, a C-47 pilot, recalled his first day in Brisbane when he spotted both Americans and Australians running up a street, "as if they were being chased." And then Ford smelled spent gunpowder.

As it developed, a wounded Australian soldier had returned home from the fighting after being away a year or more. He found no one in the house. What he did discover were baby clothes and the uniform of an American sailor. He found his wife and the American at a downtown service club where his wife rebuffed and embarrassed him. Ford reported that the husband produced a grenade and "pulled the pin and rolled it under the bar stools. All three were killed and several more were wounded."[8]

Although few incidents ended so tragically as the one Ford described, these sorts of confrontations were not uncommon. And it can be reasonably argued that they were virtually guaranteed to occur. Many Australian men were gone, fighting the Japanese or elsewhere. They simply weren't there to be had. And those that were home were ordinary. They were what the Australian women had always known—the same men with whom they had grown up. On the other hand, the Americans were, if not exotic, then different. And exciting. And, they shared the same language, more or less.

Moreover, the Americans had the magic of Hollywood working for them. Their accents, the way they carried themselves, their slang was just exactly what the women had gawped at in the movie houses as they came of age. Additionally, at least compared to what the women were used to, and with some exceptions, the Americans were kind, polite, generous, and neat.

And they were paid much more than their Australian counterparts, which gave them access to the best meals and goods and venues. Their uniforms also imparted an advantage as they were made of good material and were well fit, if not tailored. An olive-green blouse, or jacket, was paired with khaki trousers that in certain light took on a sandstone-pink hue. In fact, they were called "pinks." This improbable combination was in fact quite handsome and distinctive. And the Americans were issued two sets, whereas the Australian servicemen were given just one of their own inferior uniforms. Owning only a single set made care, cleaning, and even hygiene awkward.

Neither to be discounted was peer pressure. "I wanted to fall in love with a Yank, badly," wrote Maureen Meadows. "All the other girls were falling in love with Yanks, lots of them. Some had already been married, and while I had not ventured as far as this, I was all set to fall in love, really in love." And she didn't want just a traditional relationship. She wanted excitement. "Not the quiet, respectable, lukewarm affair I had known with Robert," she continued, "but the sort of love I had always associated with Americans—tender, thrilling, tempestuous, and no half measures."

American reactions to the Australian women were perhaps a little less ardent. The 3rd Bomb Group noted that "there were many nice-looking girls in this country, but their customs of makeup and dress differed greatly from those of the American girl. Lipstick was used very sparingly; hair was cut shorter (the climate might be an explanation of this) and the clothing styles did not have the rapid change which was so noticeable at home."

Not surprisingly, there was resentment on the part of many Australians. Their women, many of them underaged, some of them married, some of them family, seemed to have lost all their inhibitions. Particularly alarming to the sensitivities of the more traditional Australians were the attitudes of some of the youngest women who were described as having "the softness of childhood and the viciousness of accomplished whoredom."[10]

Although most encounters between the Australian and American servicemen were cordial at a minimum, there were inevitably scuffles and fistfights, and the military police rarely had a quiet night. It culminated on November 26, 1942, when a push-and-shove in Brisbane escalated into a riot involving more than 2,000 people. An Australian solider was shot and killed by an American military policeman, and many more were injured.

Although the riot was broken up that same night, tensions still simmered the following day. William Bentson was a staff officer at MacArthur's headquarters in Brisbane. "I had just left barracks and was walking to headquarters for my shift," he recounted. "When I got to Queen Street, it seemed to be at a standstill. People were everywhere. Aussies were grabbing every American they could find and kicking the hell out of them. It didn't look good, so I ran down a lane and made a run for HQ." Safe on the sixth floor he hung out a window and watched the mob. "There were three circles formed in the crowd," Bentson said, "and they were passing Americans in uniform over their heads and into the circles where they were punching and kicking them."[11]

Fortunately, although there was always an undercurrent of tension, and a pattern of regular hurt done by and to both sides, nothing as ugly as what became known as the Battle of Brisbane was ever repeated. Both the American and Australian leadership made efforts to educate their men and to better regulate when and how many were allowed in town. Discipline was tightened, as was punishment for poor behavior.

However, Australia's efforts to regulate the behavior of its women toward American servicemen—to include restricting their access to alcohol—had little effect. Many of them endured ostracism and criticism and even physical abuse by their own countrymen. Ultimately, up to 15,000 Australian brides were ferried to the United States at the end of the war, many of them married to the men who fought in the skies over New Guinea.

★★★

The twin-engine, Lockheed P-38 Lightning was the fighter that proved to be a game changer for Kenney's Fifth Air Force. Like the P-39 it was designed to be a fast, high-altitude interceptor. However, unlike the P-39, its engines were equipped with turbo-superchargers and the aircraft actually excelled as a fast, high-altitude interceptor.

First flown in January 1939, it showed great promise and set a cross-country speed record less than three weeks later when it flew from California to New York in just more than seven hours, excluding two stops for refueling. Although it was wrecked while landing in New York, the Army Air Corps ordered it into production.

The flashy P-38 with its unique twin-boom design was a public darling. But like any new aircraft, it wasn't without problems. Most famously, during high-speed dives it suffered from compressibility. That is, as aerodynamic pressures shifted on the wings, they caused the controls to "lock up" and the dive to steepen. The misunderstood phenomenon destroyed several aircraft with consequent loss of life. This was naturally unnerving to the P-38's pilots, and it wasn't until mid-1943 that a solution was devised and incorporated into the lower wing.

Other issues included uncomfortable temperatures in the cockpit. It was too cold in Europe, whereas it got so hot in the Pacific that pilots often flew in shirtsleeves and shorts. Engine failures on takeoff also frightened pilots, but this issue was cleared with proper training. And, although it was actually a forgiving and easy aircraft to fly, the operation of the various switches and knobs and dials and other controls necessary to configure it for different phases of a mission could be daunting to neophytes.

Still, it was a significant improvement over the P-40 and P-39, and clearly superior to the Zero and Oscar. Although not as nimble as the Japanese types, it still turned well, it had a better rate of climb and better high-altitude performance, and was faster and more powerful. And, especially important to Kenney, it possessed outstanding range as compared to the P-39 and P-40.

Certainly, it was a bigger aircraft than the other two, and because it had two engines, it required roughly twice as much maintenance. And two engines gave twice as many opportunities for engine problems. But if one engine failed or performed poorly or was shot up, the other engine could bring the pilot home. This was especially comforting on long, overwater flights. And happily, for the support personnel, was the fact that its Allison V-1710 engines were the same that powered the P-39 and the P-40. This eased supply and maintenance burdens.

Finally, the P-38 carried perhaps the deadliest armament of any American fighter during the war. In its nose were packed four .50 caliber machineguns and a single, 20-millimeter cannon, as well as plenty of ammunition. Because they were mounted in the nose and fired along the aircraft's longitudinal axis, these weapons delivered a concentration of firepower that couldn't be matched by wing-mounted guns. When a P-38 pilot found his mark, the target was almost literally blown to pieces.

Kenney's P-38s began arriving in crates not long after his arrival in Australia. But no matter how badly he wanted to put them into combat, it took time to get them assembled and working properly. It also took time not only to get pilots and maintenance personnel trained with the new type but also to develop the tactics, techniques, and procedures that made best use of the new fighter's capabilities.

And it didn't happen fast or smoothly. There were accidents, and many of the aircraft were missing components that had to be fabricated in Australia or brought in from the States. And the self-sealing fuel tanks with which they had been equipped proved faulty and leaked worse than if they had been shot up. It took a few months before the P-38s were ready for combat.

The 35th Fighter Group's 39th Fighter Squadron was the first Fifth Air Force unit to be equipped with the new fighter. Kenney wanted the squadron's pilots to start shooting down enemy aircraft immediately, but the type's first aerial victory wasn't conventional. On November 26, 1942—the same day as the Brisbane riot—four of the squadron's P-38s were airborne over Lae. The pilots very badly wanted the enemy fighter pilots to make a showing so that they might test their new aircraft. They each carried two 500-pound bombs with which to beat up the airfield in the event the enemy declined to engage in air combat. Over the radio they called the Japanese everything but men, certain that their transmissions would be intercepted and translated.

Finally, a Zero accelerated down the runway. Bob Faurot dived after it, but partway down remembered the bombs that he carried. He realized that no matter how capable his new P-38 was, lugging the bombs around in a fight would put him at a disadvantage. He released them, then pulled into a climb and prepared to reattack.

The bombs hit the sea a few yards past the end of the runway and exploded. The wall of water raised by the bomb caught the Zero and pulled it into the water. Faurot and his comrades gaped in disbelief. The event must have made an impression on the Japanese pilots as no more aircraft rose to meet the P-38s. When Kenney stopped by to visit with the squadron later that day, Faurot asked if he was going to receive the Air Medal. Kenney had promised it to the first P-38 pilot to shoot down an enemy aircraft. "Hell no," Kenney said. "I want you to shoot them down, not splash water on them."[12]

Kenney was joking. Faurot was awarded the Air Medal, and the 9th Fighter Squadron went on to knock down many more Japanese aircraft, but with guns instead of bombs. Moreover, the P-38 continued to evolve and became hugely successful in the Pacific. Of all the fighters in the USAAF inventory, the P-38 shot down more Japanese aircraft than any other type.

11

"MOST OF US WENT AWAY SHAKING OUR HEADS"

Through 1942, and into 1943, the Fifth Air Force's heavy bombers went without fighter protection much of the time. Many of the targets they were assigned were simply too far away—beyond the reach of the P-39s and P-40s. Although the situation improved later with the introduction of the P-38, the long-legged B-24s and B-17s still went places that the fighters could not reach. Moreover, because the bomber crews normally made their attacks at night, or near sunrise, there was no good way for the fighters to protect them in the darkness, or even to find them.

The situation would have been dire had the heavy bombers not been so well armed. They typically carried 10 .50 caliber machineguns and could put up a formidable wall of gunfire. The lightly protected Japanese Army Ki-43s and navy Zeroes were particularly vulnerable. A single Japanese fighter attacking a B-24 or B-17 was, quite frankly, outmatched. Indeed, Japanese fighter pilots were sometimes reported as being reluctant to engage the big bombers. In light of the firepower carried by the B-17s and B-24s, that reluctance was reasonable.

Moreover, the American bombers were sturdily constructed with armor plating at critical points and self-sealing fuel tanks. They were difficult to knock down. But they became less defensible if damaged, either by fighters or antiaircraft fire. The enemy pilots often ganged up on cripples as the odds of success increased against a bomber whose crew was struggling to control a fire or restore an engine or otherwise stay airborne. German fighter pilots in Europe, flying more heavily armed and armored aircraft than the Japanese, did the same.

As they typically had no fighter protection, the bomber crews escorted themselves. A damaged bomber crew could expect that one or more other crews would bring their aircraft into close formation. Their combined firepower often discouraged the enemy fighter pilots or made their attacks less effective.

Such was the case on December 18, 1942, when the 43rd Bomb Group sent a small formation of B-17s against a handful of combatants and a pair of transports sailing north of Wewak on the north coast of New Guinea. Folmer Sogaard's B-17 was attacked and hit by a flight of Zeroes, and his right outboard engine was shot out. Dark smoke—visible for miles—poured from the engine. It was akin to blood in the water, but rather than sharks, a swarm of at least eight Zeroes closed on Sogaard's bomber.

Pilot James Murphy firewalled the engines of his B-17 and raced to his friend's aid. He tucked himself into close formation with Sogaard. Once there, he repositioned his aircraft to one side or the other of Sogaard's, depending on the direction from which the Japanese attacked. "We were able to back up his guns and give them quite a time," said Murphy. Both aircraft were considerably shot up as the Zero pilots pursued them south across the Owen Stanley Range, but by sticking together they returned safely to base.[1]

★★★

The B-17 was increasingly being used by Kenney's crews as a skip bomber against shipping, a mission for which it was never intended. Flying at mast-top height, it was difficult for the crews to miss. But at such low altitudes, the B-17 was a big target. Consequently, the crews were typically sent out at night when they were more difficult to spot and to track.

But night operations were a double-edged sword. Certainly, the dark provided cover for the bomber crews, but it also provided cover for the ships the bomber crews sought to sink. Accordingly, it was difficult to find worthwhile targets on the open sea. On the other hand, it was not nearly so difficult in the crowded waters around Rabaul.

And it was to Rabaul that the B-17s were often sent, as was the case on December 30, 1942, when the James Murphy crew took off from Port Moresby and set a course to the northeast, together with six other B-17s of the 43rd Bomb Group. While most of the aircraft flew directly over Rabaul Harbor at 6,000 feet where they drew the attention of the searchlights and at least one night fighter, Murphy descended. Trolling over the water approximately 10 miles to the east of the harbor at 2,000 feet, he and his crew looked for a suitable target.

And they found it—two, in fact. A pair of transports sailed peacefully together; their foamy wakes reflected the light of the rising moon. Murphy eased his throttles back to their stops and dropped the nose of the B-17. At the same time, he maneuvered to set up for a broadside attack against the two ships. He carried four 1,000-pound bombs and planned to drop two against each ship.

"I had never seen such an opportunity," Murphy said.[2] His aircraft made almost no noise as he flew toward the two ships. At the right instant he directed his bombardier to toggle two bombs against the first ship, then concentrated on the next. Seconds later, he called for the other two bombs. Immediately, his crew shouted at him to pull up. He did so, narrowly missing the mast of the second ship. He noted that his bottom turret gunner simply "closed his eyes and prayed."

There followed sprays of gunfire from the vessels and the antiaircraft batteries ashore. Shrapnel and small-caliber rounds made staccato pings and pops as they punched into the aircraft. At the same time, fiery blasts aboard both ships dimmed the light of the antiaircraft tracers, and Murphy's headphones were jammed by the excited voices of his crew. He pushed his throttles forward and held the aircraft down, just above the water.

Several miles later he let the aircraft climb into a turn. "Both ships were filled with fire," he said, "and smoke was billowing up from the decks. It looked like an early New Year's celebration, with all of the light from the fires."

★★★

Combatants have often attributed their enemies with more power and capabilities than they actually possessed. Late in 1942, Kenney's Fifth Air Force was overwrought and still desperately lacked the forces it needed to defeat the Japanese. Indeed, formations of enemy aircraft regularly harried Allied bases in New Guinea and even as far as the Australian mainland. But as more and more American units arrived in theater, along with more and better equipment, the Allies gradually transitioned to ascendency.

At the same time, even though their air elements were still formidable, the Japanese were ever so slowly beginning to come apart. Japanese Navy ace Kazuo Tsunoda remembered this period as the Americans and Australians intensified their attacks against Lae. "We often took off three times a day," he said. "As we did not have any advanced warning the enemy could easily make a sudden attack on our airfield. We tried to do the same thing to them, but the Australians had commandos hidden in the hills reporting when we took off."[3]

The Allies were increasingly able to apply the sort of pressure described by Tsunoda, and the Japanese were increasingly unable to resist it. It was to become more and more the case—at base after base—as more American men and equipment were thrown into the fight over New Guinea.

★★★

"On January 5, 1943, I was on what most of us thought was a suicide mission," said Fred Wesche, a B-17 pilot with the 43rd Bomb Group.[4] "Most of us went away shaking our heads. Many of us believed we wouldn't come back from it." Wesche and his comrades had just been briefed that they were to attack a group of Japanese warships at Rabaul. And they were to do so not at dawn or dusk but in broad daylight—near noon. Wesche remembered that they were to fly at "something like five thousand feet over the most heavily defended target in the Pacific."

Deciphered radio intercepts and reconnaissance flights during late 1942 and early 1943 indicated that the Japanese were marshaling a convoy at Rabaul. It was to sail with men and material to Lae on New Guinea's northern coast. Kenney's Fifth Air Force, although growing in strength, operated mostly in a reactionary mode—not yet capable of influencing events on a large scale, but only able to respond to whatever moves the Japanese made. This particular Japanese move—sending a convoy to reinforce its forces on Lae—was one to which Kenney wanted to forcibly react. Accordingly, he ordered Kenneth N. Walker, the commander of his Fifth Bomber Command, to be ready to do so with as many bombers as could be mustered.

Walker, twice divorced and variously described as complex, self-centered, obsessive, and egotistical, was almost 10 years younger than Kenney, but like Kenney, he had joined the Army in 1917 during World War I. Again, like Kenney, he trained as a pilot, although his training occurred later in the war and he did not serve overseas, whereas Kenney had flown combat with distinction. This was one factor in their differing career trajectories. By 1920, Kenney was made a captain and continued to be promoted during the interwar years, whereas Walker remained a first lieutenant until the mid-1930s. Other officers joked that he was the oldest lieutenant in the Air Corps.[5]

Walker served in various capacities during the years following World War I, although his time spent at the Air Corps Tactical School from 1928 to 1934 probably defined his career more than any other. He became an almost-rabid advocate of the airpower construct that was centered on the strategic bomber. A central figure in what was dubbed the "Bomber Mafia," he and others championed the development of fast, well-armed bombers. They believed that such forces could not be stopped by fighters and would be capable of wrecking an enemy's war-making capacity. Claire Chennault, a prominent booster of fighter aviation and the leader of the American Volunteer Group, or Flying Tigers, called Walker "a radical with a blind spot."[6]

Walker's skills as a pilot and commander were perhaps best described as patchy. Hap Arnold bemoaned the totally avoidable loss of a B-12 bomber that Walker crashed during a routine landing at March Field, in California. By this point, Walker had logged thousands of hours of flight time. There were other accidents, including one that destroyed a B-17. Walker later commanded the 18th Pursuit Group at Wheeler Field in Hawaii, which operated the Curtiss P-36. It was an assignment that was perhaps intended to temper his fanatical advocacy of the strategic bomber concept.

Walker was unhappy there. Taciturn and grumpy, he turned his nose up at the specially polished and liveried P-36, "Gold Bug," that his men had prepared for him as his personal aircraft. He grew impatient with the instructions that his adjutant, Bruce Holloway, tried to give him prior to his first flight. The result was that he nearly crashed, entirely due to his own hubris.

During the remainder of his time in command, he didn't fly the P-36 more than he had to, although it was a perfectly fine little fighter. Holloway noted that, unlike most fighter pilots, Walker did not thrive on, or even enjoy, the excitement that came from flying high-performance fighters. On the other hand, Walker could be a kind and patient mentor and leader. He often engaged Holloway in personal and professional discussions. "This caused me not only to pay attention," said Holloway, "but to offer counter comments. It was a truly cherished relationship."[7]

Walker didn't stay in command of the 18th Pursuit Group for long. He was ordered back to the States, specifically Air Corps headquarters in Washington, D.C. There, he was a critical member of the small team that developed the air warfare plans that guided the creation and employment of the Army Air Forces that ultimately dominated the skies over Europe and the Pacific. Following America's entry into the war, he chafed for combat and finally received orders overseas, arriving in Australia at the start of July 1942, a few weeks ahead of Kenney. The two men knew each other, and when they met, Kenney was happy to have Walker join his team. Still, the two did not always agree, and Walker, although loyal, was his own man.

Kenney put Walker, by now a brigadier general, in charge of bomber operations. Walker immediately put his stamp on the organization as he streamlined its command structure, put efficiencies into place, and demanded greater professionalism and discipline from the men. Always hardworking, almost frenetically so, he was anxious to prove the strategic airpower theories he had helped create beginning in the early 1930s. But the number of heavy bombers at his disposal was too small to put his concepts into play in any meaningful way.

Kenney was frank in his assessment of the man.

> He was stubborn, oversensitive, and a prima donna, but he worked like a dog all the time. His gang liked him a lot, but he tended to get a staff of "yes-men." He did not like to delegate authority. I was afraid that Ken was not durable enough to last very long under the high tension of this show. His personal problem was tough because he kept himself keyed up all the time and he just couldn't seem to relax a minute.[8]

Walker and Kenney were regularly at odds. For instance, B-17s were already scoring successes with skip-bombing attacks, and Kenney was excited about the concept. But such operations didn't align with Walker's high-altitude strategic bombing notions, and he only grudgingly acknowledged their potential.

To his credit, Walker did occasionally fly combat missions as an observer. Not only did this gain him credibility with his men, but it also gave him firsthand awareness of the conditions under which they flew and fought. But Kenney didn't like it and ordered all his high-ranking commanders to stop flying combat. He had few experienced officers to replace them if they were shot down.

Notwithstanding Kenney's mandate, most of them still slipped away on the occasional mission or two. Kenney once more ordered a stop to such acts of defiance when Walker returned from a mission aboard a B-25 that was missing part of a wing. The pilot had flown into a tree. Kenney was not only worried about losing an able commander and friend but also concerned that Walker or some other commander might be shot down, captured, and tortured for information. Still, Walker disliked being told to sit on the ground.

As the disposition of the Lae-bound convoy became clearer, Kenney ordered Walker to send his bombers to attack it at sunrise on January 5. Kenney stressed the importance of arriving overhead at the break of day when he believed the defending Japanese fighters wouldn't be prepared. But Walker didn't want to make a dawn attack. Doing so would require his crews to take off several hours earlier in the black of night. He worried they wouldn't be able to rendezvous in the darkness. Instead, he wanted to make a daylight strike at noon when the crews could fly in a tight formation that would better concentrate their defensive firepower.

Kenney brushed Walker's argument aside. "The Nip fighters were never up at dawn," he said, "but at noon they would not only shoot up our bombers but would ruin our bombing accuracy. I would rather have the bombers not in formation for a dawn attack than in formation for a show at noon which was certain to be intercepted."[9]

As it developed, Walker disobeyed Kenney. The bombers, six B-17s of the 43rd Bomb Group and six B-24s of the 90th Bomb Group, took off after dawn from Port Moresby with a planned time over target of noon. Their crews probably didn't know it, but at the same time they were climbing on course, Rabaul was being bombed.

Indeed, three B-17s from the 43rd Bomb Group had been sent to attack the airfield at Lakunai, near Rabaul. The reason for the mission is unclear—perhaps it was intended to cause confusion before the main strike. Or maybe Walker sent it so that he could tell Kenney that he had complied with his orders for a dawn raid. Regardless, one of the three aircraft was compelled to turn back, but the other two pressed on. When they arrived over the Rabaul area they were stymied by a blanket of clouds left behind by a dissipating rainstorm. The two bomber crews crisscrossed the area, but Lakunai was hidden under the weather. They finally gave up and dumped their bombs on another nearby airfield, Vunakanau.

A ragtag group of fighters raced to intercept them. A mix of army Ki-43 Oscars and Navy Zeroes, they paralleled the course of the B-17s, but out of gun range. After a short time, they raced ahead to gain separation, then turned back to make head-on attacks. Neither side scored during this initial gambit, and the Japanese pilots arced back around to make individual attacks from every quarter, braving the intensive firepower of the defending gunners. When the Japanese finally turned for home, the B-17s, badly damaged, limped south toward New Guinea. The gunners aboard the two bombers claimed a total of seven enemy fighters shot down. For their part, the Oscar pilots declared they had shot down one of the B-17s.

The truth was that none of the Japanese fighters were downed, although several were damaged. One of the B-17s was badly shot up and ditched near the New Guinea coast, while the other made an emergency landing near Buna. All the crewmen in both bombers survived. In fact, no one—Japanese or American—was killed in the encounter.

Meanwhile the small force of 12 bombers motored northeast for Rabaul. Walker had disobeyed Kenney by planning the attack for midday rather than dawn. Compounding that disobedience was the fact Walker was aboard the lead B-17, *San Antonio Rose*, as an observer. The reason he decided to fly the mission in defiance of Kenney's explicit order can only be guessed at. Perhaps it was intended as a direct snub to Kenney. It is also possible that he felt the mission was so important that his presence was imperative. There is also a chance that he didn't believe Kenney would find out. At any rate, he was excited about the mission and was doubly excited about bringing along his new camera so that he might capture images of the action.

Regardless, Walker was likely not thinking of Kenney as the bombers neared Rabaul's Simpson Harbor. The overcast layer that had so vexed the crews of the early morning mission had broken up into a few puffy clouds. In the harbor and the adjacent waters, the American crews saw dozens of Japanese ships. Most were transports and merchantmen, but there was a scattering of combatants as well. There was no way for them to know, but none of the vessels below were part of the convoy for which they were searching. It had already sailed.

Strangely, and counter to Kenney's warning, the B-17s and B-24s remained unmolested by Japanese fighters—none were in sight. The aircraft drifted apart, flying at about 9,000 feet, as each crew selected a target. The first bursts of antiaircraft fire pocked the sky as the bombers closed the distance to the harbor. Soon after, the aircraft began releasing their loads.

Great geysers reached skyward as bombs splashed into the harbor. There were no direct hits, but the *Keifuku Maru*, a support ship, suffered two near misses which collapsed its sides and caused it to break in half. Other near misses set several of the ships afire. None of them sank, but some of the damage was substantial—20 men being killed aboard one vessel. No doubt influenced by the smoke and fire, the American crews claimed to have hit 11 ships—a grossly inflated number.[10]

The antiaircraft fire intensified as the bombers turned back toward the south. The crews saw fighters racing down the runways at both Lakunai and Vunakanau. B-17 pilot Fred Wesche recalled the strike: "Anyway, we went over the target and all of us got attacked. I was shot up. Nobody was injured, fortunately, but the airplane was kind of banged up a little bit. We had to break formation over the target to bomb individually and then we were supposed to form up immediately after crossing the target, but no sooner had we dropped our bombs and my tail gunner says, 'Hey, there's somebody in trouble behind us.'"

That somebody was the crew, including Walker, aboard *San Antonio Rose*. It had earlier been seen turning over the harbor—lower than the rest of the aircraft—presumably to take photographs of the raid's effects. It trailed smoke from one of its engines and was being dogged by two or three Japanese fighters.

None of the other bomber crews descended to help protect the stricken aircraft. More enemy fighters arrived, and it became clear that there was little that could be done. Wesche watched the B-17 nose over, "obviously headed for a cloud bank with the whole cloud of fighters on top of him. There must have been about fifteen or twenty fighters. Of course, they gang up on a cripple, you know . . . but he disappeared into a cloud bank and we never saw him again."

In fact, no one ever saw *San Antonio Rose* again. Walker's aircraft was one of three bombers lost on the mission—his, another B-17, and a B-24. Most of the men from the other two aircraft survived and were rescued. Still, it was a 25 percent loss rate for a raid that destroyed only one ship. Kenney couldn't afford to lose aircraft at that tempo. And the chief objective of the raid, the Lae-bound convoy, hadn't even been found.

Surprisingly, Kenney did not intend to fire Walker if he survived and was returned to Allied hands. "I told General MacArthur that as soon as Walker showed up, I was going to give him a reprimand and send him to Australia on leave for a couple of weeks."[11] MacArthur replied that if Walker did not make it back, he was going to recommend him for the Medal of Honor—the nation's highest award for valor.

Walker, who disregarded his superior officer's orders, did nothing other than get dead for his trouble. He certainly did nothing that merited such an award. Many men had been shot down, and many more would be. Mostly lieutenants and enlisted men, they typically received no special recognition. Rather, their parents were sent Purple Heart medals through the mail. But MacArthur loved attention, and decorating Walker—a brigadier general—would bring a certain degree of that.

Walker did not return. Search crews sent out in the days after the raid came back with nothing useful, although many were engaged by Japanese fighters. Indeed, a B-24 was shot down on January 6, 1943. During this time the convoy—the original target of the mission—was discovered and attacked, albeit ineffectually, on January 7.

As was typical of MacArthur, when it was announced on January 11 that Walker had been shot down, the effects of the raid were overinflated. An Australian newspaper repeated the claims that, "9 or eleven enemy ships were destroyed." The same article quoted MacArthur's comment regarding Walker's performance: "Much of the efficiency of the bombardment command of the Fifth U.S. Air Force is due to his exceptional brilliance and courage."[12]

MacArthur's staff wrote a citation for the Medal of Honor, which described several accomplishments that were artfully created out of virtually nothing. The question was reasonably raised as to whether or not Walker's actions were consistent with those required for the award. Evidently, that question was satisfactorily answered—or ignored—as President Roosevelt presented Walker's oldest son with the medal a couple of months later on March 23.

No trace of Walker or the wreck of *San Antonio Rose* has ever been found. Some accounts indicate that the pilot and copilot survived only to be captured by the Japanese on New Britain Island where they subsequently died—or were murdered. No credible evidence exists of Walker surviving, and it is assumed that he was killed by the enemy fighters, or in the subsequent crash.

★★★

The Japanese convoy that Kenney had ordered Walker to destroy at Rabaul on January 5, 1943, sailed unmolested for Lae. It included five transport ships, four destroyers, and a light cruiser. The Japanese had given it the code name of Operation 18. Shrouded by poor weather and protected by screens of fighters, it remained undetected for the first part of the voyage. However, during the early morning darkness of January 7, Squadron Leader T. V. Stokes of the RAAF's 20 Squadron, at the controls of a PBY Catalina flying boat, discovered it on course for Lae.

Stokes radioed the information to another RAAF Catalina crew led by Squadron Leader David Vernon of 11 Squadron. Vernon had just bombed and strafed the Japanese airstrip at Gasmata. Although he expended four 250-pound general-purpose bombs during that attack, he still carried four 250-pound anti-submarine bombs.

Vernon arrived at the reported location and skimmed through thin clouds looking for the reported convoy. The crew finally spotted five transports with a destroyer in the lead and one to each side. Vernon angled his aircraft toward the enemy vessels but was called off by his navigator and bomb aimer, George Leslie. The approach didn't suit Leslie and he directed Vernon to turn away and set up for a stern reattack.

Vernon added power and hauled the big aircraft into a turn, careful in the dark and the rain and the mist not to fly into the water. The roar of his two engines bounced across the waves and was no doubt subsumed by the dull reverberations created by the enemy ships as they powered their way through those same waves. Vernon and his crew remained undetected, and the enemy put up no antiaircraft fire.

Vernon was anxious not to lose contact with the Japanese ships. Dawn approached, and the Catalina was not just a large target, but also a slow one.

Darkness was the crew's only protection, and if the convoy slipped from view, they might not relocate it in time to attack before sunrise.

Directed by Leslie, Vernon brought the Catalina up from behind the convoy on roughly the same course it was sailing. The vessel they targeted was the *Nichiryu Maru*, a transport. As Vernon closed on the ship, the four remaining bombs were let go. The enemy ship was hit lengthwise by three of them and the resultant explosions were so violent that the crew believed the ship must have been an ammunition carrier.[13]

The stricken transport carried approximately 1,100 men, of which more than 400 were killed outright or were trapped aboard when it finally slipped under the surface the following day. The survivors were picked up by the accompanying destroyers. Through the rest of that day, January 7, the convoy was attacked by both American and Australian aircraft—B-17s, B-25s, B-26s, P-40s, Hudsons, Beauforts, and A-20s. However, the attacks were ill-coordinated and produced disappointing results despite the determination of the fliers.

One transport, the *Myoko Maru*, was bombed and forced to beach itself at Malahang, not far from Lae. Although its engine was destroyed and several men were wounded, there was no loss of life and the ship's mission of delivering men and material was essentially met. It was the victim of P-40s from the 49th Fighter Group's 7th Fighter Squadron. The engagement was intense, and although the Japanese accounts do not align perfectly with the American descriptions, there is no doubt that it was the *Myoko Maru* that was hit. The 49th described the action in more detail.

> The two flights designated for the bombing contacted the ships twenty miles east of Salamaua in a convoy with three other transports, three destroyers and a cruiser. First Lieutenants A.T. House, Jr., and Claude S. Burtnette picked the rear transport while five other P-40s dive-bombed the first transport. Lieutenant House's two, 300-pound bombs exploded right under the stern of the ship. Lieutenant Burtnette did not observe his bombs bursting, but saw smoke rising from the stern when he looked back. The transport went down by the stern and sank.

The declaration that the ship was sunk was clearly not true, as the *Myoko Maru* was run aground where it remained for years until it was eventually scrapped. While House and Burtnette scored hits on one ship, Franklin Nichols put his bombs into the side of another transport, "not more than three feet from the hull, probably springing the plates and severely damaging the ship." The P-40 pilots then swept down on the ships to strafe them despite heavy antiaircraft fire. "They could see the Jap soldiers," the 49th noted, "bowled over like so many ten-pins."

The 49th's 8th Fighter Squadron put up 16 aircraft later that afternoon. Half of them—two flights of four—were tasked to strafe the transports, while the other two flights were to provide cover against enemy fighters. Ernest Harris led a flight of strafers. "Before reaching the target," he said, "we were attacked by Zeros. My flight split up and engaged the enemy. I continued on and strafed one transport. I observed pieces flying from the deck of the ship but was unable to observe other damage."

Harris pulled out of his dive and looked skyward at a tumbling whirl of American and Japanese fighters. He immediately climbed toward the fight where he spotted a Zero chasing a P-40. He attacked it. "I closed in on him, shooting, and saw him burst into flames." Harris pointed his fighter at another enemy fighter and fired his guns again. The Zero shed chunks of itself, rolled out of control, and fell into a cloud layer.

"I immediately pulled up and made a pass at a third Zero," Harris said. "I pressed the attack to a very close range and fired two bursts into him and saw my bullets striking him approximately at the cockpit. The Zero began spiraling down seemingly out of control into the clouds. I dove, circling the clouds and getting under them."[14] There, burning on the water's surface was the Japanese aircraft he had just shot down. Nearby, two separate circles of disturbed water and wreckage marked the impacts of the other fighters he had destroyed.

The aerial combat that day was fierce, and the 49th put in claims for 15 enemy aircraft destroyed at the cost of one pilot. Eugene Dickey's P-40 was shot up and he bailed out. He landed in the sea only about 75 yards from the shoreline. He was last seen swimming for the beach but disappeared, and his fate remains unknown.

The Japanese convoy finally reached Lae late on January 7, 1943, minus two of its five transports, the *Myoku Maru* and the *Nichiryu Maru*. Ironically, those two ships were taken out of action not by one or more of the different types of bombers that the Allies sent after them but by a flying boat and a fighter. It was an apt example of the ethos at the time, which was to get the job done, no matter the means.

★★★

The RAAF flying boats, which had found and struck the Lae-bound Japanese convoy, Operation 18, were PBY Catalinas. Designed and manufactured by Consolidated Aircraft in the United States, the type first entered service with the Navy in 1936. Big and slow, and powered by two engines integrated into a braced parasol wing, the aircraft was often referred to as "Dumbo," presumably in reference to the Disney elephant character.

But, used by all the nation's services and many different air forces around the world, the type excelled at a huge spectrum of roles. It served as a reconnaissance aircraft and was key to the U.S. victory at Midway. It was a patrol bomber and a torpedo bomber. The PBY carried men and equipment and performed clandestine missions behind enemy lines. It also evacuated civilians and military personnel from hotspots around the world, and to the men it pulled from the sea in the combat search and rescue role, it was the most beautiful aircraft they had ever seen.

The type's ruggedness, reliability, range, payload, and endurance gave it a versatility that made it invaluable. Its effectiveness in virtually every role it was assigned was later enhanced by the addition of airborne radar. And although it was big and slow, it carried enough guns to make itself a prickly target. Over the waters surrounding New Guinea it was primarily operated by the Navy and the RAAF, but later in the war was also flown by the Fifth Air Force in smaller numbers as the OA-10. Ultimately, it provided the Allies with capabilities that could not be matched by any other aircraft.

John Jackson's leadership inspired the men of the RAAF's 75 Squadron during the dark days of early 1942 at Port Moresby. *Australian War Memorial*

Above: John Jackson following his rescue aboard a USAAF A-24 dive bomber. *Australian War Memorial*

Peter Turnbull was one of 75 Squadron's most experienced pilots and was killed at Milne Bay. *Wikipedia*

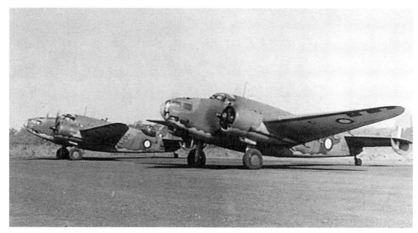

Above: The RAAF's Lockheed Hudsons performed a broad spectrum of missions.
Australian War Memorial.

Below: Muddy runways were a constant problem at Milne Bay in 1942.
Australian War Memorial

An RAAF P-40 at Milne Bay in 1942. *Australian War Memorial*

The USAAF did not have as much success with the Douglas A-24 Banshee as the Navy did with its variant, the SBD Dauntless. *Library of Congress*

Above: Australians and Americans worked together to assemble these A-24s once they arrived. *Australian War Memorial*

Above: The B-26 was more complex than the B-25 and not used as widely by the Fifth Air Force. *Wikimedia*

Below: A 22nd Bomb Group B-26 is visited by Australian infantry at Jackson Field. *Australian War Memorial*

Boyd Wagner, America's first ace during World War II, favored the P-39 over the P-40. *USAAF*

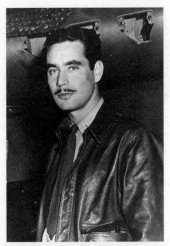

Below both: The Mitsubishi A6M Zero, code-named Zeke, was a formidable fighter. *San Diego Air and Space Museum and Australian War Memorial*

Above: The Ki-43 Hayabusa, code-named Oscar, was a lightweight Japanese Army fighter, similar in performance to the Zero. *Imperial Japanese Army Air Service*

Below: Complex maintenance work in primitive conditions was the norm. Here, men perform work on a P-40. *USAAF*

Early P-39s in formation flight. *Australian War Memorial*

A P-39 pilot
and his ground
crewman. *USAAF*

A P-39 being refueled at 30-Mile Drome. *USAAF*

Above: Intensive salvaging of wrecks and disabled aircraft kept the Fifth Air Force in business during the early part of the war. *USAAF*

Left: An early B-25, not yet modified as a convoy destroyer, sits under camouflage netting at Port Moresby. *USAAF*

Above: The Japanese Navy's Mitsubishi G4M bomber, code-named Betty, was frequently encountered over New Guinea. *Australian War Memorial*
Below: A Ki-43 attacks a B-25. *USAAF*

Left: General Douglas MacArthur is flanked by two of Kenney's airmen. *USAAF*
Right: Richard Sutherland was MacArthur's chief of staff and was almost universally disliked. *Australian War Memorial*

Top: George Brett was an ineffectual leader under Douglas MacArthur. *USAAF*

Center: The Curtiss P-40 was a tough aircraft that created a successful record against its Japanese opponents. *USAAF*

Bottom: The 49th Fighter Group and its P-40s played a role in defending northern Australia during 1942. *USAAF*

An A-20 mishap on Jackson Field, Port Moresby. *USAAF*

This RAAF PBY Catalina is loaded with two underwing-mounted 1,000-pound sea mines. *Australian War Memorial*

The RAAF's PBY Catalinas were worked as hard as any aircraft in the Southwest Pacific. *Wikimedia*

The C-47's ability to quickly transport the sick and wounded from the battlefield saved many lives. *USAAF*

The C-47's large cargo door contributed to efficiencies in loading and unloading. *USAAF*

C-47s at Wau, following the battle. *USAAF*

A C-47 is escorted by P-39s. *USAAF*

A C-47 en route to Wau. *USAAF*

Above: A Japanese bombing raid on Port Moresby on March 11, 1943, destroyed this P-38. *USAAF*

Left: Robert Faurot was the first P-38 pilot in the Fifth Air Force to down a Japanese aircraft. *USAAF*

Below: The B-17 was the Fifth Air Force's mainstay heavy bomber in the Southwest Pacific during 1942. *Australian War Memorial*

Left: Mechanics working on a P-38 under conditions its designers never considered. *USAAF*

Below: Brigadier General Kenneth Walker was killed over Rabaul on January 5, 1943, while disobeying Kenney's orders. *USAAF*

Bottom: Brigadier General Kenneth Walker was aboard the B-17 *San Antonio Rose* when it was shot down over Rabaul. *USAAF*

12

"SEND TROOPS IMMEDIATELY"

Many tasks needed doing at the start of 1943, and one of them was dealing with the approximately 4,000 Japanese that had been delivered to Lae by the convoy. It became apparent that those troops were to be sent against the Australian outpost at Wau, which had started as a gold mining town during the 1920s. Surrounded by formidable brush-covered terrain, it sat at just more than 3,000 feet elevation and was unreachable by road. Limited supplies and material could be brought in by foot on primitive tracks but only with great difficulty.

However, serviced by high-priced air transport during the early days of aviation, it had grown into a substantial community of 3,000, with hotels and other businesses as well as its own electrical grid. Still, its single, kunai grass airstrip offered challenges as it was only about 3,000 feet in length and tilted substantially toward the south. A set of mountains to the south compounded the danger, and perpetually poor weather was icing on the cake.

Crashes were frequent. Landings were made to the south toward the mountains. As the airstrip tilted dramatically upward, the sight picture presented to the pilots confused them into descending too low on the approach, and it was not uncommon for them to land with tree branches lodged in their landing gear. The mountains at the opposite end precluded them from going around for another try. Success on the first landing attempt was literally a life-or-death imperative.

Wau was evacuated at the beginning of the war, and at the start of 1943 the area was garrisoned with several hundred Australians of the quasi-guerilla Kanga Force. Their numbers were buttressed by several hundred more Papuan militiamen. Although they mounted occasional raids against Japanese outposts and patrols, their primary mission was reconnaissance.

They also aided downed Allied airmen, as they had with John Jackson, the commander of the RAAF's 75 Squadron, the previous April.

Situated as it was, only 45 miles southwest of Lae and 30 miles west of Salamaua, and as the only substantial Allied presence in that part of New Guinea, Wau was a threat to the Japanese. And the Japanese wanted to take it. Not only would doing so remove it as a potential base from which the Allies could attack their forces at Lae and Salamaua, but it could serve as a jumping-off point from which the Japanese might mount another overland assault against Port Moresby.

Moreover, they had 4,000 recently arrived troops ready for the job. The men were put aboard barges almost immediately after disembarking at Lae and were moved 20 miles south to Salamaua. Once ashore, there was no way to Wau but by foot, and Japanese patrols started moving inland by January 12. The approach to Wau from that direction wasn't as unforgiving as it was from Port Moresby, but the Japanese were compelled to carry on their backs whatever food and ammunition they needed.

Still, their numbers were great enough to overwhelm the much smaller Kanga Force. By that time, it was clear to the Allies what the Japanese intended, and it was also clear that Wau had to be reinforced. A race was underway.

Trekking men and material overland from the Port Moresby area to Wau wasn't reasonable at that time. The Allies were building a road to cover part of the distance, but its completion was months away, and it certainly would not be ready in time for the coming fight at Wau. Consequently, there was no other option but air transport. On the other hand, the air transport available in New Guinea at that time numbered less than 30 C-47s of the 374th Troop Carrier Group. The other bad news was that those aircraft were already heavily committed in support of the American and Australian troops fighting at Buna and Gona. Still, the threat facing Wau constituted an emergency, and aircraft were allocated to bring in more Australian reinforcements as well as ammunition and other supplies.

The aircraft which would play such an important role at Wau was the Douglas C-47 Skytrain—a transport aircraft. In the context of the air campaign fought over and from New Guinea, any number of candidates can be reasonably nominated as the aircraft that was most critical to the Allied cause. The P-40 certainly merits mention as having helped hold the line against the various Japanese air offensives during the early fighting. And the B-25 is definitely worthy of discussion, especially as a low-level strafer and skip bomber. The P-38 was better than any of the Japanese fighters and allowed the bombers to operate at extended ranges.

Perhaps the last contender to come to mind is the C-47. A twin-engine, low-wing monoplane, the C-47 was a militarized variant of the civilian DC-3 airliner and was an aerial pickup truck that quickly moved people, parts, and material where they needed to be. Able to accommodate 28 fully loaded combat troops or up to 7,000 pounds of cargo, it was built with an especially reinforced fuselage, strengthened floor decking, and cargo doors that could accommodate paratroopers and outsized equipment.

And when troops needed to be quickly moved to the fighting—as was the case at Wau—there was no better option than the C-47. Exceedingly rugged and reliable, it was also easy to fly and readily maintained in the primitive conditions so typical of New Guinea. Indeed, it was used in every theater of the war. No less a figure than Dwight Eisenhower declared that it was one of the four pieces of equipment that enabled the Allies to win the war—the other three being the jeep, the bazooka, and the atom bomb.

The first C-47s arrived at Wau on January 14 as the Japanese hacked through the jungle, marching ever closer. The airlift was a fitful effort as clouds regularly hid the airfield and left the C-47 crews with no choice but to return to Port Moresby with their loads. Or quite often they waited anxiously at Port Moresby with their troops and cargoes at readiness until the airfield at Wau was reported clear. Too many days, it was not. Still, it was arguable that the caution was warranted as the combination of poor weather, rugged terrain, and a marginal airfield caused three crashes during the middle part of January.

Allied planners had to be judicious with their load plans as troops without ammunition and food were useless, and ammunition and food were equally useless if there were no soldiers to which they could be delivered. And an aircraft that was grossly overloaded or sent into bad weather was worse than useless if it crashed. Likewise, losing a planeload of troops for just about any reason other than enemy action was akin to manslaughter.

Australian patrols had been clashing with lead elements of the Japanese force almost since the day the Japanese started their march. To buttress those efforts, Australian reinforcements were briefed and sent directly into the scrub soon after climbing down from the C-47s. Nevertheless, the Japanese remained unperturbed and doggedly chopped their way along old, disused tracks and, as necessary, through virgin jungle. Not only did they race against the Allied reinforcement effort at Wau, but they also hurried against the diminishing supplies of food and ammunition they carried on their backs.

The airlift bumped along. Weather and aircraft availability continued to hamper the Allied reinforcement efforts. However, the Japanese at Buna and Gona—150 miles to the southeast—were defeated during this period, which consequently freed more C-47s for the fight at Wau. An even bigger windfall was the arrival of the 317th Troop Carrier Group in Australia with more than fifty new C-47s. These aircraft had left the States earlier that month at the same time that the convoy that carried Wau's besiegers was dodging air attacks. The 317th's aircraft were hastily moved up to New Guinea and began flying missions immediately.

But it didn't matter how many aircraft were available if weather kept them on the ground. Indeed, at the end of the day on January 28, it seemed that all the effort and resources spent up to that point would prove too little, too late. Gambling that more men would be flown in that same day, the commander at Wau had sent the bulk of his forces as far forward as possible to harry and confuse the Japanese. But the gamble didn't pay off as only four C-47s found their way through the clouds and mist.

Meanwhile, the Australian defenders hunkered down against Japanese mortar rounds and machinegun fire. And then, from Port Moresby—where men and aircraft had waited anxiously all day—came the message that none of Kanga Force wanted to believe: "Flying ceased owing [to] weather."

A Japanese patrol reached the town of Wau in the early evening, less than a mile from the airstrip. Australian units fell back for the final defense as the enemy troops advanced. Heavy rain made the black of night blacker, and soldiers from both sides passed within yards of each other in the dense brush without engaging. An Australian ambulance driver watched the progress of the battle. "You could see the enemy in the blackness of night, fighting their way along the valley floor to the [air]drome by their flashes and the noise of the increasing battle. Suddenly I realized our isolation and the fact that without the airstrip we were finished."[1]

The desperate situation at Wau was not lost on the Allied leadership at Port Moresby. Everything was readied for an all-out effort to begin as soon as possible the following day, January 29. A message was sent to the commander at Wau: "All troops ready for action. Advise by most immediate message signal you will use to indicate safe for aircraft to land [at] Wau. Best of luck."[2]

The morning effort on January 29 was made up of 30 C-47s. They were scheduled to fly in five six-aircraft formations, arriving at 30-minute intervals. The pilots were reminded again of the grass airstrip's particular dangers. At 3,000 feet it was not overly short, but only the last 700 feet were usable as the remainder had been ruined by bombs and mortars. However, because the airstrip tilted so dramatically uphill in the direction they were to land, getting stopped would pose no problems. Takeoffs were to be made downhill, in the opposite direction. And because gravity would help to accelerate the aircraft, and because the aircraft would be loaded with little more than the wounded, they would have no issues getting airborne in such a short distance.

It was additionally stressed to the pilots that they had no choice but to make a successful landing on the first try. The mountains rising beyond the far end of the airstrip made second attempts impossible. Indeed, the mountain slopes wore the wreckage of several aircraft which underscored that fact. Essentially, the pilots were told that if they failed to make a successful first landing, they and everyone aboard their aircraft would die. They were also informed, probably needlessly, that the Japanese would try to shoot them down. Finally, they were reminded that this sort of hazardous duty was why they received flight pay, and that this was the day to earn it.[3]

But flight pay or not, the crews of the American C-47s, as well as the Australian soldiers they were tasked to carry, were eager to go. If they didn't understand the strategic imperative of winning the fight, they still knew that their comrades were in desperate need of help. No doubt, the great majority of them would have been happy to forego their flight pay so long as they were given a chance to fly the mission.

And, happily for the Allies, they were. But not at first light. At dawn, the airstrip was still blanketed by a layer of clouds above which American fighters droned back and forth, ready to send a signal to Port Moresby as soon as the sun burned it away. In the meantime, the Japanese renewed their attacks on the airfield with mortar, machinegun, and rifle fire. Finally, at about 0800, the men of Kanga Force raised their faces toward a brightening sky which was quickly turning from gray to blue.[4] The fighters notified Port Moresby with a message, and the commander at Wau backed it up with another: "Wau [air]drome still ours. Valley open. Send troops immediately."[5]

Loaded with men and equipment, the first C-47s climbed out of Port Moresby and turned northwest. Partway along the route they dropped down low into the creases of the mountains and valleys and canyons where they wouldn't be silhouetted against the sky and easy to detect by enemy fighter pilots. Above them flew an escort of friendly fighters.

It was demanding flying—and exhilarating were it not so dangerous. The transport pilots pushed their aircraft through mountain mists and rain showers, almost brushing the treetops as they crested the spines of various peaks and then pushed their aircraft over to accelerate down the opposite slopes. Flying through—not above—the jagged terrain, it seemed that the aircraft would catch their wingtips on rocky slopes or in the spreading branches of one of the multitudes of massive trees that reached out from the jungled ridges. Some of the soldiers—flying for the first time in their lives—wretched their breakfasts into their laps or atop their boots.

Still locked in battle with the Japanese, the mood of the defenders at Wau matched the brightening morning sky. It turned to near-ebullience an hour later as the C-47s fell like a cascade on the little airstrip. They came in flights of six, landing in quick succession. Reaching the end of the grassy landing area, three aircraft turned to the right and spun themselves around to face inward, while the other three did the same on the left. The crews did not shut down their engines but kept them turning while their cargo doors were thrown open and the troops inside jumped clear, and their cargoes were unloaded. That done, the C-47 pilots waited for the wounded to be loaded and then took off as quickly as possible so that the aircraft circling overhead could land.

The Australian soldiers went immediately from their aircraft into the fight. There were instances when men were wounded so quickly—within minutes—that they were evacuated aboard the same aircraft that flew them to the airstrip. But leaving the battlefield was no guarantee of safety as the aircraft were fired upon as they took off, just as when they had landed.

The C-47 crews of the 374th and 317th Troop Carrier Groups continued their heroic efforts until well into the afternoon of January 29. By the end of the day, 57 sorties had delivered 814 men and many tons of material. Had they not done so, the fight for Wau would likely have ended before noon.

The reinforcements did help to stymie the Japanese advance, but the situation remained exceedingly grave. The Australians were still outnumbered, and the enemy soldiers had virtually surrounded the airstrip. On the other hand, the Australians had the advantage of defensive positions and tighter and more coherent lines of communication. Fighting continued through the night.

The weather was good on the following day, January 30, and the airlift from Port Moresby to Wau resumed immediately. It was do-or-die time for the Japanese. Although they still outnumbered the Australians, the supplies of food and ammunition they carried were nearly depleted. Should they not take the airstrip that day or the next, the Allied airlift was certain to tip the advantage away and they would never succeed. The Japanese consequently peppered the airstrip with mortar rounds—each carried to Wau by hand—and made desperate rifle charges with a fierceness that took them to the edge of the airstrip on several occasions. Each time, they were pushed back into the brush.

Meanwhile, the men at the airstrip had nearly perfected the drill. Even as they endured enemy sniper fire, they unloaded the aircraft in minutes and quickly reloaded them with wounded. The pilots and crews grew more expert at operating from the primitive airstrip even though the ground was increasingly rutted by a volume of traffic the airstrip was never intended to endure. The pop of bullets punching into their aircraft was muted by the engines, as was the shouting of the Australian soldiers as they leapt out. The clanking and scraping of equipment and supplies being pulled through the cargo doors added to the cacophony.

In effect, the airstrip onto which the pilots manhandled their aircraft was not just the prize they were helping to secure but the battlefield itself. And it didn't happen without tragedy. A pilot misjudged his approach and landed too far down the already shortened landing area. He was unable to get the heavily loaded C-47 stopped, and it shot toward two other aircraft, striking one and spinning around to smash into another. One of its propellers slashed into the cockpit of the second aircraft and hacked a leg from one of the pilots. He survived.

Perhaps the most critical cargo of the entire battle was flown into Wau that morning. The men unloaded two carefully disassembled 25-pounder field guns. These were versatile artillery pieces that fired 25-pound shells of approximately 3.5 inches in diameter. Transporting such a large weapon by air—together with nearly 700 rounds of ammunition—was an achievement that proved decisive.

The guns were assembled and ready for action within two hours of being unloaded. And it was just in time. A column of approximately 300 Japanese troops—practically in parade formation—marched toward the airfield. The enemy soldiers made a perfect artillery target, and the guns went into action, literally blowing them into pieces and throwing those pieces in every direction.

Many of the Japanese soldiers who survived the initial barrage fled into high kunai grass. The Australian artillerymen switched from high explosive shells to white phosphorous. These shells blasted phosphorous fragments into the grass and into the men who hid in the grass, setting both afire. Great clots of white, suffocating, phosphorous smoke billowed skyward. The kunai grass burned black, and the Japanese burned with it. Those that didn't die immediately screamed and ran directionless, their clothes and hair and skin afire.[6]

At the same time a flight of Beaufighters from the RAAF's 30 Squadron roared overhead and sprayed the Japanese with cannon and machine-gun fire. There followed a massive blast as an ammunition dump exploded and literally lifted the surrounding earth, killing more enemy soldiers. The combined air and artillery fire stopped the enemy assault before it could take the airstrip.

That day, January 30, 1943, was the high-water mark of the Japanese attempt to take Wau. The Australians, reinforced by 66 planeloads of men and cargo on that day alone, held the airstrip while inflicting grievous casualties. The fighting continued for the next several days—as did the air-lift—but never again did the situation become so desperate. The Australian defenders grew in strength until their numbers exceeded 3,000. Finally, on February 4, the Japanese commander ordered a withdrawal.

While Japanese soldiers were grubbing and fighting through the brush and jungle around Wau—and doing it on diminishing supplies of food and ammunition—a unit likely based at Lae or Salamaua attempted to spoof the fighters assigned to escort the C-47s. The 49th Fighter Group noted these efforts.

> On the 31st of January, both the 7th and 8th Squadron pilots who herded transports to Wau, reported that a Japanese ground station attempted to confuse them with false radio chatter. A high-pitched voice chimed in on their radios in English, ordering them to do such things as land, drop their bombs, investigate plottings, etc. Occasionally, orders were given to flights which were not even in the air at the time.

It is curious that, although they were active elsewhere, Japanese air units failed to make an appearance over Wau during this period. During those several days that the weather was clear enough for the Americans to fly more than 100 C-47 sorties into the primitive airstrip, it was also clear enough for the Japanese to send fighters to interdict them. It was true that the transports were escorted by American fighters, but even so, the chaos caused by even a few Japanese fighters would have significantly disrupted operations.

It wasn't until February 6, 1943, after the battle was won, that Japanese aircraft showed in force. On that morning a flight of nine Kawasaki Ki-48 Lilly bombers, escorted by 29 Ki-43 Oscars, attacked Wau. They caught four C-47s on the ground, as well as an RAAF Wirraway. Five C-47s circling overhead fled for Port Moresby. The C-47s on the ground got airborne, but one of them crashed into a mountainside, killing its entire crew. The Wirraway was destroyed by a bomb, and three personnel were killed on the ground.

P-39s of the 35th Fighter Group, and P-40s and P-38s of the 49th Fighter Group, raced to intercept the enemy raiders. Claims, which are impossible to reconcile, were made for several bombers and more than 20 of the fighters which the American flyers mistook for Zeroes. The P-39 pilots alone claimed to have downed 11 aircraft.

David Harbour was a P-38 pilot with the 49th Fighter Group's 9th Fighter Squadron. Over the Wau area at 20,000 feet, he and the other members of his flight spotted a number of enemy fighters tangled with another flight of P-38s. "I dived with four other P-38s at a Zero breaking from the fight," he said. "He entered a cloud and the other P-38s pulled up to avoid the cloud and mountains." Harbour turned around the clouds hoping to find the enemy aircraft. Instead, he spotted another.

"I attacked with a long deflection shot from about 100 to 200 yards and saw my tracers enter his plane. He jerked left and dived into the side of the mountain from about 200 feet above the ground, instead of pulling out." Harbour snatched back on his control yoke to keep from smashing into the mountain himself. "As I climbed, I saw the smoke from the undergrowth in which the plane crashed. This Zero [Ki-43] had a wide blue or black circle [band] around the fuselage, just forward of the tail."[7]

★★★

At the same time the Allies were beating the Japanese at Wau, they were also scratching out or improving airstrips on the north side of New Guinea—particularly in the Popondetta and Dobodura areas. From there, the Fifth Air Force could better support Australian and American army units as they mopped up the remnants of the Japanese in the Buna-Gona area.

Pushing the Japanese back along the Kokoda Track to the Buna-Gona area—from where they had started their march to Port Moresby the previous year—had been one of the most miserable and grueling combat actions of the war. It had been made so by disease, a harsh environment, a paucity of material, a fierce enemy, and poor generalship on MacArthur's part. And it had been accomplished at catastrophic cost as one man of every 11 perished in the fighting.[8] It was a casualty rate that very nearly met the literal and original definition of decimation.

The campaign had been part of the larger necessity which was to neutralize or destroy the Japanese in New Guinea so that MacArthur could make the jump to the Philippines. Airpower was critical to that plan. And Port Moresby's airfield complex—as robust as it was—was not capable of supporting it. This wasn't news to anyone with a map. Should the Allies succeed in their westward advance across the top of New Guinea, Port Moresby would eventually be too far away to be relevant.

Indeed, during the summer of 1942, while the airfields at Port Moresby were still being finished and improved, the Allies were already scouting potential airfield sites near the northern coast, across the Owen Stanley Range. The area offered major advantages. Importantly, it was closer to the fighting already underway at Buna-Gona. It was also closer to major Japanese bases such as Rabaul to the northeast and Wewak to the west. Aside from allowing the bombers to hit heretofore unreachable targets—and to carry bigger loads of bombs—this proximity would also allow fighter units to protect the bombers out to greater ranges.

Another very real benefit would be the elimination of the Owen Stanley Range—and its attendant weather—as a navigational hazard. The thunderheads that typically towered over those peaks turned missions around too often. Or crews sometimes flew into shrouds of clouds only to smash into the mountains they hid. Violent thunderstorms tossed aircraft like toys or even tore them apart.

And, weather aside, the Owen Stanley Range was an imposing physical obstacle, rising to just more than 13,000 feet. Aircraft damaged in combat or suffering mechanical issues were often unable to climb high enough to fly back to Port Moresby. Trapped on the "wrong side" of New Guinea, if they were unable to reach Milne Bay at the island's far eastern tip, they had little choice but to go down in the jungle or along the coast. There they could hope for help from the natives, but they also risked injury or death by any number of causes or capture by the Japanese.

Leif "Jack" Sverdrup and his team scouted the sites that eventually became the massive Dobodura airfield complex. Sverdrup, born in Norway and educated in the United States, was a big-project engineer with a reputation for bulldogging the toughest jobs through to completion. A physically imposing man, he was running an airfield project on an island in the Pacific at the start of the war and was commissioned as a colonel directly into the Army. He personally reconnoitered potential routes for moving men and material through the Owen Stanley Range. Kenney, who appreciated a man who got things done, remembered him as a "tall, blond reincarnation of Leif Ericson."

"For some reason or other," Kenney said, "Sverdrup had worked miracles with the natives, who seemed to be willing to work harder and longer hours for him than for anyone else."[9] In fact, Sverdrup led the natives in clearing several strips out of the kunai grass during the latter half of 1942. On November 8, C-47s began bringing in elements of the 32nd Infantry Division preparatory to the Buna-Gona assault. Soon after, engineering units were brought in with their equipment to create proper airfields. With the Japanese pushed out of the area by early 1943, engineers went to work with a vengeance on an airfield complex at Dobodura. Within months, these airfields—15 of them—were at the heart of the Fifth Air Force's operations and remained so until the latter part of 1943.

★★★

Stories of air combat typically record extraordinary performances of bravery as few readers are interested in accounts of routine missions during which nothing noteworthy occurs. And only rarely found are descriptions of events during which our fathers and grandfathers utterly came apart, or broke, under the pressure of combat. However, these sorts of occurrences were part of the fighting that took place all over the world. And they were experienced by all sides. No man was perfect.

An example was described by James Murphy, a B-17 pilot with the 43rd Bomb Group. During an attack by enemy fighters, Murphy noticed that the enemy pilots concentrated on one side of his aircraft—and with some success.

> During the fight, I had asked twice why we were getting "our ass shot off" on the one side. I had not received an answer. When the Zeroes were gone, I got out of my seat and went back to the waist of the airplane. I found the gunner lying down below his gun with his head buried in his arms. I knew then why we had been hit so hard on that side. He had fired very little ammunition. I pulled out my .45 caliber pistol . . . pointed it at his head and told him to get up and get back on his gun. His eyes were ablaze and he started to cry.[10]

Murphy holstered his pistol and talked with the man, reasoning with him so that he might regain his composure. He had never previously exhibited such behavior—had in fact been a stalwart member of the crew. A short time later the man was back at his gun.

And it was a good thing. A few minutes later Murphy's aircraft was attacked again. This time the shaken gunner performed as he always had, employing his weapon with deadly accuracy, and showing no fear.

Murphy had several private conversations with the gunner following the mission. It was a difficult thing for Murphy and the tens of thousands of heavy bomber pilots like him. They commanded 10-man combat crews flying aircraft that were worth more than the small towns from which many of them came. In that role they were compelled to serve not only as skilled pilots but also as leaders, counselors, friends, and, sometimes, disciplinarians. And as most of them were still in their early 20s, they had little life experience to draw from. "I'm not sure how his problem was solved, "said Murphy, "but it was solved. He remained with us on the crew and performed in an outstanding manner on every mission for the rest of the time we were there."

13

"IT WAS MORE THAN I COULD STAND"

The sea route from Rabaul to Lae—which sat in a unique crotch of geography on New Guinea's northern coast—stretched only about 450 nautical miles. This was a distance which Rear Admiral Masatomi Kimura's 3rd Destroyer Flotilla, eight ships in all, could have sailed in a day. But they were not at sea simply to make a brisk trip down the coast of New Britain and across the Bismarck Sea. Instead, they were charged with escorting eight transport ships to Lae, on New Guinea's northern coast. Those ships were slow, and Kimura was compelled to travel at only about seven knots to maintain the integrity of the formation.

Kimura didn't like the math. His convoy, which the Japanese had given the code name of Operation 81, would be exposed to attack for much of the voyage. Although it was unlikely that Allied warships would sortie in strength to attack him, aircraft were another matter entirely. Since the heady days a year earlier when the Japanese rampaged across the Pacific almost unopposed, the Allied air forces—American and Australian—had grown considerably in strength. They had played a pivotal role in the recent destruction of the Japanese forces at Buna and Gona, and their attacks against the Japanese shipping that sailed between Rabaul and New Guinea were growing in frequency, size, and effectiveness.

A similar convoy had been caught by Allied aircraft only a couple of months earlier on January 7. Although the attacks that day and the next had been a manic mess in which the Americans and Australians attacked in small, ill-coordinated formations, or even as singles, an RAAF PBY Catalina did sink a large transport, and an American P-40 ruined another, forcing it to beach itself.

But having launched more than 400 fighter and bomber sorties, Allied expectations had rightly been higher. Consequently, they had taken lessons from this effort, and Japanese commanders were very much aware that Kimura and his destroyer flotilla might fail to get the transports safely to Lae. Indeed, wargaming exercises by Japanese planners predicted that Operation 81 might lose 40 percent of its vessels.[1]

Still, Kimura had been promised a protective umbrella of fighters during daylight when he would be most vulnerable. The promised protection, provided by both army and navy units variously based at Rabaul, Lae, and Kavieng on New Ireland, was to be continuous and in considerable strength. Rather than flying in mixed formations, one service was tasked to fly half the day, while the other was to cover the other part of the day. A6M Zeroes made up the navy's contribution while the army flew Ki-43 Oscars.

Indeed, although he couldn't see them through the clouds, Kimura knew there were more than 20 fighters orbiting overhead that very moment. He was glad for the clouds. The weather offered cover against Allied air patrols; if he wasn't discovered, he couldn't be attacked. Indeed, were it in his power, he would have made the weather worse.

The ships in the convoy carried more than 6,000 soldiers primarily from the Japanese Army's 51st Division, as well as a contingent of several hundred marines. Desperately needed material, equipment, and fuel were also embarked. All of it was necessary if Japan was going to hold the territory it had captured in northern New Guinea. Safely delivered, it would pose an enormous risk to MacArthur's ground forces. Consequently, it was not just important to the Japanese that Kimura's flotilla of destroyers succeed in getting the convoy safely to its destination, it was absolutely critical.

Kimura's eight destroyers and crews had seen considerable combat, including action in the Philippines, the Java Sea, the Battle of Midway, Guadalcanal, and elsewhere. Included in the group were the *Asashio*, *Arashio*, *Asagumo*, *Tokitsukaze*, *Yukikaze*, *Shikinami*, *Shirayuki*, and *Uranami*. Notably, the crew of the *Yukikaze* had helped to sink two American destroyers at Guadalcanal a few months earlier on the night of November 13, 1942.

The transports the destroyers escorted varied in size from 950 tons to 8,125 tons, and two of them, *Kyokusei Maru* and the *Teiyo Maru*, had been built in the West, the former in Canada and the latter in Germany. The other vessels were *Oigawa Maru*, *Taimei Maru*, *Shin-ai Maru*, *Aiyo Maru*, *Kembu Maru*, and *Nojima*. All the transports were owned by commercial companies except the *Nojima*, which was operated by the navy.

Kimura didn't know that the Allies were aware he was underway. American intelligence personnel had broken Japanese codes not completely, but to such a degree that they determined a major Japanese convoy was set to sortie from Rabaul at the end of February. "On February 25, we got some information indicating that a big Jap convoy was scheduled to arrive in Lae sometime early in March," Kenney said. "Several cargo and transport vessels escorted by destroyers appeared to be coming from Rabaul and some others were coming from Palau."[2]

Word was quickly sent to the Fifth's units in New Guinea, and the next few days were spent preparing for what Kenney characterized as "the big brawl." Normal operations were reduced to give ground crews the time they needed to ensure as many aircraft as possible were available for the coming fight. Some aircraft were flown north from Port Moresby to the new airstrips at Dobodura not only to get closer to the coming fight but also to eliminate the possibility of being grounded in the event of bad weather over Port Moresby or the Owen Stanley Range.

Kenney's staff crafted a plan that emphasized timing and the concentration of mass. Although the heavy bombers were to make periodic attacks once the Japanese were discovered—to fatigue the enemy sailors and perhaps inflict some damage—the main blow was designed to bring the full weight of the Fifth's forces to bear. In particular, Kenney wanted to hit the Japanese hard with the B-25s, which had been modified as commerce destroyers. The Allies chose the southern end of Vitiaz Strait, the passage that separated New Britain from New Guinea's Huon Peninsula, as the ideal point of engagement. There, the Japanese would be within range of the Fifth's B-25s and A-20s, the RAAF's Beaufighters, and a covering force of P-38s. They would be flung into the attack in numbers intended to overwhelm and destroy the Japanese convoy. In concert, shorter-ranged P-40s and P-39s were to attack the already-beleaguered airbase at Lae to keep fighters based there from taking off.

Of course, the focus on the Vitiaz Strait assumed that Kimura cooperated by taking the expected route. Rabaul sat on the northeastern end of New Britain, and Kimura had the option of sailing along either the southern or northern coasts of the island. The northern route would take the enemy convoy through the Vitiaz Strait, whereas the southern option would send it through the Solomon Sea and closer to Allied airbases.

The Fifth's weathermen were adamant that the weather was going to be poor—to the advantage of the Japanese—along the northern coast. And if the Americans and Australians chose to attack while the convoy was transiting along that route, they would be more vulnerable to defending Japanese fighters. Kenney and his staff considered all these factors. "We decided to gamble that the Nip would take the northern route," he said.[3]

The gamble paid off.

After sailing from Simpson Harbor at Rabaul late on the night of February 28, the convoy was discovered on New Britain's northern coast the following afternoon, March 1, by a B-24 crew of the 90th Bomb Group. Kenney's staff had kept at least two, and sometimes three, of the bombers thrashing through the storms on a round-the-clock basis. The sooner the enemy was found, the sooner he could be engaged. As it developed, the formation of eight B-17s that was subsequently dispatched to hit the convoy returned to base when their quarry disappeared under the protective cover of another storm.

Nevertheless, there was little doubt that Kimura and the ships making up Operation 81 were still advancing toward their objective. This, even though he now knew that the Americans and Australians were aware that he was at sea; the messages transmitted by the B-24 that had found his ships had been intercepted. Still, strategic imperatives overrode all other factors—the men and material carried by the transports he escorted had to be delivered to Lae.

Kenney and his men were anxious to maximize their chances of success. It was something they had failed to do in January when they had expended so much effort and produced such pitiable results. RAAF Group Captain William Garing was behind the creation of the attack scheme that ultimately proved so successful. He had flown Sunderland flying boats in the Atlantic during the first two years of the war, and urged Ennis Whitehead, who exercised operational control of Kenney's forces in New Guinea, to plan a massive, multifaceted knockout blow rather than another disorganized pell-mell rush of uncoordinated formations.

Garing made a convincing case, and Whitehead directed him to work with his staff to craft a plan. "So," Garing said, "I went, and we sat out in front of the tent of the headquarters, and we drew it in the sand, how we were going to do the battle of the Bismarck Sea."[4] The plan went from sand to paper and then directly to the participating units.

Garing also pressed for rehearsal flights. As a plan's complexity increased, so did the odds that it would come apart. Practicing the mission—while there was time to do so—would mitigate the risk of failure. "Now, the first rehearsal was dreadful," Garing said. "They were all over the goddam time scale, and Whitehead and I went, and we got all these blokes together and Whitehead tore a most unholy strip off them for their navigation and their timing." A second mock attack was subsequently flown with much better results.

A 90th Bomb Group B-24 found Kimura's convoy again on the morning of March 2. It was sailing west, north of Cape Gloucester at the western end of New Britain island. Again, B-17s were immediately sent after the Japanese ships. Their covering escort of 16 P-38s from the 35th Fighter Group arrived in the area before the bombers and quickly shot down three Japanese Ki-43 Oscars for no loss. When the first formation of eight B-17s arrived, they attacked from an altitude of 6,500 feet and hit three of the transports. One of them, the *Kyokusei Maru*, was hit with five bombs and nearly broke in half. Onboard ammunition and fuel exploded in a series of blinding blasts. Nearly a thousand survivors were rescued by two destroyers, *Asagumo* and *Yukikaze*, before the stricken ship exploded a final time and disappeared beneath the waves. The other two transports were able to continue with the rest of the convoy.

A second formation of 11 B-17s attacked shortly afterward and claimed hits on at least two ships, but none were mortally damaged. There followed several smaller attacks by B-17s and a pair of B-24s. These crews also claimed hits and near misses but failed to sink any more vessels. All were engaged by the covering force of Japanese fighters, which did inflict damage and casualties but failed to bring down any of the big bombers.

Tracking Kimura's convoy—and counting the ships that made it up—was difficult as darkness fell and the weather continued to provide cover. American intelligence experts scratched their heads, understandably frustrated, as they sifted, sorted, and struggled to make sense of the reports brought back by the heavy bomber crews. For their part, those crews couldn't possibly have seen everything. They sat more than a mile high with limited fields of view. And they made their attacks while under fire from both the defending destroyers and the covering fighters. Those considerations aside, there was still weather in the area.

Some estimates mistakenly tallied more than 20 ships—including several cruisers. And claims for sunken ships ranged as high as five. Complicating the issue of an accurate count was the fact that the two destroyers, *Asagumo* and *Yukikaze*, which had rescued survivors from the *Kyokusei Maru*, raced southeast to Lae to deliver them before sprinting back to rejoin Kimura. It was ironic that the rescued survivors arrived at their destination ahead of schedule even though their ship had been sunk. Regardless, the exact situation was unclear to the Allies as night fell on March 2.

Again, the big and slow, but venerable, PBY Catalina proved its worth. An RAAF crew, captained by Terry Duigan, used its radar to dog the Japanese ships through the night of March 2 and into the early morning hours of March 3. The Australians dropped flares and bombs, causing no damage but keeping the Japanese on edge and, more importantly, tracking their position.

Once the convoy passed through the Vitiaz Strait, it was clear to Kenney's staff that its goal was Lae. And because they had intercepted the radio reports from the Catalina crew, the Japanese were aware that the Allies knew it. Armed with this information, Kimura, for reasons not quite clear, decided not to strike as quickly as possible for Lae but rather to delay his arrival there until the following day. It is possible that he did not want to outrun the weather under which he had hidden Operation 81 up to that point. It has also been suggested that he wanted the protection that the covering force of fighters could have provided after dawn. But this makes little sense given the fact that he would have been safe from Allied air attacks had he covered the remaining distance during darkness.

An American B-17 relieved Duigan and his Catalina crew at dawn.

It was at about this time that seven plucky RAAF Beaufort torpedo bomber crews from 100 Squadron arrived in the area. The weather was still poor and only three of them actually found the Japanese. Their low-level attacks, albeit courageous, were ineffective. Only one torpedo was released. It missed.

Meanwhile, Allied airfields buzzed with activity as ground crews readied aircraft for the coming battle. Trucks and jeeps rushed here and there. Knuckles were bashed and curses flew as bombs and bullets were loaded, fuel tanks were topped, and last-minute maintenance was performed. Men slapped panels back in place and fastened them securely with screws and latches. The roar of newly serviced engines rose and fell and rose and fell again while men shielded their eyes against the dust and debris raised by the propellers those engines turned.

At the same time, aircrews were briefed as to when, where, and how the battle would be fought. The plan called for the attacking forces to rally at Cape Ward Hunt on New Guinea's northern coast, just more than 150 miles north of Port Moresby. Once joined, they were to press toward Kimura's force on a timeline that would see the opening shots exchanged at 1000.

The 43rd Bomb Group was tasked with sortieing 16 B-17s, which were to lead the entire formation, releasing their 1,000-pound bombs from an altitude of 7,000 to 10,000 feet. The 3rd and 38th Bomb Groups were each assigned to provide a squadron of 16 B-25s. Flying on the heels of the 43rd's B-17s, they were to drop their loads of 500-pound bombs from an altitude of 3,000 to 6,000 feet. These aircraft had yet to be modified as commerce destroyers and would make level bombing runs, notwithstanding the fact that such attacks had not proved to be particularly successful against moving ships. But some chance of success was better than no chance. And in fact, the *Kyokusei Maru* had been sunk the previous day by B-17s using the same tactics. Additionally, it was hoped that the bombers flying at higher altitudes would distract the enemy fighters, keeping them up and away from the aircraft that were to make masthead-level attacks to deliver the killing blows.

RAAF Beaufighters from 30 Squadron, each armed with four, 20-millimeter cannons and six .303 caliber machineguns, were charged with leading the attack down low, just as the B-17s and B-25s finished their bomb runs. Blackjack Walker recalled that their objective was to strafe the ships "from stem to stern, in which case you would probably get the bridge." Indeed, if the ship's bridge was thoroughly sprayed with cannon and machinegun fire there was a good chance that the captain and his officers would be killed or wounded, consequently leaving the crew leaderless.

Of course, the fire from the Beaufighters would also kill or wound other personnel on deck, including the antiaircraft gunners. At a minimum, forcing those gunners away from their positions was a desired objective. Not to be discounted was the material and equipment that would be damaged or destroyed.

Two squadrons of B-25s, one each from the 38th and 3rd Bomb Groups, were tasked to hurry in with, or immediately behind, the Beaufighters. These B-25s were the modified gunships, or commerce destroyers, that Pappy Gunn had helped create on Kenney's direction. At wavetop height, they were to fire on their targets not only to kill men and destroy material but also to force the antiaircraft gunners away from their positions.

Then, within range, they were to release one or more of their five 500-pound bombs. Falling away, the bombs would skip across the water until one or more slammed into the targeted ship. At that point, if a bomb did not penetrate, it would sink until its fuze, set for a multisecond delay, triggered it to explode. The resulting shock wave would heave the ship and break its structure, ideally causing it to sink.

Another reason for the fuzing delay was to give the attacking aircraft time to escape. The bombs were dropped so closely to the targeted ships—just a few hundred yards—that they lost very little speed and struck their targets at about the same time that the aircraft cleared the vessel's superstructure. Were the bomb to detonate instantaneously, there was a good chance that it would blast the aircraft out of the sky.

The last element of the attack was a squadron of A-20s from the 3rd Bomb Group. They were to follow the Beaufighters and B-25s. Their tactics were the same as the B-25s but being smaller they carried fewer guns and only two 500-pound bombs.

Posted above all the different groups were to be more than 30 P-38s from the 35th and 49th Fighter Groups. Their primary objective was to keep the Japanese fighters away from the bombers. In other words, they were to keep the Japanese fighter pilots from doing their job.

So, in short, the plan called for B-17s and B-25s to attack from medium level to distract the Japanese fighters while the Beaufighters and specially modified B-25s and A-20s flew just above the wavetops to strafe, and to smash their bombs into the transports and destroyers. Above them all, escorting P-38s were to protect them from enemy fighters. The mission's priority was the transports—Allied leadership wanted the Japanese reinforcements dead before they ever set foot in New Guinea. The secondary priority was the destroyers.

The participating units got airborne on time and headed for the rendezvous point. The 3rd Bomb Group's mission narrative recorded the mood. "Needless to say, everyone was ready and spoiling for the chance to hit the Nip where it would hurt most. What could be better than shipping, men and supplies? Off went the men of the 3rd Group to distinguish themselves against the 'little monkey men.'"

Blackjack Walker, the commanding officer of the RAAF's 30 Squadron, was beside himself with frustration. His observer was sick, and he could find no one to replace him. He watched, frantic with anxiety as his Beaufighter crews—12 of them—launched without him. "It was more than I could stand," he said. "I thought, I can't let those characters go out alone. So, I tore around the camp and I found some poor little green observer who had just come up from down south and I don't think he'd ever flown a mission, and I said, 'Get into that aeroplane.'"

None of the crews had been part of such a large operation—nearly a hundred aircraft. It was unprecedented in the southwest Pacific. "It was quite exhilarating to sit there and look at all these aeroplanes," said Beaufighter observer Frederick Cassidy, "but we knew it was going to be tough."[5] At 0930, on time, the formation turned northeast on a heading of 035 degrees toward the Japanese convoy, less than a hundred miles distant.

The weather that morning had cleared considerably, and the Americans found Kimura's convoy without trouble. His eight destroyers formed a screen around the seven remaining transport ships. Together, they steamed resolutely toward Lae. Specks, in many small groups, flitted and flashed overhead. These were the enemy fighters.

At just more than 7,000 feet, the pilots of the B-17s and of the B-25s which trailed them relinquished control of their aircraft to their bombardiers. Those bombardiers fine-tuned their approaches to the Japanese ships. For their part, desperate to ruin the work of the bombardiers, the destroyers and transports started to maneuver, leaving curving white wakes behind them. Aboard them, Japanese soldiers and sailors squinted skyward and then down toward the horizon at the thundering throng of aircraft that was about to kill so many of them.

Major Edward Larner was at the head of a 12-aircraft formation of B-25s from the 3rd Bomb Group's 90th Bomb Squadron. He led them in a steep descent down through a broken layer of cumulus clouds and toward the water. There, ahead of them, was Operation 81. Bombs from the medium-altitude B-17s and B-25s plunged into the water and exploded, sending huge columns of water into the air. Drop tanks from the P-38s also splashed into the water—some too close. The falling drop tanks indicated that the American fighter pilots were speeding to a fight with their enemy counterparts.

Blackjack Walker took off late. Now, at the controls of his Beaufighter with his hastily snatched, wet-behind-the-ears observer, he latched onto the only formation he could find—a group of P-38s. Enemy fighters were spotted as the P-38s neared the convoy, and Walker remembered the American pilots calling out to him, "They said, 'Listen, Blackjack, you better get that Beaufighter out of the way. It will be no bloody good in a dogfight.'" This was sound advice and Walker dived clear.

In the actual event, the rehearsal flights proved their worth. Although the timing wasn't perfect, the goal of overwhelming the Japanese defenses with simultaneous and devastating forces was certainly achieved. This was evidenced by the RAAF's Beaufighters and Larner's B-25s as they started their attacks at virtually the same time while bombs from the B-17s and higher-flying B-25s dropped through them. "From then on," crowed the 3rd Bomb Group's narrative, "for the next half hour, chaos reigned for the Sons of Nippon."

The Japanese believed that the low, fast-approaching Beaufighters and B-25s were torpedo bombers and turned directly into the attack to present a small, head-on target rather than a much bigger side profile. The Beaufighter pilots couldn't have been more pleased, as it allowed them to rake the destroyers with their cannons and machineguns from stem to stern. For their part, the B-25 crews were able to maneuver to make quartering and beam attacks.

Walker was in and among the fracas by that point. He declared that he'd "never seen anything like it."

B-25s going in at zero feet. In fact, I could see a Beaufighter and a B-25 were both going in at the same time and I thought, get out one of you. Anyhow, the B-25 bloke saw the Beaufighter going in so he peeled away and turned around and came in again. . . . That ship was hit, and I think it must have been an ammunition ship or something like that because a circle appeared above it and then my attention was distracted for a moment and I looked back to where this ship was . . . it had disappeared. It must have blown up.

Beaufighter pilot George Drury made a strafing pass at one of the enemy transports. He pressed so closely that he had to roll up on one wing to pass between its two masts. Almost immediately he selected another target. "My reflector sight had gone out, so I pressed the button, starting the bullets just below the waterline, pulling the nose up so that they came up the side of the ship and on to the deck which was piled high with packing cases and landing barges. I left it a mass of flames."[6]

The ferociousness of the Beaufighter crews at the outset of the battle was much admired. The 38th Bomb Group, which flew B-25s, practically gushed: "One thing every man in the battle agreed on was that the RAAF Beaufighter pilots were the 'fightenest' flyers they ever worked with. Throughout the heat of the battle, they were constantly on top of the ships—transports, destroyers and even the deadly cruisers—strafing personnel and antiaircraft posts, and firing equipment. No ack-ack [antiaircraft fire] was too hot to keep them out, and they never seemed to run out of ammunition."

Larner gave the signal for his B-25 crews to separate and select their targets. He flew directly at one of the destroyers, perhaps *Shirayuki* which was Kimura's flagship, and descended to just above the wavetops as he set up for his attack. Barreling toward the enemy warship, he checked to either side of his aircraft and saw several other B-25s still with him. He called over the radio, "Dammit, get off my wing and find your own boat!"

John Henebry led a three-aircraft B-25 element of Larner's 90th Bomb Squadron. Ahead of him was the destroyer-protected convoy. He declared that he was "scared as hell at the thought of flying right up to their sides at water level."

"Larner," said Henebry, "peeled off and bore in on the lead cruiser [destroyer]. We watched him go in strafing, get a hit and start after the next one. Well, that instilled tremendous confidence in the rest of us. If he can do it, so can we . . . and all hell broke loose then."[7]

The battle over Kimura's convoy quickly became a deadly spectacular. The destroyers lobbed five-inch shells at the B-17s and the B-25s that trailed them at medium altitude. A fiery flash and lingering smoke marked each explosion. But against the low-flying Beaufighters, B-25s, and A-20s, those five-inch guns were worthless—their barrels could not be depressed low enough, nor could they traverse fast enough. Instead, the gunners aboard the warships defended against the water-skimming bombers with streams of 25-millimeter cannon and small-caliber machinegun fire. The aircraft returned the favor; their gun muzzles flashed, and tracer streaks marked the paths of their bullets.

Overhead, mortally damaged fighters fell flaming into the water, leaving twisting tendrils of black smoke. Errant bombs sent great plumes of water skyward, while those not so errant exploded on or against the destroyers and transports. Secondary blasts added to the special hell the battle had become.

The fight down low became especially confused as aircraft wheeled around to make second, third, and even more attacks from multiple directions. No longer was it a choreographed operation. Rather, it had become a free-for-all. "It was bedlam actually," said Frederick Cassidy. "Aeroplanes everywhere. Ack-ack [antiaircraft fire] everywhere. And ships turning and speeding off everywhere. It was quite an exhilarating thing, actually."

Perhaps it was exhilarating for Cassidy and many of the other Allied crews, but it was terrifying for the Japanese in the convoy. Kimura's flagship, *Shimura*, was hit by a B-25, perhaps Ed Larner's, at the outset of the fighting. The vessel's bridge and deck were raked by gunfire, and the bomb that crashed into its side detonated the ammunition magazine. The ship broke apart and immediately began to sink. The admiral was not one of the many men killed, but he was blasted overboard and wounded. Not long afterward he was hauled from the water alive by another destroyer, *Shikinami*.

Back at the Allied airfields, radios had been rigged to loudspeakers at different points so that the ground crews and other support personnel could listen to the fight as it developed. Australian Burton Graham recorded the excitement.

A bomb-by-bomb description was coming over the loudspeakers to the crowds surrounding the operations shack. No ball game ever had a keener listening audience than this. The description came to them in the short terse sentences of the pilots in actual combat. You heard the warnings, the curses, the instructions of intrepid flight leaders. Sometimes, you hear the whir inside a crate [aircraft] when a pilot has forgotten to turn off his transmitter. You hear a pilot say that another ship has been hit and is burning. It makes the crowd cheer and stamp about like fools.[8]

The 3rd Bomb Group's mission report recounted the results of each attack made by the 90th Bomb Squadron's 12 crews. Every aircrew, except two whose bombs would not release, smashed their deadly loads into at least one enemy vessel. Even a small sample from the report is repetitive and—despite the fearsome nature of the action—soon numbs the sensibilities. It is probable that the Japanese enduring those attacks were likewise numbed but by horror and shock rather than tedious text.

> Lt. Chatt scored two direct hits and two near misses on a large destroyer or small cruiser . . . superstructure entirely blown away . . . ship made 90-degree turn and stopped immediately . . . large amount of black smoke coming from it. Lt. Howe dropped two 500-pounders on a large transport with results unobserved . . . he dropped two more bombs on a 3,000–5,000-ton transport and the ship was observed to blow up in the middle . . . Lt. McCoun peeled off onto an 8,000-ton transport gutted [sic] with fully-laden soldiers in jungle equipment . . . he laid one hit at the waterline and another in the middle of the ship . . . the ship burst into flames and large columns of smoke poured from it . . . left in sinking condition.

The 90th Bomb Squadron B-25s were followed by 12 A-20s from the 89th Bomb Squadron—also from the 3rd Bomb Group. The 89th was undermanned and some of the aircraft were crewed by men from the group's 8th Bomb Squadron which had relinquished its A-24s months earlier and was still mostly without aircraft. One of these crews was pilot Edward Chudoba and his gunner, Felix Larronde.

When Chudoba first sighted Kimura's convoy, it was already in disarray. Both the transport ships and the destroyers—those not dead in the water—were turning, circling, and otherwise maneuvering to defend against the persistent attacks of the B-25s and the Beaufighters. Chudoba descended to 50 feet and turned to attack a transport but aborted that effort when he spotted another A-20 from his group already doing so. He consequently adjusted his course slightly to target a different transport, later identified as the *Taimei Maru*.

Closing the range, Chudoba noted the twinkle of machinegun fire coming from the bow and stern of the enemy vessel. He fired his own guns from 2,000 yards and continued putting bursts into the ship until he was only 200 yards away. At that point, he toggled his two, 500-pound bombs and crossed over the transport just aft of amidships, smashing his right wing into a radio or cargo mast as he did so. An instant later he hauled the A-20 into a steep, climbing left-hand turn, escaping with only a single bullet hole in the aircraft's nose.

Chudoba could not see his bombs, but Larronde, facing rearward, could. A post-mission debrief recorded his observations: "The gunner [Larronde] definitely observed both bombs after he felt their release. The first bounded up in the air in a deflected wobble and skipped toward the bow of the ship. The other skipped straight and struck directly amidships. The latter exploded first in about 5 seconds and was followed by a tremendous flash at the bow as the second exploded."

In total, the 3rd Bomb Group's A-20 flyers claimed 12 bomb hits against seven different ships.

Kimura's destroyers were better armed than the transports they escorted, but they were still vulnerable to the ferocious attacks. Reiji Masuda was one of the crewmen assigned to the *Arashio*. Its bridge was blown away by a pair of 500-pound bombs. "On our side, we were madly firing," Masuda said, "but we had no chance to beat them off. Nobody could have survived. The captain, the chief navigator, the gunnery and torpedo chiefs, and the chief medical officer were all killed in action. The chief navigator's blackened body was hanging there, all alone." Its leadership dead and its steering most probably damaged, *Arashio* heeled out of control and careened directly into the *Nojima*, one of the transports it was charged with protecting. The *Nojima* began to sink immediately.

Masuda recalled that the *Arashio*'s steam pipes burst, scalding men and making it almost impossible to stay aboard the doomed destroyer. "We tried to abandon ship," he said, "but planes flying almost as low as the masts sprayed us with machineguns. Hands were shot off, stomachs blown open. Most of the crew were murdered or wounded there. Hundreds were swimming in the ocean. Nobody was there to rescue them."[9]

The P-38s from the 35th and 49th Fighter Groups engaged enemy fighters from the very start. Although the plan called for the Japanese Navy and Army to separately cover the convoy during different hours of each day, it is evident from aircrew reports and surviving records that fighters from both services—navy A6M Zeroes and army Ki-43 Oscars—were airborne over the convoy that morning. Estimates of their numbers ranged from 30 to 50 and more.

Stanley Andrews flew a P-38 with the 35th Fighter Group's 39th Fighter Squadron. "It was a beautifully clear day as you would frequently see in that area," he said. "You could see the coast of New Britain to the north and off to the west you could see the area of New Guinea around the tip of land near Finschhafen. The convoy of ships was spread out ahead and below us making white wakes in the deep blue sea."[10]

Andrews's appreciation of the pretty panorama below him was short-lived as Japanese fighters turned to intercept the P-38 formations. "It looked like a swarm of bees coming at us from probably fifteen thousand feet," Andrews said. "About this time, the first skip bombers were hitting and the explosions on the surface started up. Fires, splashes, black smoke and then we were into it with the Japs." Andrews and his squadron mates twisted and turned and fired at the enemy fighters they could see and were often shot up by those they didn't see. Andrews escaped with 93 holes in his aircraft, and both of his main landing gear tires were shot out. He later landed safely, albeit he didn't roll very far on his ruined tires. He was uninjured but his aircraft was scrapped.

One of the enemy fighters damaged in the freewheeling melee climbed toward the B-17 captained by Woodrow Moore and rammed it. "Both planes broke in two," remembered another of the Japanese pilots, "and the four pieces fell, jumbled together."[11] Remarkably, seven men parachuted clear of the tumbling wreckage that had been the B-17.

They might just as well have not. Rather than attacking the aircraft that were savaging the convoy—and their countrymen—several Zero fighter pilots turned instead toward the gently descending Americans. They made multiple gunnery passes, blasting the airmen into hunks of bloody meat until they hung butchered and lifeless under their parachutes.

The ferocity of the air battle intensified. Several American P-38 pilots threw themselves after the murderous Zeroes, while others continued the fights in which they were already engaged. Among those who sought to avenge their murdered B-17 comrades was Robert Faurot of the 39th Fighter Squadron who, months earlier, was the first P-38 pilot to be credited with an aerial victory against the Japanese. With him were squadron mates Hoyt Eason and Fred Shifflet. All three were shot down. B-25s of the 38th Bomb Group spotted one of the fighter pilots descending in his parachute and began to circle him. "After they identified his yellow life vest," noted the 38th's after action report, "and saw that he was a white man, they dropped him a life raft." But ultimately, Faurot, Eason, and Shifflet were all lost.

With so many fighters in the sky, the air battle developed at a confused and frenetic, almost fractious tempo. This was reflected in the mission report filed by Clay Barnes, a 9th Fighter Squadron P-38 pilot who flew as wingman to Ed Ball. "I saw enemy aircraft at one o'clock high engaged with P-38s. At the same time, I saw one enemy aircraft at 10 o'clock low.

Ball and Barnes dived at the low aircraft and fired at it with no effect. At this time, two more enemy aircraft were approaching head on and were firing at us," Barnes said. Ed Ball fired at one of the Japanese fighters and set it to smoking, but the two P-38 pilots exited the fight at high speed.

Ball and Barnes took a breather for a few minutes before throwing themselves back into the fray after spotting two more Japanese fighters. "I dove and made a 15-degree head-on shot," said Barnes. "I started firing at about 500 yards and fired a real long burst but with no observed results." The P-38 pilots streaked through the fight before turning back and spotting about a dozen enemy fighters beating up a formation of B-17s.

Barnes caught sight of an aircraft in front of him which he was unable to immediately identify. However, after it made a series of turns, it crossed low in front of him only about fifty yards away. "I saw the red ball on the wing and fuselage," said Barnes, "and fired a big burst straight into its canopy. The canopy disintegrated into sparkling pieces of glass and the Japanese plane banked steeper into a dive. I went on past and our flight made a steep 90-degree turn toward home. When we turned toward home, I saw the place where the [enemy] plane had crashed into the ocean." Barnes noted that the enemy aircraft they had fought that day "had round wingtips and were colored a dark brownish black with mottled green spots over it."[12]

Clay Tice was assigned to lead a four-ship flight of P-38s which were part of a formation of 12 aircraft launched by the 49th Fighter Group's 9th Fighter Squadron. He took off on time from Dobodura just after 0900 with the rest of the squadron but had to land almost immediately as gas streamed from a loose fuel tank cap. That issue was quickly resolved, and he launched again but was unable to chase down his squadron and attached himself to a formation of eight B-17s instead.

Flying high above the bombers, Tice had a grandstand seat from which he watched the destruction of Operation 81. Readying his P-38 for air combat, he attempted to release the two external fuel tanks he carried. They failed to fall. They were heavy and would degrade the performance of his aircraft in a fight. Not wanting to get caught by enemy fighters at a disadvantage, he turned once more for Dobodura. Descending toward the base at 350 miles per hour, he felt the left external fuel tank break free. Once he landed, mechanics removed the other tank, and he quickly got airborne again at 1045 when most of the aircraft from the morning strike were already on their way home.

Headed back toward the convoy, Tice spotted a column of smoke as he climbed through 5,000 feet. He eventually reached an altitude of 22,000 feet when he spotted a destroyer. He described it as "motionless and burning with five or six large lifeboats to the north of it. I pointed my gun camera at the ship," he said, "and was taking pictures (guns off) when I saw a Zeke emerge from beneath my nose on the same course and 4,000 feet below me."

Tice immediately forgot about the damaged destroyer and dived after the enemy fighter, which was painted dark green with a horizontal dark blue or black stripe across its vertical stabilizer. "At about 800 yards, he saw me and made a very sharp diving turn to the left." Tice likewise rolled and pulled hard to the left, attempting to cut inside the Japanese pilot's turn so that he could bring his guns to bear.

Tice was able to get the nose of his aircraft pointed in front of the enemy fighter but not as far as he wanted. "Believing that I was failing in my attempt to lead him enough," Tice said, "I fired a chance burst in a deflection shot of about 70 degrees." That burst included 30 rounds from Tice's 20-millimeter cannon and 200 rounds from his four .50 caliber machineguns.

Despite his doubts, the fire from his guns found its target. "The entire burst entered his cockpit," said Tice, "blowing all of the canopy off and throwing large chunks out of the cockpit. I could see the cannon and incendiaries bursting in the cockpit and I believe that the pilot was blown to bits."[13] The Japanese aircraft and the chunks that remained of its pilot spiraled out of control toward the sea.

The air combat that morning might have been frustrating, but it was nonetheless successful. That success was underscored by the fact that only a few of the enemy fliers dived to attack the low-altitude bombers, which slammed bomb after bomb into the ships of the convoy. And none of those bombers was shot down, although two, a B-25 and a Beaufighter, were so badly damaged they never again flew. Added to the aerial victories of the P-38s were those of the gunners aboard the bombers. Their claims were overlapping and inflated, but the effectiveness of the gunners in holding off the enemy fighters could not be disputed.

Extraordinary—almost unbelievable—reports poured in as the American and Australian crews recovered to their airfields. Allied planners tried to make sense of them all even as returning aircraft were refueled, rearmed, and readied for a follow-on strike. The men who had been part of the mission were almost wild with excitement as they shared with their ground crews—and the aircrews slated for the next mission—what they had seen and done. Men poked their fingers and hands through the holes of damaged aircraft, which were examined both out of curiosity and with the goal to get them repaired and back into service.

Indeed, an afternoon attack had been part of the plan all along regardless of how successful, or not, the morning strike had been. As had been the case in the morning, the afternoon mission was planned to be an all-out effort. However, not unexpectedly, there were fewer aircraft available. Mechanical failures, damage, and wear and tear had exacted a price, as had losses.

Weather in the form of afternoon storms also worked against the Allies. The RAAF Beaufighters of 30 Squadron were unable to clear the thunderheads that boiled over the Owen Stanley Range. Likewise, 3rd Bomb Group A-20s failed to get through as did elements of other units.

Joseph McWhirt led a formation of five B-25s from the 3rd Bomb Group's 13th Bomb Squadron out of Port Moresby. The 13th had more crews than aircraft, and he had lost a coin toss to a squadron mate, Art Small, and so had missed the morning's action. "Art was pretty tickled about winning that toss," McWhirt said." On the other hand, McWhirt was chagrined at not having taken part in the killing orgy. Now, in the afternoon, he was eager to help administer the coup de grâce to what remained of Kimura's convoy.

The 13th's crews were bounced about as they made detours to thread their way through the weather. They were consequently late when they reached the rendezvous point, which was again over Cape Ward Hunt. As it developed, many of the other units were also late, and the 13th's tardiness did not keep it from participating in the mission. Finally, just before 1500, the B-17s of the 43rd Bomb Group started north to find the ships of Operation 81 that were still afloat. They were followed by formations of B-25s from the 3rd and 38th Bomb Groups. The RAAF's 22 Squadron, with a handful of Bostons—export versions of the A-20—were also part of the formation. Above them flew 10 P-38s from the 35th Fighter Group Additional aircraft in ones, twos and small groups followed during the remainder of the afternoon.

McWhirt was eager and excited. "After having listened to the radio chatter and to the pilots returning from the morning mission," he said, "we were all hot to see what was left out there at the scene of the battle." They didn't have long to wait. Only about 15 minutes passed before the flyers spotted huge oil slicks and rafts of flotsam atop the water. In the distance, McWhirt saw smears of smoke that marked the positions of damaged Japanese vessels. Scattered across the area, miles apart in some instances, four or five transports burned. Dead in the water was a destroyer, obviously damaged. Anxious with anticipation, McWhirt and the other airmen in the formation readied for their bomb runs.

Above him, he saw strings of bombs fall from a flight of B-17s. One of the bombs made a direct hit on the motionless destroyer. At the same time, he and his crew spotted a ship in the far distance steaming away. "Three of the Flying Fortresses above us were giving chase," he said. McWhirt joined that chase with his B-25s. The vessel was a destroyer, perhaps *Arashio*, and had been pulling soldiers and sailors out of the water before fleeing the oncoming attackers.

"We could see it ahead and below us turn sharply to the left to avoid the bombs from the Fortresses," said McWhirt. The string of bombs was well delivered but straddled the destroyer rather than striking it. McWhirt's tiny formation pressed ahead for its own attack from an altitude of 5,500 feet.

"When we came over the destroyer it was completing a circle," he said. The other B-25 pilots tucked their aircraft close to McWhirt's as his bombardier made last-second adjustments preparatory to releasing their load of five 500-pound bombs. At exactly the right instant, the bombs were let go at the still-circling warship. The bombs from the other B-25s fell at the same time. The aim was good, and their luck was better. "The whole aft of the destroyer was in the pattern, concealed from above by the splash and explosion of the bombs," said McWhirt. "The destroyer slid ahead a little and stopped dead."[14]

The lead ship of the 38th Bomb Group's 71st Bomb Squadron was flown by Ezra Best. Also with the crew was the group's commanding officer, Brian O'Neill. The bombardier, Bob Renneisen, was nervous not just because of the coming engagement, but because the success of the squadron's mission rested largely with him. The squadron would release their bombs on his cue. And O'Neill—his boss's boss—would be able to see just how well he performed or did not. "As lead bombardier," Renneisen said, "I had to pick out our target and decide the course."

Best led the formation toward the floating, fiery wrecks that were what was left of the Japanese convoy. In front of him, in the nose of the aircraft, Renneisen decided to target a destroyer that seemed undamaged but was dead in the water. He refined the bombing solution as the rest of the 71st's B-25s followed. It was then that the squadron was hit by a formation of eight Zeroes. The formation's gunners responded with concentrated bursts of machinegun fire.

"I was in the middle of my run without much time to watch," said Renneisen. At the same time, he spotted another potential target, a seemingly undamaged destroyer that was actually underway. He called it out to O'Neill but couldn't understand the response over the boom of the machineguns. "I glanced up," Renneisen said, "to see tracers chasing after a couple of green-bellied Zeroes."

Finally, he heard O'Neill's exasperated voice crackle over the intercom: "Well, pick out something and let's get out of here. They're going to be all over us."

Renneisen decided to continue after his original target, which might have been the mortally damaged *Asashio*. "I kept on my dead duck, and she was really dead. Even most of the ack-ack [antiaircraft fire] was out." His aim was good, and the 71st's aircraft scored three direct hits which were followed by two more hits from higher flying B-17s. Having suffered no losses, the formation turned back to Port Moresby.[15]

None of the aircraft flying that afternoon were shot down. This was due not only to the fact that most of the antiaircraft guns aboard the Japanese ships—and their gunners—were put out of action during the morning mission but also because the enemy fighters were not particularly aggressive. For instance, when the 71st's B-25s were attacked by a group of eight fighters, Renneisen remarked that "they only made a couple of passes, and they didn't even press them home." Certainly, the escorting P-38s offered some protection, but there were only 10 of them, and when they were elsewhere or otherwise preoccupied the Japanese still didn't engage the bombers with any degree of tenacity.

Although it had long been a target of Allied air attacks, the Japanese airbase at Lae still hosted various air units and could service many more. Indeed, Lae-based fighters—if left unchecked—had the wherewithal to disrupt the Allied ambush of Kimura's convoy. Accordingly, the airfield complex was attacked by Australian and American units for several days in late February and early March. Those attacks continued through the morning and into the afternoon of March 3.

Arthur House Jr., a P-40 pilot with the 49th Fighter Group's 7th Fighter Squadron, was assigned to fly a dive-bombing mission early that afternoon. Part of a four-aircraft formation high over Lae, he led his wingman, James Martin, down at the runway in a steep dive from 9,000 feet. Heavy antiaircraft fire caused them both to pull up without releasing their 500-pound bombs. However, just a moment later they hurtled down once more through the bursting enemy shells, let go their bombs, and continued down to strafe the airfield.

The pair of them raced low above the dirt runway shooting up targets of opportunity before turning across the water to attack a barge. That done, they banked hard toward the shore and streaked at treetop level over the jungle. House then spotted a formation of 11 Japanese fighters above him and to his right. They were likely returning from the fight over Kimura's convoy. He eased his aircraft into a turn away from the enemy fighters and spotted a single aircraft above him to his left. "He [the other aircraft] started to fire at 2,000 feet," said House, "and I started to call him on the radio, thinking he was one of our airplanes."

House was mistaken. The aircraft firing at him was an enemy fighter. He looked behind him and saw his wingman, Martin, bracketed by a pair of Zeroes. At that instant he could do nothing for Martin and instead pulled up and left into the aircraft that was shooting at him. "I fired a long burst," House said. "His tracers were going behind me. My shots hit him right in the center of the front of the plane and he exploded in midair."

House had spent all his airspeed in the climb and his aircraft stalled and fell out of control to the left. Meanwhile, Martin had shaken his harassers and subsequently chased away another pair of Zeroes. A moment or two later, House regained flying speed, turned left, and squeezed off a burst of machinegun fire into another Japanese fighter which crossed in front of him from left to right. The rounds smashed into the engine and cockpit of the Zero. "The aircraft caught fire," House said, "and continued down, falling into the water just off shore."[16] Outnumbered and anxious not to exhaust their luck, House and Martin raced for the cover of the clouds that cloaked the nearby mountains and found their way home.

14

"WHAT WE DIDN'T GET, THE SHARKS GOT"

When the afternoon mission ended on March 3, 1943, a thousand or more Japanese thrashed in the water or clung to debris or huddled aboard lifeboats or landing barges that had been cut loose from the doomed transports. An additional thousand or more Japanese soldiers were aboard four destroyers which raced to transfer them to a pair of warships steaming from Rabaul. Some of the men had been rescued from sinking wrecks, only to endure another attack and another sinking. Many of them were injured. Virtually all of them suffered from shock.

The Americans and Australians started slaughtering them almost immediately. B-17s circled low overhead like great hulking metal condors while their gunners laced the sea with thousands of .50 caliber machinegun rounds. The water turned a foamy pink when the bullets found their marks. B-25s and A-20s likewise combed the area and shot up the hapless Japanese wherever they found them.

Many of the Japanese who survived the strafing did so by jumping from their rafts or lifeboats each time they came under attack. Their heads and shoulders made smaller targets and, as powerful as the .50 caliber machineguns were, the bullets stopped quickly once they hit the water.

By nightfall on March 3, it was obvious to both the Allies and the Japanese that Operation 81 was not just a failure but an unprecedented catastrophe. The 51st Division was destroyed as a combat unit. Many of its men were already dead, a thousand or more were adrift, and more than a thousand had been rescued and were on their way back to Rabaul—their starting point. Only about 900 men from the 51st reached Lae, the convoy's destination. These had been rescued from the *Kyokusei Maru*, which had been sunk the previous day by the 43rd Bomb Group's B-17s.

That the Allies had scored an enormous success was unquestioned. But exactly what had been achieved was still unclear at the end of the day, March 3. Allied intelligence personnel found it maddeningly difficult—in fact, impossible—to accurately reconcile the dizzyingly disparate claims made by the aircrews. This was especially so because multiple aircrews attacked and hit the same vessels not just in the morning but also in the afternoon. Moreover, the total number of Japanese ships remained undetermined; reports ranged from just more than a dozen to well more than 20. And the different types of vessels that made up Kimura's convoy also defied definition. Reports of cruisers, although there were none, were so numerous that it was simply accepted that they were part of the Japanese force.

What had been achieved in the air was also confusing, the P-38 pilots claimed 26 Japanese fighters shot down, whereas the bomber crews claimed seven. These figures are certainly inflated, but not to the same extent as the claims submitted by the Japanese fighter pilots. They declared they had destroyed nine P-38s, six B-25s, and three B-17s. Actually, only three P-38s and one B-17 went down.

Regardless of what was sunk and who shot down whom, the Allies knew that there were still Japanese vessels afloat as night fell. Their exact numbers and dispositions were unknown, but preparations were made to finish them off the next day, March 4. But what the ships had carried—the men of the 51st Division—was more important than the ships themselves. Should those men make it ashore, the victory that was the destruction of Operation 81 would be a hollow one; those soldiers would be reequipped and sent into the fight.

Both sides knew the value of those men. After nightfall on March 3, a trio of the surviving Japanese destroyers, *Shikinami, Yukikaze,* and *Asagumo,* crept back into the battle area and skimmed survivors from the sea. Having witnessed what Kenney's squadrons had done to the other ships in Kimura's convoy, the destroyer captains knew that it would be dangerous to be caught in the area after daylight. Consequently, although many men still floated in the jetsam and wreckage and open sea, the destroyers abandoned them and ran for Rabaul soon after midnight.

Meanwhile, at nightfall, the U.S. Navy sortied 10 torpedo boats from their base at Tufi. Slinking through the waves, two of them were forced to return after smashing into wreckage. The remaining eight plucked prisoners from the water and shot up many more. A floating wreck—one of the transport ships—was discovered and sunk by a pair of torpedoes.

Neither MacArthur nor Kenney explicitly ordered the Fifth Air Force's flyers to find and exterminate the Japanese still adrift in the Huon

Gulf. But for the most part, those men did not need to be ordered to do so; most were happy to kill the Japanese whenever and wherever they found them. News quickly spread of how the Japanese Zero pilots had shredded Woodrow Moore's B-17 crew as they descended in their parachutes. But that was only fuel on an already raging fire of atrocities that the Japanese had fed for years. These included the brutal butchering of hundreds of thousands of Chinese men, women, and children, the sneak attack on Pearl Harbor, the Bataan Death March, and the pitiless torturing, beheading, and bayoneting of Allied prisoners of war and neutral civilians.

Words can conjure images, but they can never evoke even the very smallest iota of the terror endured by the victims of the Japanese. Although it postdated the destruction of Kimura's convoy by a couple of weeks, the horror that took place aboard the destroyer *Akikaze* is representative of the sorts of grotesqueries the Japanese committed. The ship was sent to retrieve a group of German missionaries and nuns at Wewak on the northern coast of New Guinea who were suspected of collaborating with the Allies. Others—a mix of other nationalities—were collected at other stops, including Kavieng, on New Ireland. After boarding the group—which included three infants—the *Akikaze* set sail for Rabaul on March 18, 1943.

En route, the men and women, approximately 60—were individually brought to the stern of the ship. There, they were bound by their wrists, winched off the deck, shot, and then dumped into the sea. The children, alive, were simply pitched overboard. These particular murders, measured against the typical Japanese spectrum of atrocities, were mild. Death by rifle fire was quick compared to sword strokes, bayonet thrusts, evisceration, and being burned alive.

Consequently, it was only natural that many of the Allied airmen understood the Japanese to be an inhuman race of depraved monsters. One flyer, a B-17 pilot, recalled, "I wanted to vent some of my anger and kill every Japanese son of a bitch I could find."[1] The 38th Bomb Group's remarks were a bit breezier as it noted, "Considerable strafing of the Nip troops gave the gunners of the planes a little practice at shooting sitting ducks."

The 3rd Bomb Group simply declared that "as many of the survivors as possible were strafed." William O'Brien, a B-17 pilot with the 43rd Bomb Group, reflected on the gruesome fate of Woodrow Moore's crew: "It was one of those things that makes you mad—and burning mad. What we didn't get, the sharks got. Every man in the squadron would have given two month's pay to have been in on that strafing."[2]

Vengeance aside, there was inarguable logic behind the killing of the Japanese in the water. "You can't have the enemy loose at sea," said Richard Cresswell, who commanded an RAAF P-40 squadron, "even though they might be in rowing boats and rafts and so forth. You have to complete the job."[3]

In fact, the Japanese were still part of an invasion force, and should they have made it to shore—and that was certainly possible, even probable for those in boats—they would have been formed into combat units and thrown into the coming battles. And in those battles, they might kill Australian or American soldiers. On the other hand, a Japanese soldier gunned to death in the water wasn't going to kill anyone. RAAF Group Captain William Garing made that clear to one young pilot. "Well now," he said. "For every one that you sent to the bottom and the sharks got, you've saved one Australian infantryman. Don't forget it."

The strafing of the Japanese survivors began in earnest on March 4. Aside from making attacks on Lae and other targets, Allied aircraft of all types combed the sea with the primary goal of what Kenney called, "mopping up." Crews scanned the sea for whatever Japanese vessels remained afloat. They also looked for survivors of the previous day's carnage who paddled in the water or clung to wreckage or floated on the currents in lifeboats or barges.

There actually were crews who declined to fire their machineguns on the essentially helpless enemy. But there were still more than enough who were willing to do the job, either reluctantly or with enthusiasm. Australian Frederick Cassidy recalled that he and his pilot, Mostyn Morgan, had reservations. "We asked why have we got and go out and strafe these people in the water? Why can't somebody go and pick them up or just leave them there? We were just told to go and do it." Accordingly, they climbed into their Beaufighter and did so.

The mission left an impression on Cassidy. "I mean when you hit a boat, and the water would change colour, you hit a boat with about eighty people in it with four cannons and six machineguns in it, it's something." It was especially something when sharks savaged the survivors.

Garing recalled returning that morning after flying a mission in a P-40. Upon climbing down from his fighter, he struck up a conversation with Blackjack Walker. "Blackjack and I were just standing on the edge of Ward strip," said Garing, "and we saw a little boy get out of a Beaufighter and go to the side and he wretched his guts out and we walked over to him and said, 'What's wrong with you son?' and he said, 'Sir, I've never seen so many sharks.'"

Richard Cresswell noted that the experience wasn't "very nice. But the sharks had a good meal," he said. "The sea was red with blood and you could see the sharks diving up and down."

Not every Japanese in the water was shot to bits or eaten by sharks. A pair of submarines, the I-17 and I-26, rescued 234 men from March 6 through March 8. Other submarines rescued additional survivors in lesser numbers. Some men were washed onto nearby islands during the following days and weeks where they were variously captured, killed, rescued, or simply languished. A small number, 21, swam, drifted, sailed, or paddled to New Guinea.

When the massacre was finished at the close of the first week of March 1943, the tally against the 16 ships that made up Operation 81 was overwhelmingly in favor of the Allies. Every one of the eight transports was sunk, as were four of the eight destroyers. The surviving destroyers were *Shikinami*, *Yukikaze*, *Uranami*, and *Asagumo*. Japanese dead numbered nearly 3,000—approximately half of the total force. Virtually all of the 51st Division's equipment was lost, as were the supplies and material intended to support it and the forces already in New Guinea.

After the battle, Kimura himself described how he and his commanders were flummoxed by the new Allied tactics. "The big planes came skimming the waves," he said, "dropping their bombs to skip on the surface and hit into the side of the ships. Conventional evasive maneuvers proved utterly useless."[4]

"Our losses for this single battle were fantastic," declared a staff officer at Rabaul. "Not during the entire savage fighting at Guadalcanal did we suffer a single comparable blow. We knew we could no longer run cargo ships or even fast destroyer transports to any front on the north coast of New Guinea, east of Wewak. Our supply operation to northeastern New Guinea became a scrabbler's run of barges, small craft and submarines."[5] Indeed, the Japanese never again risked sending convoys—or even large surface vessels—to Lae. Their forces in northern New Guinea were subsequently forced to endure a slow, ceaseless starvation that degraded not only their combat capability but also their bodies and their spirits.

The responsibility for the Japanese failure sat stinking and directly in the laps of the air commanders who had possessed the men and aircraft to disrupt the American and Australian attacks, if not turn them back completely. That point was driven home on March 4—the day after the big battle—when approximately 100 Rabaul-based aircraft attacked Allied positions at Buna. "The Japs fired a lot of ammunition," Kenney said, "but did practically no damage. It was a good thing that the Nip air commander was stupid. Those hundred airplanes would have made our job awfully hard if they had taken part in the big fight over the convoy on March 3."[6]

Unquestionably, the greater strategic victory was the absolute denial of the sea routes the Japanese needed to move men and material. American leadership tried to burnish that achievement even further but dulled it instead by claiming to have destroyed more ships than were actually in the convoy. Kenney's initial assessment, which he delivered to MacArthur early on March 4, included six destroyers or light cruisers sunk, and anywhere from 11 to 14 transports destroyed and up to 15,000 troops killed. He gave this estimate even though his staff was still compiling incoming reports. A few days later, MacArthur inflated the claims by declaring that 22 Japanese ships were sunk.

The reasons for the miscalculations were manifold. First, there was genuine ignorance about the actual number of ships destroyed; the preliminary determination was no doubt reduced from a greater number of claims made by understandably exuberant aircrews. Second, the sinking of a given number of Japanese ships was good news, so it stood to reason that the sinking of even more Japanese ships was even better news—especially at a time when the folks back home weren't getting much of it. Third, both MacArthur and Kenney understood that the victory would focus more attention on their part of the war, and more attention might very well result in more resources. With more resources they might achieve more success. In the end it didn't change the truth, which was that Operation 81 had been utterly destroyed.

MacArthur and his considerable public relations staff were noted for regularly exaggerating the achievements of the forces under his command. Even at that point in the war, newspaper correspondents were already jaded by the communiqués issued by MacArthur's headquarters. News conferences were frequently marked by eye rolls and guffaws. To make matters worse, MacArthur was often reluctant to share credit or to acknowledge the contributions of Australian units.

The reception that Kenney received upon returning stateside just a few days after the battle reflected this cynicism. "The first thing they wanted to know," said Kenney, "was the real story about the Bismarck Sea Battle. Everyone seemed skeptical at first, but when I showed them the operations reports, it was easy to convince them that a truly spectacular victory had been won."[7] Yet doubts persisted, and Kenney complained in a message to Hap Arnold, "I do not appreciate the implication of exaggeration or falsification by myself and members of my command. I can only speculate about the motives involved."[8] MacArthur actually wanted action taken against those who later questioned the numbers he cited in his communique.

But the Navy, one of MacArthur's chief opponents, remained unconvinced of the Fifth Air Force's claims. Indeed, Secretary of the Navy Frank Knox scoffed at the reports. Angry and exasperated, MacArthur sent Richard Sutherland, his chief of staff, back to the States to set the record straight. No satisfactory resolution to this interservice ruckus was ever reached, and the inflated claims persisted until after the war.

Considering the backbiting and backstabbing that took place at the highest levels of command, it is gratifying that, among the young men doing the actual fighting, there was an appreciation of what they had accomplished. The contemporaneous perspective of a young officer of the 35th Fighter Group was as accurate and prescient as any observation made at the time or since:

> A great victory had been won by airpower over naval strength. Militarists the world over now recognized that one of the oldest principles of war—isolation of the battlefield—had been achieved with war's newest weapon—the airplane. It also proved to Allied strategists that if the sea north of New Guinea could be controlled with airpower and [with] the help of the United States Navy, there was no necessity in plowing the fifteen hundred miles through New Guinea's jungle to the tip, and the jump-off [point] for the Philippines.

There was no denying the bravery and skill of the Allied airmen, but none of what was accomplished could have happened without the ground crewmen who toiled almost ceaselessly—in starkly primitive conditions—to prepare the aircraft for combat. George Kenney certainly understood and appreciated the importance of these men. While stateside during March 1943 he met Arde Bulova, the head of the Bulova Watch Company. Bulova wanted to give a hundred watches to Kenney to be used to reward top-scoring fighter pilots. Kenney suggested that the watches be awarded instead to the best of his ground crewmen, a notion to which Bulova readily agreed.

It should additionally be noted that although the ground crewmen rarely saw direct combat, they were sometimes killed by enemy action. Notwithstanding the Bismarck Sea defeat of the previous week, the Japanese sent a force of bombers and fighters against Allied airfields at Dobodura on March 11. The enemy aircraft were thought to be friendly and consequently, no one took cover until bombs started hitting the ground.

It was on that day that the 49th Fighter Group lost its first ground crewman to enemy action. Frederick Bente was working on an aircraft when it was hit and caught fire. He burned to death. Obert Franklin's arm was hit by shrapnel and was subsequently amputated. Others were wounded but not as seriously.

★★★

American ground crewmen and airmen alike were less than impressed by the food made available to them through official channels. It was only satisfactory at its best and "very poor by our standards," observed James Peterson, an officer with the 3rd Bomb Group. "There was a limited amount of milk, butter and eggs and some fresh vegetables," he noted. "There was a decided excess of mutton and lamb."

Virtually every unit got around this paucity of decent food by way of "Fat Cat" flights to Australia. Typically, a hat was passed with a suggested contribution amount—sometimes more for officers than enlisted personnel. And then a small foraging party flew to Australia to shop for groceries. Literally.

The aircraft used were generally war-weary airframes—B-25s and A-20s—that were stripped of their fighting gear and optimized for carrying cargo. Once in Australia, they were typically loaded with fresh fruit, vegetables, milk, and eggs—and lots of booze and beer. Back in New Guinea, the food was taken to the cooks who did their best to make mealtime more nutritious and palatable. Peterson recalled that his unit was particularly committed to the concept as they kept a permanent presence in Australia. "The group had one man, sometimes two, at Cairnes, Queensland, buying food."

15

"THE ZERO EXPLODED JUST BEFORE HITTING THE WATER"

The chase over Oro Bay was almost finished. Martin Alger had been pursuing the high-altitude enemy reconnaissance aircraft for nearly 10 minutes. And now he was nearly in range.

He squinted through the gunsight of his P-38 once more. The unarmed Mitsubishi Ki-46, code-named Dinah, did not maneuver but continued fleeing straight ahead. Its only defense was its speed, and any sort of turn would allow the American to more easily close the gap.

But it didn't matter whether the Japanese pilot turned or not, Alger's aircraft was faster. He double-checked the range through the gunsight, then fired his guns. The recoil of the four .50 caliber machineguns and the single 20-millimeter cannon reverberated through his legs and seat. Tracers arced through the sky and into the enemy aircraft. The left engine belched smoke. Another firing pass put the right engine afire. "I then set behind him," Alger said, "and continued to fire until he blew up."

The burning Japanese aircraft tumbled toward the sea. A wing, engulfed in flames, broke free and fluttered down with the rest of the burning wreck. A partially open parachute somehow flapped clear of the flaming scraps of metal but failed to catch air. All of it crashed into the water and continued to burn atop the waves for several more minutes.[1]

★★★

Notwithstanding the successes that Kenney had achieved with the hard-used, worn-out mule of an outfit that he had turned into the increasingly potent Fifth Air Force, he was acutely aware of how grim the situation was in New Guinea during the spring of 1943—even following the tremendous Bismarck Sea victory. "The Allied Air Forces were going downhill fast," he said, "and if the replacements and reinforcements I was promised in Washington didn't start coming soon, I was going to be in a bad way."[2]

All of his aircraft had been flying almost daily, so long as the weather permitted and they were in flying condition. Aside from hard use and the creeping wear and tear exacted on them by the pervasive mud and dust and moisture, many of them had been shot up and repaired, or wrecked and repaired, multiple times. Some of the P-40s used to defend Darwin more than a year earlier were still in service. So hard-pressed was Kenney for aircraft that he—the commander of a numbered air force—personally directed that three near-derelict fighters located in Australia be made serviceable and sent up to New Guinea. That a general was involved in such minutiae bordered on absurdity. "Those three fighters were the last three left in Australia," Kenney said. "That scraped the bottom of the barrel."[3]

Michael Bauman, a B-26 bombardier, recounted an experience that highlighted how Kenney sometimes couldn't keep himself from performing the duties of a supply sergeant. Bauman was lazing under the wing of a broken B-26 at Port Moresby one day when someone shouted "Attention!" Startled, Bauman scrambled to his feet and saw Kenney sitting in a jeep.

Kenney put the men at ease and asked what parts or repairs the aircraft needed to be put back into service. "A tire and a wheel," replied Bauman. Kenney asked if Bauman and his crew could mount a tire and a wheel if he found them. "We'll get it on, don't worry about it," Bauman replied.

Kenney returned with both the tire and the wheel and would have pulled them from the jeep himself if Bauman hadn't shouted at him. "He stood there, looking at me kind of stupid like," Bauman said of Kenney. Immediately, Bauman and the rest of the crew wrestled the tire and wheel from the jeep and soon had them mounted on the aircraft.

In the meantime, the fight on the ground, the Salamaua-Lae campaign, which Kenney's men were charged with supporting, continued as a deadly, slow-motion slog. The fighting was certainly hard, but jungle conditions made it additionally hard. The Japanese ground troops, although they were on their heels and increasingly ill-equipped and poorly fed, were experts at defense and gave up ground only at great cost.

And Japanese airpower in the area was still to be feared. One of Kenney's chief worries was that a large Japanese raid might arrive undetected over one of his main bases and wipe it out. As it developed, nothing of the sort had happened up to that point, which contributed to Kenney's contempt for his enemy. "The Nip was dumb to begin with and did not understand air warfare. He did not know how to handle large masses of aircraft. He made piecemeal attacks and didn't follow them up. He had no imagination."[4]

But the Japanese did have enough imagination to attack Oro Bay several times during the previous months. Situated on the coast, only about 10 miles from Dobodura, Oro Bay was constructed by the Americans in December 1942 to handle cargo vessels. Once offloaded, the material they delivered was moved overland and used to prosecute the ground campaign. It was consequently an important transportation node, but not nearly so large or vital as Port Moresby, or the airfields at Dobodura. That the Japanese hit it so often was curious.

Curious or not, they were back at it on May 14, 1943. A Dinah reconnaissance aircraft shot down by Martin Alger at the controls of a P-38 that morning was an indicator that the Japanese might be considering another strike that day. And indeed, a couple of hundred miles to the northeast, 18 G4M Betty bombers were already winging toward Oro Bay from their base in New Ireland with an escort of 32 Zeroes from Rabaul.

The alert at Dobodura came at approximately 0940 and sent the men of the 49th Fighter Group's three squadrons, the 7th, 8th, and 9th, scrambling. Ground crews and pilots leaped from jeeps and trucks that raced from aircraft to aircraft. Pilots donned helmets and flight gear and strapped themselves into their cockpits while they started their engines. Ground crews pulled equipment and wheel chocks out of the way and shielded their eyes as P-40s and P-38s, engines roaring, whipped zephyrs of stinging grit into the air.

Moments later, the fighters raced airborne, turned for Oro Bay, and clawed for altitude. The flight leaders resisted the temptation to firewall their throttles lest they leave their wingmen behind. A short time later, a virtual dust storm in their wake, 32 P-40s and 16 P-38s disappeared on a heading to intercept the enemy raid.

The radar-equipped 49th Fighter Control Squadron, call sign "Cater," had radar contact with the enemy aircraft and did its best to quarterback the fight from the ground. It did so with mixed results. One flight of P-40s was called back overhead Dobodura where there was no threat and where none would develop. Other flights were directed to hold at specific points even though the pilots could clearly see the advancing Japanese force. Still other flights were ordered to turn to headings that took them away from the enemy. Garbled radio communications added to the confusion.

The P-40s were first to the fight. George Davis, leading a flight of four, spotted the enemy bombers near Cape Nelson on a southwesterly heading for Oro Bay. In the vanguard was a formation of escorting Zero fighters. Davis immediately signaled the other pilots in his flight to drop their external fuel tanks and then pushed the nose of his fighter over into a steep diving attack.

The first pass was botched and did virtually no damage. The P-40s climbed out of their dive and set up for a firing run from the side of the enemy formation. During that second attack Davis's element leader, Leo Mayo, put rounds into one of the bombers, which shed an aileron, started smoking, and fell into the sea. Immediately afterward, his oxygen mask came loose, and he dived away to get it clamped securely back over his face.

That done, Mayo was joined by Tom Farley, Davis's wingman. The two of them started toward a distant dogfight when Farley suddenly spotted another P-40 with a Zero in close pursuit. Farley fired his six .50 caliber machineguns. "But the Zero was apparently not hit," said Mayo, "and pulled straight up where I put a three-second burst into him. He continued up and over a loop, smoking. Pulling over the top of the loop he took a shot at me and dove straight for the sea. The Zero exploded just before hitting the water. Lieutenant Farley confirms this Zero."[5]

Dick Vodra was Mayo's original wingman, but his engine was balky, and he was left behind during the initial attack. Still, he found plenty of trouble when he was attacked by two Zero pilots. Despite his troublesome engine, he was able to dive away fast enough to keep from being shot down. "Two more Zeroes entered in the chase," Vodra said, "by using a front quarterly attack from above me." One of the enemy fighters mistakenly turned in front of Vodra and presented him with an easy tail shot. "The Zero started smoking and later burst into flames and crashed into shore a few miles south of Oro Bay," said Vodra.

A short time later, he spotted another P-40 with a Zero close behind. "After expending the remainder of my ammunition on him," Vodra said, "the Zero pulled up abruptly, snap-rolled and started to descend. Lieutenant Harrison . . . who was flying the P-40 being chased by the Zero, saw it burst into flames and crash into the water."[6]

Meanwhile, the leader of the flight, George Davis, had shot down a Betty after multiple passes despite, as he described it, "being pestered continually by a lone Zero who stayed with the bomber." There followed a protracted dogfight during which the Japanese pilot tried to disengage by heading north across the water for home. Davis followed and after some time finally caught the enemy fighter.

The Japanese pilot gained the advantage during the subsequent tussle and made several firing passes at Davis. "I snapped sharply to the right,"

Davis said, "and down to about 1,000 feet, and looked back, when he suddenly hit the water and a column of spray and black smoke arose from the water."[7]

The 49th Fighter Group's other P-40 pilots enjoyed similar successes. Larry Succop dived on a Betty that was separated from the main formation of enemy bombers. Coming from astern, he fired from relatively close range, killed the tail gunner, and blew chunks away from the rear of the aircraft. Pressing his attack, Succop set the left engine afire and came so close that he nearly collided with his quarry. And then, as he passed underneath the bomber, it exploded.

The concussion rocked Succop's aircraft and covered the canopy and windscreen with engine oil. Flying essentially blind, he made a turn back for Dobodura. His wingman shepherded him home and he landed without incident.

Elsewhere, John Griffith and his wingman made an ineffectual pass at the Bettys as they approached within 20 miles of Oro Bay. "Climbing in a right turn after recovery from the dive," he reported, "I sighted a Zero below and to my left." Griffith was alone as his wingman had gotten separated. Still, he jumped the Japanese fighter. "I dived on his tail and opened fire at good range and observed pieces flying from in front of the cockpit and black smoke."

Griffith heard and felt a clattering pulse as machinegun fire hit his P-40. He dived away from his pursuer while keeping an eye on the aircraft he had attacked. "On recovery from the dive [I] saw the Zero strike the water between Oro Bay and Cape Nelson." Although his propeller linkage was shot away, Griffith pulled up into his attacker, another Zero, and fired a burst.

The enemy pilot took issue with Griffith's failure to flee and quickly turned the tables by putting more holes into the P-40. Still, Griffith was able to dive away again and outdistanced his bothersome attacker. Back at Dobodura, he circled for half an hour as he tried to get his left main landing gear to fully extend. It refused and he was forced to make a crash landing from which he climbed uninjured, although his aircraft was damaged so badly it was written off and subsequently cannibalized for parts.[8]

Several of the Japanese bomber crews jettisoned their loads before reaching the docks and shipping at Oro Bay. Others were shot down. The few bombs that were dropped started scattered fires and hit a fuel barge and a warehouse but did no major damage.

Meanwhile, the 49th's P-38s joined the melee. "I observed fires along the docks and saw one single-seat fighter in flames in the water just offshore from Oro Bay," said Frank Nutter, part of Jesse Peaslee's six-ship flight. "I saw two other planes going down in flames out to sea."

Cater directed Peaslee away from the fighting, but with Japanese aircraft in sight, every pilot except Peaslee's wingman abandoned him and chased after the enemy. Nutter and another pilot engaged a Zero but did it poorly. Both of them fired their guns during the initial pass and missed, whereupon the enemy flyer chandelled into position directly behind Nutter. Now on the defensive, the two Americans ran away. "We firewalled [our engines] and finally succeeded in losing the Zero after indicating 400 [miles per hour]." The Japanese pilot accepted the fact that he had no chance of catching the fleeing Americans and turned around. The two P-38 pilots immediately reversed course and raced after him, but the Zero flew into a low bank of clouds and disappeared.

Nutter observed that the fighter he engaged that day wore an unusual camouflage scheme. "The Zero had yellow and black checkerboard wings with one-third of the wings on the tip ends painted green with an orange ball on the green background."[9] Such a combination was a very dramatic departure from the overall gray or green paint that was normally seen, and Nutter's report could easily have been ignored or discounted but for the fact that other pilots made similar observations. John Yancey, a P-40 flight leader, also declared that "all the Zeroes he saw were checkered, [and] with the usual red circles."[10] Donald Byars, a P-38 pilot, observed that a Zero he claimed to have shot down "had yellow and black checkerboard pattern on [the] upper surface of [the] wing."[11] And Bill Haney said, "The Zero had orange and black checkerboard pattern from one-third in from his wingtips to the fuselage. Wingtips were camouflaged green with red circles on the field of green."[12]

Certainly, combinations of light and shadow could distort appearances or present misleading impressions, as could the simple excitement of combat. Additionally, aerial engagements were dynamic and fleeting in nature with little time for detailed observations. Those considerations aside, it was unusual for four different pilots to make similar reports about such a peculiarity, and it is likely that some of the Zeroes encountered that day did wear an unusual camouflage scheme.

But not all the enemy fighters were painted unconventionally. Keith Oveson was treated to an incredibly close look at a gray-painted Zero when he almost rammed it with his P-40. "I saw the pilot clearly," he said, "and noticed that the gray paint along his fuselage was chipped, and also that the red circle was chipped, leaving only about three-fourths of the circle intact."[13]

Earnest Harris of the 49th Fighter Group's 8th Fighter Squadron made no such observations. He led his flight of four P-40s after the remaining Bettys as they shambled for home, their formation no longer intact. They were approximately 75 miles out to sea when the Americans made their first firing pass. Harris downed one of the bombers, as witnessed by a wingman who declared, "The airplane which Lieutenant Harris attacked did not burn, but merely belly-landed in the ocean."

The P-40 pilots continued their attacks and destroyed more of the Japanese bombers. Afterward, Harris and another pilot from his flight, Robert Howard, retraced their route and dropped down to investigate three separate fires burning on the sea's surface. "Two oil slicks were [also] visible where enemy aircraft had hit the water," Harris said, "and one Betty was floating in the water with four-to-six of its crew on the wing."[14] The two men left the Japanese flyers unmolested, satisfied that the evidence on the water was adequate confirmation of the six aerial victories for which the flight eventually put in claims.

The fighting that day was intense and wide-ranging, but Arthur Bauhof, a P-38 pilot with the 49th Fighter Group's 9th Fighter Squadron, was the only American loss. He was caught by a pair of Zeroes as described by the squadron's after action report.

> A Nip must have put a burst into the right engine of Lieutenant Bauhof's plane, causing it to begin smoking. Other Zekes [Zeroes] attacked him and he went on his back and dove into the water, his plane burning. Lieutenant Fanning circled the area about the fallen plane and observed Lieutenant Bauhof atop a rubber raft. Two flights of P-38s were later sent out to locate him and to direct a crash boat to his rescue. The crash boat was guided to the area where the plane went down, and Lieutenant Bauhof was nowhere to be found. He was last seen swimming about twenty miles due east of Cape Sudest. It was believed that sharks probably got him since several were observed in the vicinity of the searched area.

Bauhof had indeed been spotted by several different pilots who circled to mark his position for the boat that was sent from Oro Bay to fish him from the water. But he disappeared at some point, and subsequently could not be located. The crew of the boat did observe numerous, seemingly frenzied, sharks in the area but saw no sign of the downed flyer.[15]

The 49th later addressed Bauhof's demise in its monthly summary with a callous notation. "Saw him on rubber raft," it stated. "Couldn't find him when they looked, and presumed he was shark bait since there were sharks in the area where he splashed." The document did nothing to memorialize him, but instead abruptly changed subjects: "Telegrams of congrats to boys for this day's work."

It is quite possible—perhaps likely—that Bauhof was killed by sharks. They were numerous, and a very real danger. Noted Japanese fighter pilot Saburo Sakai recalled attacking a B-26 from the 22nd Bomb Group the previous year on May 28, 1942, only a couple of miles from the coast, near Lae. Another B-26 crew observed that the aircraft was engulfed in fire, but that the pilot made a good water landing and that some of the men had been able to climb atop the wings while the aircraft was still afloat.

After the aircraft sank, Sakai spotted four men in the water clustered around their life raft. Then one of the men thrust his hands into the air as he was pulled underwater. Sakai recalled the sickening scene:

> The others were beating fiercely at the water, and trying to get into the raft. Sharks! It seemed that there were thirty or forty of them; the fins cut the water in erratic movements all about the raft. Then the second man disappeared. I circled lower and lower, and nearly gagged as I saw the flash of teeth which closed on the arm of the third man. The lone survivor, a big, baldheaded man, was clinging to the raft with one hand and swinging wildly with a knife in the other.[16]

The last man also succumbed. Sakai later learned that the boat sent by the Japanese at Lae to retrieve the men failed to find even the smallest vestige. Nothing remained but the bloody life raft.

As it developed, the melee of Oro Bay on May 14, 1943, was one of the 49th Fighter Group's biggest days of air combat. The group's pilots claimed to have shot down 11 of the bombers and nine of their Zero escorts. They submitted detailed encounter reports, most of them with witnesses to buttress their claims.

But Japanese records indicated that although all of the Bettys sustained damage, only six were missing. And more curious, all of the Zero fighters were declared to have returned safely. The dichotomy between the claims of the 49th's pilots and what the Japanese acknowledged was astounding.

If the Japanese records were correct—which wasn't always the case—someone was not just mistaken. They were lying.

The overclaiming against the bombers is somewhat understandable. Many of the pilots from the 49th who got airborne that day took a shot at the Bettys. And many of them certainly scored hits. When a bomber went down, it might understandably be claimed by more than one pilot.

But the claims against the Zeroes are more difficult to reconcile. A review of the day's encounter reports shows that, among the men who claimed to have shot down a Japanese fighter, most made unambiguous, detailed reports. Examples, among others, include, "I put a long burst into the enemy aircraft and it fell into the sea," and, "I saw the Zero strike the water," and, "The Zero exploded just before hitting the water," and "The Zero started smoking and later burst into flames and crashed into the shore." These are declarative statements made for official reports which, taken at face value, leave no doubt that enemy fighters were destroyed.

As there was little incentive for the Japanese to misrepresent their losses in their own reports, the issue is clouded. However, there were those on the American side who had their suspicions about the claims. After review, Lieutenant Colonel Floyd Volk, the intelligence officer for V Fighter Command, strongly admonished those he felt needed it.[17]

On the other hand, the Zero pilots encountered that day made the American exaggerations seem minor. They claimed to have shot down 13 of the 49th's aircraft when in fact, Arthur Bauhof was the only man lost. In this matter of overclaiming, if nothing else, the Japanese consistently dominated the Americans.

Several of the 49th Fighter Group's pilots reported seeing the crew of one of the downed Betty bombers standing on its wings as it floated in the sea approximately a hundred miles north of Oro Bay. The pilot was Masao Yoshihara. His aircraft had been attacked multiple times by both P-40s and P-38s after it dropped its bombs. It was holed by both machinegun and cannon rounds and set afire, with one engine shot out. It actually limped along quite some distance before Yoshihara put it into the water.[18]

Once down, the crew of six, one with stomach wounds, exited and gathered atop the wings with a red, five-man life raft. Remarkably, the battered bomber stayed afloat for more than an hour before it slipped beneath the waves, leaving Yoshihara and his crew adrift. They were encouraged when, some hours later, they were circled by a Japanese bomber and a pair of fighters. It was apparent they had been spotted.

It came to nothing. Early that evening an American seaplane, probably a PBY Catalina, flew low overhead but did not appear to spot them. The following day, multiple American fighters flew low overhead several times. Yoshihara and his crew stripped and covered the red raft as best they could with their clothes. It apparently worked as they were not strafed, nor was anyone sent to retrieve them.

The crew drifted for eight days, during which time they survived on a cask of cider and rainwater as well as the occasional coconut. Yoshihara's hand was bitten by a shark on the same day that they pulled ashore on a deserted island. There was nothing and no one on the island and they put to sea again. After landing at two more islands and returning to the sea each time, they were finally pushed by wind and current to the coast of New Guinea near Buso, about 30 miles south of Salamaua, on May 24. There, they were met by natives and fed a meal of coconuts, bananas, and potatoes, and then taken to a Japanese unit.

★★★

The 22nd Bomb Group with its 50 B-26s had been one of the first operational USAAF units to fly over New Guinea, flying its first mission on April 6, 1942, against Rabaul. The B-26 was a fast and capable aircraft, but more complex and difficult to maintain as compared to the B-25. By early 1943 the 22nd, the only B-26 unit in the Fifth Air Force, was battle-worn and exhausted—unable to participate in the Bismarck Sea massacre. The group was subsequently equipped with the B-25—and later the B-24—to help streamline maintenance and support efforts. One of the 22nd's squadrons, the 19th, continued to operate the B-26 until early 1944, when the type was finally pulled from service with the Fifth Air Force.

16

"WE NEVER DID SEE THEM"

It was several hours before dawn on May 21, 1943, when Japanese Navy pilot Shigetoshi Kudo eased his twin-engine Nakajima J1N1, code-named Irving, underneath the B-17. Piloted by Paul Williams, the aircraft had been named *Honi Kuu Okole*. In Hawaiian, this translated roughly as "Kiss my ass." The bomber was part of a stream of B-17s from the 43rd Bomb Group tasked to hit the airfield at Vunakanau, near Rabaul, on the island of New Britain. Williams and his crew were less than 10 miles from their target.

A bright white moon hung high in the sky, but Kudo remained undetected. The aircraft he flew had been specially modified just for this sort of mission. Although the Irving was primarily a reconnaissance type, the particular aircraft he flew had been fitted with two 20-millimeter cannons in the fuselage behind the cockpit. However, instead of being configured to shoot straight ahead, the guns were canted at a 30-degree angle to fire forward and up. This arrangement allowed the pilot to keep his target silhouetted against the night sky and kept him clear of the turbulent wake directly behind.

Satisfied that his aim was good, Kudo fired. The muzzles of the two cannons burst brightly against the surrounding blackness. An instant later flashes peppered the B-17 as the rounds slammed into the aircraft and exploded. Kudo watched as the gunners aboard the big bomber sent streams of gunfire blindly through the night sky.[1]

The B-17's right wing caught fire. A load of incendiary bombs in the radio compartment sputtered and flared. These were meant to be tossed overboard by hand and there was now no way to get rid of them. The closest crewmen drew their arms up around their faces and recoiled from the heat. At the front of the aircraft the bombardier, Gordon Manuel, jettisoned the aircraft's primary load of 14 300-pound bombs.²

The bomber was already doomed when Kudo closed on it again and fired another burst. It tipped over toward the water, fully afire. As it fell, only two, perhaps three, of the 11 men it carried jumped clear before it hit the water and exploded in a searing blue-white flash.³

One of the wings was blown skyward. It missed Gordon Manuel by only a few feet just seconds before his parachute settled him gently into the sea alongside the flaming debris. The water crackled and hissed, and steam rose from the burning swells. Manuel surfaced, spit water, and spotted another parachute. He cursed when Kudo arced after it and fired his guns.

Manuel was lucky to have escaped, but his left leg was broken. And both were riddled with shrapnel. There was a gash on his head; he had hit some part of the B-17 when he bailed out. And he had somehow sustained a blow to his mouth as evidenced by a tooth jutting out between his lips. Moreover, he had no survival equipment other than a Mae West life preserver, a few matches, and a pistol with six rounds. He was also deep in enemy territory and five miles from land.

Only barely lucid enough to do so, he struggled toward shore, suddenly tortured by thoughts of friends back home and grief-stricken at the loss of his comrades. Several times he thought he heard sharks slashing through the water, and he once pulled his pistol—having given up and intending to end his life.

But he stopped himself and put it back in its holster. Exhausted and in shock, he resumed his shoreward thrashing, repeating prayers as he did so. During that time, although he didn't see it, another B-17 fell flaming earthward, another victim of Shigetoshi Kudo's guns.

It was daylight when Manuel finally pulled himself onto a small reef. He rested there until midday, then swam the last few hundred yards to shore. He wasn't there long when a Japanese Zero cruised by, low above the beach. Worried he might be seen, Manuel hobbled into the brush that pushed against the beach.

★★★

Gordon Manuel was still alive a few days later. During the time since his aircraft had been shot down, he had hidden in the brush behind the beach, alongside a small freshwater stream. He emerged only a few times each day to soak his wounded legs in the salt water and to forage for food. Although he had wrapped his broken left leg with a heavy vine, it still pained him mightily, and he was compelled to crawl wherever he went.

He didn't know it, but he had come ashore on New Britain near the island of Induna on the Matala plantation. Rabaul sat 25 miles to the northwest. Worse, a Japanese encampment was situated less than a mile away, near the village of Put Put. But for all he knew, he was miles from anywhere and anyone.

Manuel's food options were limited. The numerous coconuts on the ground were dry and hard and defied his efforts to crack them open. He tossed them at the fresh green coconuts that hung tantalizingly above him but was unable to knock any of them loose. Snails he brought up from the beach and ate raw were barely palatable. But wrapped in leaves and steamed over a fire he found them tasty.

On the morning of the fifth day since he had been shot down, Manuel struggled to his feet and stumped slowly inland, intent on getting a better awareness of his surroundings. The wounds on his legs were festered and painful, and the break in his left leg caused him unceasing agony. Expecting to penetrate a deep, dark jungle, he was startled when he stumbled onto a road, only 60 yards from his hiding place. He was even more startled when he spotted a pair of almost-naked native men at the edge of the road. Uncertain as to their allegiance, he raised a hand, looked directly at them, and declared loudly that he was a friend.

And that he was hungry.

★★★

The sudden cacophony of hammer-like strikes that rattled across his B-25 startled Bill Webster nearly out of his seat. Shards of glass zipped across the cockpit and blasts of wind-whipped smoke stung his eyes. The airplane shook so badly that he struggled to control it.

This was not supposed to have happened. On this morning, July 9, 1943, he was on a routine weather reconnaissance mission over the Huon Gulf. It was a cream puff sortie that still counted as a combat mission even though the enemy was rarely encountered. That was why, as the 3rd Bomb Group's 8th Bomb Squadron's operations officer, he had assigned it to himself. He had already been shot down once—at the cost of his two front teeth—and he had a newborn boy back home that he had never seen. He felt he owed himself an easy one. He had been so confident that it would be a benign nothing of a flight that he had allowed the group's weather officer, Frances Murphy, to ride along.

Webster looked to his left and saw a Ki-43 trailing his aircraft only 50 or 100 feet away. Robert Widener, his copilot, reported another to the right. The top turret gunner wasn't firing at the Japanese fighters because he was dead—shot to death. "We never did see them," Webster said. "All of a sudden there were seven of them. And after the turret was knocked out, they were virtually flying formation, really, literally. They were so close I could see the pilots, you know, see their heads in the cockpit."

The right engine, afire, vibrated badly. Webster feathered the propeller and shut the engine down. At the same time, he pushed the nose of the aircraft down and tried to maneuver away from the peppering machinegun fire that the enemy fighters sent after him. The B-25, still burning, descended in a right-hand spiral through a deck of clouds with the enemy fighters following them down. A moment later the right landing gear dropped from its nacelle under the engine and into the windstream. The lock holding it in place had melted.

The aircraft's diving turn steepened almost into a rolling dive. "By this time," Webster said, "they had stopped firing at us because, hell, we were going in."

Webster and Widener struggled to pull the aircraft out of its dive and to put it down—under control—into the water. Webster pulled down the escape hatch, which was positioned directly above his head, and struggled out of his parachute harness and lap belt. At the same time, he pressed down hard on the left rudder, rolled the control yoke in the same direction and pulled back on it with all his might.

Remarkably, the B-25 responded to Webster's control inputs and came out of the spiral just a few feet above the water. An instant later, it shed the right wing and smashed into the waves. Just overhead, the Japanese fighter pilots roared through the flying debris that had been part of Webster's B-25.

Webster was violently ejected through the escape hatch, and he tumbled a considerable distance through the sky before smashing into the water. His right side was badly scraped, and his uniform shredded. His Mae West, shot through by a machinegun bullet, was ruined. At the edge of consciousness, he righted himself and sputtered to the surface, spitting out seawater and blood.

Frances Murphy looked up through the water from where he lay in the quickly sinking bomber. The light that reached him through the rectangular shape of the escape hatch was fading quickly, just as was his awareness. Although he couldn't see them, and likely did not have the mental capacity to care, other members of the crew were struggling to the surface that very moment.

Above Murphy, Bill Webster saw his radio operator, Lawrence Allport, break the surface. Copilot Robert Widener did the same a few seconds later. And then, after half a minute, Frances Murphy, who had been aboard the aircraft as a simple observer on what was to be an uneventful sortie, floated unconscious to the surface. The body of the top turret gunner, Alfredo Davis, was trapped in the bomber.

The Japanese fighters made several passes over the point where Webster's B-25 had hit the water, but there was little that remained on the surface other than the four men—Webster, Widener, Allport, and Murphy—and the tire from the right main landing gear. Whether the enemy pilots failed to fire on the surviving men was because they didn't see them, or because they simply didn't want to is unknown.

The four men came together, having no raft and no specific idea of where they were. Webster recalled a technique he had learned from the Boy Scouts. He shed his boots and kicked vigorously to propel his head and shoulders out of the water at the very crest of a wave. During that brief instant he spotted a small spire of rock jutting from the water. He subsequently rallied his comrades and paddled toward it.

Murphy was only barely conscious, and Webster and Widener took turns towing him. It was only an hour or so before Webster struck something solid with his hand as they neared the islet. It was a coral reef—one of several that the group dragged themselves across before crawling onto a small beach situated in a cove. The rest of the islet—Musik Island—was a sharp, jagged rock that plunged steeply into the water. Vines and stunted trees clung to the little carbuncle of land wherever they could find purchase.

Murphy was the most badly injured of the four men, and he retched alarming quantities of water and blood. Webster worried that he might have sustained a punctured lung, or worse. Aside from alarming Webster, the noise of the injured man's suffering also became tiresome after several hours. Happily, another sound reached the stranded group. "I suddenly heard a new noise, a faint voice," said Webster. "Nobody in our foursome was talking, yet I could swear I heard a human voice like a native laughing. It grew louder along with splashing sounds."

An outrigger canoe paddled by three natives and another man rounded a point and slid into the tiny cove. The four Americans spent a few apprehensive moments until they confirmed that the little craft carried no Japanese. Webster had feared the cliché of a fully uniformed Japanese officer complete with boots, a samurai sword, and a stateside education. "But it turned out to be an Australian coastwatcher named Sergeant Pomeroy," he said.

Pomeroy operated from a hidden outpost south of Salamaua and reported on Japanese air and naval activity. It had been a busy time as the

Allies were advancing on the Japanese bases at Lae and Salamaua. Just a few days earlier, the Americans had made an amphibious landing at Nassau Bay, not too far from where Webster and his crew had gone into the water.

But Pomeroy had watched helplessly as the Japanese fighters hacked the B-25 out of the sky and into the sea. The crash was so violent that Pomeroy didn't believe there could have been any survivors. Nevertheless, on the slim chance that there might be someone yet alive, he darkened his skin so as not to arouse suspicion if he were spotted by the Japanese. Then, with his Papuan friends, he put to sea at great risk.

It was a short trip of only three or four miles. Webster and his comrades had no idea they were so close to the mainland as it sat out of sight on the other side of the rocky little island upon which they had pulled themselves. The Americans were jubilant with relief when they realized that Pomeroy was an Australian and not a Japanese soldier. After a brief celebration, Pomeroy brought the four flyers aboard the canoe, leaving two of the natives behind. Precariously balanced on the little craft, the men pushed away from the island and paddled toward the main island of New Guinea.

The small group sailed without encountering any trouble. "About an hour later we got near land," said Webster, "and Sergeant Pomeroy was able to signal a nearby LCI to take us off his hands." The LCI, Landing Craft Infantry, was involved in the amphibious operation at nearby Nassau Bay, and its crew pulled Webster and his companions aboard. Webster, grateful at his rescue, handed his silver pilot's wings and captain's bars to Pomeroy. Pomeroy's native helpers were excited and gratified to receive fishhooks, chewing tobacco, and a small handful of Australian coins. Webster and his men—including Frances Murphy, who survived despite his injuries—were just a few more ticks on the ledger that carried the names of so many Allied flyers saved by the coastwatchers and their Papuan friends.

The LCI put the rescued crew ashore at Nassau Bay a short time later. Webster was essentially uninjured except for coral cuts on his feet—he had shucked his boots during his swim to Musik Island. A medic examined him and called out to a coworker who was busy cataloging bodies. The man found a pair of boots that were Webster's size, 11C, and pulled them from their deceased owner. They fit perfectly, and Webster wore them until the end of his combat tour four months later.[4]

17

"SELL THE P-47 OR GO BACK HOME"

The first Republic P-47 Thunderbolts, together with the men of the 348th Fighter Group, reached Australia on June 20, 1943. They had been promised by Hap Arnold to Kenney when the latter had traveled back to Washington, D.C., a few months earlier. Although he would have rather had P-38s, Kenney was happy enough to receive the P-47s, especially as they arrived with the fully trained men of the 348th.

The P-47 was a huge and massively powerful fighter. Empty, it weighed in at 10,000 pounds as compared to the P-39 at 6,500 pounds, and the even lighter Mitsubishi Zero at 6,100 pounds. Powered by the Pratt & Whitney R-2800 radial engine, its top airspeed exceeded 400 miles per hour, and it had a service ceiling above 40,000 feet. It was heavily armored and carried a total of eight .50 caliber machineguns. On paper, the Japanese had nothing to match it.

The P-47 had only entered combat a few months earlier in Europe and its performance to that point had been unremarkable as, like most new fighters, it experienced teething issues. Virtually everyone in the Fifth Air Force, excepting Kenney, the 348th's men, and the 348th's commander, Neel Kearby, looked down their noses at the big tubby aircraft that was known as the "Jug." "Besides not having enough gas," Kenney said, "the rumors said it took too much runway to get off, it had no maneuverability, it would not pull out of a dive, the landing gear was weak, and the engine was unreliable."

Kenney knew better. Within a few days he arranged a mock dogfight between Neel Kearby in a P-47 against George Prentice, the commanding officer of the still-forming 475th Fighter Group, in a P-38. Although he was confident in the P-47, Kenney padded the odds against the P-38 as he knew that Prentice would be attending a celebration the night prior and would likely be flying with a hangover. "I sent for Kearby," Kenney said, "and told him I expected him to sell the P-47 or go back home."

It worked just as Kenney had hoped.

> Prentice was surprised at the handling qualities of the P-47 against his P-38 and admitted that Kearby "shot him down in flames" a half dozen times. He still preferred his P-38 but began warning everyone not to sell the P-47 short. At the same time, he wanted to go to bed early that night and "have another combat with Neel tomorrow." I interfered at this point and said I didn't want any more of this challenge foolishness by them or anyone else and for both of them to quit that stuff and tend to their jobs.[1]

Kenney was a smart leader and not above the use of guile to get what he wanted.

★★★

A constant theme of air operations over New Guinea—indeed, over every theater of the war—was that nearly as many aircraft were lost to mechanical failures and accidents as were downed by the enemy in direct combat. That fact was underscored on July 13, 1943, when the 49th Fighter Group's 9th Fighter Squadron scrambled 14 P-38s to intercept a Japanese raid over Salamaua.

Francis Love flew one of those aircraft. It started to develop engine trouble as the formation turned over the coast looking unsuccessfully for the enemy aircraft. But Love wasn't the only pilot with engine issues. The squadron had been struggling mightily with engine maintenance during that period, and five pilots had already aborted the mission.

Love made six. The squadron reported that "a pilot observed a P-38 making a 150-degree turn to the right and head out to sea." Not soon after leaving the formation, Love decided to do a bit of freelancing on his own after spotting another aircraft low over the water. "I went down to investigate," he said.

Despite his engine trouble, Love rolled over in a steep dive and started after the unidentified aircraft. After having spent time at altitude, his windscreen was cold. The humid air warmed as he reached lower altitude, and condensation quickly covered his windscreen.

Love couldn't see. He pulled back on the control yoke, but too late. His P-38 smacked the water and, incredibly bounced back airborne. "Both engines were on fire," he said, "and I hauled back on the stick and the plane came back up out of the water." Love climbed the burning fighter up to about 500 feet and jumped clear.

"I couldn't get my little rubber boat out as I left in such a hurry," he said. "I did have my Mae West on, though, so it kept me afloat.

"The searching planes and boats couldn't locate me," Love said. "I saw sharks twice, once within ten feet of me. I wasn't cut or bleeding anywhere, so they didn't bother me. I guess the Good Lord was with me."

Love had gone down in the water only about four miles from shore at roughly 10 a.m. But tide and currents kept him from reaching land until the same time the next day. Exhausted, he crawled into the jungle and slept until late afternoon. Once he woke up, he made his way back to the beach where he met friendly natives. As was so often the case when the natives encountered downed Allied flyers, they looked after Love, giving him food and water, and even finding him a pair of boots to replace those he had kicked off as he swam for shore.

There followed several days of trekking along the coast. But swamps and rivers barred the way, and the natives were reluctant to move Love by boat. After returning to almost the same point at which he came ashore—worse for the wear—Love spotted an aircraft flying low above the beach. It was squadron mate William Bleeker. Love signaled vigorously and caught Bleeker's attention. Once he returned to base, the 9th sent an L-4, essentially a militarized Piper Cub, to retrieve their lost comrade.

Love was obviously delighted to be returned to the squadron but was also extremely grateful for the care and kindness with which the natives had treated him. "Two of them stayed with me all of the time," he said. "We gave them a handful of shillings, some cigarettes, matches and some tea. They were very pleased over this. I still have a grass mat that one of them made for me to sleep on."[2]

On July 14, 1943, the day after Love went down into the water, and at about the same time that he struggled ashore, another 49th Fighter Group pilot was shot down in the same area. Donald Lee, a P-40 pilot with the 7th Fighter Squadron was sent with 14 others to escort a formation of C-47s. The mission was uneventful until the P-40s were directed to intercept a flight of enemy aircraft that developed to be a scattered group of five or six Aichi 99 dive bombers, which carried the code name of Val.

The older, slower, and heavier Val was typically "easy pickings" as compared to the Zeroes and Oscars with which the 7th's pilots typically tangled. Lee dived on one of the enemy dive bombers and opened fire. It was an unfair fight as his six .50 caliber machineguns were far more powerful and delivered massively overwhelming volumes of fire as compared to the single, small-caliber machinegun of the Val's rear gunner.

But the Val's rear gunner won. There was a banging rattle when machinegun rounds slammed into Lee's aircraft, and it took only a moment or two for him to realize that the coolant system had been shot up. The P-40's engine quickly overheated, and Lee turned toward Lasanga Island.

He didn't make it and was forced to bail out as the aircraft descended through 1,000 feet. He broke his arm as he did so, and when he came down in the water, he was lucky to shed his parachute before it dragged him down and drowned him. However, he wasn't able to inflate his life raft.

Lee's squadron mates circled his position as he flailed and wrestled with the life raft. "Several others were thrown to him by other pilots," noted the unit narrative. Robert DeHaven was one of those other pilots. "I got the life raft out from underneath me and put it in the crook of my arm and cranked the canopy back and held onto the lanyard," he said. "And then I put the flaps down and flew across him and tried to shove it over the side to drop it down to him." As DeHaven released the raft, the white powder in which it was packed enveloped him in the cockpit, cutting off his vision for a few desperate seconds. "I had sunglasses on," DeHaven said, "but I didn't know what had happened for a moment and I just about joined him in the drink!"[3]

DeHaven's raft and those of the others splashed down too far away and Lee was unable to reach them. And it got worse. "Two schools of sharks formed a semi-circle around Lieutenant Lee," said the narrative. DeHaven confirmed it. "We covered him as long as we could," he said. "While we were there and watching the sharks around him, we'd let them get in so close then we'd get on a strafe and we'd kill one and the rest of them would take off for the one that we had hit. A lot of blood in the water."

Lee's squadron mates started for home as they ran critically low on gas. However, Lucius LaCroix stayed with Lee long enough for a flight of A-20s to relieve him. The A-20 pilots orbited overhead, marking his position until a crash boat arrived and hauled him from the water.

18

"MAKING FOOL OF THE JAP MAN"

The four airfields in the Wewak area—Dagua, But, Boram, and Wewak itself—constituted a lesser analog to the near-impregnable air bastion at Rabaul. Chopped out of the jungle—much of it by hand—it was not as well-developed as Rabaul, nor did it have port facilities on the same scale. Still, it was a powerful air stronghold even though the Japanese had come ashore there only in December 1942. The Japanese Fourth Air Army, once completely in place and equipped, would be able to launch strikes from Wewak that might very well stymie the Allies as they hop-scotched westward.

It had to be neutralized.

Fortunately, by mid-August 1943, Kenney's Fifth Air Force had a plan, as well as the men and the aircraft, for doing just that. Before then, his meager force of bombers could reach Wewak, but his fighters—even the P-38—could not. And without fighter protection, the losses to Japanese interceptors would be crippling. Certainly, as they had done before, his crews could bomb Wewak at night when the threat from Japanese fighters was greatly lessened, but they couldn't do it as accurately as they could during the day. The number of raids to inflict the damage required, if it could be achieved at all, would cost too many aircraft, too many lives, and take too much time. Somehow, a means to give the bombers the fighter protection they needed had to be found.

An obvious solution was to base the fighters forward, closer to the target. This was actually a notion with which the Americans had wrestled for months as they prosecuted their air campaigns against Lae and Salamaua and other Japanese bases. Operating out of the airfield complexes at Dobodura and Port Moresby, the Fifth Air Force's fighters were able to spend very little time over the most distant targets. And if their rendezvous with the bombers was delayed, or botched by weather or incompetence or bad luck, the fighters didn't have enough fuel to make things right by waiting, or catching up, or by making their way around thunderstorms or through layers of clouds. A forward base could mitigate these issues.

But identifying where to put such an airfield had proved thorny. As big as the island was, New Guinea's harsh geography—its mountains and valleys and swamps and jungles—was not well-suited for hosting extensive airfield complexes. And the fact that the Japanese had a say in the matter made things additionally problematic.

"We had surveyed Kokoda, Wau, Dona, and a dozen other places, but none were suitable,"[1] Kenney said. Finally, in May 1943, an Australian patrol was favorably impressed by the Watut Valley as a potential site for air operations. Shortly afterward, with a handful of Americans in tow, they hacked their way across the inhospitable terrain until they reached a site near the village of Marilinan, about 40 miles west of Lae. In fact, they hadn't been the first to recognize its suitability as they discovered a short, overgrown airstrip that had once been used by miners.

The scouting party induced local natives to chop the runway clear of the tall Kunai grass. Additional reconnoitering—by air this time—confirmed that the Marilinan site could be enlarged and improved. However, the area just a few miles north, near Tsili Tsili, was recognized as superior, and the decision was made to develop it as the main airbase with two large intersecting runways connected by taxiways leading to dispersal areas and hardstands. There was adequate space to bivouac the ground troops needed to protect it, and for the maintainers, logisticians, and other personnel that would be necessary to make it operational.

Such an airfield would take time and resources to build. And it would make a juicy target within easy range of Japanese bases, especially the Fourth Air Army units at Wewak. But combat attributes and fighting spirit aside, this was the sort of logistical and engineering undertaking at which the Americans excelled, and it was a capability which the Japanese could not match.

Work at Marilinan—about 200 miles from Port Moresby—began immediately when troops of the 871st Airborne Engineer Aviation Battalion and its equipment were brought in by C-47s escorted by fighters. Trucks were cut in half, loaded aboard the aircraft, and then welded back together upon reaching the destination. The same was true of other heavy equipment—small tractors and graders and other engineering kit. By June 20, 1943, a rudimentary road had been built from Marilinan to the Tsili Tsili site, and round-the-clock work also began there. It wasn't long before aircraft began using the newly built runways.

Loading and unloading the C-47s as quickly and efficiently as possible was critical to the success of the effort. Doing so was not only key to increased sortie rates, but also necessary to keep them safe. After the C-47s touched down at Tsili Tsili, their fighter escorts orbited overhead to defend them against Japanese air attacks. If it took too long to get the cargo unloaded, the fighters, low on fuel, were compelled to return to base and leave the C-47s unprotected.

Mundane training at seemingly ordinary tasks made all the difference. A salvaged C-47 wreck was dragged into place at Port Moresby to establish and refine loading methodologies. "At first," Kenney said, "it took forty minutes to load a jeep . . . and about the same time to unload it. After a few days of practice, the time was reduced to two-and-a-half minutes to load it and two minutes for the unloading procedure. The trucks bringing supplies from the warehouses to the airplanes were loaded in reverse, so that cargo fed automatically and kept the balance in the plane correct."[2] Very soon, the unheralded air freight crews at Tsili Tsili were so effective that the C-47s could land, unload, and take off again at a rate exceeding 30 aircraft each hour. By the middle of July, the airfield at Tsili Tsili was handling more than a hundred C-47 sorties each day.

Remarkably, especially since their ground units regularly patrolled the area, the construction work at Marilinan and Tsili Tsili went unnoticed by the Japanese. Or, if it was noticed, it was not considered worthy of attention. Regardless, the work continued at breakneck speed entirely unbothered by the Japanese.

This was due in part to a bit of subterfuge undertaken by Kenney and his staff. Kenney ordered his officers to "send someone to Garoka and get the natives to start clearing a strip right away. I didn't care about making anything more than a good emergency field, but I wanted a lot of dust raised and construction started on a lot of grass huts so that the Japs' recco [reconnaissance] planes would notice."[3] In truth, the rudimentary fields served as more than emergency strips and decoys; they were also used to fly in supplies for nearby Australian ground units.

Regardless, Kenney was most interested in using the primitive airstrips to keep the Japanese distracted. And to the natives who were doing most of the work, he wanted it made plain "that we were playing a good joke on the Japs, that we were trying to get them to send some bombers over."

The decoy work at Garoka and nearby Bena Bena paid off. The Japanese bombed them several times, using resources they could ill afford to waste. Kenney received reports that the Papuans delighted in being part of the scheme and that during an attack, "they would roll around on the ground with laughter and chatter away about how we were 'making fool of the Jap man.'"[4] Meanwhile, the work at Tsili Tsili progressed so well that the Fifth started to move combat units into place.

This creation of an operational airfield out of nothing but wilderness—and in such a short time—is all the more remarkable when it is considered that everything necessary to do so was flown in. This included the equipment, the material, and the people. Stockpiles of fuel and other supplies grew until they were adequate to meet Kenney's plans.

The task of simply getting stuff clear of the aircraft and to where it needed to go was exhausting, especially in the heat and mud and dust. The bomber and fighter crews might have received the lion's share of the glory during the air campaign over New Guinea, but that glory was made possible by the largely unrecognized cargo haulers, the C-47s, and the men who operated and serviced them. And not to be forgotten were the men who managed the cargoes they carried. Moreover, it should be considered that, in reality, this movement was really the last leg of a logistics chain that began on the other side of the globe, in the United States. No other nation possessed the wherewithal to equal what the Americans were doing.

★★★

To most of the Fifth Air Force's flyers, the work at Tsili Tsili during mid-1943 was simply background noise. Or they knew nothing about it whatsoever. Indeed, they continued to train and to fight. And that training and fighting continued to be deadly.

For instance, on July 27, 1943, the 38th Bomb Group's 71st squadron sent crews to a nearby reef to practice skip bombing. Among them was the crew of Ercoli Ducci, one of the squadron's old hands, and a popular officer. Something went awry during one of Ducci's practice runs when the bomb bounced high off the water and smashed into his B-25. The bomber's horizontal stabilizer was torn away, and the aircraft slammed into the water. The entire crew was killed.

A boat recovered three bodies that same day, and the bodies were interred during a memorial service at the airfield the following day. Such an event was rare as bodies were so infrequently recovered. A boat with two squadron members returned to the crash site the following day, and tragedy struck again when the boat exploded. A life raft was dropped to the men, who managed to get aboard and paddle to a small island. "This island is used for a target for bombing practice and strafing," noted the squadron diary that same day. "And a flight of B-17s, not knowing the men were there, dropped bombs which landed only twenty feet from Sgt. Malachick. Both Lieutenant Peters and Sergeant Malachick will probably be in the hospital for quite some time."

Peters and Malachick were able to go to a hospital because the standard of medical care had grown alongside the Fifth Air Force's ability to fight. Not only was more and better equipment brought in, but more care facilities were created, and more medical staff arrived. And very importantly, improvements to general health and hygiene practices were implemented down to the unit level as reported by the 35th Fighter Group's medical cadre:

> The sanitary conditions in and about each camp area were good. Each kitchen was covered, screened, and the floor cemented. Liquid garbage was disposed of through grease traps and soakage pits. Latrine tops were scrubbed daily either with soap or a weak creosol solution. They were frequently burned out. All drainage ditches throughout the areas were treated with an oil solution, two times weekly, for mosquito control, and efforts were made to keep the high grass cut throughout the different camp areas.

These practices and others helped to maintain the health of the men, but no one escaped New Guinea without getting sick. Malaria—spread by mosquitoes—was the greatest threat. The men slept with mosquito netting and were required to take daily doses of Atabrine—a synthetic antimalarial—to fight the disease. It was effective, but it turned the skin of the men yellow. Dengue fever was another mosquito-borne disease, viral in nature and less harmful. Dysentery was usually caused by poor food hygiene and, among other symptoms, emptied men's bowels, often to the point that they were incapable of working. Scrub typhus was particularly deadly. It was passed by mites, and treatments for it were rudimentary and largely ineffective.

One pilot remembered those mites, or chiggers as they were also known. "The one thing that bothered us the most were chiggers. And I still bear scars on both my ankles from scratching these silly things. We always wore Aussie flying boots. They were very comfortable, and they were excellent for flying. And the chiggers would get down in that fleece lining. Drive you crazy."

The pesticide DDT was used liberally and effectively to kill the various critters that acted as disease vectors. Although much maligned in later years for its negative environmental effects, it undoubtedly saved many lives in the Pacific during World War II. Aircraft and ground vehicles were modified to spray encampments with it, and men were often inadvertently doused with clouds of the stuff.

A host of fungal infections and skin rashes—lumped together as "jungle rot"—were ubiquitous, and together with diarrhea, afflicted virtually everyone at one time or another. Or even all the time. Additionally, lacerations, abrasions, and other wounds, if not immediately treated, typically became infected.

Ultimately, the Allies were able to keep their men healthy enough to fight. Although it was common for men to work or to fly while they were not fully healthy, the ratio of medical casualties to combat casualties— always high—steadily declined as time went on. It was a credit not only to more and better material and equipment, but to the men who did the daily and oftentimes dull work that was necessary to keep New Guinea's seemingly numberless diseases at bay. "They also served" who scrubbed latrines, mowed drainage ditches, and daubed standing water with motor oil.

★★★

On August 11, 1943, a Japanese reconnaissance aircraft finally discovered the true extent of what the Americans had done at Tsili Tsili. Curiously, the reaction was not immediate, and it wasn't until August 15, after another reconnaissance flight, that a raid of seven Ki-48 Lilly bombers, escorted by more than 30 Ki-43 Oscar fighters, was dispatched to attack the essentially completed airfield. The newly operational radar unit at Tsili Tsili failed to detect the enemy force, and surprise was nearly complete. Men squinted skyward at the sound of the Japanese aircraft. Their sudden realization that the enemy was overhead and preparing to kill them was accompanied by splashes of adrenaline that fueled their sprint for cover.

But the men aboard the 12 C-47s of the 374th Troop Carrier Group that were in the process of landing could not seek cover. The timing could not have been worse. The transports, just as they had during the previous several weeks, were on another presumably routine mission to deliver more personnel and material; half of them were safely on the ground when the enemy raid began. But the remaining aircraft were now targets—unexpected prey—for the Japanese fighter pilots.

An escort of a dozen P-39s from the 35th Fighter Group's 40th and 41st squadrons was the only protection the C-47s had. Until that day, the 35th's pilots considered these sorts of missions tedious; rarely did they offer any sort of action. Now, they found themselves in a fight not only for their own lives but also for those of the men in the transports and their comrades on the ground.

In fact, elements of the 35th were in the middle of a move to Tsili Tsili aboard those same C-47s. The unit's diary noted that "the headquarters squadron personnel who were in those transports that day will long remember it—the cold fear of being in an unarmed transport under attack by enemy fighters—and the thrill of seeing one of their own squadrons come in to save the day."

But not everyone's day was saved. The 35th's dental officer, Robert Heller, and his assistant, Virgil Dockery, were aboard one of the C-47s. "When a Japanese fighter made an initial attack on the transport," noted the group's diary, "Corporal Dockery was seriously wounded in the shoulder. The plane burst into flames and the occupants rushed forward when the pilot said he would crash-land between the trees." But the pilot, Enoch Burley, never got the chance as he was killed when enemy fighters made another pass. The burning plane fell to the ground and exploded. Incredibly, Heller was blown clear of the fiery crash and survived.

The battle devolved into a free-wheeling aerial bloodbath. The considerably outnumbered P-39 pilots, whose job at the start of the day was to protect the C-47s, chased after the Japanese bombers. The bombers were not only easier targets but were attacking the airfield. The Japanese fighter pilots—whose mandate was to guard those bombers—attacked the fleeing C-47s which the P-39 pilots were supposed to protect.

The enemy bomber crews arced around Tsili Tsili and readied to release their bombs while the P-39s climbed desperately after them. The two aircraft were contemporaries as the Japanese aircraft entered service in 1940 and the American fighter became operational only a year later. The P-39 might not have been equal in every respect to the Zero, but its original purpose was to intercept and knock down bombers. On this day its performance was nearly textbook.

Once they closed the distance to a few hundred yards the Americans started shooting. The gunners aboard the Ki-48s returned fire, but the bombers did not waver in their formation except to tumble from the sky flaming, many of them before releasing their bombs.

The P-39 pilots pressed their attacks and the Japanese bombers continued to fall, but not without exacting a toll. Frank Topolcany shot up one of the Ki-48s and followed it earthward. Either he was hit and killed by a gunner aboard one of the bombers or his fighter became unflyable, or he simply lost situational awareness. Regardless, he smashed into the ground at high speed only an instant after his quarry and less than a hundred yards away.

Topolcany was not the only 35th fighter pilot to go down that day. The Japanese Oscars started the fight with an altitude advantage and outnumbered the P-39 pilots nearly three to one. And they climbed and turned better. The thousands of men on the airfield might have been excited at the sight of the bombers being so readily handled by their own side, but that excitement was tempered by the fact that, aside from Topolcany's fiery death, two more P-39 pilots were forced to take to their parachutes, and another crash-landed. All three men survived, although one foundered about in the jungle for nearly a week before being rescued. Two of the Oscars were shot down.

Elsewhere on the airfield, Chaplain Keith Munro led a worship service. The din of battle reverberated across the airfield, and he rushed to get his flock to safety. It was for nothing. One of the burning Japanese bombers smashed into the chapel and exploded in a spectacular fireball. Munro—who had a 10-week-old daughter he had never seen—and five other worshippers were killed. A few weeks later Munro was memorialized in his hometown newspaper as having perished "with God's word on his lips in the explosive crash of a bomb-laden Japanese bomber in the New Guinea jungle."[5]

Meanwhile, those C-47s still airborne scattered to escape the fighting. Stuffed with cargo and personnel, they raced as fast as they were able, their pilots hugging the hills and skimming the trees and writhing unpredictably to make themselves difficult targets. The aircraft captained by Charles Cathcart was one of those which was carrying men from the 35th Fighter Group. It was last spotted as it disappeared over the horizon with Japanese fighters in close pursuit. Eventually knocked down into the smothering jungle, its wreckage and the bodies of Cathcart and the other men remained undiscovered, despite an intensive search, until 1950.

Robert Heller, the dentist who had been thrown clear of Enoch Burley's C-47 when it was shot down, was found after the day's fighting. He was the only man from the aircraft still living. Flown back to Port Moresby, he was hurried to the hospital but died shortly afterward.

As it developed, the Japanese lost six of the seven bombers it sent against Tsili Tsili that day, and the raid was an unqualified failure. Aside from Chaplain Munro and the handful of men killed in the chapel, six more men were killed elsewhere on the airfield, and two C-47s were also destroyed on the ground. But there was no damage that impeded activities in the slightest, and work continued apace. Tsili Tsili was fully able to meet the mission for which it was created—supporting operations against Wewak and other Japanese bases.

The Japanese tried to change that fact the very next day, August 16. They launched a raid that included, once more, seven Ki-48s and more than two dozen Oscars. A C-47 mission of 24 aircraft had already landed by the time the Japanese arrived. The enemy aircraft ran into a buzzsaw in the form of 15 P-38s of the 475th Fighter Group and 32 P-47s of the 348th Fighter Group. It was the P-47's combat debut in the Southwest Pacific.

Contrasted with the previous day, it was the Japanese who were outnumbered, and they paid dearly. The attack was entirely ineffective, and the Americans—including three P-47 pilots—put in claims for a total of 15 enemy aircraft destroyed. Leonard Leighton was the first Thunderbolt pilot to score. Alone, he chased after a Japanese fighter and sent it down flaming with his massive fighter's eight .50 caliber machineguns. But he also became the first P-47 pilot to be lost over New Guinea. Almost immediately, he was jumped from behind and likewise crashed into the ground, dead. He had struck off on his own, and his death was subsequently used as a learning point as described by the 348th's unit diary: "From this unfortunate loss, the all-essential lesson of staying in at least a two-ship element was impressed upon the pilots of the group." Leighton was the day's only American casualty.

★★★

At about the same time that the P-47 was entering service with the Fifth Air Force, the B-17 was leaving. Having provided outstanding service with the 19th and 43rd Bomb Groups, it was replaced by the longer-legged, albeit less-lovely B-24. The B-24 extended the reach of Kenney's air force, and the transition to a single type streamlined maintenance and support efforts. Except for a few aircraft used for special transport and other utility duties, the B-17 was removed from combat operations in the Fifth Air Force by the end of 1943.

★★★

At the same time, Kenney's fighter forces were buttressed in August 1943 when the P-38-equipped 475th Fighter Group was declared ready for combat operations. Even before he left the States in 1942, Kenney had badgered Hap Arnold for as many P-38s as possible. It had paid off, and he had three squadrons flying combat by early 1943. They had proved their worth ever since, and Kenney never ceased campaigning for more.

He struck a deal of sorts with Arnold that led to the creation of the 475th Fighter Group. Arnold allocated him 75 of the aircraft, but Kenney was responsible for finding the men to fly and maintain them, as Arnold didn't have enough to spare. Consequently, Kenney mandated that his existing fighter squadrons—regardless of whether or not they flew

P-38s—were to give up men to staff the 475th. He emphasized that those men were to be proven performers rather than green newcomers or men the squadrons were anxious to be rid of.

The order struck a nerve, and although it was obeyed, it did little to endear the 475th to the rest of Fifth Air Force. The new fighter group was officially brought into existence in May 1943 and was flying combat by August. The 475th—made up of established combat veterans—went on to become one of the most successful fighter units of the war.

19

"MY GOD, WHAT A SIGHT!"

Searchlights tracked the B-24s as they passed through the night sky, one by one, and dropped their bombs on the airfield complex. A broken layer of clouds reflected the light in all directions and a thin, eerie white glare shone back toward the ground. Bright flashes of antiaircraft fire pocked that glare, and the crews blinked reflexively as each explosion bounced brief, blinding bursts of light into the cockpits of the big bombers. One of the men wrote how "one position poured up intense continuous fire which looked like a giant Roman candle shooting up golden rain."[1] Illumination flares, exploding bombs, and raging fires further corrupted the darkness.

The crews were compelled to maintain stable flight on a steady course to ensure their bombs were delivered accurately. So, rather than maneuvering to escape the enemy fire, they motored resolutely through it. Inside, hunched over their equipment during the final few seconds before releasing their bombs, the bombardiers struggled to see the target through the chaotically illumined murk that was the sky above Wewak in the early morning hours of August 17, 1943.

Yanks from Hell, a B-24 from the 90th Bomb Group piloted by Joseph Casale, was hit and caught fire immediately. "I saw Joe Casale go down," said squadron mate Dustin Swanson. "He started his bomb run in front of me and they received a direct hit. He went down in flames. It was not easy, going in for our run, after that." *Yanks from Hell*, ablaze and with 11 men trapped inside, tumbled into the jungle and exploded.[2]

★★★

The Fifth Air Force often had immediate requirements to enhance the performance of its aircraft that simply could not be met in time by the formal engineering processes used back in the United States. Kenney gave his own engineering, maintenance, and support personnel great latitude to experiment and develop ad hoc solutions in the field. One of the contrivances that resulted from these activities was an expendable fuel tank for the B-25.

It was little more than a sheet metal cube—and associated plumbing—which fit into the same space as the disused bottom turret. It sat on an aluminum frame and was designed to be jettisoned once the fuel it carried was used. Doing so was an imperative as it was not self-sealing; if it was hit by enemy fire the aircraft would quickly become a flying torch. Even empty, residual fuel and fumes gave it the characteristics of a vapor bomb. Moreover, the top gun turret could not be rotated with the tank in place.

Testing of the new tanks was complete during the first half of August 1943, just in time for the Fifth's upcoming campaign against Wewak. The B-25 already had enough range to make the flight from the Port Moresby area to Wewak, but the new auxiliary tanks gave it enough fuel to deal with contingencies such as rerouting to avoid bad weather or running at especially high engine settings if forced to flee enemy fighters.

★★★

The men rubbed their eyes and yawned in the early hours of August 17, 1943, as they stepped from the predawn darkness into the briefing tent. Their clothes, a mix of mostly uniform items—some of them threadbare—hung limp on their bodies in the sticky-hot, unstirring air. The muted hum and buzz and chirp of nighttime jungle creatures washed across the compound. It was occasionally interrupted by a shriek or howl, the cause of which the men could only guess at.

These were the B-25 crews of the 38th Bomb Group's 405th Bomb Squadron. The hour was earlier than typical, and they knew that the day's mission must be a big one. Still, most of them were surprised, and troubled in various degrees, by the announcement they were headed to Wewak. It had loomed ever larger in their minds—a formidable bogeyman—as the Japanese built it up during the previous several months into a giant base from which they intended to stop the Allied advance west across New Guinea.

Although they didn't know it, a mixed force of 38 B-24s and 12 B-17s were returning from Wewak that very moment. That night attack, at the cost of three B-24s, had cratered runways, destroyed aircraft and material, and killed men. As the bombers completed their attack, an observer described the scene, "with flames leaping from many fires, heavy ack-ack [antiaircraft fire] stabbing intense white gun flashes, and pom-poms throwing up streams of golden tracers."[3]

The Japanese defenders at Wewak—almost 500 miles away—were stirred up and alert. At that very minute, they picked through the smoke and ash of wrecked buildings and aircraft and bodies to assess the damage done by the Fifth Air Force's bombers. The attack, and its scale, was new to them.

The 405th's B-25s took off at dawn through a low layer of haze and clouds. Shortly afterward, each aircraft punched up through the murk into the lightening sky and joined the mission leader who orbited in a lazy circle above the airfield. Their specific objective was the Dagua airfield, west of Wewak. Their sister squadron, the 71st, was slated to hit the airfield at But, a few miles farther west of Dagua. An additional three squadrons of B-25s from the 3rd Bomb Group were slated to attack the airfields at Wewak and Boram. The simultaneous and overpowering attack against the four different airfields was intended to dissipate and weaken the Japanese fighter defenses.

The 405th's B-25s were flying their first mission with the new auxiliary fuel tanks, and all was well. Once the squadron assembled into formation, it pressed west to pick up the 71st at Durand. Unlike the 405th, the 71st's crews made an ass-hash of their takeoff through the clouds. Individual crews chased after each other as they flailed about in the early morning light. Unable to join as a squadron, the 71st was forced to abort the mission; it was not only an embarrassment, but it also undercut the strength of the bomb group's mission by half.

For its part, the 71st recorded its failure as almost a nonevent, noting only that "twelve of our aircraft took off this morning en route to But [airfield] to bomb and strafe enemy aircraft on the [air]drome. Due to correct rendezvous being messed up, our aircraft returned to their base." Aside from grumbling, there was nothing the 405th could do about the 71st's poor performance, and the squadron pressed west toward Marilinan to meet up with the three squadrons of B-25s from the 3rd Bomb Group, as well as an escort of P-38s.

Once their B-25s burned enough gas from their main fuel tanks, the 405th's crews started to transfer fuel from the new auxiliary fuel tanks. Meanwhile, near Marilinan, the squadron rendezvoused with the P-38s, which flew high above them in a protective screen. Together, the 405th and the P-38s flew lazy orbits and waited for the B-25s from the 3rd Bomb Group to arrive. But they failed to show, and the 405th gave up and pressed west toward Wewak. Together with its escort of P-38s, the squadron took care to avoid the Japanese airbases at Lae and Madang. Once past Madang, the B-25 crews prepared to jettison the auxiliary fuel tanks.

But they would not fall away. Crew after crew checked and rechecked that the straps and fittings which held the tanks in place were disconnected.

But the tanks—stuck in place by friction—remained stubbornly unmoving. Desperate, the men shoved and kicked them. Their efforts went largely unrewarded as only three crews were able to push the balky tanks out of their aircraft. It seemed that the entire day was jinxed. The formation leader aborted the mission, and the squadron followed him as he arced back toward Port Moresby.

There were three aircraft that did not follow him. They were the crews that had been able to dump their tanks. Captained by William Gay, Garrett Middlebrook, and Berdines Lackness, they continued flying west. The raid, against which the Japanese had yet to play a part, and which had been planned to include five squadrons of B-25s and their P-38 escorts, was now reduced by poor flying, equipment hiccups, and who-knew-what-else to a tiny flight of three aircraft from the 405th Bomb Squadron.

It wasn't for lack of trying on the part of their sister squadron, the 71st. After fouling its initial rendezvous in the early morning, the squadron tried again. This time the formation of 12 aircraft covered about half the distance to Wewak but gave up once more after failing to join with escorting P-38s over Bena Bena.

In truth, it was folly for the 405th's three crews to continue. They were alone—the P-38s had turned back with the rest of the squadron. They were also headed toward the largest enemy airbase complex on the island of New Guinea. It was protected by all manner of antiaircraft guns and more than a hundred fighters. And it was nearly 600 miles from home.

Garrett Middlebrook considered all this and more. There was a valid argument that the decision to continue rather than follow the rest of the squadron was a failure to follow orders. They might even be disciplined in the uncertain event they survived. And Middlebrook realized that there were moral aspects attached to pressing ahead with such a risky attack. He questioned his authority to continue and thereby put the rest of his crew in such peril, regardless of his personal desire to continue the mission—or not.

His decision to go echoed the sentiments expressed by so many men from so many nations in so many wars: "I must confess in complete frankness that neither my duty to the Air Corps nor my patriotism to my country had any bearing upon my decision. I was solely persuaded in my commitment to the mission because of the loyalty I felt toward Gay and Lackness, damned fools that they both were."[4]

William Gay led the three-ship formation low and just above the haze-shrouded treetops using the terrain to shield the flight from Japanese observers and radars. Their route to the airfield at Dagua would take them past the airfields at both Wewak and Boram, which increased the odds that they would be discovered and intercepted by Japanese fighters. The anxiety of the three crews heightened with each passing mile.

Nevertheless, Gay successfully led them along a series of ridges south of the coast. On the other side—on the flat coastland—were the Japanese, unaware but deadly. The little flight of B-25s didn't see Wewak to their right on the other side of the jungled crest as they skirted it, but were relieved to continue unchallenged. They enjoyed the same good fortune and relief when they flew past Boram.

And then came the time to turn toward the target—the heavily defended airfield at Dagua. Fear swelled in the guts of each man at the thought of what awaited their little formation. Gay made a right climbing turn to leap the ridge. Middlebrook and Lackness maneuvered to follow, careful to not drop a wingtip into the trees. At the apex of their climb, the ocean and coastline burst into view. And so did the airfield and its runway, which ran parallel to and almost atop the beach.

It was time for business. Training and instinct pushed up through the dread the three crews shared. "My God, what a sight!" said Middlebrook. "And how quickly my tormenting fears vanished." The unfolding panorama that so emboldened him contrasted sharply with the already beat-up airfields he and his squadron mates had previously attacked at Lae and elsewhere.

Dagua, despite the heavy bomber attacks of a few hours earlier, was essentially a combat-ready, real-life diorama of a working military airbase, complete in every detail. It burgeoned with aircraft and material and equipment, and it bustled with activity. Mechanics, support personnel and crews busied themselves all over the airfield. Arming and refueling operations were underway at several locations, and a trio of Ki-43 fighters got airborne at the far end of the airfield. More fighters were lined up on the seaward side of the runway. And up to 50 light and medium bombers were clustered in twos and threes on the near side of the runway. The three B-25 crews could not have been presented with a better target.

Middlebrook and the other pilots let the noses of their bombers drop toward the airfield, pushed their throttles forward and raced down the sloping hills. Flying at nearly 300 miles per hour, Middlebrook fired his guns into a stack of gasoline drums that erupted so violently the flames nearly enveloped his aircraft.

He kept firing and watched his rounds rip into a bomber, a Mitsubishi Ki-21 Sally. The aircraft exploded with such ferocity that it lifted another nearby bomber into the air. It slammed back to the ground and burned. Middlebrook fired his guns at another bomber and watched awestruck as it blew up and immolated two Japanese as they ran past. Behind him, he heard and felt his gunners shooting at other targets of opportunity. To his right, his copilot Paul Thompson released clusters of parafrags. The little bombs drifted gently earthward before bursting into fiery showers of red-hot shrapnel that shredded aircraft, material, and men.

Smoke dust and fire roiled the airfield. Japanese antiaircraft crews sent lines of machinegun and cannon fire arcing after the three B-25s. Gay and Lackness and their crews, like Middlebrook, made flaming wrecks out of aircraft that only a minute earlier were ready for combat. Middlebrook barely bothered to stop firing his guns. His rounds seemed to slam into worthwhile targets whether they were aimed or not.

The devastating power of the B-25's forward-firing guns was demonstrated to Middlebrook once more. He saw his bullets smash into a fighter with such force that it was pushed forward into another. He kept his finger on the firing button. "The steady fire from my guns passed through plane after plane, a score of items of equipment and many human bodies," he said.

And then, less than a minute after it began, the attack was over. The three B-25s raced across the beach and skimmed low over the sea as they reconstituted their formation with William Gay again in the lead. Behind them, the maelstrom they created sent columns of smoke skyward.

The calamity the B-25 crews made of Dagua receded behind them, but trouble did not. A Ki-43, likely one of the trio of fighters which had taken off as they started their attack, prepared to dive on them from the top of a chandelle. But having lost so much airspeed, the Japanese aircraft was an easy target, and the B-25 gunners laced it with .50 caliber rounds. The fighter tumbled burning into the water, almost literally knocked from the sky.

It marked the beginning of a running gun battle with more than a dozen determined Japanese fighters. Fleeing as fast as their aircraft could go, the B-25 pilots dived for the sea. Leveling off just above the waves, their propellers whipped spray into the air behind them. Rarely did they climb above 20 feet. Flying so low made them difficult targets as it was impossible for the Japanese to attack from below, and firing passes from above could not be too steep for fear of flying into the water.

The enemy pilots were skilled and aggressive, but one was especially so. This expert pilot flew an all-black aircraft, whereas the others were silver with blue-green lines painted in a wavy pattern across their fuselages and wings. The pilot of the black fighter pressed his attacks with a cunning that frustrated the defending gunners.

The three-ship of B-25s pointed landward and flashed across the beach south of the mouth of the Sepik River, flying only high enough to keep from plowing into the jungle. Flocks of tropical birds flapped screeching into the air, blown from their treetop perches by the fast-moving bombers. The black-painted Japanese fighter and the others followed, crisscrossing the air around the B-25s with machinegun fire. But still, although each of them was holed by the enemy guns, none of the bombers was mortally hurt.

As skilled as the Japanese fighter pilots were, the American bomber crews were equally accomplished. Gay, Middlebrook, and Lackness had each flown more than 50 combat missions. On this day Middlebrook and Lackness clung tightly to Gay to better concentrate the defensive fire of their experienced gunners. Gay expertly took advantage of every crease in the terrain as he led his wingmen down, over, or across it to spoil the aim of the enemy pilots. Middlebrook marveled at his squadron mate, declaring, "Gay was supremely effective in matching wits and skill with our enemy."

The fight twisted and turned over more than 150 miles of sea and jungle. And then, the engines on the B-25s—after being flogged so hard and for so long—began to overheat. Should the race last much longer, the engines would fail or catch fire. If the Japanese didn't kill the little band of flyers, a crash into the jungle would. Moreover, the engines were consuming fuel at an unsustainable rate. Worse, all but one of the gunners were out of ammunition. Still, Gay kept the formation speeding low over the green carpet of trees, wriggling it just barely out of harm's way each time an enemy fighter attacked.

The attacks were dogged and calculating. The black fighter sliced through the formation so closely that Middlebrook could see the pilot was a solid man with a "fleshy" square face, and that he wore his goggles up on his forehead. The other Japanese pilots, if not so skilled and daring, were nevertheless keen and showed no signs of shirking or cowardice.

And then it was over.

Past Madang, the Japanese pilots—by now also low on fuel and ammunition—gave up the chase. They simply winged away and were gone. Aboard the B-25s, the barely mastered terror that had gripped the crews for nearly 40 minutes gave way to incredulous relief and then, almost immediately, to exhaustion.

Once he was certain the enemy was gone, Gay reduced power to his engines to lessen the stress they were enduring, and to save fuel. His wingmen did the same. The three pilots threaded a route between the Owen Stanley Range and a line of thunderclouds before touching down without fanfare at Durand with almost no fuel remaining. Without the gas from the problematic auxiliary fuel tanks, they would have gone down into the jungle long before reaching home.

Middlebrook shut down his aircraft's engines and climbed down from the cockpit. Still soaked in sweat, he recalled his happiness at seeing his men safe. The day's singularly terrifying mission had further strengthened the comradely bond they shared. "My only interest," Middlebrook said, "was confined to the miracle I saw before me. My four fellow crewmen stood looking at me, all physically normal although I doubted that they would ever be the same mentally again."

Rather than being censured or rebuked for having pressed to the target alone, the men were rewarded. Kenney liked audacity in his men, and their actions had been audacious in the extreme. Photographic intelligence and post-mission interviews indicated that the three crews together had destroyed 17 aircraft on the ground, and damaged another 20, while also destroying a considerable quantity of fuel and other material. Additionally, they were credited with shooting down three fighters during the high-speed, low-altitude escape from Dagua. Gay, Middlebrook, and Lackness were each awarded the Distinguished Service Cross. The other crew members received the Distinguished Flying Cross.

Although they didn't know it at the time, the three squadrons of the 3rd Bomb Group for whom the 405th had waited vainly over Marilinan that same morning actually did make their planned attacks on Boram and Wewak. At Boram, most of the aircraft were readying to taxi for takeoff when the 3rd's crews swept across the airfield, guns firing. Many Japanese pilots and ground crews burned to death on the spot.

Sustaining no losses and claiming a minimum of 65 aircraft destroyed at the two airfields, the 3rd's results highlighted what could be achieved by coordinated full-strength attacks—and Kenney's specially modified B-25s. Indeed, so violent was the strike at Boram—and so closely parked were the Japanese aircraft—that they exploded one by one down the line as if each were a gunpowder keg.

Notwithstanding the success of the attacks on August 17, there still remained plenty at Wewak that needed to be destroyed. The Fifth had the men and aircraft necessary for the job and consequently launched more raids on the following day, August 18, 1943. A mixed force of 17 B-24s and 9 B-17s escorted by 74 P-38s led the day's attacks but were stymied by poor weather. Their bombs did little damage.

However, strafer-modified B-25s from the 38th and 3rd Bomb Groups followed immediately behind the heavy bombers. Ralph Cheli, the deputy commander of the 38th, led the mission at the head of the group's 405th

Bomb Squadron. The 405th's sister squadron, the 71st, did not bungle its rendezvous that day and followed closely behind. In total, the 38th's formation included 28 B-25s which managed to stay together despite scattered curtains of rain that drummed against the aircraft and intermittently cut visibility dangerously low. While in a speedy descent through 1,500 feet about 30 miles from Dagua, the group was jumped by a force of approximately 10 Ki-43 Oscar fighters which the B-25 crews misidentified as Zeroes, or Zekes. More Japanese fighters milled in the distance.

The 71st was heavily engaged. William Skinner, the top turret gunner aboard B. F. Herman's aircraft, was exceptionally deadly. He spotted an enemy fighter attacking from the 11 o'clock position. "But instead of pressing the attack home," the squadron's after action report noted, "the Jap banked up sharply on his side, exposing the top side of his plane." Skinner blasted the enemy fighter with a burst from his twin .50 caliber machineguns. It caught fire, broke apart and crashed into the sea. An instant later, Skinner spun his turret around and the B-25 vibrated again as he fired his guns at another fighter attacking from the 2 o'clock position. This aircraft, like the other, burst into flames and tumbled into the sea. The 71st's crews claimed a total of eight Japanese fighters shot down.

The 38th's after action report noted, "The Zekes [actually, Ki-43s] appeared to be lying in wait just offshore and dived on our formation out of the clouds from slightly above our altitude." The report also described the appearance of the enemy aircraft. "Most intercepting Zekes were camouflaged green and brown with large red roundels on top of wings. 2 or 3 were a dull silver." Regardless of how their aircraft were painted, the enemy pilots were aggressive and apparently intent on knocking out the 405th's lead flight, Cheli's, in order to break up the group's attack.

Although the Japanese fighters concentrated the weight of their efforts on the front of the formation, they also attacked other aircraft. John Donegan's bomber in the flight behind Cheli's was particularly hard hit. It skidded out of position and over the water when its rudder controls, parts of the horizontal and vertical stabilizers, and the entire right aileron were shot away. There, away from the group, it staggered to stay airborne as the enemy fighters intensified their attacks.

"I lost most of my elevator control," Donegan said, "and when the formation made its run over the target, I couldn't turn sharply enough to stay with them." The enemy fighters attacked the lone B-25 from every direction, and Donegan adjusted his flight path to fire with his nose guns at an aircraft making a head-on pass. It fell away, smoking.

The B-25s in the 38th's main formation continued to fight back. The fire from their .50 caliber machineguns lashed out at Ki-43s, which pressed their attacks "to minimum range." Seemingly out of nowhere, a lone Ki-61 Tony appeared—sleek and menacing—and made a head-on attack. It passed through the group's formation in a flash and disappeared, neither doing nor suffering harm.

Cheli's aircraft was only a couple of miles from Dagua when it was hit. Pilots from the 71st reported, "Smoke, then streaming fire was seen to come from the right engine of Cheli's airplane." The flames burned all the way to the cockpit, and it was apparent to the rest of the crews that the aircraft was doomed. Cheli could have pulled up and exchanged his airspeed for altitude, thereby giving himself and his crew an opportunity to take to their parachutes. "We were flying so tightly, however," said a comrade, "that if he had done so he would have broken up the formation and ruined the attack, besides exposing others to isolated interception."

This notion that the attack would have been "ruined" if Cheli had pulled out of his run was not true. Certainly, there would have been an instant or two of distraction, but the rest of the 38th's crews would have continued strafing and bombing, just as the mission required. And there was no way of knowing what was going on in Cheli's mind. Perhaps he did not know how badly his aircraft was hit. But he absolutely knew that parachuting into the arms of the enemy during a devastating attack that he was personally responsible for leading was a high-risk proposition. If his comrades didn't inadvertently kill him and his crew, there was a very good chance the Japanese would kill them quite on purpose.

Cheli, his bomber burning fiercely, continued straight at Dagua. The B-25s he led spread out a bit more so that they didn't shoot each other as they ripped the parked Japanese aircraft with their guns. Clusters of parafrags fell from their bellies. The explosions they created as they settled to earth added to the ferocity of the attack.

Once across the airfield, Cheli angled his B-25 out to sea. The enemy fighters continued to swarm him despite the efforts of squadron mate William Pittman, who climbed into them, guns chattering, in an effort to protect his leader. He was in turn set upon by the Japanese and was rescued only when a flight of P-38s dived into the melee. Cheli's aircraft, still afire, sent a plume of spray skyward when it hit the water a couple of miles from the coast.

Meanwhile, the swarm of Japanese fighters continued to savage John Donegan's lurching bomber. "We were flying by ourselves for about five minutes, and it seemed as though all the Japs wanted to take a crack at us personally," Donegan said. One of the fighters hit the cockpit area hard. Donegan was badly wounded in his right arm. Next to him, copilot Charles Peebles was hit in the left shoulder and head. Bleeding profusely and slumped over his control wheel, he intermittently lost and regained consciousness. Donegan turned to see the crew's navigator, Victor Scammel, folded onto the floor and bleeding from his head; jagged shards of metal had penetrated his skull. Donegan had no idea how the men at the back of the bomber were faring—the intercom system had been shot out.

Even though Donegan's ship was separated from the main formation, the gaggle of Japanese fighters grew so large that it attracted a group of P-38s. The American fighter pilots rocketed into the fight with a ferocity that sent the enemy scrambling. The subsequent galaxy of climbing, twisting, turning air combat spun in a wheeling orb around the damaged B-25. All around them, Donegan's crewmen watched wide-eyed as tracers arced through the sky and fighters disintegrated and spun into the sea.

Donegan had very little control of his aircraft and flew it by using differential power to his engines, which he kept almost at full throttle. He limped away from the fight and attached himself to a flight of three other B-25s. He raised the leader of the three-ship on the radio and asked to be taken to the nearest friendly airfield. They punched into a layer of clouds—where they couldn't be spotted by enemy fighters—and flew on instruments for several minutes. When they emerged into the clear they discovered themselves under terrific antiaircraft fire and directly over the airfield at Wewak. The other B-25s turned sharply away, but Donegan was unable to follow, and his aircraft was hit again.

Still, the damaged bomber flew on. Donegan spotted another pair of B-25s and struggled to join them. "I gave the plane everything she had," he said, "which was quite a bit in spite of her damage. The hydraulic system was out and the bomb bay door[s] kept coming open."

Donegan closed to within a mile of the other two B-25s, but at that point they were attacked by a group of fighters. The pilots of those fighters soon discovered Donegan's crippled bomber and regrouped to make several overhead passes on it. With no good options, he put his aircraft into a steep dive and raced for a layer of clouds.

But the enemy scored again. The top turret gunner, Donald Bybee, was struck in the face when the Plexiglas of his turret, and the gunsight, was shot away. Bybee, now exposed to the slipstream, nevertheless stuck to his guns and continued firing until Donegan plunged the B-25 into the security of the clouds.

Anxious to throw the enemy pilots off course, Donegan made a right turn inland while still shrouded in the weather. When he finally flew out of the clouds there wasn't another aircraft—friend or foe—in sight. "I kept worrying about the engines," he said. "I didn't dare slow them down to normal speed for fear of going into a spin, and I worried about keeping them gunned, especially after that hammering we'd taken."

There was the additional problem that Donegan and his crew, with the aircraft running low on fuel, were no longer sure of their position. Joseph Carroll, the radioman, had suffered a glancing blow to his elbow from a machinegun round, but was otherwise uninjured. He crawled through the bomb bay and up into the front of the aircraft. Taken aback by the chaos he found, he nevertheless got to work. Victor Scammel, the navigator, was a bloody mess and was his first priority. Carroll pulled bandages from the first aid kit and did his best to staunch the bleeding. He additionally gave Scammel a syringe full of morphine.

Peebles, the copilot, was next. "I helped him back out of the seat and tore off my sweat shirt to make bandages for him and the pilot." Carroll then crawled back through the bomb bay to check on Bybee, the top turret gunner. "He said he was all right," Carroll said, "but he looked pretty bad, with blood all over his head."

Carroll wriggled back to the front again where Peebles was proving willful in his strong desire to help Donegan. "I'd just get him down on the floor," Carroll said, "when he'd want to get up at his controls again." Carroll wrestled Peebles, who was obviously suffering from shock, up and down several times.

Scammel, the most gravely wounded, slipped in and out of awareness. He tried to make sense of his charts and scribbled directions to Donegan, but they were unreadable. Should they not get pointed in the right direction soon, the aircraft would run out of gas before they got home. Finally, Scammel—despite his injuries—put Donegan on the correct course.

Donegan had been grappling with his broken bomber for almost three hours when Jackson airdrome hove into view. He directed Bybee and Carroll to bail out, unsure if he could successfully land the ship. Both were wary of doing so. They were a crew, a team, and to this point they had succeeded at staying alive with Donegan at the controls. They disobeyed him and stayed aboard.

The middle of the runway was blocked by an aircraft. Despite Donegan's radio calls for it to be moved, it remained in place. He circled the field five times, waiting for someone on the ground to drag the aircraft clear. "I couldn't wait [any] longer with Scammel and Peebles apparently bleeding to death," he said. He finally lined up to land in the grass to one side of the runway. His landing gear, with the hydraulic system shot out, stayed stuck inside the aircraft. The bomb bay doors, which had fallen open multiple times already, caused him additional worry.

Donegan made his approach at 170 miles per hour—well above normal landing speed. Carroll tried to crank the flaps down by hand so that Donegan might be able to reduce his airspeed. However, something went awry and the aircraft tipped out of control just as it touched down. "We scraped and jolted along," Donegan said, "throwing up a huge cloud of dust."

The B-25 remained tough to the end, neither catching fire, breaking up, nor tipping over. Within minutes, emergency crews pulled the men clear and took them to the airfield's hospital. They all survived, as did their aircraft, which, despite being holed more than 250 times, was repaired and eventually returned to service.

★★★

While the 38th Bomb Group ripped the Japanese at Dagua and But on August 18, the 3rd Bomb Group, at the cost of two B-25s, did the same to the airfields at Wewak and Boram. They additionally sank four cargo vessels anchored offshore. The entire Wewak complex—and the Japanese Fourth Air Army—was a shambles.

MacArthur's staff parsed the data fed to them by the Fifth Air Force and released a communique that described the work the American flyers had done on August 17 and 18. It stated, "Photographs reveal the total destruction of 120 enemy planes and severe damage to at least another 50." The dispatch also estimated that more than 1,500 ground personnel were killed. This was a gross exaggeration.

Kenney, who was no stranger to hyperbole, was not to be outdone. After all, he led the Fifth Air Force. He bragged about the two days of strikes, "It was doubtful if the Nips could have put over a half dozen aircraft in the air from all four airdromes combined."

Kenney was anxious to keep the Wewak complex beaten down and sent two more large strikes against the complex on August 20 and 21. Rather than a niggling "half dozen," the Japanese launched many dozens of fighters to oppose the strikes. Still, the American formations overwhelmed the defenders and destroyed most of what had been left undamaged.

A Japanese officer, Colonel Kazuo Tanikawa, reflected on the reduction of Wewak and its impacts on Japan's war in New Guinea:

We lost 100 planes including light bombers, fighters and reconnaissance planes. It was a decisive Allied victory. We were planning to retain the balance of power and were making plans to bomb Port Moresby and other areas. A few days before our projected plan . . . we were bombed at Wewak and our airpower was severely crippled.[6]

Although it is apparent that the Japanese acknowledged the Wewak strikes to be as debilitating as MacArthur and Kenney declared they were, the number of aircraft they acknowledged to have lost was less. The truth was that no one—neither the Americans nor the Japanese—knew how many Japanese aircraft had been made unflyable. Making such a determination was not an exact science.

The American intelligence staff at the different units compiled and forwarded photographic evidence and aircrew reports from the missions, as well as information from postmission reconnaissance flights. To this, damage assessment experts applied the latest techniques and methods to arrive at an estimate.

Aircrew reports were useful to some extent, but only to make approximations. This was because the perspective of each individual was limited, and when everyone's perspectives were combined, there were considerable overlaps, as well as considerable gaps. For instance, the pilot and copilot in each aircraft could not see what damage was done by their parafrags as they settled to earth and exploded well behind them. On the other hand, the crewmen in the rear of each aircraft could see what damage the parafrags did but could not see what was happening to the front. Moreover, attacks were typically made in waves of aircraft, and there were often duplicate claims against the same targets. Too, combat produced fears and anxieties—even terrors—that sometimes compromised the observations and recollections of the crews.

And to be sure, there were disagreements among the photo analysts about which aircraft were wrecked to a degree that they could not be put back in service. Simply put, the Americans could make an estimate but didn't have the luxury of physically examining each aircraft individually.

But the Japanese did. Although it was easy enough in most cases for them to distinguish between a flyable aircraft and one that would never be, deciding if an aircraft that had sustained damage might be put back into service was more problematic. For instance, if an aircraft was easily repairable assuming a critical part was readily available, then it might be considered only damaged. But if that critical part was not on hand and was not anticipated to ever be available—and if it could not be cannibalized from another aircraft—then it would never fly again.

Some damage took time to assess. Seemingly minor machinegun damage might, upon detailed examination, be found to have compromised important structures which forever destroyed the flyability of an aircraft. On the other hand, many good parts might be salvaged from a wreck to make several otherwise nonflyable aircraft airworthy again.

But such work required skilled labor and specialized equipment that might not be available. The one man capable of making a particular repair might have been killed in a raid or fallen to disease. Indeed, properly evaluating all the aircraft based at each of Wewak's four airfields would have taken several days or more. Even then, the number was still subject to change as the availability of resources changed, and as more detailed examinations of specific aircraft were made.

In the end, however, exact numbers of aircraft damaged or destroyed didn't matter. What mattered was achieving the desired effects. And Kenney and his men had done that. The Japanese Fourth Air Army at Wewak, utterly battered, was incapable of fielding offensive operations of any meaningful size in the short term. Or even defending itself. It was for all intents and purposes nearly dead.

But only nearly.

★★★

Among the Japanese fighter types that defended Wewak was the Kawasaki Ki-61 Hien. It was powered by a derivative of the same liquid-cooled, inline DB-601 engine used by early variants of the Luftwaffe's primary fighter, the Me-109, which was manufactured by Messerschmitt. Consequently, the forward fuselage and cockpit enclosure resembled the German aircraft to such a degree that when first encountered by Allied pilots in 1942, it was mistaken for a license-built copy. Later, there was speculation that it might have been an Italian Macchi C.202. As a result, it was given the code name Tony.

However, aside from the engine and the resemblance, the Ki-61 was a distinctly different aircraft. And as compared to the Zero and the Oscar, the Tony was faster and better armed, but not nearly so maneuverable. Additionally, it suffered from manufacturing difficulties and was challenging to maintain in the miserable environment of New Guinea. Nevertheless, when flown by a competent pilot, it was a worthwhile adversary and certainly the equal of the P-40, if not superior.

20

"BUT HE WAS ALWAYS CHEERFUL"

By now, several months after he was shot down and rescued by friendly natives, Gordon Manuel had established himself as "mastah." This pidgin English title was typically applied to white men, and it was one that Manuel welcomed. The villagers to which he had bound himself had essentially put him in a position of leadership, even though he relied entirely upon them for food, shelter, and protection.

But such was the case only with his particular group of natives, several of whom became fast friends. They had done so at great risk. The population had been ordered to capture any Allied flyers they found and turn them over to the Japanese authorities. Were they to hide and protect such airmen, they would be tortured and killed.

Many natives did cooperate with the Japanese either out of fear or in exchange for small rewards. Outside Manuel's protective circle were natives who threatened to inform the Japanese of his location. His friends turned the tables by threatening to tell the Japanese that the would-be tipsters had actually been complicit in hiding him.

Manuel took charge of the situation and called the headmen of all the different villages together. He variously appealed to them, bullied them, and cajoled them. He explained that the Japanese were destined to lose the war as evidenced by the Allied air raids against Rabaul, which were accelerating in size and frequency. Exaggerating somewhat, he told them that if they turned him over to the Japanese, the Americans would be very angry and would behead them when they finally arrived. But should they shelter and guard him—and any other Allied flyers—they would be rewarded with great treasure.

It worked. Although he never let his guard down, Manuel no longer lived in constant fear of capture. In fact, he organized the natives into reconnaissance parties to scout the area's defenses, including its airfields. Should he escape, it was information he believed would be valuable to Allied planners.

★★★

A few days after the mid-August raids on Wewak, a Japanese crewman from one of the Lily bombers shot down on August 15 over Tsili Tsili was captured by an Australian patrol. He cooperated readily during his inter-rogation, and the information he shared confirmed that the Allies were gaining the upper hand in New Guinea. Although his complaints—poor food and living conditions, disease, and air attacks—were similar to those of his American and Australian counterparts, the challenges the Japanese faced seemed more desperate and acute.

Moreover, he and his comrades loathed their aircraft, the Ki-48. It was slow, vulnerable to fighter attacks, and mechanically unreliable. And it carried such a small bombload that some crews questioned whether or not their sacrifices were worthwhile. After the Wewak attacks of mid-August, their morale was no doubt worse.[1]

★★★

Ralph Cheli, who had so selflessly led the 38th Bomb Group across Dagua in his burning B-25 on August 18, 1943, was memorialized with the Medal of Honor only a couple of months later. The citation closed with a note that venerated the man's bravery: "Although a crash was inevitable, he cou-rageously elected to continue leading the attack in his blazing plane. From a minimum altitude, the squadron made a devastating bombing and strafing attack on the target. The mission completed, Major Cheli instructed his wingman to lead the formation and crashed into the sea." Most assumed the award was posthumous.

But Cheli was not dead.

Although the details are unknowable, he and two others of his crew, Raymond Warren and Clinton Murphree, the radioman and aerial gun-ner respectively, survived the crash and were captured by the Japanese. They were subsequently sent to Rabaul. American prisoners already there recalled Cheli arriving "badly burned and banged, but otherwise okay."

Although he and his crew were officially listed as Missing in Action, or MIA, as was common when there was any possibility of survival, it was generally assumed that they were dead. But indications otherwise were received in early 1944. An unofficial German broadcast stated that Cheli was a prisoner of the Japanese. A subsequent transmission declared that Warren and Murphree were also being held. In May 1944 the Army contacted Cheli's wife with the text of a letter. It had been broadcast from Japan and was represented as having been written by Cheli. It stated, among other things, that he was a prisoner.

However, through the duration of the war, the Japanese were criminally dissembling and outright cruel with respect to the way they reported—or did not—the status of prisoners of war. There was simply no way to confirm whether or not Cheli was alive.

Meanwhile, just as he had been a much-admired leader in the 38th Bomb Group, Cheli was similarly well-regarded by his fellow prisoners. "Cheli was [the] ranking officer at our camp at that time and the Japs really made life hell for him," the men recalled. "They held question and answer sessions with him ten times a day and beat him when he stubbornly refused to answer anything beyond his name, rank and serial number. He was always given the worst kind of work detail."

"But he was always cheerful," they said. "Always adamant he wouldn't talk [give information to the Japanese]. He didn't, either. Finally, the Japs got disgusted with him and decided to ship him to Japan." Cheli and approximately 20 other prisoners were marched out of their camp on the evening of March 5, 1944. The Japanese told the remaining prisoners that the group was to be embarked aboard a ship bound for Japan. Later, the prisoners repeated what their captors told them: "At 9:30 our own planes [American] attacked the ship berthed there and Cheli died instantly in the bombing." Another story told by the Japanese was that the men were queued up on a beach at Talili Bay, waiting to be transported to nearby Watom Island, when they were killed by an American air attack.[2]

The Japanese were liars. On March 4 and 5, 1944, they murdered Cheli and 31 other prisoners and buried them in a mass grave. Later, as the end of the war approached, they exhumed the bodies and cremated them to cover their crimes.[3]

★★★

Yoshikazu Tamura, a Japanese soldier at Wewak, reflected on the death of his friend who was killed offshore as part of a working party.

> A few days ago, my friend was killed by enemy shells in this bay. However, the bay with its white waves does not look any different. . . . The landscape of the headland is as lush as before. . . . However, how devastated I feel! He left us after a work session, sending his regards to other members of our section. The next morning, this friend could not

be found anywhere and now he is at the bottom of the sea after an attack by enemy planes. What an unfortunate fate he had. However, it is no use lamenting. We hope he is in a peaceful slumber and becomes a god protecting the nation.[4]

It is human to want to feel sympathy for Tamura and his friend. However, such feelings are tempered by an awareness of the manifest cruelties that Tamura's comrades, and perhaps Tamura himself, inflicted on those who were not of the same race.

Although none of the American flyers who hit the airfields at Wewak were aware of it, the Japanese there were committing bestial atrocities. Among the running figures the aircrews occasionally saw dodging their bombs and machinegun fire were some of the approximately 3,000 Indian prisoners of war that were held at Wewak. Most of them were captured when British and Commonwealth forces capitulated at Singapore in 1942. They were subsequently taken to Wewak while crammed into the holds of ships. The conditions were so horrid that many died even before they reached New Guinea.

Starved and beaten—and imprisoned in a squalid camp situated in a stinking swamp—the Indians were forced to work up to 14 hours at a time in the miserable heat. Wracked by exhaustion and given only meager rations, they frequently succumbed to sickness. Among the encyclopedic list of tropical diseases that afflicted them, beriberi was one of the most ubiquitous. Caused by a diet deficient in thiamine, beriberi was painful and caused feet and legs to swell to massive, cartoonish proportions. In one instance, a particularly sadistic Japanese officer, Colonel Takano, savagely beat a group of men who were afflicted with the disease because he believed they were not working fast enough.[5]

And, as happened at other camps elsewhere in the Pacific, the Japanese took away groups of prisoners and used them as live targets for marksmanship training. Those who weren't killed outright were bayonetted. Protests at their condition brought only harsher treatment from the Japanese. One Indian officer, Captain Nirpal Chand, was beheaded for objecting to the abuses his men were forced to endure. Before being taken away, he implored his men: "Don't worry. If I am killed, some of you will see the good times which are ahead and tell your tales. The Japs cannot finish the whole lot. If I die for your rightful demands, I shall consider it a great honour and credit to me." Chand's execution was botched, as it took two sword strikes to remove his head.

But it was cannibalism that was the most shocking and depraved of the many crimes the Japanese committed. An Indian prisoner, Captain R. U. Purzai, described the sickening evil practiced by the Japanese.

> Of 300 men who went to Wewak with me, only 50 got out. Nineteen were eaten. A Jap doctor, Lieutenant Tumisa, formed a party of three or four men and would send an Indian outside the camp for something. The Japs immediately would kill him and eat the flesh from his body. The liver, muscles from the buttocks, thighs, legs, and arms would be cut off and cooked.[6]

Ironically—and tragically—the Indians were also savaged by Allied air raids against which the Japanese refused to allow them to take cover. Chint Singh remembered, "In August 1943 we were working on the airstrip at Wewak and Allied aeroplanes bombed the area. This was the first big air raid and about five or six Indians were killed and about 13 were wounded."[7]

Colonel Takano, whose viciousness knew no bounds, took the injured men to their camp and threw handfuls of sand at them. "Why are you crying?" he shouted. "This is not my fault. It is Roosevelt and Churchill!" A Japanese medical officer left the Indians with a pitiable supply of medical stuff, but the wounds of the injured men became infected, and they all died shortly afterward.

21

"GREAT GUSHING GOUTS OF FUEL IGNITED"

Although they probably didn't consider it regularly, most of Kenney's men knew implicitly that the war in New Guinea was a ground campaign, even though they saw very little of it, or the men doing the fighting. Their role was to kill Japanese, or to at least destroy the means by which the Japanese might harm their comrades who sweltered and struggled unseen in the scrub and jungle. All of Kenney's units contributed. The fighters and bombers killed and destroyed, and the transport crews made certain that all the organizations—ground and air—had the material they needed.

This ground war in New Guinea did not follow the traditional model of linear fortified positions with attacks in the form of overwhelming frontal assaults or rapid flanking gambits during which troops were moved through key towns and cities on established lines of communication. Rather, when the Japanese came ashore, they normally, but not always, did so at locations that were lightly defended, or not defended at all. And then they typically stayed in place and hacked away at the jungle to build airfields from which they could control the sea, air, and ground out to a certain distance. And they constructed piers and other infrastructure from which they could offload the shipping that kept them supplied.

Only infrequently, as was the case during the assault up the Kokoda Track, did the Japanese strike overland to seize Allied positions. Such treks through the jungle were practically prohibitive—the men were exhausted, ridden with disease, and short of food and material before the fight began. The Japanese never took a significant Allied position in New Guinea by attacking any distance through the jungle.

More typically, attacks were made from the sea, as was the case with the poorly considered Japanese attempt to take Milne Bay. The Allies, often better led and always better supplied, were more successful. Supported by

Kenney's Fifth Air Force, which softened enemy defenses before and during the actual assaults, they were never repelled. Still, the Allies preferred to bypass Japanese enclaves, fighting for them only when it was deemed necessary.

However, left unmolested—especially if they were resupplied—the isolated enemy garrisons could be dangerous, Consequently, it became one of Kenney's responsibilities to ensure that the bypassed Japanese positions were kept from threatening the flanks and rear of MacArthur's hop-scotching ground forces. This Kenney did with regular air strikes that kept the Japanese hunkered down. Perhaps more effective was the interdiction of enemy shipping—vessels large and small—which carried badly needed material and equipment. This strangulation of the Japanese lines of communication kept the stranded garrisons impotent and on the edge of starvation.

It was a strategy created and espoused by others. After some convincing, MacArthur—who once wanted to seize the exceedingly formidable Japanese fortress at Rabaul—was convinced of the value of the "bypass and isolate" concept. Predictably, he claimed it as his own. Regardless of who originated the idea, it saved men, material, and equipment, and characterized the Allied advance across New Guinea toward the Philippines.

★★★

When the first Allied air units started operating out of Port Moresby during March 1942, their most frequent opponents were the Japanese pilots who flew from the recently captured airfield at Lae, and less often from Salamaua, 20 miles south. When the Australians and Americans dared to hit Lae during this period it was generally done with small numbers of aircraft and at great risk—the Japanese Zero pilots were fearsome foes. And it seemed that the Japanese almost always replied in kind with retaliatory raids against Port Moresby.

There developed a tit-for-tat pattern of reciprocal attacks that continued well into 1943. By that time, although they still struggled, the Allies had more and better aircraft, pilots, and material support. By the end of 1942, the Allied flyers not only began to dominate but started to turn Lae and Salamaua into virtual punching bags. By March 1943 and the Battle of the Bismarck Sea, it became dangerous for the Japanese to operate from either location. It also became difficult to keep the units there provisioned.

A series of hard-fought ground clashes followed during that spring and summer as the Allies—primarily the Australians—gradually pushed the Japanese north and west, back toward Salamaua and Lae. This offensive was supported by the Fifth Air Force both with movements of men and material and with firepower.

Ultimately, the Allies prevailed in the brutal fighting that forced the Japanese out of Salamaua toward Lae. Salamaua was captured on September 11, 1943. Overland and amphibious assaults tightened the noose around Lae, and the Japanese there were finally ejected less than a week later on September 16. With the enemy cleared, the Allies immediately began using the airfield.

At the same time that the Allies were closing on Lae and Salamaua, they made an airborne assault on Nadzab, 20 miles northwest of Lae, in the Markham Valley. On September 5, 1944, 48 B-25s raced low over the Markham Valley. They plowed the drop zone with machinegun fire at the same time that they dropped parafrags against no discernible targets. The B-25s were followed by a flight of A-20s, which deployed a thick smoke screen. Close on the heels of the A-20s were 79 C-47s from which just more than 1,500 American and Australian paratroopers jumped. Above them flew 108 fighters in a protective screen.

And flying in the midst of it all were Kenney and MacArthur in two separate B-17s. Both had been keen to watch the operation. It unfolded like clockwork not only due to the detailed planning and briefing but also because the entire effort was unopposed both in the air and on the ground. Casualties were three paratroopers killed in accidents.

Nearby Japanese units were chased away, and Nadzab was developed during the next several months into the major Fifth Air Force airfield complex in New Guinea. Nestled in the relatively gentle terrain of the Markham Valley, it enjoyed more moderate temperatures and was characterized by savannah-type vegetation rather than thick jungle. The men based there found it more comfortable than both Port Moresby and Dobodura. And most important from an operational perspective was the fact that it was closer to where the fight was headed.

★★★

On September 7, 1943, three companies of Australian soldiers, or "diggers," of the 2/33rd Infantry Battalion, Australian Imperial Force, sat in 18 different trucks waiting to be driven to Durand Airfield at Port Moresby. There, they were to climb aboard American C-47s which would fly them to the newly captured airfield at Nadzab. It was early morning, not quite 0430, and dark.

Less than a mile to the west beyond a low ridge sat Jackson airfield, or 7-Mile Drome. It was already busy, and the Australians heard the rumble of aircraft engines through the thickets of trees. One roar grew steadily louder and seemed to come directly at them, although they could see nothing beyond the ridge. And then, a hulking form appeared—a dark shape against a darker sky. The men grabbed their hats and variously cursed or laughed as it passed only dozens of feet above them. A few of them reached skyward in mock attempts to touch the bottom of the big bomber.

Howard Wood of the 43rd Bomb Group's 403rd Bomb Squadron peered from his cockpit and watched the previous B-24 disappear in the dark. He checked his engine instruments again and confirmed that all was as it should be. His aircraft was loaded with almost 3,000 gallons of fuel for the mission—a reconnaissance flight to Rabaul. It also carried four 500-pound bombs and plenty of ammunition for the aircraft's guns. The other 10 men in his crew had already called over the intercom that they were ready to go. He noted an edge in the voices of some but didn't blame them. Rabaul could be a rough target.

Ready for takeoff, Wood advanced the throttles of his aircraft and swung it around so that it pointed down the center of the runway. Satisfied, he pushed the throttles further forward to takeoff power. The engines growled and the aircraft rolled slowly at first before gradually accelerating. Wood unconsciously leaned forward in his seat, trying to see better, while his flight engineer called off the airspeed. Wood sneaked peeks at his instrument panel as he concentrated on keeping the aircraft on track.

And then, finally, at flying speed, he horsed the aircraft into the sky and called for his copilot to raise the landing gear. He checked the attitude gyro and then looked outside again, and then back to the attitude gyro, and then to the vertical speed indicator to confirm that the aircraft was climbing.

It was not.

The Australian soldiers, weighted down with ammunition and grenades and other war kit, shifted uncomfortably in the trucks. They heard another bomber roaring toward where they sat. All eyes were on the ridgeline as they waited for the aircraft to burst into view. It did, but unlike the previous B-24, this aircraft was not in a gentle climb and in fact, was not climbing at all. Rather it came directly at them.

The bomber paralleled the downward slope of the ridge just above the scrubby trees as it descended. The left wing hit a tree and separated from the rest of the aircraft. Great gushing gouts of fuel ignited and rushed in torrents toward the Australians, as did the burning wreck that was the rest of Wood's B-24. There wasn't time for the men to leap from the trucks and run. One of the aircraft's propellers spun itself free from its engine and slammed into a truck. The four bombs the aircraft carried broke free and caromed downhill over the rough ground. The caps protecting the nose fuzes were torn away and three of the four bombs detonated.

Some men were blown to pieces, others were incinerated where they sat. Still others, the lucky ones, were thrown clear with minor injuries. Those who could, ran. Some of them were afire. Ammunition aboard the trucks and from the aircraft cooked off.

Rescue operations began immediately and continued through the day. The Australians suffered 60 dead with many more badly wounded, burned, and disfigured, while all 11 crewmen aboard the B-24 were killed. No cause for the accident was definitively determined, although some witnesses declared that one of the engines on the left wing was burning. The official USAAF report assigned blame to the pilot. News of the incident was quickly quashed in the interest of morale. The exigencies of war prevailed, and those men who survived unhurt were sent to Nadzab the following day.[1]

22

"TICKLING A GIANT'S THROAT WITH A FEATHER"

Rabaul and its military complex sat on the northeastern tip of New Britain Island. Since seizing it from Australia in February 1942, the Japanese had transformed it into an enormous air and naval fortress from which they attacked Allied positions in New Guinea, the Solomon Islands, and as far away as Australia. Indeed, it was a near-impregnable bastion that stood at a strategic pivot point nearly 700 miles northwest of the central Solomon Islands, and just more than 400 miles northeast of the island of New Guinea. Virtually every Japanese ship or aircraft that traveled to either region passed through Rabaul first.

The actual town of Rabaul was situated on the northern edge of Simpson Harbor, a superb anchorage protected by rising terrain on three sides. Scores of cargo vessels regularly sheltered there, as did naval combatants of all sizes. The area was defended by air units based at four different airfields, and it was garrisoned by more than 80,000 troops who had dug miles of tunnels and innumerable fighting positions from which to defend against an amphibious assault.

Doing anything substantive about Rabaul was bound to be costly. The most hopeful optimists considered a plan that leveraged the geography surrounding Rabaul. Indeed, the area was characterized by lively volcanic activity which had nearly destroyed the town as recently as 1937. But the hopes of those optimists were dashed by a report that came out at the same time that Allied staffers were drafting detailed plans to destroy, capture, or at least neutralize the Japanese there.

On July 9, 1943, the *Adelaide Advertiser* carried an article:

> The Commonwealth Government, after a full investigation, rejected as impracticable a proposal that the volcano at Rabaul should be bombed

219

in an effort to start an eruption as a new and terrifying weapon against the Japanese. Discussing the question today, an expert said that the largest conceivable bomb blast would have about the same effect on a volcano as "tickling a giant's throat with a feather." The blast of even a large bomb would merely ruffle the surface, and would not be sufficient to cause an eruption.[1]

Rabaul, it seemed, would have to be dealt with the old-fashioned way.

So long as the Japanese operated freely and in force from Rabaul, MacArthur could not secure the Southwest Pacific. He wanted to take Rabaul, but doing so would have been possible—if at all—only at an enormous cost in men, equipment, and time. The enemy was well-trained, well-entrenched, well-led, and exceedingly well-motivated.

An elaborate plan that culminated in the capture of Rabaul was created in cooperation with the Navy and with guidance from the Joint Chiefs of Staff. Operation Cartwheel included 13 separate supporting operations in both the Solomon Islands and New Guinea. The objective was to eliminate the Japanese bases controlling the approaches to Rabaul. Enormous in scope, it required participation not only by the Army and the Army Air Forces but also the Navy, the Marine Corps, and forces from Australia and New Zealand. It began well enough with the unopposed seizures of Kiriwina and Woodlark Islands in June 1943, and with assaults at various points in the New Georgia Islands.

These and subsequent operations met their objectives, but many were costly. Moreover, they were dramatically smaller compared to the effort that would be required to capture Rabaul. This was apparent to even the most junior staffer. The Joint Chiefs of Staff back in Washington, D.C., were not junior, nor was George Marshall, the Chief of Staff of the Army. After evaluating the resources required against what was available—and considering that the planned invasion of Europe was the priority— Marshall decided that the plan to seize Rabaul was a mistake. He subsequently directed MacArthur to isolate and bypass it instead.

MacArthur initially objected. He didn't want to look over his shoulder every time his forces moved west toward the Philippines. And bypassing Rabaul would rob him of an opportunity to burnish his public star with a real and meaningful victory. This was especially important to him since his defeat in the Philippines. On the other hand, MacArthur realized that bypassing Rabaul would eliminate the risk that his forces might be dragged into an especially bloody and potentially protracted battle that could delay his advance toward the Philippines. Should that happen, his generalship might once again get called into question, or even cause him to be stripped of his command.

Certainly, MacArthur and his staff knew from the very beginning that Rabaul would have to be dealt with, regardless of whether it was taken or isolated, but until the latter half of 1943 there was no way to do either. U.S. Navy submarines poached Japanese vessels as they sailed to and from the area, but they couldn't stop all the maritime traffic, and they certainly could do nothing about the forces ashore. In truth, bombers were the only means by which Rabaul—and the men who defended it—could be directly hit.

But during 1942 and much of 1943 the Allies were only able to send raids of just a few aircraft at a time, and mostly under the protection of night. These efforts amounted to little more than harassment. A ship or two might be damaged or even sunk, or several aircraft might be destroyed on the ground, but these were losses the Japanese could and did replace. They made little material difference.

The situation had changed by the latter half of 1943. Kenney's Fifth Air Force was no longer the tottering wreck whose men were forced to pick over the carcasses of dead aircraft to find the parts they needed to mend other, almost-dead aircraft. Instead, it was a burgeoning force of increasingly well-trained men that was growing larger and better every day. It was capable of delivering big blows on a scale that could have only been dreamed of a year earlier.

As part of the modified Cartwheel plan, an amphibious assault at Empress Augusta Bay on Bougainville was scheduled for November. Additionally, two more landings were planned at Gasmata and Cape Gloucester on New Britain Island in December. Gasmata sat less than 200 miles from Rabaul. Consequently, Japanese air units needed to be kept at bay. Kenney and his Fifth Air Force were charged with doing so, and Rabaul was the primary target.

The first big strike was scheduled for October 12, 1943. Planned for 349 aircraft, it was the biggest mission the Fifth had ever put together. A force of 114 B-25s from the 345th, 38th and 3rd Bomb Groups, together with a dozen Beaufighters from the RAAF's 30 Squadron, were tasked with hitting three of Rabaul's four airfields—Vunakanau, Tobera, and Rapopo. They were to mow across them low and fast, strafing and dropping parafrags as they did so.

These low-level attacks were intended not only to destroy but also to decoy. At the same time the B-25s were scheduled to strike the airfields, a total of 87 B-24s from the 90th and 43rd Bomb Groups—flying at high altitude—were to hit shipping in Simpson Harbor. Their probability of success would be greatly enhanced if the defending Japanese fighters were either engaged down low with the strafers or being blown to pieces by the strafers. Protecting the entire strike were to be 125 P-38s which would stage through the airstrip at Kiriwina Island for fuel and recover there, afterward.

The B-25s were staged forward from Port Moresby to Dobodura on October 11, as were the 12 Beaufighters of the RAAF's 30 Squadron. Takeoff took place the next morning at 0730 when the four squadrons of the 345th Bomb Group roared airborne. The 345th, which had started operations only a few months earlier in July, was proof of America's burgeoning might. Comprising four squadrons, it was the first fully manned, fully trained, fully equipped bomb group to arrive from the States.

The B-25s of the 38th and 3rd Bomb Groups took off after the 345th, but the dust raised by so many aircraft forced the Australian Beaufighter pilots to wait on the ground until visibility improved. Consequently, the main force pressed toward Rabaul without them. Once they took off, the Australians wasted no time and raced after the Americans.

The B-25s approached New Britain Island at low level to escape detection. Upon making landfall, the 3rd Bomb Group set a course for Rapopo while the 345th and the 38th Bomb Groups—six squadrons in trail formation—angled for Vunakanau. The odds of achieving surprise seemed small, especially as the 345th and 38th passed close by the Tobera airfield, where an estimated 20 to 30 fighters were lined up wingtip to wingtip and others were just taking off. That the B-25 crews had the discipline to fly past such an easy and lucrative target was remarkable.

In fact, the 12 Beaufighters of 30 Squadron were supposed to be attacking Tobera that very moment. Instead, they were still well out to sea and hurrying to catch the other elements of the raid.

★★★

The growl of an engine rose and fell, then rose and fell again. A mechanic jumped to the ground from where he stood on the fighter's wing, while another mechanic continued to test the engine from the cockpit. Other men in other revetments fussed with their own aircraft. Above them all, a trio of twin-engine bombers buzzed placidly around the airfield as they practiced landings, and a pair of fighters taxied toward the takeoff area. In the distance, a transport aircraft arced in a turn toward the airfield. At its edge, men walked unhurriedly between administrative buildings, or stopped and chatted or smoked in small groups. It was a typical morning for the Japanese at Vunakanau.

And then, great chunks of earth jumped skyward as a storm of .50 caliber machinegun rounds ripped the runway and the ground. One of the taxiing fighters exploded in a great orange fireball and lurched into the wall of a revetment. Men looked to the east as they ran for cover and saw the first wave of B-25s racing low across the airfield in a wide line abreast.

Each of the American bombers carried eight forward-firing machineguns, and the barrels of each streamed smoke as they spat deadly rounds into aircraft, men, and machines. Combined, the forward-firing guns of each bomber fired thousands of rounds. Tail, waist, and top turret gunners fired even more rounds at targets of opportunity.

At the same time, the bright white blossoms of parafrags dropped from the bellies of the bombers and fell softly toward the ground. The violence with which they exploded contrasted sharply with the gentleness of their descent. Deadly curtains of shrapnel rocketed in every direction, wrecking equipment and cutting men apart. Smoke and screams boiled across the airfield.

Clinton True, the commander of the 345th Bomb Group, led the B-25s. The mission narrative reported the effects of his attacks. "A Zeke that had left the runway and was airborne," it noted, "was strafed and seen to crash. The plane was seen by other crews and is known to have been destroyed definitely. [Para]Frag clusters were dropped among other planes and six were believed destroyed. One Zeke on landing strip was strafed and believed destroyed."

Kenneth Dean, another pilot with the 498th, had successes similar to True's. "Lieutenant Dean attacked along the strip and definitely destroyed or damaged severely, three airplanes. One inline engine fighter taxiing on the strip was strafed and tracers were seen to hit the fuselage from the tail up to the cockpit. This plane suddenly swerved to the side and stopped." Other 498th crews added to the score.

That first squadron of 12 B-25s, the 498th, was followed by five more—the three other squadrons from the 345th Bomb Group and two from the 38th Bomb Group. Trailing each other in approximately one-minute intervals, each successive squadron found it more and more difficult to find worthwhile targets. The best ones had been destroyed by the preceding crews, and those that remained were increasingly shrouded in smoke and dust.

So many aircraft attacking on such a broad front were constrained to a certain degree. For instance, a pilot at one side of the formation couldn't attack a target that wasn't more or less in front of him. He might be forced to attack nothing more valuable than a set of outbuildings or a garden plot.

Changing course just a few degrees could put him in the line of fire of other aircraft, or put other aircraft in front of his own guns. Indeed, the pilots were compelled to maintain tight discipline to achieve the desired destruction without shooting each other down.

That discipline unraveled occasionally, as was the case when the 345th's 500th Bomb Squadron made its attack. A fighter took off directly in front of the squadron and several pilots chased after it. George Cooper, on the formation's south side, had to turn his flight out of the way to keep from being rammed or shot.

At Rapopo, the scene was similar. The 3rd Bomb Group's B-25s blasted and bombed the aircraft parked there, and blew away the wing of a twin-engine, Mitsubishi Ki-21 bomber that was on its takeoff roll. All of the crew were killed.

Mayhem characterized the scene on the ground. Crews aboard aircraft that were readying to take off were immolated when their aircraft were set afire. Men were killed outright or were grievously wounded by the big .50 caliber machinegun rounds. At Rapopo, a Japanese doctor, Tetsuo Aso, noted the effects of the parafrags as they touched the ground and detonated. "Petty Officer Ohira and a few others on the floor died instantly," he said. "Sergeant Matsui was carried on a stretcher to the clinic with a big hole in his chest and his lungs hanging out, looking like balloons." Aso could do nothing, and Matsui died a short time later.[2]

It was apparent that even though the Japanese had multiple radar stations and ground observers in the area, the defenses received little warning of the attack. Gun crews raced toward their positions but were sent fleeing for cover time and again by successive waves of gunfire and parafrags. Likewise, only a few Japanese fighters were able to take off during the attack. They did so at tremendous risk. Although one B-25 of the 38th Bomb Group was shot down by fighters, few of the American low-level attackers sustained any damage.

The first formations of B-25s were already homeward bound very low over the water as 30 Squadron's Beaufighters finally neared the coast. Above the B-25s flew an escort of P-38s. The B-25 crews mistook the Australians for Japanese bombers and climbed toward them, guns firing, but their aim was poor, and they did no damage. The P-38s positioned themselves for an attack, but the Beaufighter leader, Bill Boulton, raised them on the radio and called them off before they fired. Both sides continued their separate ways.

After leading his squadron over the coast and pressing inland toward Tobera, Boulton noted that "huge chimneys of smoke and fire spreading over about three miles were rising from Vunakanau." It was then that his formation crossed under a group of nearly twenty Japanese fighters readying to land at Tobera—many with their landing gear already down. "But they soon put them up again," said Boulton. "Our appearance was evidently a surprise, but with the Zeroes airborne we knew we were [in] for it."[3]

A running fight followed as the Beaufighters closed ranks and raced for Tobera. The pilots took fleeting shots when Japanese fighters crossed in front of them, but at the airfield there was little to shoot at. And that was because most of the aircraft they had been tasked to destroy were airborne and trying to shoot them down.

Once past the airfield the Australians pulled for home. The Beaufighters were powerful and fast and eventually outstripped the Japanese fighter pilots who finally gave up the chase. However, one of the Australian pilots, Derrick Stone, left the protection of the formation to climb after a Zero and was soon lost to sight. His remains and those of his wireless air observer, Edward Morris-Hadwell, were not recovered until decades after the war.

High above it all, the B-24s of the 90th and 43rd Bomb Groups flew into a hornet's nest. Alerted by the B-25 attacks at Vunakanau and Rapopo, the crews of the big antiaircraft guns—and the guns aboard the naval combatants—put up a forceful defense. Augmenting that defense were most of Tobera's fighters, as well as those from Lakunai, which had not been attacked. Survivors of the massacres at Vunakanau and Rapopo—in ones and twos—joined them.

Arthur Rogers, the commander of the 90th Bomb Group, was stunned at what awaited his bombers as they neared Simpson Harbor. In the distance, black smoke and dust roiled the sky over Vunakanau. More ominously, a dense layer of antiaircraft bursts flashed and boiled directly in front of him, and above that churned a formation of Japanese fighters. "I was amazed and flabbergasted," he said, "to see just ahead, the biggest swarm of enemy fighters I had ever seen in the air at one time."[4]

It didn't matter what enemy defenses awaited Rogers and his B-24 crews; their mission was to bomb the ships below them. They pressed toward the harbor in formation as Japanese fighters paralleled their course, outdistanced them, then turned to make head-on attacks. Muzzle flashes winked from the guns mounted in their wings and noses. The front and top turret gunners aboard the bombers answered with their twin, .50 caliber machineguns.

Finally, the B-24 crews released their loads. The 1,000-pound bombs cascaded toward the harbor, and near misses sent geysers of sea-spray skyward, momentarily obscuring the ships. Other bombs found their marks as evidenced by great explosive blasts that were followed by fire and smoke. Warehouses and stockpiles ashore were set ablaze, and soldiers and sailors and civilians ran here and there, some to save their lives and some to save valuable material and equipment.

When the last of the B-24s released their bombs and winged for home, the sea around Rabaul and the town itself was shrouded in smoke and fire. White wakes marked the paths of enemy vessels as they fled the harbor for open water. In the distance Vunakanau and Rapopo still burned.

Enemy fighters, a mix of Zeroes and Ki-43s and Ki-61s, dogged the big American bombers. An engine on the B-24 captained by Hampton Rich was shot out. Tipped off by the smoke and fire, the enemy fighter pilots focused their attacks on the newly crippled bomber. Rich's squadron mates did not slow to protect him, and the P-38s tasked with protecting the formation were nowhere to be seen.

Unable to keep up or to maintain altitude, Rich and his crew fell further behind and dropped toward the water. Hopelessly alone, the B-24 was set upon by more Japanese fighters, which shot out at least one more engine. Finally, several other B-24 crews circled back to defend him, but it was too late. Rich's bomber continued to fall until he set it down in the sea more than 75 miles from Rabaul. The enemy pilots strafed the wreck until it exploded. There were no survivors.

The Japanese fighters continued their attacks for at least another 50 miles. It seemed to the B-24 crews that the Japanese would never run short of fuel or ammunition. Despite the guns carried by each bomber, and the combined effects of those guns when the bombers flew in formation, two more B-24s went down. Most of the rest were damaged.

MacArthur, as was typical, overstated the success of the raid. "It was a crushing and decisive defeat at a most vital point for the enemy," he declared. "Once again, surprise was predominant. Rabaul has been the focus and very hub of the enemy's main advanced air effort. I think we have broken its back. Almighty God once again blessed our arms."

Estimates of Japanese losses were grossly overblown at 177 aircraft, three destroyers, three large cargo vessels and 43 smaller vessels ranging from 100 to 500 tons, as well as 70 smaller boats. In reality, although several smaller craft were destroyed, only one large cargo vessel was sunk. This was the *Keisho Maru*. Certainly, a number of other cargo ships were damaged, as were a handful of combatant ships. But in terms of tonnage sunk, the results were less than remarkable especially considering the level of effort that was expended.

Aside from the material ashore that was blown to bits or burned, the real damage was done by the B-25 units at Vunakanau and Rapopo. Although the number of Japanese aircraft that was destroyed was not 177 as MacArthur claimed, the actual number probably exceeded 50. Perhaps more critical were the skilled mechanics and other highly trained personnel who were killed or badly wounded. New aircraft could be manufactured and sent to Rabaul in a matter of weeks. On the other hand, it took years to develop a competent mechanic, without which the aircraft were useless.

The same was true of pilots. Although the number killed that day was small, Japan was training new ones too slowly and not very well. This became more apparent as the war continued.

★★★

Although his men had inflicted real damage on the Japanese at Rabaul, Kenney knew that the October 12 raid was not a killing blow. He never expected that it would be and had already planned a series of additional raids intended to keep the Japanese back on their heels. Only by maintaining constant and overwhelming pressure could Rabaul be neutralized. In fact, a raid was launched the very next day, October 13, but poor weather kept it from reaching its objective. And it did so at a price.

Gerald Johnson was leading the P-38s of the 49th Fighter Group's 9th Fighter Squadron that day. They were part of an escort of more than a hundred P-38s for the 70 B-24s that the Fifth was able to put airborne for the mission. Johnson joined with the bombers north of Kiriwina and continued northeast on a course for Rabaul. However, the weather grew uncooperative after less than an hour. Johnson noted, "We hit thin clouds at 20,000 feet. The bombers proceeded through these, and I could see blue sky above so took my squadron through to clear weather."

Darkening clouds loomed ahead, reaching up to 30,000 feet. "The bombers by this time," said Johnson, "were scattered and taking different courses and altitudes through the weather. I approached the frontal area, my flights above and behind me." By now, with the B-24s on divergent paths and altitudes, it was apparent that the raid to Rabaul was not going to happen.

"Then I made a gentle, diving turn to the left through the edge of some rain, picking up ice on the propeller hubs." Johnson's pitot tube iced over, and he consequently lost his altimeter and airspeed indicator. He continued his descending turn until he popped clear of the weather. Checking to his rear, Johnson saw no one from his squadron.

When Johnson had turned left and descended, the rest of the formation had turned right. "The weather didn't look so good from the start and kept getting worse," recalled Gordon Fanning, one of Johnson's pilots. "I could see a solid mass of clouds ahead and bombers and fighters disappearing into it." Fanning's flight leader, Theron Price, turned right and started down. Heavy rain throbbed hard against the aircraft. "I followed," said Fanning, "until he and his wingman disappeared into the clouds which were so thick it was necessary for us to fly on instruments." When he finally cleared the weather, Fanning caught a fleeting glimpse of one other P-38, but nothing else.

Milby Marling was also in Price's flight. At one point, in the thick gray gloom of the clouds, he sneaked a quick peek away from Price to check his instruments. They showed he was in a steep, diving turn and flying much too fast. He broke away from Price, regained control of his aircraft, and flew clear of the clouds. There was no one else in sight.

None of the aircraft made it to Rabaul, and three of the 9th Fighter Squadron's P-38s failed to return, Theron Price among them. There was no way of knowing for certain what happened to the missing pilots, and three days of searching turned up nothing, but Gerald Johnson offered a theory: "I believe the reason for the loss of these pilots was due to mid-air collision. All pilots had sufficient experience to turn out of the rain."[5]

New Guinea's treacherous weather proved—as it had and would many more times—to be as deadly a foe as the Japanese.

Meteorological conditions continued to stymie the Fifth's plans against Rabaul for the next several days. Rather than letting his units sit idle, Kenney sent them against targets in New Guinea that would need attention at some point anyway. These targets included Wewak and Alexishafen among others, as well as enemy barges and army units in the coastal regions. For their part, the Japanese didn't sit idle either, sending sizable strikes to Oro Bay on October 15 and 17. Both efforts were badly beaten by defending American fighters.

Gambling against the weather, the Fifth sent another mission against Rabaul on October 18. The plan was for eight squadrons of B-24s to hit the airfields at Vunakanau and Lakunai. Presumably, the two airfields would be too badly damaged to recover the defending fighters, which would then be forced to land at Rapopo and Tobera. Subsequently, as those fighters were being refueled, five squadrons of B-25s from the 345th and 38th Bomb Groups were to attack from low level and blow them to bits. Another squadron from the 345th was assigned to hit shipping in the harbor.

Weather en route kept the high-flying B-24s from reaching Rabaul. Some hit secondary targets while others returned directly to base. The fighter escorts—the P-38s—also aborted the mission. But Clinton True, who led the B-25s at the head of the 345th Bomb Group, pressed on. A recall order was sent, but True pretended not to hear it as he led the six B-25 squadrons lower and lower through sheets of driving rain, until they flew just above the water at an altitude of 50 feet.

The visibility was so poor that 345th pilot George Cooper slid his side window open so that he could see the waves well enough to keep from flying into them. Commenting as to whether or not True heard the radio transmission that recalled the mission, Cooper said, "He heard it. I heard it—we all heard it." True's decision to press on without a fighter escort was contrary to standing orders.[6]

Contrary or not, it was a decision that caused the Japanese considerable hurt. The force of 50 B-25s finally broke into the clear, made landfall, and headed inland. The two squadrons of the 38th Bomb Group arced left toward Tobera while the four squadrons of the 345th Bomb Group leaned right toward Rapopo. Strafing and dropping 100-pound parachute-suspended demolition bombs, or parademos, the treetop-skimming 345th and 38th destroyed an estimated forty aircraft at the two airfields.

It wasn't until they swung for home that they were attacked by a force of approximately 50 Zeroes. Roughly half of the enemy aircraft stayed at altitude, wary of a fighter escort which in fact had turned back due to the en route weather. The B-25s closed ranks, and their combined defensive firepower proved to be effective as the crews claimed a dozen enemy attackers shot down. None of the B-25s were lost.

Meanwhile, the 345th's 500th Bomb Squadron—which was sent to attack shipping in the harbor—fought a separate battle. Reduced by mechanical failures to only six aircraft, the two flights of three strafed targets of opportunity before dropping down so low that the blast of their propellers flattened the waves behind them. They adjusted their flight paths and flew directly at a pair of freighters.

Max Mortensen and Ray Geer dropped 1,000-pound bombs which straddled one of the ships. The bombs were fused for five-second delays, and when they detonated, they blew the vessel out of the water and capsized it. A corvette maneuvered wildly in front of them. Thane Hecox released two 1,000-pound bombs, which hit directly in front of it. A few seconds later, just as the ship passed over them, they exploded and essentially rendered the ship and its crew into small pieces.

The other flight of three B-25s, led by Lyle Anacker, set another freighter's superstructure afire with heavy machinegun fire. Closing the distance, they dropped six 1,000-pound bombs. One struck the ship and bounced into the water, while the other five detonated nearby and lifted it out of the water.

And then, they were caught by enemy fighters.

Ralph Wallace's right engine was hit, and he was forced to shut it down before it shook itself from the wing. The other two aircraft in the flight, captained by Anacker and Harlan Peterson, slowed to protect him and his crew. It wasn't long until the Japanese pilots shot up Peterson's left engine, which began to smoke. At the same time, the left landing gear extended. Peterson was unable to maintain flying speed, and the aircraft hit the water, tail down. A half-dozen enemy fighters strafed it before it sank.

Wallace and Anacker fled down New Britain's southern coast for an hour and 10 minutes as they fought the relentless Japanese fighter pilots. Seven enemy aircraft were claimed shot down by the two crews. "One nervy Jap," noted the postmission report, "eased into formation between the two B-25s and flew for more than a minute not more than 50 feet away from either Mitchell. The gunners did not dare to fire for fear of hitting their other plane. The Jap pilot was described by one gunner as a 'mean-looking bastard.'"

Wallace's crew scrambled to move more ammunition to the guns while the radioman hunched over his set and transmitted calls for help. A gas line ruptured, spraying fuel through the middle of the aircraft. The men took turns covering the leak with their hands while trying not to pass out from the fumes. Spent shell casings and gasoline sloshed about their feet. The copilot, Edward Hicko, slid back his side window and fired his .45 caliber pistol at the enemy fighters as they made their firing runs. He took bullets in his belly and a hand for his troubles.

Anacker's aircraft was badly hit, and he turned north toward the enemy-held shore of New Britain, pursued by a flight of enemy fighters. Wallace turned south for Kiriwina and battled the remaining enemy aircraft. "Some of the Japs appeared anxious to finish him off," declared the postmission report, "and became daring in their maneuvers which resulted in four, and a possible fifth, crashing to the water as they wheeled low to attack Lieutenant Wallace, who was flying at about 30 feet."

The remaining Japanese fighter pilots winged for home one by one as they ran short of fuel and ammunition. Finally, there remained only one Zero. Its pilot saluted Wallace and his crew with several slow rolls, then waggled his wings and flew away. Far to the north, Anacker's B-25 was shot into the water. Anacker was killed, but two of the crew survived and swam to shore. There, they were befriended by natives and brought to an Australian coastwatcher. Months later, they were returned to American control.

The air war over New Guinea would have been fought much less effectively if not for Paul "Pappy" Gunn. *Wikipedia*

An early P-38 over New Guinea. *Australian War Memorial*

A head-on view of two P-38s in New Guinea. *Australian War Memorial*

Right: A 25-pounder like those transported to Wau by C-47. *Wikipedia*

Below both: The RAAF's Bristol Beaufighter was tough, fast, and well-armed. *Australian War Memorial*

Above: An RAAF Bristol Beaufighter over the Bismarck Sea. *Australian War Memorial*

Left: Wing Commander Brian "Blackjack" Walker flew the Beaufighter during the Battle of the Bismarck Sea. *Australian War Memorial*

Below: A view over the shoulder of a pilot of an RAAF Beaufighter. *Australian War Memorial*

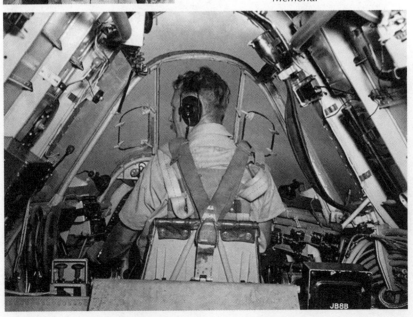

Japanese ships burn during the Battle of the Bismarck Sea. *Australian War Memorial*

Although less well-liked than the B-17, the B-24 carried a larger bomb load farther. *USAAF*

Left: A Ki-41, code-named Helen, burns at Dagua, part of the Wewak complex. The
line of Ki-61 Tony fighters appears unharmed. *USAAF*
Right: At Dagua, B-25s deliver a low-level strafing and parafrag attack. *USAAF*

An airstrike against Boram, part of the Wewak complex. Note the B-25 at the top of the photo and the shadow of another B-25 on the runway. *USAAF*

B-25s make an apparently unsuccessful low-level attack against Japanese shipping. *USAAF*

Above left: A B-25 flies low over the runway at Wewak. *USAAF*
Above right: Two bombs fall from a B-25 on a skip bombing mission. *USAAF*

A Japanese Ki-21 bomber, code-named Sally, is about to be shot down. *USAAF*

A B-25 attacks shipping in Simpson Harbor, Rabaul. *USAAF*

A Japanese freighter burns in Simpson Harbor, Rabaul. A cruiser is in the foreground. *USAAF*

Above both: Parafrags fall on enemy aircraft at Vunakanau, near Rabaul. *USAAF*

The 345th Bomb Group's B-25s dropped white phosphorous bombs at Rabaul on November 2, 1943. *USAAF*

A Japanese Ki-43, code-named Oscar, was shot down over Cape Gloucester, December 1943. *USAAF*

Above: Native Papuans clear a road near Dobodura. *USAAF*

Left: The P-47, although quite capable, never was as well-liked as the P-38 by pilots in the Fifth Air Force. *USAAF*

Below: A 49th Fighter Group P-40 being refueled. *USAAF*

P-40 mechanics prepare a new Allison V-1710 engine for installation. *USAAF*

The Vultee Vengeance was not put into combat by the United States but was effectively flown by the RAAF. *Wikimedia*

Above: The P-40 was an especially tough aircraft that performed well in the Southwest Pacific. *Australian War Memorial*

Below both: The Kawasaki Ki-61, code-named Tony, was not as maneuverable as the Zero or Oscar but was faster and better armed. *USAAF and Wikipedia*

The Navy's PBY Catalina was a welcome sight for downed USAAF flyers. *Wikimedia*

Generals Ennis Whitehead, George Kenney, and William Knudson. *USAAF*

Generals William Knudson, Ennis Whitehead, and George Kenney. *USAAF*

Gordon Manuel was aboard this B-17 when it was shot down. The photo has been censored with white patches. *Australian War Memorial*

The phosphorous bombs used at Rabaul made it difficult for Japanese antiaircraft gunners to see. *Australian War Memorial*

Kenney's parafrags proved to be devastating weapons. *USAAF*

A 49th Fighter Group P-40 Warhawk readies for takeoff. *USAAF*

The death of a 312th Bomb Group A-20 crew at Kokas, New Guinea, after being hit by antiaircraft fire. *USAAF*

Thomas McGuire's P-38, *Pudgy*. *Wikipedia*

Above: Japanese air power at Hollandia was wrecked before it could be used. *USAAF*

Thomas Lynch was a leading P-38 ace when he was shot down and killed by antiaircraft fire in March 1944. *USAAF*

Aviation legend Charles Lindbergh, right, shared a tent with leading P-38 ace, Thomas McGuire. *USAAF*

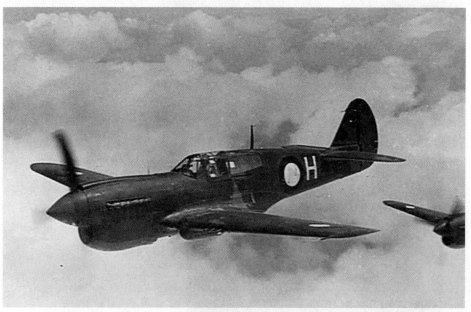

The RAAF used the P-40 very effectively until the end of the war. *Australian War Memorial*

The CAC Wirraway was a useful trainer, utility aircraft, and general hack but was never intended as a combat aircraft. *Australian War Memorial*

Left: George Kenney. *USAAF*
Right: Gordon Manuel evaded the Japanese on New Britain Island with the help of native friends. *USAAF*

23

"HE WAS LYING"

The all-B-25 effort on October 18 proved to be a success, but Clinton True—who led the attack despite the recall order—was in hot water. Kenney had earlier issued orders that no bombing mission was to continue to any target unless it had a fighter escort. True knew that the P-38s tasked to escort him had turned back in the face of the dismal weather. And although he denied it, he was almost certainly aware of the message which canceled the attack.

On the one hand, Kenney admired True's aggressiveness. On the other hand, that aggressiveness was in direct defiance of his orders. "When True returned," Kenney said, "I called him over to headquarters and bawled him out for disobeying our standing instructions that bombers were also to turn back if the fighters had to."

Kenney queried True about the circumstances along the route to Rabaul and whether or not he knew the P-38s had aborted the mission. True denied any knowledge of it. "He was lying," Kenney said, "and he knew that I knew it, but he was sticking to his story." Kenney let it stand and congratulated True on the success of the mission. He later rewarded him with the Distinguished Service Cross.[1]

★★★

The number of Japanese aircraft at the different airfields at Rabaul at any one time during this period was difficult to determine as photo reconnaissance was not always complete or accurate, and the Japanese destroyed many of their records. Estimates sometimes ranged north of 300. But the number of aircraft counted on the ground didn't translate to equal numbers of aircraft in the sky during the Allied raids. A senior Japanese officer explained:

In 1943, at any one time, only 50 percent of the planes were ever available, and on the next day following an all-out operation only 30 percent would be available. By the end of 1943, only 40 percent at any one time would be serviceable. . . . From 1943 on, it [low aircraft serviceability] was due to lack of skill on the part of maintenance personnel and faulty manufacturing methods. Inspection of the aircraft and spare parts, prior to their delivery to Rabaul, was inadequate, and there were many poorly constructed and weak parts discovered.

★★★

Rabaul, the entire complex, was still a burgeoning base for Japanese air and naval operations despite the Fifth's attacks. Reinforced with fighters from the Japanese base at Truk in the Caroline Islands, it remained as potent as ever. It had not been neutralized or reduced, and certainly could not be bypassed. Consequently, more raids of varying effectiveness were sent on October 23, 24, 25, and 29. Excepting the mission of October 24, which was another low-level strike by B-25s, these follow-on raids were high-altitude efforts flown by B-24s and escorted by P-38s. It should also be noted that the RAAF sent small numbers of Beaufort bombers on night raids on several different occasions.

During this same period, on November 1, 1943, the 3rd Marine Division went ashore at Cape Torokina at the north end of Empress Augusta Bay, on Bougainville. This was a critical part of Operation Cartwheel. The Marines were uncontested at the beach, but a powerful enemy naval force made up of cruisers and destroyers sortied from Rabaul that same day to interdict the landing. This force was engaged by a U.S. Navy force of similar size and composition, and in the fierce battle that followed—in the early morning dark of November 2—the Japanese were turned away.

Kenney planned strikes against Rabaul to coincide with the landing on Bougainville. But it wasn't until November 2 that the weather cleared enough for his pilots and crews to deliver. It was to be a multi-axis attack made up of 76 B-25s protected by 73 P-38s. Shipping in Simpson Harbor was the primary target.

The force started to launch early on November 2 but was recalled because of weather before most of the crews got airborne. The second takeoff, just before 1100, experienced no issues, and the three bomb groups pressed toward New Britain. Along the route, they picked up the P-38 escort that had been staged forward at Kiriwina Island.

The plan called for the four squadrons of the 345th Bomb Group to fly a course to the east of Simpson Harbor before racing down the slopes of the volcanoes toward the town of Rabaul. Along the way, skating through the sky just above the terrain, they were to strafe enemy antiaircraft positions and other targets of opportunity. At the same time, they were to smother them with parafrags. This was intended not only to kill or neutralize the enemy gun crews but to attract the attention of the enemy fighter pilots and draw them away from the anchorage. Essentially, the 345th was blocking and tackling for the 3rd and 38th Bomb Groups, which were tasked with hitting the shipping in the harbor.

The aircraft of two of the 345th's squadrons carried 12 100-pound white phosphorous bombs each. Should the strafing and parafrag attacks fail to be effective, the white phosphorous bombs would blanket the area with a thick, cloying veil of white smoke. With their vision blocked, the enemy gunners—at least for a short time—would be just as useless as if they were dead.

These white phosphorous weapons also had a psychological effect. They burst with a flash followed by great, terrifying white tentacles of choking smoke and sizzling bits of phosphorous which set fire to whatever they contacted. This included people. Almost impossible to extinguish, the phosphorous burned through clothes and skin and created great, painful lesions.

The 498th Bomb Squadron was at the head of the 345th's formation. As the squadron flew east of Rabaul, it was fired on by three destroyers. After making landfall, the squadron was attacked with aerial bombs dropped from above by a fighter. "Three aerial burst bombs which exploded, throwing long red streamers were dropped by enemy fighters," the squadron recorded. "One bomb exploded on same level as bombers, but 100 yards in front. One hit the ground before exploding. One dropped from 1,500 feet burst 700 feet above the bombers."

Unperturbed and undamaged by the strange weapons, the 498th's crews continued to Rabaul, bombing and strafing antiaircraft positions and other targets of opportunity. Although attacked by dozens of enemy fighters as they egressed, they sustained virtually no damage.

The 500th Bomb Squadron—loaded with white phosphorous bombs—followed the 498th. The aircraft flown by Albert Krasnickas was hit by antiaircraft fire, which caused one or more of its phosphorous bombs to ignite. Smoke and fire immediately enveloped the aircraft as it tipped over in a death roll and smashed into the ground, instantly immolating the crew.

Max Mortensen's bombs were also hit, and although the resultant explosion was not nearly so violent, he still struggled to see through the eye-stinging smoke that swirled through the cockpit. He immediately jettisoned his bombs and feathered the right engine which seemed to have likewise caught fire. The smoke inside the aircraft cleared and he was able to fly the aircraft back to Dobodura. The squadron's mission narrative noted that "the plane was still smoldering and glowing from the phosphorous [even] hours later."

The 345th's squadrons, as planned and expected, attracted the Japanese fighters as they hit their targets and ran for home. Zeroes fell on them, and P-38s, in turn, chased after the Zeroes. Black trails of smoke creased the sky, marking the death dives of both Japanese and American fighters. Geysers of spray marked where they hit the water. Fiery explosions belied their impact points on land. Antiaircraft fire from both ships and shore alike fired into the increasingly chaotic melee that was the air fighting above Rabaul.

George Cooper, a flight leader with the 499th Bomb Squadron, flew to the south, along the eastern part of Simpson Harbor. The phosphorous bombs of one of his wingmen, Bill Parke, were hit. Parke salvoed the bombs, saving himself and his crew. Cooper fired at a line of floatplanes not far from shore, setting four of them afire. Other members of the 499th shot up targets at Lakunai airfield.

On schedule and on plan, the B-25s of the 38th and 3rd Bomb Groups—the antishipping aircraft—raced north across the water. The volcanoes surrounding Rabaul rose to their left. High above, the P-38 pilots readied their aircraft for combat and released their external fuel tanks. The bomber crews spotted the empty husks tumbling down like so much trash. A line of destroyers peppered the sky above them with antiaircraft fire— none of it was low or close enough to do them harm.

Both bomb groups swung left to the west, crossed the shore, and climbed the slopes of the volcanoes north and east of the harbor. Their engines strained and their airspeed dropped precipitously. At the crest of the pass which led down to the harbor they sprayed the antiaircraft crews that were still alive with torrents of gunfire. Nose guns, top and tail turret guns, and waist guns sent converging cascades of vibrations through each aircraft.

A staggering panorama of fire and smoke showed itself as the two bomb groups accelerated down the slanting sides of the volcanoes. Crashed aircraft burned, as did warehouses and other buildings in the town. A skein of white phosphorous fog, denser in some places than others, drifted and collected in gullies and other low places. Bright tracers chased after fleeing bombers which flew so low, they blasted the scrub behind them, or left flattened paths of water in their wakes.

Dick Walker, a pilot with the 3rd Bomb Group's 13th Bomb Squadron, recalled that morning's briefing: "Hearing the latest word on the extent of the Japanese defenses was pretty much a prediction that all of us would not be coming home," he said. "The twelve crews that were assigned to fly the mission sat gray-faced and quiet during the briefing." He had gotten spit out of the squadron's formation as it turned toward Simpson Harbor, and his wingman had already been shot down. Now alone, he flew as low and as fast as he dared. Ships that shot at his aircraft risked hitting other ships.

Walker zig-zagged between them before lining up on a freighter. "That ship's superstructure looked like the Empire State building towering in front of me, but I drove in, released my bombs and hauled back on the yoke," he said. Walker's B-25 barely missed the ship and his bombs slammed home only a second or so later. Subsequent photographs showed the freighter's stern underwater.[3]

James Hungerpiller, a pilot with the 38th Bomb Group, let the nose of his B-25 drop toward Simpson Harbor and felt the bomber accelerate as it flew—together with the other aircraft of the 71st Bomb Squadron—just above the sloping terrain. The anchorage in front of him was filled with both cargo ships and naval combatants, and the sky was already dirty with battle smoke of all sorts. Smoke gushed from the stacks of ships that hurried to get up steam, while smoke of a different pallor rose from burning vessels and buildings ashore.

Hungerpiller crossed the beach and stopped his B-25's descent just above the water. John Orr, flying to Hungerpiller's right, did the same. Dazzling streaks of tracers belied the paths of the antiaircraft fire that criss-crossed the harbor and which only barely cleared the superstructures of the dozens of ships that sat or sailed on its surface. It took the two pilots just seconds to select their targets.

Ahead, sitting broadside to Hungerpiller's path, were two destroyers, one behind the other. He dipped a wing, altering his course so as to fly directly at them, while Orr, unable to target the destroyers without running the risk of smashing into Hungerpiller, aimed his aircraft at a merchant vessel. As they closed the distance to their targets, both pilots triggered their machineguns and sprayed the decks of the enemy ships. Hundreds of bright flashes winked back at them as the projectiles found their marks.

Only a second or so before reaching the destroyers, Hungerpiller let go two bombs. Fred Bossi watched from where he manned a waist gun on Orr's aircraft. "I saw one of the bombs score a direct hit on one of the destroyers," he said, "and cause an immediate explosion and fire. The other bomb skipped on the ship's deck and fell in the water some fifty feet past its prow, and among the swimming sailors."

Both pilots climbed to about 200 feet. Orr looked to his left and saw Hungerpiller's left engine afire. Hungerpiller pulled his damaged B-25 into a hard right turn and passed directly underneath Orr, losing both altitude and airspeed. "As I last saw the plane," said Orr, "it was heading toward two heavy cruisers anchored near shore on the west side of the harbor. The left engine was burning fiercely and there appeared to be a secondary explosion and fire as if the left main and left auxiliary wing tanks had ignited."

His aircraft no longer capable of flight, Hungerpiller and his crew smashed into the water and perished.[4]

Raymond Wilkins commanded the 8th Bomb Squadron. He had been the only pilot to return to Port Moresby following the disastrous A-24 raid north of Gona more than a year earlier. Now, his B-25 already damaged by antiaircraft fire, he rocketed down toward the harbor directly at a destroyer. He released a 1,000-pound bomb which punched into the side of the vessel. It exploded violently, and the ship started sinking immediately. Behind him, while he took aim at a large transport, the remainder of the 8th's crews scored hits and near misses on a grab-bag of freighters and combatants. Again, his bomb found its mark, and the big ship burned furiously.

Constrained from maneuvering by nearby aircraft and ships, Wilkins was compelled to fly directly at a cruiser. He sprayed the big ship with machinegun fire while flying into a virtual curtain of antiaircraft shells. One of his vertical stabilizers was shot away, and then, as he turned to avoid running into another aircraft, his left wing was nearly shot away. He and his crew cartwheeled into the water. He was posthumously awarded the Medal of Honor for his actions that day.

Meanwhile, the P-38 fighter escorts did their best to protect the B-25 crews. It is impossible to untangle exactly what happened where and when—and to whom by who—but the fighting took place at all altitudes and across a broad arena. Virtually all accounts mention the ferocity of the air engagements and the huge numbers of aircraft.

The P-38 pilots were outnumbered. Although a force of 75 of the fighters was planned for the mission, mechanical difficulties forced a number of them to turn back early, and only about 60 actually reached Rabaul. Conversely, it was estimated that the Japanese launched more than a hundred fighters.

For this reason, and because it seemed that the Japanese pilots on this particular day were well-trained and aggressive, the P-38s endured substantial losses. But one of these, Leo Mayo, a pilot with the 475th Fighter Group, was not killed by a skilled and aggressive pilot. Mayo spotted a Ki-61 and closed on it from behind at high speed and started firing at about 200 yards. The enemy fighter blew up, and a piece of debris knocked off

Mayo's right wing. Although he was able to parachute clear of his wrecked aircraft, he came down very near the shore and was likely captured and killed.

On the other hand, no one seemed to know what happened to Lowell Lutton, another P-38 pilot with the 475th. Two of the pilots in his flight aborted the mission for mechanical difficulties, and he had lost the other at some point during the fighting.

"In the last few minutes of the fight, I turned to the right of Lieutenant Lutton to intercept an enemy aircraft making a diving attack from the right," said Arthur Wenige, another 475th flight leader. "Having scared him off, I started straightening out and saw Lieutenant Lutton tack on[to] the rear of my flight. I called to him on the radio and said, 'Let's go home,' then I transferred my attentions to enemy aircraft in the area. No longer than one or two minutes later, I noticed that Lieutenant Lutton was no longer behind me."[5] Lutton was never seen again, and had quite possibly been picked off, unnoticed, by a Japanese fighter pilot.

Francis Love, a P-38 pilot with the 49th Fighter Group, likewise disappeared. This was the same Francis Love who had inadvertently flown his P-38 into the water the previous July. On this day he was the fourth man in the flight led by Norman Hyland. "We were passing over Simpson Harbor at approximately 3,000 feet," said Hyland. "This is where I last saw my second element [numbers three and four in the flight]. Lieutenant Love was tail man in the flight. The Zeroes were thick and the antiaircraft fire was heavy. I can't say that Lieutenant Love was shot down or whether he ran out of gas on the way home."[6]

Because of the dynamic nature of air combat, it was not uncommon that individual fighter pilots were seen one minute and then never again. The fights often moved at high speeds and the distances covered were considerable—an aircraft could be swallowed by the sky very quickly. Moreover, other pilots were frequently preoccupied, either trying to shoot another aircraft down, or trying to be not shot down.

A final example on that same day underscores this reality. Kenneth Richardson flew P-38s with the 475th Fighter Group. His flight was assigned as low cover for the B-25s over Simpson Harbor. "As we approached the south end of the harbor," recalled Francis Lent, Richardson's flight leader, "we noticed six-to-seven Zekes [Zeroes] making for the B-25s." Racing to protect the B-25s, Lent and his flight were attacked by the same enemy fighters. "As we succeeded in chasing the first Zekes away, we were attacked by seven or eight more Zekes from above," said Lent. "Three of them attacked me and chased me toward New Britain. I looked around and saw four Zekes chasing Lieutenant Richardson over Rabaul Harbor. This was the last I saw of Lieutenant Richardson."[7]

★★★

The November 2 raid against Rabaul had been an astonishing spectacle. Photographs taken during the attack supported this, as did accounts from the enemy. "An appalling sight met my eyes," said a Japanese soldier. "Through the palm trees I saw one of our ships enveloped in black smoke and a moment later I saw a pillar of flames shoot up to the sky and the ship exploded and sank. All other ships must have suffered the same fate, as columns of black smoke were emanating from them."[8]

Kenney was giddy at the successes his crews claimed, and he declared, "Never in the long history of warfare had so much destruction been wrought upon the forces of a belligerent nation so swiftly and at such little cost to the victor."[9] This was a ridiculous exaggeration, especially as compared to the Battle of Midway the previous year during which the Navy sank four Japanese aircraft carriers.

What the Fifth Air Force actually claimed after performing a critical assessment of the raid was three large destroyers and eight merchant ships sunk, as well as a handful of smaller vessels. The intelligence analysts also noted significant damage to a number of other ships—including a cruiser— as well as the destruction of warehouses and stores ashore. Although noteworthy, this tally was hardly historic and was in fact reduced later in the war. For their part, the Japanese indicated that no combatant ships were destroyed and that only a bare handful of cargo ships were sunk.

Aircraft claims were even more excessive. Supposedly, 67 of approximately 125 Japanese fighters were shot down, but the total was much smaller. On the other hand, the Japanese declared they had shot down a total of 48 B-25s and 95 P-38s. They later raised this total to more than 200. Actual Fifth Air Force losses were a fraction of that, at eight B-25s and 10 P-38s. This overclaiming by the Japanese made the American claims seem quite judicious.

Still, the loss rates for both the B-25s and P-38s on this mission approached 15 percent—a number which was absolutely not sustainable. And considering the speed, altitude, armament, and survivability advantages of the P-38 over the enemy fighters, it is difficult to characterize the performance of the P-38 pilots during the raid as anything but poor.

The disparity between claims and actual losses for both ships and aircraft defy accurate resolution. The Japanese destroyed many records at war's end and were often reluctant to talk about their losses, or had incomplete knowledge. In particular, definitively determining aircraft losses was very problematic. Pilot reports were notoriously unreliable, either purposefully or because of the confusion and excitement of air combat. During the strikes of October and November 1943, reconnaissance photographs showed consistently high numbers of aircraft at the different airfields at Rabaul, even after the big raids. This was attributed to the arrival of reinforcements, principally from Truk.

However, although aircraft were no doubt received from Truk, those numbers are uncertain. The reality was that claims for aircraft destroyed were grossly inflated and that the aircraft being counted at Rabaul were mostly the same ones that had been there all along. Additionally, aircraft claimed as destroyed might have been only damaged, and could have been quickly repaired and put back into service.

That Rabaul's air elements weren't yet defeated was underscored by the fact that the Japanese launched offensive missions against various targets through the entire period. In fact, a strike of more than eighty aircraft had been sent against the Allied forces at Cape Torokina, at Bougainville on the morning of November 2. If the Japanese had been neutralized, no one had bothered to tell them.

Although it sometimes was not done well, it was easier to monitor ships, especially combatants of destroyer size or larger. This was due to the simple fact that ships were big and easier to track. Allied intelligence organizations had awareness—albeit incomplete—of what combatants were in service and where they were. Over time, it became apparent when particular ships were sunk.

Also, not to be discounted is the basic fact that ships were difficult to sink. They were large, they were made of steel, and they were especially designed *not* to sink. Sailors were well trained in damage control, and a vessel that seemed certain to go under one hour could be saved during the next, long after attacking aircraft were gone. Moreover, a great deal of fire and smoke did not necessarily translate into mortal damage as fires could be extinguished and smoke didn't sink ships. Moreover, vessels could be raised if they went down in shallow water and weren't too badly damaged.

There might also have been political motives for the overstated effects of not only the raid of November 2 but of the entire series of raids. In terms of resource allocation, the war against Japan was secondary to the war against Germany, and Kenney had always played second fiddle. If he could show his superior—Hap Arnold—that he was making good use of what he had been allocated, then Arnold might be more inclined to send him more. The overclaiming might have had the desired effect because Kenney did receive more resources. On the other hand, this might have been because the nation's industrial complex was finally running at top speed, and there was simply more equipment to give.

Additionally, there was little upside for Kenney's other boss, Douglas MacArthur, to temper the estimates of destruction. If Kenney's airmen looked good, then so did he. What he really wanted was Rabaul eliminated as a threat. If that goal was accomplished, he had little reason to fiddle with the details of ship and aircraft losses.

The next raid against Rabaul took place on November 5. It had as its objective the interdiction of a sizeable force of newly arrived cruisers that threatened the recently landed Allied forces at Bougainville. A Navy strike from two aircraft carriers, supported by high altitude B-24s and escorting P-38s, damaged six of the seven cruisers. Most of them fled to Truk the following day, thereby negating the threat.

★★★

It had been more than five months since Gordon Manuel had been shot down. Now, on November 6, 1943, with a party of his native friends, he was on the move to find and join Allan Roberts, an Australian coast-watcher. The group was traveling on a road which ran along the coast when they halted and went to ground upon spotting a lone figure walking down the beach.

Manuel squinted against the glare of the beach. The man was not a native, nor was he Japanese. And if he was a white man, he was totally ignorant of how dangerous it was for him to be moving in the open. Manuel stood up and the man spotted him and waved.

They approached each other and Manuel—having been so far and long removed from his own culture—choked when the other man shouted at him, asking if he was an American. The man was Owen Giertsen, who had last been seen in his P-38 during the swirling dogfight over Rabaul just a few days earlier, on November 2.

Part of a 475th Fighter Group formation covering a low flight of bombers, Giertsen had followed his flight lead, Fred Champlin, up and around a cloud. "Immediately after this," said Champlin, "Lieutenant Giertsen was attacked by enemy aircraft from above and behind. I called the enemy aircraft into Lieutenant Giertsen and he immediately broke down and to the left." Champlin turned in the other direction, then "swung back" and shot the enemy aircraft off of Giertsen's tail. Under attack himself, Champlin dived into a bank of clouds. The last time he saw Giertsen, he was flying in the clear and headed for Kiriwina Island. "I believe that

Lieutenant Giertsen ran low on gasoline," said Champlin, "and was unable to reach Kiriwina."[10]

Champlin might have been confused. Actually, Giertsen's aircraft had been badly hit during the first attack. He was still in control of the aircraft when he escaped by diving into a cloud layer but was forced to ditch and subsequently drifted ashore aboard his life raft having sustained no real injuries except a gash on his face.

Giertsen reviewed the latest news with Manuel—war, sports, and otherwise—as they walked with the natives down the beach to where Giertsen had set up an ad hoc camp. Manuel was ecstatic at having connected with a fellow American after having been isolated from everything familiar for so long. But he started with horror when he spotted Giertsen's parachute. He had hung it high in a tree where it billowed big, white, and bright for all the world to see. On Manuel's orders the natives quickly pulled it down and stashed it in the jungle, along with his life raft. When all traces of Giertsen's existence had been erased, Manuel's party, larger now by one, continued cautiously along the coast road.

★★★

The Fifth Air Force—in cooperation with the Navy—had big plans for Rabaul on November 11. However, weather en route turned back most of the effort with only a few B-24s striking the airfield at Lakunai. The Navy attacked later from a different direction and enjoyed better luck, sinking a destroyer and heavily damaging a cruiser. A Japanese force of approximately 120 aircraft was subsequently sent to attack the Navy's aircraft carriers. It developed to be a disaster as 38 of those aircraft were shot down and the Navy suffered little damage.

It was becoming apparent to the Japanese that their navy could operate out of Rabaul only at great risk. This was especially true as Operation Cartwheel continued to develop and more Allied bases were established in ever-closer proximity. Consequently, Japanese combatant ships ceased to maintain a regular presence at Rabaul following the retreat of the cruiser force in early November.

In December 1943 the responsibility for continued air operations against Rabaul, and for delivering the coup de grâce, was passed to Admiral William "Bull" Halsey, the commander of the South Pacific Area. Beginning in December 1943, his organization continued the hard fighting with land-based Navy, Marine Corps, and Royal New Zealand Air Force units, as well as those from the Thirteenth Air Force. Specifically, this organization was known as Air Command, Solomons, or AirSols.

Marine Corps SBD dive bombers—essentially the same aircraft as the A-24—and TBF Avenger torpedo bombers were the primary attack aircraft. Protected by Marine Corps F4U Corsairs, Navy F6F Hellcats, and Royal New Zealand Air Force P-40s, they flew raids that sometimes exceeded 200 aircraft. And they flew them almost as often as the weather permitted. Japanese sea and ground targets were gutted as were the defending fighter aircraft. One Japanese Zero pilot observed, "It was obvious that so long as we continued the battle in its present fashion, the Americans would grind us under."[11]

A statement from another Japanese pilot indicates that he and his comrades understood the futility of their efforts, and that their defeat was inevitable. "Prior to the beginning of 1943, we still had hope and fought fiercely. But now, we fought to uphold our honour. We didn't want to become cowards. . . . We believed that we were expendable, that we were all going to die. There was no hope of survival—no one cared anymore."[12]

As had been the case with Kenney's Fifth Air Force fliers, it was nearly impossible to determine actual numbers of enemy aircraft destroyed during this period. Postwar assessments of aircraft claimed destroyed by both sides highlight this. The Allies acknowledged losing 151 aircraft but tallied 789 Japanese aircraft destroyed from December 17, 1943, to February 19, 1944. This contrasted with the Japanese who absurdly declared they downed 1,045 Allied aircraft at the cost of only 142 of their own.[13]

Those numbers aside, the AirSols missions were so effective that large cargo vessels ceased using Rabaul in January 1944. Finally, when the Japanese bastion at Truk was hit by aircraft carrier raids, Japan's leadership realized that operations from Rabaul were no longer tenable. The remaining aircraft were withdrawn on February 19, 1944, and the once-mighty fortress was left toothless.

Keeping it toothless required continued raids on a much smaller scale through the end of the war. And losses to Japanese antiaircraft fire still occurred. However, for all intents and purposes, the U.S Navy, the Marine Corps, and the Royal New Zealand Air Force completed the neutralization of Rabaul. The considerable number of Japanese trapped there were little more than free-range prisoners of war who teetered on the brink of starvation.

★★★

One of the fallouts from the series of Fifth Air Force raids against Rabaul during October and November 1943 was the beating that the P-38 units sustained. Enemy action, mechanical failures, and accidents took a significant toll. As deliveries from the United States weren't enough to make up the losses, the P-38 squadrons that were not part of the all-P-38 475th Fighter Group were compelled to give up their aircraft to the 475th and transition to the P-47.

24

"WE TENDED TO BLACK OUT"

An American-made aircraft, the Vultee Vengeance was a big, heavy beast of a dive bomber that was underpowered and ugly. A single-engine design, it had a bomb bay that carried two 500-pound bombs and provisions to carry two additional 250-pound bombs, one under each wing. Its crew included the pilot and a rear gunner who also served as the radio operator and navigator. The wings were fitted with four .50 caliber machineguns, two each, and the gunner operated two more of the same caliber. But the USAAF considered the Vengeance obsolete and never sent it into combat. Australia, however, anxious for aircraft—any aircraft—ordered several hundred of the type at the outset of the war.

They might have been obsolete, but at least they were delivered late, and when they did finally arrive in Australia many of them required refurbishment before they could be put into service. It wasn't until September 1943 that 24 Squadron, one of five RAAF Vengeance squadrons, was sent to fight in New Guinea. MacArthur wanted them to support ground operations on the Huon Peninsula.

"When you are at 10,000 feet and you go into a dive," said Ronald Barker, a Vengeance gunner, "you put [the] dive brakes out and it holds you perfectly steady as you come down. You come down vertically, I am facing backward, the pilot is facing forward, and the plane is coming down vertically." Barker noted that the pullout from the dive imparted brutal forces and that "we tended to black out. Tremendous stress when you came out of that dive." He was especially impressed with the toughness of the aircraft: "The wings never waggled [and] the plane never shuddered."[1]

As big as the Vengeance was, Barker observed that "they were a beautiful plane to fly, and fully aerobatic. We could loop it." Indeed, the

Vengeance had a set of controls in the rear cockpit so that the gunner could fly in the event the pilot was incapacitated.

24 Squadron, and later, 21 and 23 Squadrons, bombed Japanese units directly engaged with Australian and American troops. Initially operating from Tsili Tsili, and then Nadzab, the Vengeance units were usually escorted by RAAF P-40s. Obsolete or not, the Vengeance was effective as it provided air support during the campaign to secure the Huon Peninsula. "We bombed 100 yards ahead of our troops," said Barker. "We would get a telephone message [afterward] to say that Colonel So-and-So and his troops were holed up and you bombed ahead of them and you did a magnificent job."

Barker waxed almost poetic at times. In one instance the Vengeance units supported Australian infantry units as they came ashore preparatory to taking Finschhafen in September 1943. "Coming out of this clear, blue, sunny sky, beautiful and peaceful, except that they [the Japanese] opened fire on us. And the Australians had gone ashore and were digging in and as we came down, we bombed the positions ahead of them, and the sand was flying up around the aircraft, we flew through clouds of sand."

He was reflective as his unit supported Australian infantry during the fierce fighting for Shaggy Ridge at the end of January 1944. Killing the Japanese there, or chasing them away, was critical to the eventual goal of capturing Madang. Barker knew that his brother was somewhere below him, part of that fighting. "It was a most unusual feeling," he said, "and while you don't get used to it, you are so hardened to warfare that you realize that he may be there and he may not be, he may be dead."

Robert DeHaven, a pilot with the 49th Fighter Group's 7th Fighter Squadron, joined one of the Australian patrols that Barker was supporting during this time. He could not have been more impressed by the Australian fighting men.

> And we spent about four days with them, living as primitively as any human beings could. But the innate good nature of these people, the fighting qualities of these men, was just—it was just unbelievable unless you actually saw it. They were absolutely fearless. They were, as I said, completely good-natured. You couldn't upset them. They could live under the worst conditions, literally sleeping in water.

Barker was proud of the role he played in supporting these same men. But as well as he and his pilot and 24 Squadron and the other Vengeance squadrons might have performed, they were all sent home for good during

March 1944. The chief reason was that there were other aircraft already in service with long-established maintenance and sustainment capabilities that were able to perform the same missions as well, or nearly as well—the P-40 and P-47 among them. And they required a crew of only one, rather than two. Moreover, as fighters, those types did not need fighter escorts. Additionally, the RAAF was receiving B-24s during this time, and standing down the Vengeance units made pilots and crews available to man the big bombers.

Regardless, Barker and others were proud of what his squadron had achieved with the Vengeance. "Up to from early September [1943] to the middle of December, we accounted for more than 1,000 Japanese troops that we had killed in our various operations." They killed many more in the subsequent three months. He and his comrades also derived satisfaction from the numbers and types of targets they had hit. "Sometimes it would be barges hidden out. Sometimes the Japs would come down at night to bring their supplies down to their troops and they would hide in under the trees and the coconut palms hanging out, and our target was to go and attack them. And the Americans and Australians were always pleased with the support we gave them."

Finally, Barker had great admiration for the aircraft itself, the much-maligned Vengeance and the service it had given 24 Squadron during six months of combat against the Japanese. "Despite all of the operations that we went out on, we only lost four planes and we got every crew member back," he said. "These planes were so well built and strong that you could put them down [crash land them] and then raise them up eventually, put the wheels down and a new propeller . . . and then fly them off. That's how good they were," he said. "We probably are the only squadron [of any type aircraft] in the RAAF that never lost a man on active service."

★★★

On the ground, the Allies advanced steadily west across the top of New Guinea during the latter part of 1943. Barker and his fellow Vengeance crews, as well as the crews of virtually every other aircraft in the Fifth's inventory, flew thousands of air support sorties during this period. Aided by those sorties, the Australians captured Finschhafen at the tip of the Huon Peninsula on October 24, 1943. They also, together with the Americans, gained control of Saidor at the beginning of February 1944.

★★★

Kenney's airmen made steady progress during the latter half of 1943. The Japanese, although they still mounted air strikes, were forced to the defensive. But keeping them there required the Fifth Air Force to hit the same targets repeatedly. Wewak, with its four separate airfields, was attacked regularly as the Japanese kept reconstituting their forces there—they refused to let it die. The mission of December 1, 1943, was representative.

The plan for the 90th Bomb Group's strike against Wewak that day included a bit of razzle-dazzle. The 319th and 320th Bomb Squadrons—with six B-24s each—were to attack from inland while the 321st with its six aircraft was tasked with attacking from seaward at virtually the same time. The intent was to confuse and divide the attention of the Japanese defenders. Accordingly, once they cleared the Owen Stanley Range and passed down the Ramu Valley, the three squadrons motored west along the coast until reaching a point about 50 miles from Wewak. There, the 321st turned north over the water to set up for its off-axis attack.

The concept was good, but the execution was flawed. Clouds caused the 319th and the 320th to separate, and the 321st was still too far out to sea as the other two squadrons approached Wewak. Moreover, the Japanese were ready, perhaps tipped off by a reconnaissance flight flown by one of the group's B-24s early that morning. Ki-61 Tony and Ki-43 Oscar fighters climbed to intercept the American bombers. Antiaircraft crews readied their guns and squinted skyward.

The 319th led the way into especially heavy antiaircraft fire. *Pistol Packin' Mama*, piloted by Richard Adams, was hit in the number three engine, which was destroyed. Adams shut it down and increased power on the other three to maintain position. Approaching the release point, the bomb racks of the lead aircraft malfunctioned, and responsibility for getting the squadron's bombs on target was passed to Adams's bombardier, Fred Blaney. Blaney expertly assumed the task and a moment later the 319th's bombs exploded in the middle of the Wewak airfield.

But the Japanese weren't done with *Pistol Packin' Mama*. Soon after releasing its bombs, the aircraft was hit by both fighters and antiaircraft fire. The number four engine was set afire and Adams was compelled to shut it down. With both engines on the right wing gone, the remaining two engines strained to keep the aircraft airborne. Of course, the harder they worked, the more liable they were to fail. The crew of *Pistol Packin' Mama* began to jettison whatever wasn't fastened down to lighten the aircraft.

Their efforts were for nothing. The badly damaged bomber steadily lost altitude, and Adams made ready to put it into the water. Ditching the B-24 was notoriously difficult and dangerous. The roller-style bomb bay doors usually buckled, which essentially turned the bottom of the fuselage into a giant water scoop. The weight and impact of so much water typically smashed the aircraft to a stop almost immediately and broke the fuselage in half.

In this instance, *Piston Packin' Mama* caught a wingtip in the waves and cartwheeled across the water. Miraculously, six of the men—all in the front half of the fuselage—managed to escape the sinking bomber and climb into a life raft. The B-24 quickly filled with water and disappeared with the remaining four members of the crew. Squadron mate Stanley Robeck and his crew flew low overhead and marked their position.

The 90th's B-24 crews were harried on the mission by a mix of approximately 50 Ki-61 and Ki-43 fighters. An outnumbered escort of two squadrons of P-47s from the 348th Fighter Group did a credible job of deterring the Japanese fighters, but there was no way they could turn back every attack. Consequently, the gunners aboard the bombers were kept busy.

The smoke and dust from the attacks by the 319th and 320th were already starting to dissipate as the 321st approached Wewak from the north. Antiaircraft fire exploded over the target, and enemy fighters turned to catch the lone squadron. The six-aircraft formation of B-24s pushed through both without sustaining serious harm, and the formation dropped its bombs.

Flying at the rear of the formation was Oliver Sheehan's aircraft, *Ten Knights in a Bar Room*. Shortly after leaving the target area, a Ki-61 climbed to make a nearly head-on firing pass from below. Clarence Roper, the right waist gunner in the squadron's lead aircraft, said, "The Tony made a pass, skidding past our nose and on by the formation, and in so doing hit Lieutenant Sheehan's plane."[2] Following his attack, the Japanese pilot dived and arced away preparatory to making another pass.

It wasn't immediately apparent that the enemy fighter had done any damage. Bryant Poulsen, flying opposite Sheehan, noted that the other pilot "maintained his position in formation for a minute or two without showing signs of being damaged." But then, Sheehan's number two engine—the left inboard—started streaming grayish-white smoke, and the aircraft lost altitude. Intense flames were spotted at the waist position, and crewmen from other aircraft reported spotting debris and one, two, or three parachutes falling away from *Ten Knights in a Bar Room*.

Poulsen started down after Sheehan and his crew to protect them from additional attacks. But such protection was unneeded. "The fuselage of his plane broke into flames," Poulsen said, "and in a few seconds his plane began falling apart. When I saw the fuselage break in two just aft of the bomb bays, I took my attention from him and resumed my position in the formation." In the meantime, the Ki-61 pilot attacked the squadron again but did no harm. He rolled over and dived after the flaming wreckage that was Sheehan's aircraft, catching up to it just as it smashed into the jungle.

Minutes later, the 319th's sister squadron, the 320th, was jumped by Japanese fighters which concentrated on *Lobo*, the B-24 captained by Lawrence Smith. Smith's bomber was attacked by three Ki-43 Oscars, which James Sfarnas, a bombardier aboard another of the squadron's aircraft, misidentified as Zeroes. "One of them dived below our formation, shooting out two of Captain Smith's engines," said Sfarnas. "Another Zero, from above and behind our formation, came in and shot out the whole tail turret, and the tail gunner [William Bundy] dropped out with no chute on."[3]

"While still over land," Sfarnas said, "one man in the waist jumped from the camera hatch and was strafed by Zeroes as he went down." *Lobo*, still under control, crossed the beach and flew over the water while more men continued to bail out. When last seen, it was approaching land again at about a thousand feet. Although a PBY was dispatched to search the area the following day, *Lobo*'s wreckage was never found, nor were any of its crew.

The B-24 immediately behind *Lobo*, piloted by Harold Mills, was also attacked as the 320th fled Wewak. The life of the right waist gunner, Buddy Andrews, was saved by a section of armor plate that absorbed the impact of a 20-millimeter cannon shell that otherwise would have torn away his chest. The crew's tail gunner, Phillip Smith, was not so lucky. Andrews recalled that Smith, hit in the head and leg, staggered up to his position. "A groove cut to the bone across his forehead. He crawled out of his turret and tapped me on the back. There he was, standing with blood all over him, which scared the fool out of me." Smith was tended by the rest of the crew and survived the flight back to Port Moresby, where more than 200 holes were counted in the aircraft.

There was dissatisfaction among some of the 90th's crews about how the mission was executed, as was indicated by Dustin Swanson, who led the 321st Bomb Squadron that day.

When we got to the target things were pretty screwed up and the group leader [Ellis Brown] called and said to go in one way and then went in a different way himself. That sort of left me out on my lonesome with the squadron and before I made my run we were hopped by fighters. I made my run and got the devil out of there. It was a pretty screwed up deal today, and the major who led the group can take a lot of the blame. I guess every squadron made a different run.[4]

Following the mission, the six survivors from Richard Adams's *Pistol Packin' Mama* bobbed in the current away from where they had crashed, approximately 20 miles northeast of Finschhafen. They tended their wounds while simultaneously staying alert for rescue aircraft as well as the Japanese—and sharks. Little of note occurred, and they continued to drift through the night. Remarkably, they spotted and retrieved the body of William Ball, one of the gunners who had been in the back of the bomber. The decision was made to not keep Ball's body in the already crowded raft, and they performed an ad hoc ceremony before returning him to the sea just before dawn.[5]

The following day, the men were alarmed at the sight of several fighters orbiting overhead. Alarm turned to relief when the aircraft were recognized as P-47s. There followed much arm waving and other signaling which the pilots returned with wing waggles. A short time later, the men were retrieved by a PT boat and returned to safety.

The raid of December 1, 1943, achieved its objective of keeping pressure on the Japanese units on Wewak. A handful of aircraft were destroyed on the ground, as were buildings and material. Although only three B-24s were lost, the Japanese fighter pilots and antiaircraft crews claimed a total of 10 American aircraft. Not to be outdone in the over-claiming department, the 348th's P-47 pilots claimed four enemy fighters destroyed, and the 90th's B-24 gunners put in a tally for six additional fighters. Japanese records—which could very well have been wrong—admit to zero losses for that day's combat.

The 16-aircraft formation that hit Wewak that day was small—even tiny—when compared to the raids then being mounted against the Germans on the other side of the globe. It should be considered, however, that although only three B-24s were lost on the raid, those three aircraft constituted almost 17 percent of the attacking force. It was a loss rate that was not sustainable by any air force, and it is fortunate that such losses were not a regular occurrence.

★★★

Gordon Manuel and Owen Giertsen and their native friends were still pressing through the jungle on New Britain Island as they searched for the coastwatcher's camp. They reached the bank of the Mevelo River near its mouth, and after regarding its breadth and depth for a moment, Manuel suggested they wade across. His native friend frowned as he considered the notion, then bent down and tossed a rock into the current. Nothing happened, and the man picked up a larger rock and threw it into the water.

Immediately a large shark broke the surface and gnashed at the current where the rock had entered the water. An instant later it rolled, flashed its white belly skyward, and then dived away. As the other men reflexively stepped back from the riverbank, the native hurled another rock at a long, dark object at the water's edge. It thrashed away, revealing itself as a big crocodile.

The native looked at Manuel. Manuel looked at Giertsen. Then, they both looked at the beaming native, laughed, and headed upstream to a narrower point where they lifted a log across to the other bank. Especially careful of their footing, they crossed their makeshift footbridge, thereby foiling the sharks and crocodiles of the Mevelo.

Later that day, Gordon's native guides rushed him and Giertsen from the road on which they had been traveling. There were Japanese troops coming from the opposite direction. Prone in the brush next to Giertsen, who likewise pressed his body down into the ground, Gordon tightened his grip on his rifle and watched the road. Although he could hear the relaxed gabbling of the Japanese soldiers, he could not yet see them. He knew that all around him, invisible in a way that he could never hope to emulate, were the native men who made up the rest of the group.

And then, there they were. A squad of uniformed Japanese strolled idly on the road in no particular order and without any obvious purpose. They certainly weren't looking for the two Americans. Manuel felt Giertsen's body tense and saw him ease his face against his rifle's stock as he took aim. Manuel grabbed Giertsen's shoulder and shook his head when the other man looked at him. They might very well kill several of the enemy soldiers, but doing so would cause the Japanese to flush the area with troops to find and capture them. It was best to let them pass.

Both men watched the Japanese walk out of sight. Shortly afterward, their idle chit-chat faded from earshot. A moment later, Manuel's native friends stepped from their hiding places, and the group resumed its trek.

A few days later, near the end of November 1943, Manuel stopped on a signal from his native friend. He was tired, scratched, and bruised, and his feet were bleeding. Carefully, without making any noise or sudden movements, he took in his jungle surroundings. And there, right in front of him, was a man in uniform. It was Allan Roberts, the Australian coastwatcher. Manuel was excited and happy to finally meet the man. Roberts had been on the island for about a month and was gracious in welcoming Manuel and

Giertsen. The Australians and their own native helpers were comparatively well-provisioned and more importantly had a radio. Roberts used that radio to pass the news that both Manuel and Giertsen were alive and well. He used it again about a week later to pass similar news when natives brought two more recently downed Americans—P-38 pilots.

These were Edward Czarnecki and Carl Planck. Although Czarnecki had been flying missions for only a few months, he had already been credited with six aerial victories. He had gone down on October 23 after an engagement with enemy fighters. A member of the 475th Fighter Group, Czarnecki was spotted going down by his comrade Charles Ratajski, who was cruising down the New Britain coast at 10,000 feet, hunting for enemy aircraft.

"I noticed aircraft near the water," Ratajski said. "There were two aircraft, about two hundred yards from each other. One was a P-38, the other a single-engine airplane which looked like a Zero." The P-38 was easily recognizable, while the other aircraft was not. Ratajski peered down at the two aircraft skimming just above Wide Bay. "There were no Allied single-engine aircraft around, so it must have been a Zero," Ratajski said. "I watched them and after about thirty seconds, both of them landed intact in the water. Both of the pilots got out of the airplanes. The P-38 pilot seemed to be waving something white."[6]

The other pilot, Carl Planck, had been credited with two aerial victories. He flew for the 49th Fighter Group and was part of a formation escorting B-25s on the mission to Rabaul on November 2, 1943. His flight ran into heavy antiaircraft fire and flew into clouds to avoid it. When he flew clear of the clouds, the rest of his flight was nowhere to be seen. But he spotted an enemy fighter, a Zero, and immediately attacked, setting it afire with three bursts. Seconds later, he made a head-on pass with another Zero. His gunfire apparently killed the pilot as the aircraft's guns ceased firing. Planck kept firing, intent on exploding the enemy fighter. However, he pressed the attack too close and smashed into his target, essentially destroying his left engine and damaging the left boom and vertical stabilizer.[7]

His aircraft crippled, Planck dived away to escape other enemy fighters in the area. Unable to return to Dobodura, he put the aircraft down in the water not far from where Manuel had come ashore so many months earlier. Although he had smashed his head, he was otherwise unhurt, and friendly natives led him to Allan Roberts.

Manuel's native friends were nervous and not nearly so excited about joining with the coastwatchers. He soon learned the reason. Roberts had been the chief constable at Rabaul, and his second-in-command, Malcom

English, had also been part of the Australian law enforcement organization. Essentially, both men had been in a position of power over the native population and were not particularly beloved.

Nevertheless, there was no significant friction between the natives and the Australians. Rather, it was Manuel who became frustrated. Although he got along well with Malcolm English, and with the third Australian, David MacAvoy, who had recently seen combat in North Africa, he believed that Roberts was too cautious. Over the course of a month, the Australian spooked and ordered the movement of their camp three different times at great effort. The radio equipment and its batteries alone weighed nearly half a ton. Moving it and all the other gear up and down through the brush and jungle—often in the rain—was difficult and exhausting.

Manuel thought the moves were unnecessary and too hard on everyone. Roberts himself was sick with dysentery. To be fair, Roberts had reason to be nervous; the Japanese would torture and murder them if they were caught. The two men clashed, but Roberts was in charge, and Manuel did as he was asked or directed. Ultimately, Manuel maintained a degree of distance from Roberts, which helped reduce the prickliness of their relationship.

Airdrops by B-24s helped ease the situation at Christmastime, seven months after Manuel had been shot down. Aside from supplies needed by the coastwatchers, Manuel personally received new boots, uniforms, a carbine and, best of all, letters from his squadron. He was excited. Barring a disaster such as discovery by the Japanese, he could expect a submarine to spirit him and his comrades back to friendly hands sometime soon.

Moreover, Manuel's spirits were likely buoyed by news of developments on New Britain. The heightened number of air raids over Rabaul—he had seen and heard them—had already given him reason to believe the Allies were gaining the upper hand, but he likely grew doubly excited when American forces came ashore at Arawe on the southwest coast of New Britain on December 15, 1943. Granted, Arawe was 150 miles or more from his location, but it was good news regardless. The additional news that the Marines had landed on the western end of New Britain at Cape Gloucester on December 26 was icing on the cake.

Although Manuel didn't know it, these landings were part of Operation Cartwheel—the effort to neutralize Rabaul. That Rabaul still needed neutralizing was indicated by the fact that air units based there opposed both landings, especially that at Cape Gloucester, with a great deal of vigor. Fortunately, the Fifth maintained air superiority over both locations and neither landing was ever jeopardized.

★★★

All sorts of units were required to keep the Fifth Air Force functional. These included engineering, medical, and support organizations, among others. These performed their duties with varying degrees of competence and went more or less unheralded. Such was the case even with a few of the Fifth's flying units.

One of these, the 418th Night Fighter Squadron, had arrived in New Guinea at the end of 1943. It operated a mix of about 10 P-70s, which were A-20s equipped with radars and otherwise modified for night operations. It also flew a smaller number of P-38s, two of which had likewise been kitted out as night fighters. Equipped and trained as it was, the unit was a bit of an odd duck, not assigned to any overarching fighter group but instead reporting directly to the Fifth Air Force's Fighter Command.

The P-70's radar was problematic to maintain, which made it difficult to conduct training. The small number of aircraft—of two different types—also hindered the aircrews as they struggled to keep their flight currency. Moreover, the 418th wasn't getting much attention from anyone that mattered as there wasn't enough damage being caused by the few Japanese night raiders to warrant the unit receiving top priority for parts, material, equipment, and personnel.

Indeed, the 418th had only about a dozen or so of its mixed bag of aircraft ready to fly on any given day. Consequently, the squadron's achievements during its first few months of operations were not noteworthy, and it had shot down only one Japanese dive bomber. And that was achieved with a P-38 during daytime.

The fact was that the number of Japanese aircraft that the 418th destroyed was far less than the number of its own aircraft that it destroyed in accidents. An example occurred on April 9, 1944, when Richard Ferris took off from Finschhafen in a P-47 for what the squadron described as a "test-hopping" flight. As the 418th didn't operate P-47s, the reasons for him at the controls of one can only be guessed at.

Regardless, the aircraft exploded as it climbed through 5,000 feet, and what was left of it plummeted earthward. Ferris tried desperately to escape as the wreck fell, inverted. He finally slipped free of the cockpit but was badly battered when he smashed hard into the tail of the fighter just before it slammed into the water. A Navy vessel was close at hand and hauled Ferris aboard almost immediately. Sadly, he drew his last breath at the same time.

★★★

The pilots of the 49th Fighter Group's 9th Squadron were grumpy at being ordered to give up their P-38s to the 475th Fighter Group following the fighting over Rabaul. In place of their much-loved Lightnings, they were flying the pudgy P-47. Where the P-38 was fast and exotic, the P-47 was only fast. Rather than exotic, it looked like a Sunday roast with wings.

But it was effective as evidenced by Gerald Johnson's encounter report of December 10, 1943. It described a fight which took place over Gusap between the four P-47s he led and eight K-61 Tonys. Johnson spotted the enemy fighters several thousand feet below. "The Tony's were dark in color," he noted, "and had red roundels on the wings and fuselage. They appeared to be old planes as the surfaces of the wings were shiny where the paint had worn off."

Johnson led his flight in a diving attack, but their speed built up so quickly that they had no time to fire their guns. The enemy fighters scattered, and individual dogfights developed during which Johnson made head-on attacks. "I hit one Tony in the engine," Johnson said, "and it started burning. The pilot bailed out and an Australian patrol shot him on the ground."[8]

Less successful were Raymond Swift and Ralph Wandrey, whose guns would not fire. "I was hit once in the left wing," said Wandrey. "I made two more feints at Tonys which broke away before firing. I then left the combat and came home."[9] The episode probably did little to endear the P-47 to the two men.

★★★

Many units wrote and printed newsletters for their men. They were nothing fancy but were a means of promulgating necessary information as well as gossip within the unit—news of new babies and such. They also included corny jokes and other humor. Some of the writers adopted made-up names and bylines which added much-needed color.

One wag who called himself "Jazbo of New Dubuque" contributed to the 36th Fighter Squadron's newsletter and addressed the censoring of letters home. It was a tedious task, the value of which was questioned not only by the letter writers but also by those responsible for doing it—usually officers assigned for short stints. Jazbo commented:

> The Intelligence Officer is clamping down on censorship, so fellas, don't get any wild ideas in your letter writing. . . . So, please don't mention the number of planes we have in commission, or compare this place with Moresby, Milne Bay or Nadzab. And another thing . . . use of vile

words, lewd phrases, etc., is strictly SNAFU. So don't write shit, fuck, or any similar prolific [*sic*] phrases.

Jazbo also took a jab at the system—or lack of a system—which determined the requirements for the award of military decorations. It had been a contentious topic ever since such awards were first conceived, and that contentiousness persisted during World War II in New Guinea. During the early fighting men were decorated for actions that would have received only passing notice later. Moreover, the awards process was cumbersome, and men frequently received medals a year or more after the event for which they earned them. Jazbo's humor was telling.

> In answer to repeated inquiries concerning the awarding of medals to pilots and men of this command, Jazbo has taken down the musty files and come up with some sensational reports. To wit: If you wanna wear a Distinguished Flying Cross, go out and shoot down 5 enemy aircraft, or 3 enemy aircraft in one combat. No more of this "box top" stuff, i.e., 25 missions for an air medal, an additional 50 for a D.F.C. If you prefer a Silver Star, do something gallant on the field of battle: Shoot a Jap or shoot one of our cooks. And if you really desire to wear the Medal of Honor . . . shoot two cooks.

Less humorous was the experience of John Henebry of the 3rd Bomb Group. He had taken a major general from MacArthur's staff on a reconnaissance flight over the northern coast of New Guinea. They went only as far as Lae, which was already in Allied hands. Essentially, it was nothing more than an airplane ride.

Not long after, Henebry was congratulated by a friend for being awarded the Distinguished Service Cross, which was eclipsed in importance only by the Medal of Honor. Henebry declared that he had received no such honor. His friend was confused as he had been aware that Henebry's passenger, the major general, had been awarded the Distinguished Service Cross for the mission and reasonably assumed that Henebry—who actually flew and commanded the mission—had received the same award.[10]

Although Japanese air units in New Guinea were increasingly hard-pressed during late 1943 and early 1944, they also delivered newsletters of a sort—these were propaganda leaflets that they dropped on Allied positions, usually at night. One cartoon leaflet in particular sought to sow discord between American and Australian servicemen. It started with a frame that showed an American having sex with an Australian woman. The next frame showed an Australian soldier pursuing a Papuan woman through the brush. The message was that while the Australians fought and died in the faraway stink and heat of New Guinea's jungles, the Americans were taking their wives and girlfriends to bed. Of course, the Americans were doing plenty of the same sort of fighting and dying as the Australians, but the message was wrapped around a kernel of truth.[11]

The Allies also dropped leaflets. Because flying was flying, men sometimes died in the doing. The 110th Reconnaissance Squadron sent four P-39s to the area west of Madang and Alexishafen on February 16, 1944. The pilots carried the leaflets in the cockpit with them and simply tossed them overboard through a window—the P-39 had hand-cranked windows much like an automobile.

While dumping his leaflets, one of the pilots, Paul Swanson, left the rest of the flight in the vicinity of Ulugum plantation and motored at very low altitude for the nearby coastline, gradually losing height as he did so. There was no indication that his aircraft had been hit by antiaircraft fire or that he was in any sort of distress. The P-39 finally disappeared below the treetops and disintegrated in a fiery explosion.

Leaflets were found in the air intake scoops of two of the other aircraft when their pilots landed. The scoop—mounted atop the fuselage directly behind the cockpit—provided cooling air to the engine. It was almost certain that many of the leaflets Swanson tossed overboard were caught by his aircraft's air intake scoop. His engine, choked of the air it needed, overheated and failed. Unable to climb high enough to bail out, or fly far enough to reach the sea, Swanson was doomed to crash into the trees. That no one considered such a hazard when the pilots were sent on the mission simply underscored the hurried nature of operations and the inexperience of the men who ordered, supported, and executed those operations.[12]

25

"I DON'T REMEMBER A LOT BEING MADE OF IT"

Gordon Manuel had been hiding from the Japanese on New Britain Island for more than eight months. Now, on the evening of February 5, 1944, after having bid farewell to his native friends and protectors, he spotted the submarine that sat just offshore of Open Bay. With him were Giertsen, Planck, Czarnecki, and a contingent of coastwatchers, to include Allan Roberts who was ill and under orders to evacuate. After so much time running and hiding—and having finally recovered from his wounds—Manuel trembled with anticipation. At the same time, he was sick with worry that catastrophe would strike just as his rescue was imminent.

It did not.

Still, it took all his willpower to keep from shouting at the figures who paddled the two rubber boats toward shore. Desperate to escape the island, he silently urged them to hurry. The minutes felt like hours before they eased through the surf and splashed ashore. They were sailors, four of them, from the submarine *Gato*. Manuel and his comrades rushed them but celebrated only a moment or two before helping to lift the rubber boats back into the water and climbing aboard.

Manuel's anxiety lifted incrementally with each paddle stroke that took them farther into the bay. They were through the surf line—that much closer to the waiting submarine—when one of the sailors exclaimed and pointed back toward the shore. Manuel looked and saw a light, a flashlight, blinking in their direction. His stomach somersaulted when the sailors spun the boats around and started paddling back toward the light. Back toward the terrifying green hell of a prison that was the Japanese-held island.

Once ashore, they were approached by three men—two Australians and an American. The Australians, flying a Boston, had been shot down

three months earlier while strafing. The American was shot down by a
Ki-45 near Rabaul while piloting his F-4, an unarmed photo reconnaissance variant of the P-38.

The merciless nightmare that Manuel was living continued to tor-
ment him. Instead of immediately putting back into the water, the group
was compelled to wait. A pair of sailors had disappeared into the dark. A
shout was raised but there was no answer. Manuel was beside himself with
apprehension, as the risk of being discovered by the Japanese was still very
real. Finally, the two missing men trudged grudgingly back up the beach
from where they had been looking for mementos. Manuel was incredulous
at their carelessness—at their failure to understand that they were endanger-
ing the lives of everyone in the group.

Happily, the Japanese failed to show, and an hour or so later Manuel
and the rest of the group were safely aboard the *Gato*. Excited and unable
to sleep, Manuel showered, ate a hearty meal, and explored the submarine.
He spent the rest of the night on the deck and watched the sea and the stars
as the boat sailed on the surface toward friendly waters. At dawn, he went
below as the *Gato* submerged to hide from enemy aircraft.

Manuel was safe. Weeks later, following an interview with a much-
impressed Kenney, he returned to the States.

★★★

William Felch of the 38th Bomb Group's 823rd Bomb Squadron leaned
forward and looked across his copilot at the B-25 flown by John Difilippo.
"When I first saw the plane, it came up abrupt, the fuselage burst into
flame from [the] front to [the] full length of [the] fuselage with most of
the flame in the fore part of the ship. The wheels lowered to about halfway and the bomb bay doors were open. The plane started to roll away,"
Felch said, "from my ship into almost a vertical position and disappearing
into the smoke over the target. I am of the opinion that the plane crashed
immediately."[1]

No one saw Difilippo's aircraft crash because the smoke and fire and
flying debris over Kavieng, New Ireland, was so dense. The pilots of the
different waves of B-25s that roared low over the town and harbor that
afternoon—February 15, 1944—were forced at intervals to use their instruments to maintain straight and level flight. The crews felt their aircraft lifted
by rushes of scorching hot air created by the conflagrations that once were
supply dumps, fuel storage points, warehouses, and the aircraft of their
comrades. Antiaircraft fire of all calibers laced through it all, adding to the
terror.

Kavieng, a major Japanese air and naval base, and supply point, sat at the northwestern tip of New Ireland, only about 150 miles northwest of Rabaul. The initial plans for Operation Cartwheel targeted Kavieng for seizure, just as had been the case for Rabaul. But MacArthur and Kenney and other Allied leaders realized that Kavieng, again, much like Rabaul, could be effectively neutralized by air and sea, thereby saving men, equipment and time.

The Fifth Air Force's mission that day was a major part of that neutralizing. Prior to that, Kavieng had received only passing attention, although B-24s were sent against it during the preceding few days. However, this particular mission was intended to eviscerate the Japanese. The 3rd Bomb Group's A-20s opened the day's fighting with attacks against shipping in Kavieng Harbor. It cost them three aircraft and crews.

One of those A-20s was flown by William Pearson. In the confusion of the attack, he followed another A-20 too closely, and when a bomb from that aircraft exploded, his right engine was hit. Pearson immediately shut the engine down and feathered its propeller, but the fire continued.

Squadron mate Craigie Krayenbuhl spotted Pearson and together with his flight leader chased him down. The two of them separated and pulled up on both sides of the stricken bomber in order that they might give him some sort of assistance. "As we drew abreast of Lieutenant Pearson," Krayenbuhl said, "his right wing hit the water and the ship cartwheeled wing-over-wing and broke into about three or four pieces."[2] Krayenbuhl and his flight leader circled the wreckage three times but could see no survivors.

B-24s followed the A-20s and pounded the airfield and the town from high altitude. But the killing blow was to be delivered by a force of 28 B-25s from the 38th Bomb Group and 47 more from the 345th. They were covered by an escort of P-38s.

Not counting a 345th bomber that crashed on takeoff, killing all its crew, John Difilippo's aircraft was only the first of several more B-25s lost that day. The aircraft flown by Eugene Benson of the 38th Bomb Group's 71st Bomb Squadron was hit in the left engine, which immediately caught fire. At the same time, the aircraft's landing gear extended partially, and the crew felt the B-25 slow and roll into unbalanced flight. Benson's navigator activated the engine's fire extinguisher while Benson and his copilot, William Smith, fought to maintain control of the aircraft. The flames did go out momentarily. However, the tire—which shared the wing's nacelle with the engine—burst into flames, and the engine caught fire again.

In truth, it didn't matter whether or not the left engine was burning because the rest of the aircraft was consumed by fire. Benson and Smith turned away from Kavieng and prepared to put the aircraft down. In the meantime, the crew's tail gunner—at risk of being cooked alive—leaped from the aircraft. His parachute opened just before he reached the water. He was never seen again.

Benson and Smith did their best to align the aircraft's course parallel with the sea's swells, which were running at more than 10 feet. They cut the good engine and successfully dropped the aircraft into a trough between two waves, and the aircraft jolted quickly to a stop. The force of the water was such that the radioman—who had been horrifically burned—was snapped out of the aircraft and drowned.

Benson, Smith, and the navigator pushed themselves out and clear of the aircraft and into the water. They had no life raft, and Smith paddled back to the still-burning B-25 but was turned away by the flames. The three men clung to Smith's parachute and watched following flights of B-25s burst clear of the burning cyclone that had been Kavieng. Someone aboard one of those aircraft took them for the enemy and sprayed them down with .50 caliber machinegun fire. Fortunately, he was a poor marksman.

If the 38th Bomb Group's crews were blinded by smoke and fire, the men of the 345th Bomb Group, which followed the 38th, were blinded even more. Debris was blasted as high or higher than the 345th's aircraft flew, and the explosions from the bombs they dropped sent more into the air. When the last of the B-25s left Kavieng behind, there was little of value that was not burning.

But it hadn't been cheap. Aside from the three A-20s lost by the 3rd Bomb Group and the two B-25s lost by the 38th Bomb Group, the 345th lost four more. One of them went down when a fuel dump exploded so violently that it blew both wings from the aircraft. Another of the 345th's aircraft disappeared still under control, but with an engine out. Two others went into the water not far from Kavieng.

Nathan Gordon, a PBY pilot with VP-34, was assigned with his crew to cover the mission to Kavieng that day. Orbiting a safe distance away with a covering flight of P-47s, he received notice there were crews in the water. Despite being awed by the smoke and fire rising from Kavieng, he nevertheless pointed his aircraft directly at it.

Spotting a life raft and marker dye, Gordon weighed the risk of putting down into the heavy swells and potentially destroying his aircraft against rescuing a downed crewman. He had never landed in seas so high. Not wanting to leave a man behind, he settled the PBY onto the water as gently as he could but was rewarded by a popping crack as seams in the hull were ripped apart. While his crew worked to plug the gaps through which the water rushed, he motored the flying boat across the heaving waves to the raft.

There was no one in it.

Gordon coaxed his damaged aircraft airborne again and, aided by two B-25 crews from the 345th Bomb Group, made three more landings to rescue three more crews, including Benson, Smith, and their navigator. All the crews were within range of Japanese mortar, cannon, and machinegun fire, and Gordon and his crew and their aircraft were bracketed by explosions and gunfire, while the B-25s made strafing runs against the enemy positions or kept tabs on other downed crewmen. Here, the massive swells worked to the PBY crew's favor as they lifted the big aircraft up where Gordon and his crew were easily targeted, and then seconds later dropped them out of sight.

Each man in the water was desperately exhausted and most were wounded. With the waves tossing the aircraft almost out of control at times, Gordon risked chopping them to pieces with the PBY's propellers and once was forced to shut down both engines as enemy fire dropped atop them. Gordon's men, working against the waves and throwing and hauling rescue lines, exhibited almost superhuman strength as they wrestled each man— most of them waterlogged dead weight—into the aircraft.

The rescued men fell onto the decking of the PBY almost delirious with joy at having been pulled to safety. And then, once the aircraft got airborne—presumably for home and safety—grew just as urgently sick with fear and dread as Gordon descended back within range of the enemy guns and landed atop the aircraft-breaking swells to recover other men.

The rescue of each man was a standalone feat of heroism. Gordon and his men pulled 15 downed flyers from the water at Kavieng. It was an act of comradely devotion and duty seldom rivaled. For his actions that day, Nathan Gordon was awarded the Medal of Honor, and each member of his crew was recognized with the Distinguished Service Cross.

Throughout the Pacific, PBY crews rescued hundreds of downed airmen. But doing so wasn't as simple as flying to a certain point, landing, and hauling them aboard. In fact, the missions were often quite complex and demanded the consideration of a number of factors.

Actually finding a man or crew in the water was perhaps the most difficult task. The distances involved and areas covered could be huge, and accurately determining locations was difficult. A lone pilot in a fighter trying to pinpoint the location of a downed squadron mate in the middle of the sea was likely to be less accurate than a trained navigator aboard a big bomber. The PBY crews used various search patterns to maximize their chances, but fatigue was a constant enemy as the crewmen watched the water for hours on end—and often without success. Moreover, a life raft was a tiny object—difficult to spot. And a man in the water without a life raft truly had little chance of being found.

Additionally, the PBY crews often flew without fighter escorts. Fighters simply didn't have the endurance required to protect the big aircraft for hours and hours. And without escorts, the PBYs were vulnerable to enemy fighters. Although they were tough and carried defensive weapons, they were also slow and unwieldy. Moreover, they were vulnerable to ground fire as had been the case with Nathan Gordon and his crew at Kavieng. And the simple act of landing on the water demanded multiple considerations, including wind direction and speed, wave sizes, orientation and types, and the presence of hazards such as rocks or reefs.

Perhaps most wrenching of all were the decisions the PBY pilots sometimes had to make. They faced dilemmas that were never presented to fighter pilots or bomber crews. There were instances when the PBY pilot had to decide whether or not to leave men in the water where they would endure an almost certain death. This was particularly the case when the weather or sea state was so bad that the PBY might be destroyed in a rescue attempt. There was little to do in those cases other than drop a raft, or additional supplies. Pilot Albert Richards articulated this pain.

> There is nothing more sickening than to see a guy shot down, make it into the sea, get out O.K., and into a raft, and cover him all the remaining daylight hours, knowing it is impossible to land. With thirty knots blowing and the consequent heavy seas. If you did try to land you would only be risking the lives of seven men to save one. For years you wake up from a dream where you see him wave to you as it gets dark, and the next day you go back and find nothing.[3]

All that being said, the PBY crews could be as prone to accidents or mishaps as any others, as indicated by a mission summary narrative from the 38th Bomb Group's 71st Bomb Squadron. One of its B-25s was sent out in company with a PBY. "On the morning of April 15, 1944," it noted, "One B-25D-1 took off at 0755 from Nadzab to search for missing members of an A-20 believed to be forced down in the vicinity of Valif Island off the north coast of New Guinea."

Eugene Benson piloted that B-25. "Because of our greater speed," he said, "we were able to make S-curves covering more area while keeping the Catalina in sight." Less than three hours later, Benson and his crew spotted a life raft with two men aboard, and the PBY crew quickly landed to recover the survivors. "The weather was overcast," Benson remembered, "and a rather stiff wind was blowing, and the Catalina had a difficult time getting airborne because of the heavy seas. It finally got off but when about fifty feet up, it suddenly stalled and crashed into the sea, exploding into a huge fireball."

Benson and his crew radioed this news, and another PBY was quickly dispatched. "We flew as low as possible to check the crash and could see some debris in the water, but no survivors. The second Catalina arrived, landed and searched the area but unfortunately with no better luck."[4] The deaths of the PBY crew hit Benson particularly hard. He was one of the men rescued by Nathan Gordon and his crew at Kavieng on February 15.

The commitment of the Allies to do their utmost to rescue downed aircrews was starkly different than that of the Japanese. A ranking Japanese fighter pilot admired the courage of the Allied rescue crews, noting that he and his fellow pilots thought them very brave. He reflected on the attitude of the Japanese leadership, "They could not tolerate the possible loss of a large flying boat merely to effect the certain rescue of one aircrew."[5]

He additionally noted how his comrades accepted that attitude. "Any man who was shot down and managed to survive by inflating his life raft realized that his chance for continued survival lay entirely within his own hands. Our pilots accepted their abandonment stoically. At any rate, the entire Japanese Navy failed to evince any great interest in rescue operations of this nature."

★★★

There had been no Japanese fighter opposition over Kavieng during the big strike on February 15, 1944. But one of the escort pilots still managed to score that day. The nation's leading ace, Richard Bong, was flying a P-38 with the 49th Fighter Group's 9th Fighter Squadron. Flying on his wing was his good friend and another high-scoring ace, Thomas McGuire.

"There were no enemy air sightings and nil interception over the target area during the attack," Bong said. However, on the return flight he spotted a Ki-61, a Tony, on a course for Rabaul. "I made a 180-degree turn to the left and started after him." Bong and McGuire raced after the enemy pilot, who showed no indication that he was aware he was being stalked. It is likely he never knew until the last few seconds of his life. "At about 75 yards," said Bong, "I opened fire and observed the enemy plane to blow up in midair and crash into the water."

The dead enemy pilot was the 22nd of an eventual 40 victims claimed by Bong.

★★★

Kenney enjoyed positive publicity nearly as much as MacArthur, and he was especially pleased when it was catalyzed by the performance of his men. During World War II, there wasn't much that generated more publicity in the context of air combat than did the idea of the "ace," a fighter pilot who shot down five or more enemy aircraft. The concept was born in the skies of World War I and indirectly popularized by air heroes such as Billy Bishop, Raoul Lufbery, Eddie Rickenbacker, and Manfred von Rich-thofen—the Red Baron. Following the war, the flying ace became a staple of comic books such as *G-8 and His Battle Aces*, *Flying Aces*, and *Sky Aces*.

An ace race enabled, if not created, by Kenney was well underway in the skies of New Guinea by early 1944, and it was well-covered by the press. The competition included Richard Bong, Thomas McGuire, Thomas Lynch, and Neel Kearby. All were P-38 pilots except Kearby, who commanded the all-P-47 348th Fighter Group but was moved by Kenney to a staff job in November 1943. Kearby chafed at the assignment but still managed to get himself into combat.

Kenney, then the commanding general of the Fourth Air Force in the United States, had saved Bong's flying career in early 1942 before either had shipped overseas. Bong got himself in trouble for flying his P-38 down San Francisco's Market Street, among other low-level aerial hijinks. Kenney chewed the young man up but admired his spirit and saved him from severe discipline. Bong proved to be a superb combat aviator and quickly racked up aerial victories. Kenney kept an eye on him. Never given a squadron command, his assignments as an "instructor" were such that he could fly almost whenever he wanted.

Both Lynch and McGuire started flying combat in the P-39—McGuire in the Aleutians. Both were strong personalities and well respected, and both scored steadily after transitioning to the P-38. At the start of 1944, all four pilots vied to become the first USAAF pilot to match and exceed Eddie Rickenbacker's World War I record of 26 aerial victories.

However, Neel Kearby was killed by a Ki-43 pilot near Wewak on March 5, 1944. He bailed out but died of his wounds as he hung in his parachute from a tree. At the time he had been credited with 22 enemy aircraft downed in air combat. Only three days later, on March 8, Thomas Lynch was killed while strafing barges with Bong near Aitape. His aircraft was hit by antiaircraft fire, and he climbed to gain altitude but wasn't high enough for his parachute to deploy when he jumped. His remains were never recovered. He had 20 enemy aircraft to his credit.

Joe Forster was a nine-victory ace who flew P-38s with the 475th Fighter Group. Notwithstanding the hullabaloo about who was the top-scoring ace, he believed that it wasn't something that most of the pilots aspired to. "I don't remember a lot being made of it," he said, "though we all had grown up with stories of World War I [aces]. Most of us wanted to get to the fight, mix it up by making a couple of passes, and take whatever shots we could, then go home so you could do it again another day. When you got that fifth confirmed, somebody might buy you a drink and say, 'Congratulations, ace,' but otherwise that was about it."[6]

Certainly, credit must be given to the high scorers, and their achievements should be acknowledged. On the other hand, it should be recognized that it was the average fighter pilots, in the aggregate, who did most of the killing, and who did the yeoman's work of protecting the bomber crews. And who were good teammates, just as the high-profile aces were. "You didn't judge most guys by their victory score," said Forster. "Mainly, you wanted to fly with people you trusted, who were good pilots and would be there when you needed them."

26

"EVERYONE EXCEPT MACARTHUR LOOKED SKEPTICAL"

Following a period of extensive air attacks, the Allies launched an amphibious assault on February 29, 1944, against Los Negros in the Admiralties, which sat about 275 miles north of New Guinea's Huon Peninsula. Manus, the largest of the Admiralties, was also seized, and the campaign was over by the end of May. By this time, Allied air superiority in the region was unchallenged, and the final outcome of the fight for the Southwest Pacific was really never in question.

The capture of the Admiralties was the final element of Operation Cartwheel and completed the neutralization of Rabaul and Kavieng and even, to a degree, Truk. The number of lives saved by neutralizing those bases rather than attempting to take them is difficult to quantify, but it was considerable. Moreover, as a naval base the Admiralties offered an excellent fleet anchorage with good infrastructure. Likewise, its airfields extended the reach of Allied air units.

★★★

As formidable as it might have been following its seizure and development by the Japanese in December 1942, Wewak had never achieved its objective of bottling up the Allied advance westward across the top of New Guinea. Instead, it had been a place where Japanese aircraft and crews were sent to be destroyed and killed before they had an opportunity to do the Allies any real harm.

But in early 1944 the Japanese expended considerable resources to lift Wewak from the ashes. Anticipating Allied assaults at Hansa Bay, and even Wewak itself, more than 150 aircraft were moved into the complex. Consequently, the Fifth Air Force looked to drive a stake into the heart of the enemy stronghold with a string of powerful raids during March 1944.

Heavy bombers and strafers, escorted by fighters, wrecked the place over again—repeating the work they had done the previous year.

But the defending Japanese Army fighter pilots—flying Ki-43s and Ki-61s—proved remarkably resilient, even downing and killing leading ace and P-47 pilot Neel Kearby. Aerial combat was regular, intense, and costly. Nevertheless, Kenney had more and better resources.

Many of those resources were airborne on March 15, 1944. Among them were 16 P-47s of the 49th Fighter Group's 9th Fighter Squadron which were escorting a B-24 strike. They encountered Ki-61 Tonys and Ki-43 Oscars.

William Huisman was part of a flight that was attacked by a single Ki-61 that was painted black on top and silver on the bottom. "The Tony made a tail pass at our flight and made a diving right turn," Huisman said. The P-47s dropped their external fuel tanks and dived after the Japanese fighter. "I followed the Tony down to 2,000 feet and gave him a long burst. The Tony started to smoke and split-essed into the water."[1]

Fred Helterline's experience was less positive. Part of the same flight as Huisman, he stuck with his flight leader until he split away to cover Huisman's attack on the Tony. "I left to rejoin," he said, "and turned out to sea to get a little altitude. Two P-47s shot at me and scored several hits before I could call them off."[2] Shaken but unhurt, Helterline returned safely to base.

Worse was the fate dealt to Warren Danson, a P-38 pilot with the 8th Fighter Group's 36th Fighter Squadron. His wingman, James McLaughlin, recalled that enemy fighters were spotted ahead and below them. "Captain Danson dropped his tanks and made two passes at the enemy. My engines were not functioning properly. However, I stayed with him as much as possible."

Following his second pass at the enemy, Danson leveled his wings and went into a descent. "I attempted to follow him," McLaughlin said, "but due to loss of power in both engines was unable to keep him in sight."[3] Danson was never seen again.

Although it was costly to the Allies, it was clear to both sides that the Wewak complex could not endure such a heavy series of attacks indefinitely. But the Japanese hadn't given up entirely and sent a convoy to reinforce and resupply the complex at the same time the Fifth Air Force was delivering its killing blows. Just after midnight on March 18, two B-24s of the 43rd Bomb Group—newly equipped with airborne radar sets—discovered a destroyer northwest of Wewak. After straddling it with a pair of bombs and leaving it damaged, the two bombers continued west toward Hollandia and discovered a six-ship convoy. They attacked and claimed one freighter sunk and another hit. On the way back to their base they dumped their last bombs on the crippled destroyer—just for good measure.

However, the convoy continued to Wewak, arriving in the early evening of March 18. The freighters, two of them, were quickly emptied of their troops and cargoes before they hurried for Hollandia with an escort of three small submarine chasers the next morning, March 19. They didn't go unnoticed, and a formation of 40 B-24s was diverted from its original target at Cape Boram and directed to hit the ships. Despite this seeming overkill, the bombers sank only one of the freighters, the *Yakumo Maru*.

This lackluster showing was followed up by a force of 56 B-25s and 33 A-20s with an escort of P-38s. It was more than enough to do the job a dozen times over. The Mitchells and Havocs fell on the hapless Japanese like a massive swarm of ill-coordinated hornets. Machinegun fire and bombs came at the enemy ships from every direction. That there were no mid-air collisions or aircraft shot down by friendly fire was a minor miracle.

And, happily for the Americans, it wasn't a fair fight. The 345th Bomb Group's 498th Bomb Squadron led the attack, and its report on the mission fails to capture the near-chaos of the attack but illustrates quite well the overwhelming firepower the force delivered.

A/P [airplane] 371 bombed the vessel identified as a Fox Tare Charlie. Three 500-pound bombs dropped by A/P 425 hit the superstructure of the ship, two 1,000-pound bombs dropped by A/P 371 hit at [the] waterline and on the bow, and two 500-pound bombs dropped by A/P 417 hit the stern of the ship. The vessel was smoking and listing as the planes pulled away and the destruction was completed quickly by following squadrons. The vessel and the wreckage of the two escort vessels [that were] sunk were strafed.

Pilot John Soloc of the 3rd Bomb Group was also part of that raid. Picking out one of the freighters, he brought his A-20 down low over the water and pushed it as fast as it would fly. An antiaircraft round smashed into his aircraft, disabling an engine. He nevertheless continued his attack to very close range, released his bomb and pulled his aircraft skyward.

He didn't pull soon and hard enough. His aircraft's wing and one of the propellers smashed into the ship's mast. The A-20 lurched noticeably and staggered away from the freighter.

Soloc's bomb smashed into the ship as he coaxed his aircraft away from the coastline. Behind him, squadron mate Wade Vukelic dropped his own bomb, just as Soloc's slammed into the ship. A geyser of water and flame and debris shot into the sky, and Vukelic instinctively ducked as he flew through it.

Soloc meanwhile tried to nurse his aircraft away from the water. However, having sustained so much damage, and flying on only one engine, and with no hydraulics and a bomb bay door that refused to close, the A-20 wouldn't stay airborne. Soloc set it down in the water and managed to escape, but his gunner, Donald Bradley, drowned when the aircraft sank.

After the 3rd Bomb Group returned to base, Vukelic's gunner checked the aircraft for damage and found a piece of paper stuck in one of the engines. Snatched midair from the debris cloud created when Soloc stuffed his bomb into the Japanese freighter, the paper was a certification for satisfactory completion of repairs made to the *Taiyei Maru*. It had been issued by the British Register Corporation for Shipping and Aircraft on November 30, 1936.

Soloc wasn't found following the attack, but he was spotted in the water by John Henebry the following day. Henebry guided a PBY Catalina to his location and Soloc was safely recovered. For his trouble, Soloc was given a week to recover in Australia before he returned to duty.[4]

Every ship and escort that made up the little convoy was sunk. And as they had done following the Battle of the Bismarck Sea the previous year, the American flyers strafed everything and everyone in the water. The devastation was so complete and the attack so overwhelming that the Japanese never again attempted to send a convoy to Wewak.

And so, Wewak died. Finally. The runways at the four different airfields were pocked with unrepaired bomb craters. Battered husks of aircraft, and pieces of aircraft, sat scattered and unrepairable. Whatever men and aircraft that survived were ordered to fall back to Hollandia at the end of March 1944.

And with supply lines essentially severed, there was little for the Japanese there to do other than tend the tiny gardens that kept them— only barely—from starving to death. The supply issues were made even more dire as surviving Japanese Army units came out of the jungle and converged on the area. Just as Rabaul was isolated and powerless, so now was Wewak. And just as was the case at Rabaul, the Allies continued to send missions against Wewak to keep the Japanese from reconstituting their forces there.

★★★

The next big Allied operation was the scheduled seizure of Hansa Bay, 90 miles east of Wewak. But with Wewak neutralized, Kenney and others considered that a greater return on the investment that had been made up to that point in men, material, and equipment could be achieved by putting aside the plan to take Hansa Bay. Instead, it was proposed to leapfrog both Hansa Bay and Wewak to seize the big Japanese air and naval complex at Hollandia. Kenney took the idea to MacArthur, who was convinced of its soundness even before Kenney stopped talking.

It was an ambitious gambit. Hollandia was in Dutch New Guinea and sat approximately 220 miles west of Wewak. The Japanese were scrambling to transform it into a major air and naval complex, one that was capable of seriously challenging the Allied march west. They had tried and failed to do the same at Wewak, but if Japan was to have any hope of stopping the Allied advance, Hollandia was where it would have to happen.

The Japanese flew aircraft by the hundreds into the three major airfields there. But there were issues. The aircraft were ferried by pilots who were then returned to the Philippines to retrieve more. The fact was that although Hollandia was becoming home to a tremendous number of aircraft, there weren't enough pilots to fly them all. Nor were there enough mechanics, tools, or spare parts to maintain them.

Moreover, the airfields had not been developed enough to handle all the aircraft. Because there weren't enough protective revetments, they were parked wing-to-wing in lines that were two or three deep. Although certainly aware that doing so was risky, the Japanese leadership was not unduly concerned as Hollandia was outside the range of the Fifth Air Force's fighters. And the Fifth Air Force's bombers went nowhere without fighter protection.

Kenney, who was responsible for establishing air superiority over Hollandia before any amphibious assault could take place, let the Japanese believe what they believed. He sent B-24s in ones and twos to raid Hollandia at night. These did little damage, but he didn't care as he wanted the Japanese to be confident that they were all that the Fifth Air Force could muster. At the same time, he sent strong raids against Hansa Bay and other targets to keep the Japanese distracted.

Importantly, Kenney had recently received 58 new P-38s with additional internal wing fuel tanks which gave them the range to escort the B-24s to Hollandia. But he wanted more of them and ordered his aircraft modification experts to fit the same sorts of fuel tanks to another 75 of the P-38s he already had on hand. In the meantime, he decreed that no P-38s were allowed west of Tadji, near Aitape, which sat 125 miles east of Hollandia. He didn't want the Japanese to know that his fighters could range the airfields at Hollandia. Should they become aware of that, they might start dispersing their aircraft, consequently making it more difficult to find and destroy them.

The Joint Chiefs of Staff approved the plan, while also canceling the seizure of the Japanese stronghold at Kavieng, on New Ireland, 150 miles northwest of Rabaul. A target date of sometime between April 15 and April 20 was set for the seizure of Hollandia—dubbed Operation Reckless. Admiral Chester Nimitz, Commander in Chief, Pacific Ocean Areas, committed to supporting the amphibious assault with two fast carrier groups and a handful of escort carriers, but was concerned about the Japanese air units there. "Nimitz," said Kenney, "kept bringing up the threat of the Jap air force at Hollandia and said that he didn't want to send his carriers to Hollandia with 200 to 300 Jap airplanes in there at the time he arrived. I promised to have them rubbed out by April 5th. Everyone except MacArthur looked skeptical, especially when I said I did not expect I would start to hit Hollandia before March 30, when my long-range P-38s would be in position."[5]

Kenney was as good as his word. Escorted by P-38s, 65 B-24s, flying at medium altitude, dropped more than 14,000 parafrags on various targets on March 30, 1944. Just as they had been at Rabaul, Wewak, and elsewhere, the parachute bombs proved to be especially effective, and the smoke from fuel and supply dumps, parked aircraft, and antiaircraft positions rose black and heavy. Roughly three dozen Japanese fighters rose to contest the strike, and 10 were claimed shot down. Not a single American aircraft was lost.

The next day's strike was essentially a repeat of the first. A force of 68 B-24s protected by 70 P-38s hit the complex again with similar results. Some of the B-24s were loaded with heavy bombs, which cratered the enemy airfields. Again, Japanese fighters were engaged by the P-38 pilots, who claimed 14 aerial victories. The Fifth's losses on this date were a single P-38.

Other strikes were flown in support of the Hollandia operations, but to other locations. One of these, on April 1, 1944, was a six-aircraft mission by the 38th Bomb Group's 822nd Bomb Squadron. It was sent to make an unusual medium altitude strike, rather than a low-level sweep, against enemy personnel and supply dumps on Tumleo Island, just a mile off the coast from Aitape where an amphibious assault—Operation Persecution—was scheduled for the same day as the landings against Hollandia.

Tragedy struck the 822nd's little formation as it passed Tadji, only a few miles from Tumleo. The life raft on the lead aircraft flown by Robert Payne broke free of its compartment and smashed into the left elevator. The aircraft careened wildly and then plunged earthward.

The B-25 went out of control so violently that three of its five 500-pound bombs broke free of their shackles and crashed through the bomb bay doors. While Payne and his copilot tried righting the aircraft, the other crew members struggled to keep from being battered to death. It is remarkable that Weslie Brown, the radioman, was able to throw himself clear and deploy his parachute.

And then, Payne regained control of the aircraft. He jettisoned the two remaining bombs and turned for home while the rest of the squadron completed the mission. At the same time, Brown descended in his parachute directly into Japanese hands.

After his capture he was taken to the local headquarters, and an eyewitness account declared that "the Japs beat him until he was senseless. He was beaten all through the night and when he lost consciousness, water was thrown on him to revive him, then he was beaten again." Brown's body was taken away the following day.

Meanwhile, Kenney's photographic intelligence experts determined that the two strikes flown against Hollandia on March 30 and 31 had destroyed a combined total of 138 aircraft on the ground, with dozens more badly damaged. Kenney's men were kicking Hollandia apart before it even became operational. His staff planned a massive knockout blow for April 3, 1944.

It was the largest raid Kenney's men had ever assembled and included a combined total of 309 bombers and fighters, and a handful of photo-reconnaissance aircraft. The B-24s, 66 of them, targeted antiaircraft positions with 1,000-pound bombs, and were followed by 96 A-20s who swept the three airfields at very low level to strafe and drop 100-pound parademolition bombs on parked aircraft. Sweeping up the mess were 76 B-25 crews who also strafed and dropped parafrags. P-38s ensured that the ineffectual Japanese fighter response stayed that way, claiming 25 of them. Again, as had been the case on March 31, a single P-38 was the only loss that day.

But other crews had close calls. Robert Best of the 345th Bomb Group's 498th Bomb Squadron brought up the rear of the formation. Flying at treetop level, he crested a ridge just prior to reaching Hollandia airfield and was immediately presented with a face full of Japanese fighter. A Ki-43, with four P-38s in hot pursuit, was pointed directly at him. The enemy aircraft was only an eyeblink away from smashing directly into his cockpit. In that brief instant, with the two planes closing at more than 500 miles per hour, the enemy pilot instinctively fired his guns and flashed past, only a few feet over the top of the Best's aircraft. Rounds shattered the top turret and slammed into Best's left wing. The gunner, Frank Leach, was not critically injured, but was hurt badly enough to receive the Purple Heart.

Behind Best was the 345th's 499th Bomb Squadron, led by Julian Baird. Just prior to reaching Hollandia airfield he ordered the squadron into a nine-aircraft line-abreast formation. The airfield—having already been hit by more than a hundred A-20s and B-25s—was a mass of smoke and fire and dust. Speeding just above the ground at more than 200 miles per hour, he struggled to distinguish the enemy aircraft on the ground that had not already been wrecked from those that had.

As did the rest of the squadron, he strafed the best-looking targets and dropped clusters of parafrags. At the far end of the airfield the white blossoms of the 498th's parafrags settled to the ground and detonated with black-orange bursts. Above and behind him he heard and felt the rattle of the turret and waist guns.

Then, the left engine was hit by antiaircraft fire. Although it continued to put out power, it was smoking, and the oil pressure dropped. Not wanting to disrupt his squadron's formation, Baird stayed in the lead position and angled toward the Cyclops airfield, where he continued to strafe and bomb. Once clear of that target, he turned the squadron toward Humboldt Bay, his attention fully directed on his bad engine rather than the enemy.

After dodging a concentration of antiaircraft fire, Baird feathered the engine and led the 499th east along the coast, climbing as he did so. Although there was no sign of fire, he knew he was not out of trouble. The single remaining engine was forced to work at higher power settings to keep the aircraft airborne, and at those higher power settings it was more likely to fail. Should it fail, he and his crew would be forced to bail out over enemy territory.

Upon reaching Tadji, he directed one of his flights of three to detach and return to the squadron's base at Nadzab. Past Alexishafen—where Australian soldiers were fighting that very day—he ordered the other flight to head for Nadzab. His two wingmen stayed with him until they all put down at the recently captured airstrip at Saidor. Once safely on the ground, he and his crew climbed aboard the other two aircraft and headed home.

The Japanese air elements at Hollandia were effectively destroyed by the time the last Fifth Air Force aircraft winged for home on April 3, 1944. "The photographs indicated a total number of 288 wrecked and burned-out aircraft," said Kenney. "Congratulations came in from Admiral Nimitz, who, after all, had a right to be interested, along with a nice message from General MacArthur, which he sent to me uncoded so that even the Japs could read it."[6]

The raids against Hollandia continued although there was little to no fighter resistance, and the airfields became secondary targets. The focus shifted to supply dumps and troop concentrations and anything that might oppose the coming assault. At the same time, missions were run against all manner of targets up and down the coast.

Still, among them all, Hollandia remained most important.

27

"PART OF A BURNED BODY SLIPPED FROM THE B-25"

Robert Huhn of the 38th Bomb Group leaned forward and peered through the shreds of clouds at the coastline. Wind-whipped waves, only a couple hundred feet below, leaped skyward. Rain throbbed hard against his aircraft, and gusts of wind bucked it harder. He knew that somewhere in that direction, just beyond the beach, was Saidor, a forward airfield. On this return flight from the strike against the Japanese air complex at Hollandia on April 16, 1944, the storm had not just broken his squadron apart but had scattered the entire force of nearly 300 aircraft.

He had lost contact with the other two members of his flight near Madang as they turned and descended through the clouds toward the water. Boiling thunderheads and lightning strikes lashed the crews with a fury the likes of which Huhn had never seen. Earlier, he and his copilot, Fred Rodgers, had watched an out-of-control P-38 smash into the water. The pilot could not have survived.

Huhn checked the aircraft's fuel and considered his options. He could continue down the coast toward Finschhafen, but there was no guarantee that the weather there would be any better than it was over Saidor. Or, he could alter course slightly and divert to Gasmata, on New Britain Island. It was 275 miles to the east and was probably—but not definitely—clear of the storm.

Huhn peered toward the coast again and was discouraged by what he didn't see. Saidor was hidden by clouds. Nevertheless, a veteran of 35 missions, he decided to take his chances with the storm and make a play for the hidden airfield. He didn't relish a flight to Gasmata during which he would be racing his fuel tanks toward empty over the Bismarck Sea.

Huhn rolled the control yoke of his B-25 to the right, toward the coast. It disappeared in the clouds, reappeared, and then was gone again.

Huhn let the aircraft drop closer to the sea and leaned further forward to stare through the rain-washed windscreen. Rodgers kept an eye on the aircraft's airspeed and altitude and, like Huhn, looked for any sign of land. Both of them were startled when a P-38, landing gear down, flashed in front of them and was gone. The machine they flew didn't care about the near-collision, and its two engines thrummed steadily—resolutely— through the storm. His wits on edge, Huhn called on the intercom to let the crew in the back of the aircraft know his plan.

There was land. The aircraft crossed the beach where big breakers smashed white against the sand. And then, the airfield was almost directly ahead. Huhn turned hard to set up for a landing, flying as low and as close to the airfield as he dared. He directed Rodgers to lower the flaps and landing gear and to watch for rising terrain. He didn't want to smash into a hill while his eyes were padlocked on the runway. Reversing his turn, he lined his aircraft up for the approach, then completed the remainder of the landing checklist.

"Plane #337 [Huhn's] landed at Saidor at 1630K," recorded the 405th's narrative report, "when visibility was reduced to less than one half mile. This plane collided on the runway with a P-38 [actually, an F-5, the photoreconnaissance version of the P-38] landing simultaneously from the opposite direction and both airplanes were totally destroyed by the result- ing fire. The pilot of the P-38, the pilot [Huhn] and navigator [William Barron] of our plane were killed in the crash. The copilot [Fred Rodgers]," the report continued, "died the following day as a result of severe burns. The radioman [Joseph Carroll] and the gunner [M.E. Daniels] are confined to the hospital at Saidor, the radioman suffering from severe burns and the gunner suffering shock and lacerations received when he was thrown clear of the wreckage."

Alfred Colwell was a crewman who had landed aboard a B-25 a short time earlier. He witnessed the crash. "Somehow one man got out of the B-25 okay," he said. "Another was dragged out badly burned (died later); the others were cremated."

There had already been several crashes, and aircraft and pieces of aircraft cluttered the runway. Still, crews were flying overhead that were low on fuel and had little choice but to attempt a landing. "The A-20s began coming in anyhow," Colwell said, "the first one almost missing the burning wreckage but clipped off a wing; the second blew a tire, his nose wheel collapsed, and he skidded through the burning planes—both fellows got out okay."

The crash crew at Saidor scrambled to make order out of the bedlam and hooked a cable onto a part of Huhn's aircraft that was not afire. "The boys with the winches," Colwell said, "walked right into the burning, exploding mess, hooked on to it, and dragged it from the strip. Part of a burned body slipped from the B-25."

The day became known as Black Sunday because the Fifth's losses far exceeded those of any other day of the war. In total, 37 aircraft were lost or destroyed, and 54 pilots and crewmen were killed. And the Japanese were responsible for none of it.

Weather did it. New Guinea's weather had exacted tribute from the flyers of both sides since the start of the war, but it had never taken so much as it did that day. The mission had already been delayed by weather during the previous couple of days and was postponed due to weather again that morning. But the date for the amphibious assault against Hollandia—April 22, 1944—was approaching, and the participating units were ordered to take off despite the fact that conditions over the target were reported by weather reconnaissance aircraft as poor.

The takeoff was accompanied by grumbling. Late afternoon thunderstorms were as predictable as sunrise at that time of year, and the delayed departure meant that the crews would be forced to pick their way home through thunderheads and showers. Their grumbling would have been more strident had they any understanding of the scale and ferocity of the yet-to-exist monster that would block their way home.

Except that a few units overshot the target area and burned too much fuel, the mission was a success. Weather along the route and over the target was reasonable, and not a single aircraft was lost to antiaircraft fire or fighters. Moreover, much of what remained in Hollandia that was worth hitting was hit. Altogether, it was little more than a long-range training exercise.

The return leg started with an almost casual attitude. There being no indication of Japanese fighters, the P-38 pilots stunted around the bombers, showing off with mild aerobatics or flying close formation and waving at the crews. Of course, all this burned more fuel, but they had plenty to burn owing to the lack of air combat.

And then, near Madang, there rose a mountainous mass of fearsome convective weather. As the different formations continued east toward the wall of thunderheads it became apparent that they rose from the ground to an altitude higher than they could fly. Most of the aircraft turned over the water where they could descend below the weather without running into a mountain.

The clouds were thick, and the rain was heavy. Group formations fell apart and broke into squadron formations which subsequently came apart into separate flights. And then, individual aircraft were spit out of those flights, as Huhn and his crew had been. Although most crews made it back to their bases, a considerable number were compelled to land elsewhere, and it was several days before the Fifth Air Force had an accurate accounting of where its aircraft and crews were. Of course, that accounting was incomplete as many of the aircraft were simply missing and remain so to the present day.

Rescue operations continued for some time after the mission. One of the recovered crews included A-20 pilot Charles Davidson and his gunner, John McKenna, of the 312th Bomb Group. Davidson became separated from the rest of his squadron and was unable to clear the weather. Out of fuel, he spotted a patch of kunai grass and decided to put his aircraft down. He gave McKenna the option of parachuting clear, but the gunner elected to stay with the aircraft. Davidson lowered full flaps, left the landing gear retracted, and set the aircraft down into the high grass.

His flying was good, and neither he nor McKenna were hurt. Davidson destroyed the aircraft's radios, lest they somehow be recovered by the Japanese, then settled down with McKenna as dusk turned into night. "That night it started to rain," McKenna said, "so we slept in the plane. We had some candy—Charms—and dry biscuits, only food in the plane."[1]

After an uncomfortable night in the cramped confines of their A-20, both men got up early. "We got out the parachutes," he said, "and smoke bombs for signaling in case anyone came over. During the morning, a P-47 came over and we set off a smoke bomb. The P-47 circled the area and dropped messages, but they fell in the trees and we could not recover them."

The P-47 pilot stayed overhead the two fliers until relieved by a formation of A-20s. Like the P-47 pilot, the A-20 crews also dropped messages. And like the P-47 pilot, their aim was poor and neither Davidson nor McKenna recovered them.

Later, another A-20 dropped supplies, as did a pair of B-24s, which showered the two men with food, blankets, a pair of rifles, a submachine-gun, mosquito nets, coveralls, and gloves. A small liaison aircraft, an L-5, overflew them late in the afternoon and delivered a note which announced "there were many Japs in the area" and that they should move. They were instructed to move in the direction of another downed A-20 crew.

Davidson and McKenna hurriedly broke camp with as much gear as they could carry. "At midnight," Davidson said, "there was a downpour. It was impossible to keep warm and the water soon was over our heads at our campsite, so we found higher ground with water to our waists."

Dodging voices that they suspected belonged to a Japanese patrol, the two men left their resting spot. They had lost their pistols and the submachinegun in the swamp, and their compass was eventually ruined. By the evening of April 18, they were back at the crash site. It wasn't a safe place to be as it was strafed by a pair of Japanese aircraft early the next morning.

That day, April 19, they were visited by several aircraft and instructed to use air-dropped machetes to cut an airstrip out of the kunai grass onto which an L-5 could land to extract them. Resupplied by more airdrops with food and two new carbines and other stuff, the men worked hard on the airstrip for the next several days. They were eventful days as the Japanese aircraft returned two more times to strafe their wrecked A-20, and friendly crews kept their morale up with more supplies.

They also tried to assist the two men with their ad hoc airstrip. "P-40s dropped 12 belly tanks," said Davidson, "setting the grass afire, but rain put out the fire." An axe was dropped to them and they were instructed to chop down a set of trees at the end of their little airstrip.

It was eventually determined that the airstrip—soaked by repeated rains—could not be satisfactorily completed. The men were dropped a life raft and food and other supplies and were directed to make for the Gogol River, a mile or so away. This they did and managed to paddle downstream about five miles before nightfall.

They continued their journey on April 27, more than 10 days since they had run out of fuel. "That morning we saw our first crocodile," said Davidson, "which was tremendous in size." The maneater was only about 20 feet from the men when they saw it. "We shot at it and killed it with about fifteen shots. We proceeded with caution and traveled slower thereafter."

Almost continuously rain-soaked, Davidson and McKenna continued down the river for the next several days. Aircraft dropped a bigger, five-man raft for them. They transferred their gear to this larger craft and continued their journey. Rather than staying close to the bank they chose to float down the center of the widening river because of the increasing numbers of crocodiles they encountered. Knowing the risk of alerting enemy patrols with gunfire, they still felt threatened enough to kill two more of the massive reptiles.

Finally, at midday on May 1, an L-5 dropped a message and more food. They were almost to the mouth of the river. Moreover, nearby Madang had been captured by the Australians. Once the two men reached the mouth of the river, the Australians would send a boat to recover them. Nearing the beach, the two men pulled their raft out of the water.

> We found a deserted Jap camp, probably a headquarters, because of the numerous telephone lines leading to it. There was about 30 or 40 Jap bodies in the area, and decomposing. There was a bridge destroyed by bombs, a truck in the river, and three dead Japs on the shore. We reached the bay about 1400, and half an hour later were picked up by an Australian corvette.

The rescue of Davidson and McKenna highlighted a great dichotomy between the capabilities and attitudes of the Allies and the Japanese. The Americans launched dozens of sorties and dropped considerable quantities of material to rescue the two men. It was expensive and time-consuming and put wear and tear on aircraft that could have been used elsewhere. But it was something that the Americans had the will and morality to do, as well as the means. On the other hand, it was something the Japanese would have never done for their own crews, regardless of whether or not they had the wherewithal to do so.

It is often said that successful people don't dwell on negatives. This applied to Kenney and the losses his units sustained on April 16, 1944. Although he acknowledged that "it was the worst blow I took in the whole war," he spent only a paragraph addressing Black Sunday in his wartime memoir, which ran nearly 600 pages.[2]

Nevertheless, Kenney and his Fifth Air Force must be given credit for their achievements at Hollandia. Supported by naval shore bombardment and aircraft from Nimitz's carriers, the Army's units encountered little opposition when they went ashore on the morning of April 22, 1944. During the next several days, only 152 men were killed. After the airfields had been secured, 380 burned and wrecked aircraft were counted. The great Japanese air complex at Hollandia was dead almost before it started operations.

Other good news for the Allies at this time was the closure of the Huon Peninsula campaign. Australian units secured Madang and the surrounding area, including Alexishafen, at the end of April. Although considerable numbers of Japanese troops escaped overland to the northwest, many of them succumbed to disease, starvation, and exposure before linking up with other forces at Wewak, Hansa Bay, or elsewhere.

★★★

It was about this time that the increased production of P-38s in the States made itself felt in New Guinea. The 49th Fighter Group's 9th Fighter Squadron had been made to give up its P-38s to the 475th Fighter Group following the fighting over Rabaul during late 1943. The squadron had been given P-47s in their place, and many men were not happy about it.

"The P-47s remained with the group for a short time only," recorded the group's historical narrative. "And in April 1944, the 9th Squadron again was equipped with P-38s. The return to the twin-engine planes was welcomed by all pilots and crew chiefs who never became reconciled to the Thunderbolts."

★★★

The Papuans had no interest in P-38s or P-47s, or in fact in the war except for the hurt that it did them. They hadn't started it, they didn't understand what it was about, and they knew little of the two sides doing the fighting. Yet, it was being fought on their land, and they were caught in the middle. And, as described by one man, they endured its savagery.

"Another bad thing [that] happened to us during the war period," he said, "was the Japanese soldiers raped and attempted to rape some of our women and we couldn't do anything to them, so we had to run away as quickly as possible into the bushes to hide for our safety." Dislocated from their homes, he and his community struggled.

"We wandered into the bush too long thinking how long [until] the war will [be] finished and saved our lives in the bushes," he said. "One day we thought about going to the beach to get fish so that we would eat. We went to the beach and while we were fishing in the river, within minutes [an] American war plane flew above us, and dropped a bomb, and fired machineguns, killing six and injuring four of our people."[3]

The Japanese regularly moved into Papuan villages, sometimes staying for weeks or more at a time, other times passing through for only a few days or less. The Papuans had little say in the matter and either fled or made nice with the Japanese and stayed put. Experiences varied. The Japanese sometimes went on rampages during which they murdered and raped. At other times and locations, they exhibited tolerance toward the natives, if not respect.

Regardless, the Allies wanted to kill the Japanese wherever they might be. Consequently, the Fifth Air Force regularly sent bombers to strafe and bomb villages which were suspected of harboring Japanese. There was something horrifyingly ironic about sending modern, fast-flying aircraft to bomb and strafe grass huts and garden plots.

There were problems of course. First, there was no guarantee that the Japanese would be in the targeted village or villages. Second, one village looked very much like another, especially when flying at a couple of hundred miles per hour while navigating with poor, or no, maps. Consequently, the wrong villages were sometimes targeted. Moreover, there was a good chance that, while destroying a village, Papuans instead of Japanese might be killed. This could ruin any goodwill that those particular natives might have harbored for the Allies.

John Henebry, the commanding officer of the 3rd Bomb Group, refused to do this sort of strafing. "Strafe everything that moved," he said of the orders he was given in early during 1944. "The command was based on intelligence that Papuan nationals along the route were assisting the beginnings of a Japanese evacuation of the Huon Peninsula," he said.

But as he flew his aircraft down toward a native village, he couldn't do it. "People were standing in the open, looking up at our low-flying planes, by now used to our presence, trusting. I vividly remember the faces of the women and children." Neither he nor the other members of the flight fired their weapons. Back at base, he made his opinion known up the chain of command. "By the next day the orders had changed," he said. "We were to leave the villages untouched."[4]

That might have been the case during that particular time for Henebry's unit, but the practice continued. On May 14, 1944, the 345th Bomb Group was directed to hit the village of Takar on New Guinea's northern coast, about eight miles southeast of Wakde Island. The strike—made from medium altitude with nearly 200 500-pound demolition bombs—included all four of the bomb group's squadrons.

"The bombing was excellent," noted a squadron account. "Withdrawing to the left and making a wide circle out to sea in order to lose altitude, our planes came in again on the same heading to make their strafing runs." There was no assessment of the damage done.

The bombing that day was in support of a greater plan that Kenney was developing to move his forces west and north in preparation for MacArthur's advance on the Philippines. "We needed airdromes," said Kenney, "I was abandoning the Dobodura area and Port Moresby as operating bases." Nor, he noted, were many of his other bases relevant—Kiriwina Island and Milne Bay being examples. They were all too far from the action.

Even Hollandia wasn't far enough west for his airmen, and room there was limited.

I needed four or five more good-sized fields to bring the Fifth Air Force and the Thirteenth into play. The area around Maffin Bay looked like a possibility for airdrome development, but I wanted to keep on going and take over Biak where the Nips already had three coral runways. Coral was good. Where there was plenty of coral, the engineers could give us a field in a matter of a few days.[5]

MacArthur wasn't initially sold on the idea, nor were others. But after considerable discussion, plans were made to seize Wakde and Biak. Wakde was quickly taken beginning on May 17, and American troops went ashore at Biak on May 27. All the landings were preceded by air bombardment, and that support continued until the enemy was dead.

With a couple of exceptions, Japanese air units were unable to seriously challenge the Americans. The bomber crews, protected by fighters, operated under an umbrella of almost total air superiority. The 3rd Attack Group described the targets struck by its A-20 crews over Biak on May 27: "Targets of opportunity, as well as designated known targets consisted of coastal defense gun positions, positions of the Jap ground forces, air strips, coastal roads and trails, and villages known to be occupied by the enemy."

But the ground fight at Biak proved to be much more vicious than anticipated. The defending Japanese were dug into a formidable line of cliffs. Every yard gained came at a cost and sometimes had to be taken more than once. The big prize was the island's main airfield, Mokmer, and the Army fought doggedly to blast the Japanese clear of the place.

Elements of the 49th Fighter Group were sent ashore at Bosnek Beach on June 5, 1944. "A battery of field artillery on the beach was methodically lobbing shells over the hills and cliffs toward Jap positions," noted the unit's monthly narrative. "However, the most disappointing news was that our infantry were unable to get and keep the airstrip from which we were to operate."

The 49th's men and equipment were moved three miles up a rough road toward Mokmer and then directed to bivouac in a small, hot, dusty stretch of coral and dirt where they were to wait until the airfield had been captured.

Strung along either side of the road we were boxed in by swamp, cliffs, field artillery and antiaircraft units. The battery of 105s [howitzers] barked night and day, their muzzle blasts flapping our canvas and eardrums. Up the road a few hundred yards was a much-disputed water hole which the Japs counterattacked daily. Mortar fire, fire from rifles and machineguns, plus the 105s kept everyone on edge. The first night, two red alerts sounded and we witnessed the heaviest flak we had seen in some time.

While the 49th's men squatted in their little hellhole during the next three weeks, the Japanese demonstrated that although their air units on New Guinea had been crushed, others were still active. On June 9, a Ki-61 fighter flew low and fast over the encampment, neither doing nor sustaining harm. And each evening, bombers came over in twos and threes in raids that were little more than harassment, but which still kept the men on edge and unable to sleep. Notwithstanding the generally poor aim of the enemy bombers, the 49th's men were frustrated by the island's coral composition, which made it extremely difficult to dig protective trenches.

"At 0130 on the morning of June 12, [1944], it happened," read the unit's narrative. "After a prolonged series of red alerts, a stick of six 'daisy cutters' sliced across our area." Even as dirt and debris continued to shower down from the explosions, men crawled from where they had been sleeping or sheltering and into a cauldron of smoke and dust and fire. Wounded men screamed and the dead lay still and quiet, some of them in pieces.

The men assessed the situation as best they could in the dark and hurried to load the wounded on the vehicles that were still operable. Within 20 minutes they were on their way to the newly erected field hospital. They left behind a smoking, bloody, and dusty devastation.

The bombs had cut down Alpheus White, Quintin Rizor, and Arnold Hayworth in midstride as they ran for protection. There was nothing to do for them. Five men in another tent were killed. William Smoots was blasted dead in his sleep while his two tent mates were blown into the air, suffering only light injuries. Jacob Shelman had already taken shelter in a slit trench. He screeched at his tent mates to hurry to him just as the bombs fell. The bombs did what Shelman's friends failed to do. They blew the two men atop Shelman, in his trench. Remarkably, they sustained only minor injuries.

It wasn't until early the next month, July 1944, that the 49th started operating from Mokmer. Even then, they were not safe from the starving Japanese, who continued to snipe them and even made small foraging raids into the unit's living area. Indeed, the Japanese continued fighting in small groups and as ones-and-twos for months until they were finally killed or starved to death.

28

"WE HAD HOPED TO CATCH A FEW JAP PLANES IN THE AIR"

Essentially, although the Japanese were capable of mounting occasional raids from distant outposts, the air war over New Guinea had been won by the middle of 1944. The once-powerful bastions at Rabaul and Wewak were reduced to husks and were bypassed, as was Kavieng. Lae, Hollandia, and others had been captured and turned into Allied airbases. Although there remained many tens of thousands of Japanese soldiers in New Guinea, they were isolated and starving. And they were being kept that way in large part by airpower.

★★★

Leonard "Tony" Duval looked past the head and shoulders of Kenneth Lindsay as the jungled terrain of New Guinea slid underneath the A-20. Duval was prone in the life raft compartment of the 3rd Bomb Group aircraft which Lindsay flew. Below and behind him in the midsection compartment were two enlisted men—gunners. They had taken off from the airfield at Hollandia a short time earlier. Lindsay was flying them to Biak where Duval and one of the gunners were to sign for a different A-20 and ferry it back to Hollandia.

Duval had just rejoined his unit, the 3rd Bomb Group's 90th Bomb Squadron, that same morning, July 16, 1944. He had been recovering in Sydney, Australia, from wounds sustained during an attack against the Japanese airfield at Waren the previous month—June 19, specifically. With the rest of the 90th Bomb Squadron, he had raced down a mountainside to drop his load of bombs while flying through a curtain of Japanese anti-aircraft fire.

An instant after releasing his bombs, his aircraft was hit by a cannon shell in the bomb bay while the doors were still open. "It went off inside the bomb bay between me and the gunner in back," he said. "Another shell hit and took part of my cockpit away and cut the safety harness that held me." Moreover, part of Duval's right engine was torn away, and pieces of shrapnel punched into his left arm and right leg.

Duval kept the aircraft flying for a few minutes, but the badly damaged A-20 wouldn't stay airborne. It dropped lower and lower until it smashed into the water about 20 miles from Waren, just a few miles north of Mios Noem Island. The impact smashed Duval's face into the instrument panel and broke his nose.

Dazed and adrenaline-charged, he had clambered clear of the sinking bomber and freed the life raft. Anxiously looking for some sign of his gunner, James Foxworth, Duval climbed into the raft and stayed close to the slowly sinking wreck that had been the A-20. A short time passed before it slipped beneath the waves. Foxworth went down with it.[1]

Now, airborne in an A-20 for the first time since that mission, Duval no doubt reflected back on that day, and on the loss of James Foxworth. However, this particular flight was nothing more than an administrative mission—a milk run. Nothing was expected to happen. And nothing did happen. At least for a while.

Then, at the coast, Lindsay spotted a Japanese gun emplacement and its crew. The men in the rear of the A-20 clutched at whatever handholds they could find as Lindsay wracked the aircraft around in a hard turn. Once he gained enough separation, he turned hard again and pointed at the Japanese position. He fired the aircraft's .50 caliber machineguns, and the enemy fired back.

Lindsay's aircraft lurched as enemy rounds tore into the tail section of the A-20. He struggled to keep the aircraft out of the treetops but failed and smashed into a grove of palm trees. Barely airborne, Lindsay pointed the mortally damaged bomber out to sea.[2]

Only a few hundred yards from shore, the aircraft rolled on its back and plunged nose-first into shallow water. The tail of the aircraft flew away and the two gunners were killed and thrown from the wreckage. Lindsay was crumpled into the cockpit and badly injured. Just as had been the case the previous time he had been aboard an A-20, Duval was shocked and disoriented, but not badly injured.

"I got out on the wing and helped Lindsey out of the cockpit, but he was hurt very badly," said Duval. "I placed him on the wing." Duval heard rifle fire and looked toward the beach where he saw about a dozen Japanese soldiers wading through the water toward him, firing their weapons as they did so.

Duval emptied his .45 caliber pistol at the advancing enemy but ultimately threw it into the water and gave himself up. The Japanese shouted and shoved him as he struggled to drag Lindsay to the beach. Lindsay's scalp had essentially been torn away, his back was injured, and he had a broken arm and leg. Once ashore, Duval saw that the Japanese had already recovered the bodies of the two gunners which had been stripped of their clothes.

After Duval carried Lindsay to where the Japanese were bivouacked, the Japanese stole their watches and other valuables. Duval struggled mightily to remove his high school ring. He only succeeded when one of the enemy soldiers drew a knife and stepped forward, preparatory to removing his finger. Afterward, the two men were trussed with cords from their parachutes. Lindsay was kept close to a fire, whereas Duval was tied to a stake underneath a hut.

After dark, Duval was startled by the sharp report of a pistol shot. The Japanese had shot Lindsay. Duval knew that Lindsay was suffering and likely would not survive and was relieved that his comrade's misery was over.

One of the Japanese boiled some rice that evening and carefully poured the hot water through the floor and onto Duval's head. "I leaned forward," he said, "and it went on down my back on the parachute cord. It got wet and gooey. I pulled on the cord until I got my hands loose. I waited until everything was quiet and got the rope off my feet and just crawled off in the jungle."

Duval was free. He hid in a large stump through the rest of the night then spent the next day mucking his way across swamps and streams until arriving at a sizeable river. He tried to swim it but was swept to the sea. He succeeded on his second attempt but was left exhausted. After resting for a period, he stepped back into the jungle.

Duval was immediately surrounded by Japanese soldiers, who stripped him naked. "I was bound hand and foot with my hands behind my back while they excitedly asked questions," he said. The Japanese leader grew frustrated when Duval failed to tell them anything but his name, rank, and serial number. He kicked Duval then spit on him. Duval grew angry and kicked him back. The Japanese prevailed in the one-sided contest when he slashed Duval across the forehead with his sword.

"When I came to," Duval said, "I was lying on my stomach on the beach with my face in the sand. They grabbed my feet and dragged me, face down up the beach." He passed out, and when he woke, he found himself alone in a hole in the sand, covered with palm fronds.

Duval crawled out of the hole, found a section of a tin can and cut himself free. That done, he stumbled once more into the jungle. There followed several days of misery as, torn by thorns and bitten by mosquitos and sucked at by leeches, he crashed through the brush or stumbled along native trails.

He was a pitiable sight, naked but for a loin cloth he had fashioned out of a piece of cast-off clothing. Incredibly, he encountered Japanese soldiers, many of them wounded, who were in little better shape. As dirty as he was—and dark-complected and small in stature—he was mistaken for Japanese. He simply grunted and kept walking when they called out to him.

Duval's feet were grossly swollen from coral cuts and insect bites and other insults. He stopped occasionally to wash them in the ocean and was once shot at by a sniper. Eventually entering a village, he sneaked into a Japanese officer's hut and stole a pair of canvas trousers, a pith helmet and a swagger stick. He only barely cleared the village in time to escape the withering fire of three A-20s. The results were staggering. "They were all gone," Duval said. "There wasn't a soul in sight. So, I just walked through the village. It was just clear. There wasn't anything there."

Afterward, Duval sat on the beach, soaking his feet and legs. He pressed and picked at his legs to remove thorns and splashed water on wounds that the stolen trousers had rubbed raw. He hadn't been there long when a destroyer hove into view and started firing over his head at a set of gun emplacements dug into a cliff above the village through which he had just passed. Scrambling into a nearby cave, he hid there until the gunfire ceased, at which point he returned to the beach. "I was walking along there, no shoes, no drawers. I had a pith helmet and a swagger stick. All of a sudden, from behind a big log, these five GIs stood up, about 100 feet away. I tried to holler at them, but no sound came out."

Duval only narrowly missed being shot as the men thought he might be a Japanese soldier. Considering instead that he might be a native, the soldiers held their fire and approached him. Duval finally found his voice and explained that he was an American pilot. "They got me a cup of coffee, and some soup," he said. "I had been dreaming every night about a cup of coffee. By the time I was finished, I was so stiff I couldn't move."

Duval was evacuated to a hospital and debriefed by intelligence authorities about what he had seen and done. It was determined that he had walked an incredible 103 miles in five days. He was sent back to the States following his recovery and spent much of the rest of the war lecturing other men on survival techniques, using his own experience as an example.

★★★

"We have been able to find no Japanese aircraft in New Guinea," wrote famed aviator Charles Lindbergh on July 5, 1944. Lindbergh had been in the Pacific theater for about two months. He had wanted a commission and combat assignment when the United States entered the war but was denied. His fame, his prewar engagements with the Nazis, and his controversial opinions on Jews, isolationism, and other issues worked against him. More-over, he had resigned his reserve commission as a political protest before the war. To top it off, President Roosevelt didn't like him.

Still, Lindbergh was a patriot and wanted to serve his country. He did quite a bit of consulting with various aviation concerns and in early 1944 wangled an assignment with the Chance-Vought division of United Air-craft. Chance-Vought manufactured the F4U Corsair, which was operated by Marine Corps and Royal New Zealand Air Force units in the South Pacific. Working with them, Lindbergh not only tested aircraft and offered suggestions for improving maintenance and performance but also went on combat missions. These sorties were officially forbidden but were unof-ficially winked at.

Flying out of Green Island and Emirau, Lindbergh flew missions against Rabaul and Kavieng. The once-powerful Japanese air units in the area had all been destroyed, and the primary dangers were antiaircraft fire, weather, and mechanical failure. Lindbergh joined Marine pilots on several missions to strafe and bomb targets of opportunity, none of which were remarkable. On one mission his flight was reduced to strafing fishing nets in the middle of Rabaul's Simpson Harbor.[3]

At that point of his life, notwithstanding his prewar political missteps, Lindbergh was still very much able to trade on the currency that was his celebrity. His wartime journal describes lunches and dinners with admirals and generals and local luminaries, missions aboard PT boats, and side trips to native villages. Indeed, his time in the Pacific was a sort of air combat adventure safari—made all the more unusual by the fact that he was a civil-ian. Lindbergh's activities as such were unique. The notion of a nonmilitary celebrity flying regular combat missions was preposterous.

Following his time with the Marines, he made his way to New Guinea—anxious to see how he might be able to help Kenney's men. On June 18, a few days after arriving at Nadzab, he dined with Ennis Whitehead—Kenney's right-hand man—and discussed the Fifth's opera-tions. Lindbergh was impressed and declared that Whitehead "has done an exceptionally fine piece of work here in New Guinea."[4]

Left on his own the following day, Lindbergh explored one of the flight lines. A noted prig, he was unimpressed by the informal artwork that adorned so many of the aircraft. "The cheapness of the emblems and names painted on the bombers and fighters nauseates me at times—mostly naked women or 'Donald Ducks'—names such as 'Fertile Myrtle' under a large and badly painted figure of a reclining nude."[5]

From Nadzab, on June 26, Lindbergh flew a borrowed P-38 to Hollandia, now a major Allied base. The threat from Japanese fighters was so diminished that he passed several unescorted C-47s along the route. Upon landing, he observed, "Wreckage of the Japanese Air Force was strewn in between the revetments around Hollandia airstrip—shoved out of the way by bulldozers to make room for our own fighters and bombers and transports. Broken fuselages, engines and wings everywhere, most of them marked with the red-ball insigne of the Japanese rising sun."[6]

Lindbergh ensconced himself with the 475th Fighter Group and, with just a handful of hours of experience at the controls of the P-38, talked his way onto the schedule for a mission the following day, June 27, 1944. The 475th was assigned to escort B-24s on a strike against the Japanese airfields at Jefman and Samate, at the far northwestern tip of New Guinea in the region known as the Vogelkop. A few Japanese aircraft were reported to still be operating from both airfields, and the Lightning pilots hoped to force them into a fight.

"We had hoped to catch a few Jap planes in the air," Lindbergh said, "but no luck." Lindbergh's flight circled the two airfields, giving the enemy antiaircraft gunners an opportunity to sharpen their skills. After a time, the Lightning pilots grew bored and went hunting for barges.[7]

They were successful as they found several vessels snugged up to the shore where they were camouflaged with jungle vegetation. "I curved in over the top of one ridge at an indicated speed of 250 m.p.h.," Lindbergh said, "missing the trees by not over ten feet, partially straightened out while I was shooting, and pulled up the mountainside." His guns eventually jammed but not before setting a barge ablaze.[8]

Just as Lindbergh was put off by the sometimes-lurid nose art that decorated many of the Fifth Air Force's aircraft, he was jolted by the attitudes of the young men doing the fighting in New Guinea. "It was freely admitted that some of our soldiers tortured Jap prisoners and were as cruel and barbaric at times as the Japs themselves. We claim to be fighting for civilization, but the more I see of this war in the Pacific the less right I think we have to claim to be civilized." He additionally noted that he wasn't certain that the behavior of the Americans in that context was much better than that of the Japanese.[9] During those instances when he articulated his disapproval, it seemed that his opinion was usually acknowledged but rarely embraced.

While he worked with the 475th, Lindbergh shared living quarters with rising ace Thomas McGuire. The two men grew chummy, although McGuire often bullied Lindbergh, which sometimes raised eyebrows or caused stifled laughs. Of course, Lindbergh was a global personality and perhaps the most famous pilot that ever lived. He was hardly intimidated, although he often acceded to McGuire's sometimes frivolous demands.

During this period, there was frustration at the slow progress being made at Biak. The Allies were anxious to use the Japanese airfields there, but that was not possible until the enemy troops were driven away. Consequently, MacArthur ordered the seizure of Noemfoor Island—and its airfields—which sat 60 miles west of Biak. The 475th was tasked with providing fighter protection overhead Noemfoor on the day of the invasion, July 2, 1944. Incredibly, Lindbergh, a civilian, was assigned as a flight lead for a flight of four P-38s. As it developed, the mission was uneventful.

The reality was that meaningful targets in New Guinea—especially active enemy airfields and aircraft—were thin by mid-1944. Kenney's fighter pilots might have been frustrated at the paucity of targets against which to practice their skills, but that paucity was exactly what the Allies had worked to establish since the start of the war. It was one of many key indicators that they were winning. So then, with their New Guinea hunting grounds exhausted, the Fifth's fighter units had to go farther afield to find new game, either west to the Moluccas or Celebes, or north to Palau or the Philippines.

Lindbergh stood ready to help. He already knew how to extend the range of the P-38 so that it could reach those areas where the enemy was still flying. As he put more missions under his belt, Lindbergh noted that he was returning to base with significantly more fuel than the 475th's pilots. "The trouble," he wrote at the time, "is that the newer pilots, and many of the old ones, cruise their engines at too high an RPM [revolutions per minute] and often leave their mixture controls in auto rich during an entire flight."[10] In contrast, Lindbergh ran his engines hotter by leaning the fuel mixture to the engines, reducing the RPM and increasing the manifold pressure. It did create more stress on the engine—and consequently more work for the mechanics—but the greater range was worth the cost.

But before he shared these techniques, he had to visit with powerful people. The news that Lindbergh was flying combat had gotten out, and he left Nadzab for Brisbane to speak with Kenney and MacArthur. Kenney hadn't even realized that Lindbergh was in the Pacific, much less flying his P-38s in combat. "I told him," Lindbergh said, "that the last thing I wanted to do was cause anyone embarrassment at headquarters. Kenney was very decent about it all."[11] Still, Kenney didn't want Lindbergh to fly combat for all the obvious reasons, but Lindbergh pushed back, asking "if there wasn't some way around the regulations?"

Kenney couldn't resist the challenge. Lindbergh said that Kenney's eyes twinkled and that he declared he might be able to use Lindbergh as an "observer." "But, of course," Kenney said, "That would not make it legal for you to do any shooting. But if you are on observer status, no one back in the States will know whether you use your guns or not."

Kenney steered Lindbergh into the office of his old nemesis Richard Sutherland. Kenney wanted Sutherland to paper over Lindbergh's illegal combat flying with official-looking orders that would make that illegal flying seem not illegal. Lindbergh and Sutherland chatted about mutual friends before Lindbergh explained that he could help the Fifth's P-38 pilots extend the aircraft's operating radius out to 700 miles or more when, at that time, they were typically flying out to only about 400 miles. But to do so, he would need to fly the missions with them.

Sutherland grew excited, as he knew that the leap from New Guinea to the Philippines would be greatly aided by such a range extension. He took Lindbergh to see MacArthur, who likewise showed enthusiasm. "MacArthur said it would be a gift from heaven if that could be done," said Lindbergh, "and asked me if I were in a position to go back up to New Guinea to instruct the squadrons in the methods of fuel economy which would make such a radius possible." Lindbergh answered that he would be happy to do so. "He said I could have any plane and do any kind of flying I wanted to, and that an increased fighter radius would be of very great importance to his plans."

Lindbergh was as good as his word. He gave classes and individual instruction to the 475th as well as other units. Typically, the reactions to his methods were guarded, but when they yielded the results he promised, they were widely and enthusiastically embraced. Lindbergh continued to fly missions and later was credited with downing a Japanese reconnaissance aircraft near Ceram.

29

"HE CURSED AND SHOUTED"

The starving men looked down at their fallen comrade. He gasped and wept. Barefoot and naked, his limbs—which looked like stretched parchment over sticks—shivered uncontrollably and his bowels leaked across the ground. Flies crawled over his face. Lacking the strength to get up, he cursed and shouted for the men hovering above him to leave, to go on. First one, then another, and finally the rest of them turned and walked up the barely visible trace through the jungle. One of the Japanese men turned and muttered a few words of encouragement. Perhaps his friend on the ground might catch up to them after he rested.

★★★

Japan's 77th Hiko Sentai had flown combat with distinction since before America's entry into the war. An army unit, it fought against the Chinese and later against the famed American Volunteer Group, or Flying Tigers, as well as the British, in Burma and Malaya and elsewhere. After stints in Japan and Sumatra, it was sent to Burma again.

But New Guinea is where it went to die. Ordered to Wewak with other units at the end of February 1944, it was summarily bashed to pieces during March by the overwhelming American raids. By the end of that month, what was left of it was directed to fall back to Hollandia. When the Allied assault on Hollandia began on April 22, 1944, the 77th Hiko Sentai—along with other units—was ordered not to fight but to escape on foot, west through the jungle.

The march was not an organized retreat but rather a life-or-death battle against the jungle. What began as a movement of more than 7,000 men degenerated into broken formations and groups of men who quickly consumed the provisions they carried and subsequently competed for what little food they found along the route. The formations and groups fell further apart into little bands, or even individuals, for whom survival became the ultimate goal. And survival depended on eating whatever they could forage from the jungle. They were no longer military men but rather starving specters stumbling almost blindly through the trees and brush and swamps of western New Guinea.

Most of them—6,000—disappeared. Unknown, unmarked, unheralded. Dead. The remainder emerged from the jungle that summer near Geelvink Bay as little more than skeletons. Most of those were evacuated, but so few men of the 77th Hiko Sentai survived that it was never reformed. The group—effectively destroyed—was a fitting analog to what had become of the formidable Japanese air forces that once dominated the skies over New Guinea.[1]

George Kenney, the architect of the Allied air campaign over New Guinea, had little regard for the Japanese air commanders and the way they had employed their forces. To be sure, Japan had never been able to deliver to its air forces the same resources that Kenney eventually received. But neither, as Kenney noted, did they leverage the advantages they had early in the war. "The Nip just did not know how to handle airpower," Kenney said. "Just because he knocked us off on the ground at the beginning of the war, when we were asleep at Pearl Harbor and in the Philippines, he got a reputation for being smart, but the way he had failed to take advantage of his superiority in numbers and position since the first couple of months of the war, was a disgrace to the airman's profession."[2]

Indeed, Japanese airpower had been disgraced and essentially destroyed not only in New Guinea but also in the South Pacific, specifically in the Solomons and the islands leading to the northwest and Rabaul. Accordingly, the Army Air Forces component of that effort, the Thirteenth Air Force, was moved under Kenney. And so too was the Seventh Air Force which had been doing its fighting in the Central Pacific. The three air forces were organized under a parent command, the Far East Air Forces, on August 3, 1944. With so many resources at his disposal, Kenney was well-situated for the coming fight in the Philippines and beyond.

And by mid-October 1944, many of those resources—men, material, and equipment—were aboard the shipping that choked Hollandia's Humboldt Bay. There were no longer any major Japanese forces in New Guinea that hadn't been isolated. Consequently, during the previous couple of months, although strikes were flown against scattered enemy troop concentrations and supply dumps, most units were prepared to move at the same time that they concentrated on training and performing much-needed maintenance on their aircraft. The 3rd Bomb Group was an example, as it noted in its monthly summary for August 1944:

> The month of August was truly a month of inactivity for the 3rd Bombardment Group—26 combat mission being the total flown. Activities for the month were confined to ground support strikes and the destruction of enemy troops and supplies. Operations carried out against enemy airdromes were of a routine nature for the purpose of keeping the dromes in an unserviceable condition.

New Guinea had become a place from which raids were sent to destroy the Japanese who sat in the path of the next great objective, the Philippines. The enormous refinery complex at Balikpapan was hit again and again and again. Enemy bases in the Celebes and the Moluccas and elsewhere were gutted.

But most units focused primarily on preparations to leave New Guinea. Although seemingly mundane, it is almost impossible to overstate the complexity of the planning and the level of exhaustive work that was required for such a movement. Aside from the finger-smashing, backbreaking labor necessary to pack and organize everything, it all had to be loaded onto trucks and moved to a harbor or bay or beach. There, it had to be embarked in accordance with specific and strict maritime requirements. That it was completed satisfactorily, if not efficiently, by barely trained men with limited communications—and equipped with little more than pencils and clipboards—was astonishing.

Once aboard the ships, the men were crowded into every inch of space that wasn't stuffed with material or equipment. Precariously placed cots and piles of personal gear made moving awkward. Men tripped and cursed. They smoked and read and gambled with cards and dice and bitched about the food and the water and the lack of mail. Most of them stayed topside away from the hellish heat and misery and stink of the ship's hold.

Then, on the night of October 23, 1944, with little noise or fanfare, the ships stirred. Anchors were weighed and hatches were battened. Here, there was a muted clank. There was a low rumble. In the distance a hurried exchange of muffled shouts bounced across the water. Cargoes were checked secure a final time and many of the men sleeping topside rose and stepped to the rails. A freshening breeze swept their faces as their ships swung their bows seaward and pushed through the gentle swells.

Literally hundreds of ships—transports and combatants—sailed from New Guinea for the Philippines. So many men, so much material, and so much firepower had never before been sortied on the Pacific. Indeed, the flotilla was many dozens of times the size of Operation 81, the Japanese convoy that had so frightened the Allies, and which they had so devastatingly destroyed in the Battle of the Bismarck Sea only the previous year.

The men watched the dark jungled hills and slopes of New Guinea slowly disappear in the black of the night. There, and in the waters surrounding it, they left more than two years of dead comrades behind. Most of them moldered in graves that would never be found, or at the bottom of the sea. But who they were, what they were and how they lived would remain with the survivors who watched the island—the battlefield—disappear.

★★★

The battle is over. The men are gone. But what they were and what they did is not.

EPILOGUE

New Guinea remained important as a logistics and training base through most of the rest of the war, at least until the fall of Manila in 1945. In fact, until the Australians seized Wewak in May 1945, the airfields there were used as a sort of combat training target for crews newly arrived from the States. Indeed, the Japanese obliged by sending up desultory volleys of antiaircraft fire, although it was hardly as voluminous as it had been when Wewak was in its heyday. Still, despite the elimination of Japanese airpower, men continued to die because flying was dangerous, and flying in New Guinea was especially so.

The brave men of the RAAF were left—together with their brothers in the Army—to mop up the mess. That is, the Japanese remaining on the island. It was deadly work as the Japanese were dangerous so long as they were alive. They also assaulted isolated Japanese positions in the Solomons and executed amphibious assaults on Borneo. The rationale for doing so, especially since the Japanese could have been left to rot, is still debated. But the devotion, perseverance, and toughness of the Australians is not.

George Kenney enjoyed the well-deserved accolades he received following the war. He was made the first commander of the new Strategic Air Command and was given other collateral assignments. As might be imagined, his straight talk and ambitious ideas—which sometimes raised eyebrows while he was a wartime commander—got him into a number of political imbroglios. He finished his career as the commander of the Air University and retired in 1951. He passed in 1977 at age 88.

General Douglas MacArthur accepted the Japanese surrender on September 2, 1945. Following that surrender he was essentially the de facto ruler of Japan for several years, setting policy and directing the administration of the country and its postwar recovery. At the same time, he made a halfhearted bid for the Republican nomination during the 1948 presidential campaign. It did not succeed.

At the outset of the Korean War, MacArthur was once again in charge. China's entry into the conflict startled him—and the rest of the world—and the political intrigue associated with this, as well as his plans to end the war, got him crosswise with President Truman. He was relieved of command in 1951 much to the amazement and shock of the American public. Truman later declared, "I fired him because he wouldn't respect the authority of the President. I didn't fire him because he was a dumb son of a bitch, although he was, but that's not against the law for generals. If it was, half to three-quarters of them would be in jail."[1]

MacArthur nevertheless came home to parades and parties and subsequently led the life of a revered icon, receiving various salaries, honorariums, and other tributes. He and his wife made their home in a penthouse at the Waldorf Towers in New York City. He died in 1964 at age 84.

Missionary James Benson was the only survivor of the group that had fled into the hills above Gona when the Japanese came ashore on July 21, 1942. Although he had unsuccessfully tried to give himself up earlier, he was eventually taken into custody and sent to a prison camp in Rabaul, and then to other camps on New Britain where he suffered much illness and hardship. Meanwhile, he was believed dead and was widely mourned by friends and family. Benson was finally liberated by Australian troops after the Japanese surrender in 1945 and returned to his missionary work in New Guinea, where he passed in 1957.

Although Gordon Manuel didn't know it when he was shot down on May 21, 1943, two other men had successfully bailed out of the same B-17. One was copilot John Rippy. The other was one of the waist gunners, Robert Curry. Unlike Manuel, their luck didn't hold, and both were quickly captured by the Japanese and taken to a prisoner-of-war camp at Rabaul. On November 25, 1943, while Manuel was trekking the jungle looking for Australian coastwatcher Allan Roberts, Rippy was murdered by the Japanese. Likewise, Curry was cruelly slain a couple of weeks later on December 9.

Manuel, who with the help of his native friends had evaded the Japanese on New Britain Island for nine months, was commissioned as a second lieutenant following his return to the States. He eventually reached the rank of captain but became ill and passed away in 1950 at age 33.

Paul "Pappy" Gunn was reunited with his family following the liberation of Manila. They stayed in the Philippines, and he resumed his career in the airline business. While flying a charter on the night of October 11,

1957, he was caught in a thunderstorm, flew into a mountain, and was killed. The ending was almost an insult to a man who had done and braved so much. He was 57.

Following the deaths of top fighter pilots Thomas Lynch and Neel Kearby in March 1944, there were only two real contenders remaining in the race to become America's premier ace in the Pacific. They were Thomas McGuire and Richard Bong. Both were dead before the war ended.

McGuire was flying over Los Negros Island in the Philippines on January 7, 1945, when the flight of four P-38s he was leading encountered a single Ki-43. The Japanese pilot was skilled and didn't hesitate to throw himself at the four Lightnings. McGuire's wingman got into trouble and McGuire sped to his aid. Turning hard and low over the jungle at only a few hundred feet, he stalled his aircraft, which tumbled into the jungle and exploded. He had 38 enemy aircraft to his credit.

Richard Bong had been credited with 40 aerial victories and was sent home with the Medal of Honor the previous month, December 1944. In the summer of 1945, he was test-flying the nation's newest jet fighter, the Lockheed P-80, out of Burbank, California. Newly married, he was killed shortly after takeoff on August 6 when the aircraft's engine failed, and he crashed to the ground in a horrific fireball. He remains the nation's highest-scoring ace.

Following the war, Charles Lindbergh advocated making the Nazis accountable for their war crimes and was equally strident in his warnings against the Soviet Union and communism. Later, in 1954, he was very pleased when President Eisenhower commissioned him back into the service and made him a brigadier general in the Air Force reserve. He remained in the public eye and became an ardent conservationist while also turning toward a more spiritual life. Notwithstanding his new spirituality or his marriage—or perhaps because of them—he took three separate German mistresses and fathered seven children between them. He wrote through much of the remainder of his life, often warning against the dangers of advancing technologies. He passed away in 1974 at age 72.

The last Japanese holdouts in New Guinea gave themselves up in 1955, 10 years after the end of the war. The only survivors of a larger group, four airmen surrendered themselves to authorities at Hollandia. They were sent home as ragged curiosities—relics.

The Papuans were not the same after the war—they couldn't be after colliding head-on with twentieth-century warfare. Their journey since then has seen highs and lows, and there is hope that the highs will outnumber the lows as time passes.

NOTES AND REFERENCES

Unless noted otherwise, the official quotes for specific missions are derived from the group and squadron mission summary reports for that particular day. That being implicit, and to save clutter and page count, I did not footnote those quotes. These reports are held by the Air Force Historical Research Agency at Maxwell Air Force Base, Alabama.

For readability, I often spelled out acronyms from the mission summary reports. For instance, "A/P" was changed to airplane, and "A/A" was changed to "antiaircraft fire." The reports were also sometimes lightly edited for grammar, spelling, and clarity, as were selected letters, diaries, or interviews. This improved readability without detracting from accuracy or the intent of the original document's creator.

NOTES

PRELUDE

1. "Nadzab Airfield (Nadzab No. 1 Strip, East Base) Morobe Province, Papua New Guinea (PNG)," Pacific Wrecks—World War II Pacific War and Korean War, April 19, 2021. https://pacificwrecks.com/airfields/png/nadzab/index.html.

CHAPTER 1: "IT WAS TRICKLING DOWN MY LEGS"

1. Arthur Tucker, Interview by Edward Stokes, Australian War Memorial, June 1, 1989. All subsequent quotes from Tucker are derived from this source.

2. John Henry Stephen Pettett, Interview by Edward Stokes, Australian War Memorial, June 20, 1989. All subsequent quotes from Pettett are derived from this source.

3. Robert Crawford, Interview by Australians at War Film Archive, May 14, 2003. All subsequent quotes from Crawford are derived from this source.

4. "Saved Port Moresby," *Cairns Post*, December 28, 1942, 4.

5. William Bellairs, Interview by Australians at War Film Archive, February 2, 2004.

6. Antiaircraft Defense, New Guinea Forces, *On Target, With the American and Australian Ack-Ack Brigade in New Guinea* (Angus and Robertson Ltd., 1943), 62.

7. William Allan Whetters, Interview by Edward Stokes, Australian War Memorial, June 9, 1989. All subsequent quotes from Whetters are derived from this source.

8. Russell Murphy, Ms. *RAAF Personalities* (Canberra, 1998), 3.

9. Peter Jeffrey, Interview by Edward Stokes, 3 Squadron Research, Australian War Memorial, July 2, 1990.

10. *44 Days: 75 Squadron's Defence of Port Moresby 1942 (Part 2)*. Australia, n.d. https://www.youtube.com/watch?v=Fm0egzs8HmA.

11. 75 Squadron Operations Record Book, W. L. Wackett.

12. Leon Kane-McGuire, *Lost without Trace: Squadron Leader Wilbur Wackett, RAAF* (Airpower Development Centre, 2011), 69.

13. Michael Veitch, *44 Days: 75 Squadron and the Fight for Australia* (Hachette Australia, 2017).

14. Bob Piper, "One-Way Flight," *Una Voce, Journal of the Papua New Guinea Association of Australia, Inc.* 4 (December 2004): 34–35.

15. Memo, *Progress and Situation Report as of 1200, January 1, 1942,* John Davies, Commanding Officer, 27th Bomb Group (L), to General Claggett, Headquarters U.S. Air Corps Troops, Amberley Field, Australia, January 1, 1942.

16. Veitch, 68.

CHAPTER 2: "HE NEVER SAID A WORD"

1. Michael J. Bauman, Interview, The National Museum of the Pacific War, August 1, 2005. All subsequent quotes from Bauman are derived from this source.

CHAPTER 3: "I DECIDED TO GO TO HORN ISLAND"

1. Unless otherwise noted, the description of the movement of the 35th and 36th Pursuit Squadrons from Australia to New Guinea, and their subsequent combat actions, was derived from their respective official squadron histories. Those histories can be sourced from the Air Force Historical Research Agency on reels A0734 and A0735. The documents, reflecting the haphazard organization and resources of the time, are poorly organized, written, and reproduced, sometimes contradictory, and often conflict with other sources.

2. 75 Squadron Operations Record Book, Ellerton, May 4, 1942.

3. Michael Claringbould, *P-39/P-400 Airacobra Vs A6M2/3 Zero Sen* (Osprey, 2018), 38.

4. "Pacific Wrecks—P-39D-Be Airacobra Serial Number 41-6982," Pacific Wrecks—World War II Pacific War and Korean War. Accessed February 12, 2024. https://pacificwrecks.com/aircraft/p-39/41-6982.html.

5. "Pacific Wrecks—A6M2 Model 21 Zero Manufacture Number 1575 Tail V-110," Pacific Wrecks—World War II Pacific War and Korean War. Accessed February 12, 2024. https://pacificwrecks.com/aircraft/a6m2/1575.html.

6. Report, Boyd Wagner to Commanding General, USAFIA, Melbourne, Report on first action against Japanese by P-39 type airplane, May 1942.

7. Air Force Historical Research Agency, 39 Flying Training Squadron, Maxwell AFB, 2010, 11.

8. Report, Gordon Grant to Secretary of Air Board, Melbourne, 8 May 1942.

9. Report, Flight Lieutenant P. B. Turnbull to Senior Administrative Staff Officer, North Eastern Area, Townsville, April 30, 1942.

10. Report, Royal Australian Air Force, No. 75 Squadron, Enemy aircraft casualties claimed in combat and ground attacks at Moresby, operational sorties and other relevant information, for the period March 21 to May 3, 1942.

CHAPTER 4: "A VERY ATTRACTIVE AND POLISHED GENTLEMAN"

1. Department of Defense (DOD), Efficiency Report, George H. Brett (General Headquarters American Expeditionary Force, Summer 1918), n.p.

2. Frederic H. Smith Jr. Oral history, n.d., AFHRA, June 1976.

3. Kenney, General George C., Oral Reminiscences of General George C. Kenney. Oral history, MacArthur Memorial, Norfolk, VA, July 1971, 16–17.

CHAPTER 5: "HE HAD AVOIDED COMBAT OFTEN"

1. Wesley E. Dickinson, *I Was Lucky: Anecdotes in the Life of Wesley Edward Dickinson* (Create Space, 2002), 125–39.

2. MACR #15937, Headquarters, 89th Bomb Squadron, 3rd Attack Group.

CHAPTER 6: "HE HAD NO PARACHUTE"

1. Curran Jones, Interview by the American Fighter Aces Association, September 6, 1989.

2. Air Force Historical Research Agency, 39 Flying Training Squadron, Maxwell AFB, 2010, 13.

3. Barrett Tillman and Henry Sakaida, "Silver Star Airplane Ride," *Naval History Magazine* 15, no. 2 (April 2001).

4. Daniel Ford, "Interview with a Zero Pilot," Japan at War: Interview with a Zero Pilot. Accessed February 12, 2024. https://www.warbirdforum.com/komachi.htm. All subsequent quotes by Komachi are derived from this source.

5. Peter Williams, "'The Greatest Fighting Spirit': Memories of a WWII Japanese Pilot," *Traces Magazine*, March 15, 2014. https://tracesmagazine.com.au/2014/01/the-greatest-fighting-spirit-memories-of-a-wwii-japanese-pilot/.

CHAPTER 7: "FATHER, DON'T TRY TO PERSUADE THEM"

1. James Benson, *Prisoner's Base and Home Again: The Story of a Missionary P.O.W.* (J. Spencer & Co., 1959), 31–45.
2. Alan Gill, "Recalling the Gona Tragedy—and Its Martyrs," *Sydney Morning Herald*, July 27, 1977.
3. Matthew K. Rodman, *A War of Their Own: Bombers over the Southwest Pacific* (Air University Press, 2005), 49.

CHAPTER 8: "I WOULD BE LOYAL TO HIM"

1. Message, GHQ SWPA, MacArthur, to Marshall, 30 June 1942.
2. Douglas A. Cox, *Airpower Leadership on the Front Line: Lt Gen George H. Brett and Combat Command* (Air University Press, 2006), 57.
3. George C. Kenney, *General Kenney Reports: A Personal History of the Pacific War* (Air Force History and Museums Program, 1997), 7.
4. Ibid., 27–30.
5. Karl James, "The Track," A historical desktop study of the Kokoda Track, 2009. https://www.dcceew.gov.au/sites/default/files/documents/awm-kokoda-report.pdf, 18.
6. George Dick, *Beaufighters over New Guinea: No. 30 Squadron RAAF, 1942–1943* (Royal Australian Air Force Museum, 1993), 32.
7. Kenney, 89.
8. Ibid., 94.
9. Ibid.
10. Keika Tamura, "Human Face of War: War Correspondent's Experience of War, Okada Seizo," Australia-Japan Research Project. Accessed February 13, 2024. http://ajrp.awm.gov.au/ajrp/ajrp2.nsf/30017f4131c6b2acca256cfb0023646c/7f98853c86ed1ff0ca256d2b001b1142?OpenDocument.

CHAPTER 9: "WE PRAY FOR ABSOLUTE VICTORY"

1. Herman Wolk, "The Genius of George Kenney," *Air & Space Forces Magazine* 85, no. 4 (2002, April 1).
2. Kenney, 56.
3. Brian Walker, Interview by Ken Llewellyn, Australian War Memorial, February 17, 1993. All subsequent quotes from Tucker are derived from this source.
4. Kenney, 54.
5. Ibid., 63.
6. Ibid., 235.

7. Ibid., 103.

8. Robert MacMahon, Interview by Eugene Valencia, American Fighter Aces Association, circa 1960s.

9. Kenney, 12.

10. Ibid., 77.

11. Gabrielle Chan, *War on Our Doorstep: Diaries of Australians at the Frontline, 1942* (Hardie Grant Books, 2004), 188.

12. Steven Bullard, *Japanese Army Operations in the South Pacific Area: New Britain and Papua Campaigns, 1942–43* (Australian War Memorial, 2007), 150.

13. William Crawford and Ted Saucier, *Gore and Glory: A Story of American Heroism* (McKay, 1944), 65–69.

CHAPTER 10: "ONE'S HEAD LYING ON ANOTHER'S CHEST"

1. Kenney, 126.

2. Ibid., 141.

3. Peter Dunn, "16 November 1942 Crash of a B-24 Liberator at Iron Range, 4 Aircraft Destroyed, 11 Men Killed," Australia at War, February 7, 1999. https://www.ozatwar.com/ozcrashes/qld230.htm.

4. Peter Dunn, "Graphic Diary Details of the Carnage Following Crash of a B-24 Liberator at Iron Range on 16 November 1942," Australia at War, June 11, 2020. https://www.ozatwar.com/ozcrashes/qld230diary.htm.

5. Frederick Knight, "90th Bombardment Group B-24 Liberator," Asisbiz, September 25, 2022. https://www.asisbiz.com/il2/B-24/90BG.html.

6. Kenney, 144.

7. Timothy Gann, *Fifth Air Force Light and Medium Bomber Operations during 1942 and 1943: Building Doctrine and Forces That Triumphed in the Battle of the Bismarck Sea and the Wewak Raid* (Air University, 1992).

8. Ernest C. Ford, *My New Guinea Diary* (White Stag Press, 2010), 76.

9. Maureen C. Meadows, *"I Loved Those Yanks"* (G. M. Dash, 1948), 50.

10. Donald Friend, *Painter's Journal* (Ure Smith pty. Limited, 1946), 67.

11. Ken Wright, "Culture Clash: Americans in World War II's South Pacific," *America in World War II* 6, no. 2 (March 2007): 26.

12. Kenney, 150.

CHAPTER 11: "MOST OF US WENT AWAY SHAKING OUR HEADS"

1. James T. Murphy, *Skip Bombing* (Praeger, 1993), 77.

2. Ibid., 80–81.

3. Peter Williams, "'The Greatest Fighting Spirit': Memories of a WWII Japanese Pilot," *Traces Magazine*, March 15, 2014. https://tracesmagazine.com.au/2014/01/the-greatest-fighting-spirit-memories-of-a-wwii-japanese-pilot/.

4. Frederick Wesche III, Interview by Shaun Illingworth and Kathryn Tracy, May 10, 2001. All subsequent quotes from Tucker are derived from this source.

5. Martha Byrd, *Kenneth N. Walker: Airpower's Untempered Crusader* (Air University Press, 1997), 44.

6. Ibid., ix.

7. Ibid., 79.

8. Ibid., 102.

9. Kenney, 116.

10. Richard Dunn, "The Search for General Walker: New Insights," *Airpower History* 61, no. 3 (2014): 12.

11. Kenney, 176.

12. "U.S. Air General Lost at Rabaul," *Sydney Daily Mirror*, January 11, 1943.

13. Silvano Jung, "Wings beneath the Sea: The Aviation Archaeology of Catalina Flying Boats in Darwin Harbour, Northern Territory." Thesis, Northern Territory University, 2001, 108–9.

14. Ernest Harris, Encounter Report, 49th Fighter Group, 8th Fighter Squadron, January 7, 1943.

CHAPTER 12: "SEND TROOPS IMMEDIATELY"

1. Phillip Bradley, *The Battle for Wau: New Guinea's Frontline, 1942–1943* (Cambridge University Press, 2008), 169.

2. 17th Infantry Brigade, War Diary, January 1943, 15.

3. Ford, 242–44.

4. 17th Infantry Brigade, 29.

5. John D. Poole, *Jungle Skippers: The 317th Troop Carrier Group in the Southwest Pacific and Their Legacy* (Air University Press, 2017), 29.

6. Ibid., 48.

7. David Harbour, Encounter Report, 49th Fighter Group, 9th Fighter Squadron, February 6, 1943.

8. Eric Larrabee, *Commander in Chief: Franklin Delano Roosevelt, His Lieutenants, and Their War* (Naval Institute Press, 2019), 329.

9. Kenney, 136.

10. Murphy, 88–89.

CHAPTER 13: "IT WAS MORE THAN I COULD STAND"

1. Edward J. Drea, *MacArthur's Ultra: Codebreaking and the War against Japan, 1942–1945* (University Press of Kansas, 1992), 67.

2. Kenney, 197.

3. Ibid., 199.

4. William Garing, Interview by Edward Stokes, Australian War Memorial, June 8, 1989. All subsequent quotes from Tucker are derived from this source.

5. Frederick Cassidy, Interview by Australians at War Film Archive, April 28, 2003. All subsequent quotes from Cassidy are derived from this source.

6. Burton Graham, *None Shall Survive: The Graphic Story of the Annihilation of the Japanese Armada in the Bismarck Sea Battle by the U.S. Fifth Air Force and the Royal Australian Air Force: The War against Japan, 1943* (F. H. Johnston Pub., 1946), 66–67.

7. Jim Fausone, "Raymond Wilkins," Home of Heroes, October 12, 2021. https://homeofheroes.com/heroes-stories/world-war-ii/raymond-wilkins/.

8. Graham, 73.

9. Development, PodBean. "67—Pacific War—Battle at the Bismarck Sea, February 28–March 7, 1943: The Pacific War—Week by Week," February 28, 2023. https://thepacificwar.podbean.com/e/67-pacific-war-battle-at-the-bismarck-sea-february-28-march-7-1943/.

10. Air Force Historical Research Agency, 39 Flying Training Squadron, Maxwell AFB, 2010, 21.

11. Gregory P. Gilbert, *The Battle of the Bismarck Sea, March 1943* (Airpower Development Centre, 2013), 68.

12. Clayton Barnes, Encounter Report, 49th Fighter Group, 9th Fighter Squadron, March 3, 1943.

13. Clayton Tice, Encounter Report, 49th Fighter Group, 9th Fighter Squadron, March 3, 1943.

14. George Kennedy, "Bismarck Sea Victory," *Washington Star*, September 29, 1943.

15. 38th Bomb Group combat narrative, Battle of the Bismarck Sea.

16. Arthur House, Encounter Report, 49th Fighter Group, 7th Fighter Squadron, March 3, 1943.

CHAPTER 14: "WHAT WE DIDN'T GET, THE SHARKS GOT"

1. Murphy, 119.

2. J. Paul O'Brien, "Bombing Diary," *Flying* 24, no. 3 (March 1944).

3. Richard Cresswell, Interview by Australians at War Film Archive, September 17, 2003. All subsequent quotes from Cresswell are derived from this source.

4. Hara Tameichi, *Japanese Destroyer Captain* (Ballantine, 1967), 120.

5. Eric M. Bergerud, *Fire in the Sky: The Air War in the South Pacific* (Basic Books, 2009), 592.

6. Kenney, 206.

7. Ibid., 210.

8. John Correll, "George Kenney's Fighting Spirit," *Air Force Magazine* 98, no. 4 (April 2015).

CHAPTER 15: "THE ZERO EXPLODED JUST BEFORE HITTING THE WATER"

1. Martin Alger, Encounter Report, 49th Fighter Group, 9th Fighter Squadron, May 14, 1943.

2. Kenney, 236.

3. Ibid., 239.

4. Ibid., 241.

5. Leo Mayo, Encounter Report, 49th Fighter Group, 8th Fighter Squadron, May 14, 1943.

6. Richard Vodra, Encounter Report, 49th Fighter Group, 8th Fighter Squadron, May 14, 1943.

7. George Davis, Encounter Report, 49th Fighter Group, 8th Fighter Squadron, May 14, 1943.

8. John Griffith, Encounter Report, 49th Fighter Group, 7th Fighter Squadron, May 14, 1943.

9. Frank Nutter, Encounter Report, 49th Fighter Group, 9th Fighter Squadron, May 14, 1943.

10. John Yancey, Encounter Report, 49th Fighter Group, 7th Fighter Squadron, May 14, 1943.

11. Donald Byars, Encounter Report, 49th Fighter Group, 9th Fighter Squadron, May 14, 1943.

12. Bill Haney, Encounter Report, 49th Fighter Group, 9th Fighter Squadron, May 14, 1943.

13. Keith Oveson, Encounter Report, 49th Fighter Group, 9th Fighter Squadron, May 14, 1943.

14. Ernest Harris, Encounter Report, 49th Fighter Group, 8th Fighter Squadron, May 14, 1943.

15. S. W. Ferguson and William K. Pascalis, *Protect and Avenge: The 49th Fighter Group in World War II* (Schiffer, 1996), 162.

16. Saburō Sakai, Martin Caidin, and Fred Saito, *Samurai!* (Nelson Doubleday, 1978).

17. Ferguson and Pascalis, 162.

18. Richard L. Dunn, "Masao Yoshihara's Story: May 14th–25th, 1943," Masao Yoshihara, June 15, 2002. https://j-aircraft.com/research/rdunn/masao_yoshihara .htm.

CHAPTER 16: "WE NEVER DID SEE THEM"

1. Jeff Groves, "Shigetoshi Kudo, the First Nightfighter Ace of the Pacific War," Inch High Guy, February 23, 2021. https://inchhighguy.wordpress .com/2021/02/17/shigetoshi-kudo-the-first-nightfighter-ace-of-the-pacific-war/.
2. Quentin J. Reynolds, *70,000 to 1* (Random House, 1946). The description of Gordon Manuel's ordeal is derived from this book. Page citations are not provided.
3. MACR #2459, Headquarters, 64th Bomb Squadron, 43rd Bomb Group.
4. William H. Webster, Interview by David Gregory, February 13, 1999.

CHAPTER 17: "SELL THE P-47 OR GO BACK HOME"

1. Kenney, 264–65.
2. Francis Love, *Francis Love, Flier, Missing in Action, Writes Vivid Story of His Rescue* (Unknown, n.d.).
3. Robert DeHaven, Interview by Eugene Valencia, American Fighter Aces Association, Circa 1960s. All subsequent quotes from DeHaven are derived from this source.

CHAPTER 18: "MAKING FOOL OF THE JAP MAN"

1. Kenney, 251.
2. Ibid., 270.
3. Ibid., 253.
4. Ibid., 263.
5. Hal Johnson, "Dies in Pulpit—Local Chaplain Killed While Conducting Tropical Service," *Berkeley Gazette*, August 26, 1943.

CHAPTER 19: "MY GOD, WHAT A SIGHT!"

1. L. J. Fitz-Henry, "Japs' Worst Blow in Pacific: 120 Planes Destroyed," *Brisbane Courier-Mail*, August 19, 1943.
2. Allen D. Boyer, "Shooting Up Wewak," *America in World War II* (August 2018).
3. Fitz-Henry.
4. Garrett Middlebrook, *Air Combat at 20 Feet: Selected Missions from a Strafer Pilot's Diary* (Global Group, 1989), 423–48.
5. "Pronounced 'Kelly,'" *Time*, September 6, 1943.
6. George Odgers, *Air War against Japan, 1943–1945*, Vol. 2 (Australian War Memorial, 1968), 70.

CHAPTER 20: "BUT HE WAS ALWAYS CHEERFUL"

1. Michael Claringbould, "Tsili Tsili Lilly," *Flight Path* 29, no. 2 (2017).

2. Casualty Branch, Status Review and Determination Section, "Status of Crew of a B-25 Aircraft Missing in Action in the Southwest Pacific Area since August 18, 1943," SR&D No. 1218, August 19, 1944; Mary Stubbs, Chief Investigator, Memorandum for Chief, Casualty Branch, "Subsequent Review and Determination of Status under the Missing Persons Act," SR&D No. 1218-A, December 3, 1945; MACR #16528, Headquarters, 405th Bomb Squadron, 38th Bomb Group.

3. C. Kenneth Quinones, *Imperial Japan's Allied Prisoners of War in the South Pacific: Surviving Paradise* (Cambridge Scholars Publishing, 2021), 415.

4. Tamura Yoshikazu, "Diary of Tamura Yoshikazu: Military Life and Death," AJRP. Accessed February 16, 2024. http://ajrp.awm.gov.au/ajrp/ajrp2.nsf/pages/NT000088CA?openDocument.

5. Manimugdha S. Sharma, "Japanese Ate Indian PoWs, Used Them as Live Targets in WW II," *The Times of India*, August 11, 2014.

6. Ibid.

7. Narinder Singh Parmar, *Chint Singh: The Man Who Should Have Died* (Shawline Publishing Group, 2021).

CHAPTER 21: "GREAT GUSHING GOUTS OF FUEL IGNITED"

1. "The Worst Aviation-Related Disaster in Australian History: USAAF B-24D 42-40682, 'Pride of the Cornhuskers.'" LiberatorCrash.com, 2022. https://www.liberatorcrash.com/.

CHAPTER 22: "TICKLING A GIANT'S THROAT WITH A FEATHER"

1. "Bombing of Rabaul Volcano Rejected," *Adelaide Advertiser*, July 9, 1943.

2. Lex McAulay, *Into the Dragon's Jaws: The US 5th Air Force at Rabaul October–November 1943* (Banner Books, 2012).

3. Geoffrey Hution, "Devastating Allied Raid on Rabaul," *Canberra Times*, October 15, 1943.

4. McAulay, 26.

5. MACR #1256, Headquarters, 9th Fighter Squadron, 49th Fighter Group.

6. Jay Stout and George Cooper, *Jayhawk* (Casemate, 2020), 120.

CHAPTER 23: "HE WAS LYING"

1. Kenney, 316.

2. Henry I. Shaw and Douglas T. Kane, *Isolation of Rabaul* (U.S. Government Printing Office, 1963), 453.

3. Dick Walker, "Raid on Rabaul on 2 November 1943 as Told by Dick Walker," 13th Bomb Squadron, 3rd Bomb Group: Their part in the raid on Rabaul, on 2 November 1943, 2015. https://www.ozatwar.com/usaaf/rabaul 2nov43.htm.

4. MACR #1218, Headquarters, 71st Bomb Squadron, 38th Bomb Group.

5. MACR #1262, Headquarters, 431st Fighter Squadron, 475th Fighter Group.

6. MACR #1315, Headquarters, 9th Fighter Squadron, 49th Fighter Group.

7. MACR #1951, Headquarters, 431st Fighter Squadron, 475th Fighter Group.

8. McAulay, 74.

9. Kenney, 321.

10. MACR #1259, Headquarters, 431st Fighter Squadron, 475th Fighter Group.

11. Shaw and Kane, 498.

12. Gilbert, 19.

13. Shaw and Kane, 503.

CHAPTER 24: "WE TENDED TO BLACK OUT"

1. Ronald Barker, Interview by Australians at War Film Archive, September 23, 2003. All subsequent quotes from Tucker are derived from this source.

2. MACR #2085, Headquarters, 321st Bomb Squadron, 90th Bomb Group.

3. MACR #1316, Headquarters, 320th Bomb Squadron, 90th Bomb Group.

4. "Mistake over Wewak—December 1, 1943 Mission," Pacific Wrecks—World War II Pacific War and Korean War. Accessed February 16, 2024. https://pacificwrecks.com/aircraft/b-24/42-72806/mistake-over-wewak.html.

5. MACR #13824, Headquarters, 319th Bomb Squadron, 90th Bomb Group.

6. MACR #1235, Headquarters, 432nd Fighter Squadron, 475th Fighter Group. NOTE: Other sources indicate that Czarnecki bailed out of his aircraft.

7. MACR #1096, Headquarters, 9th Fighter Squadron, 49th Fighter Group.

8. Gerald Johnson, Encounter Report, 49th Fighter Group, 9th Fighter Squadron, December 10, 1943.

9. Ralph Wandrey, Encounter Report, 49th Fighter Group, 9th Fighter Squadron, December 10, 1943.

10. John P. Henebry, *The Grim Reapers: At Work in the Pacific Theater: The Third Attack Group of the U.S. Fifth Air Force* (Pictorial History Pub. Co., 2002), 154.

11. Boyer, 130.

12. MACR #3737, Headquarters, 110th Reconnaissance Squadron, 71st Reconnaissance Group.

CHAPTER 25: "I DON'T REMEMBER A LOT BEING MADE OF IT"

1. MACR #4600, Headquarters, 843rd Bomb Squadron, 38th Bomb Group.

2. MACR #16315, Headquarters, 13th Bomb Squadron, 3rd Bomb Group.

3. Albert Richards, "One Hung Up," *Air Classics* 10, no. 9 (September 1974): 58.

4. Gene Benson, "A Sad Day," 38th Bomb Group Association—Stories from the Front. Accessed February 21, 2024. https://www.sunsetters38bg.com/index .php/articles/stories2/a-sad-day.

5. Martin Caidin, Masatake Okumiya, and Jiro x Hirokoshi, *Zero* (ibooks, 2014), 357–58.

6. Joe Forster, Interview by Barrett Tillman, 2006.

CHAPTER 26: "EVERYONE EXCEPT MACARTHUR LOOKED SKEPTICAL"

1. William Huisman, Encounter Report, 49th Fighter Group, 9th Fighter Squadron, March 15, 1944.

2. Fred Helterline, Encounter Report, 49th Fighter Group, 9th Fighter Squadron, March 15, 1944.

3. MACR #3735, Headquarters, 36th Fighter Squadron, 8th Bomb Group.

4. Charles Martin, *The Reaper's Harvest* (Halstead Party Press, 1945), 22.

5. Kenney, 377.

6. Ibid, 381.

CHAPTER 27: "PART OF A BURNED BODY SLIPPED FROM THE B-25"

1. Charles H. Davidson, Escape and Evasion Report, 388th Bomb Squadron, 312th Bomb Group, May 8, 1944; Rusty Trosclair, "Local Veteran Recalls 'Black Sunday' Flight," *The Courier*, June 11, 2003. https://www.houmatoday.com/ story/news/2003/06/11/local-veteran-recalls-black-sunday-flight/26809980007/.

2. Kenney, 388.

3. Kevin Mongagi, Interview by Voices from the War, June 13, 2016.

4. Henebry, 149–50.

5. Kenney, 395.

CHAPTER 28: "WE HAD HOPED TO CATCH A FEW JAP PLANES IN THE AIR"

1. Memo, 90th Bomb Squadron, 3rd Bomb Group, to Commanding General, U.S. Army Forces, Western Pacific, October 24, 1945.

2. Arthur Veysey, Leonard T. Duval, and Richard V. Saunders, "Leonard T. Duval," Accessed February 17, 2024. https://3rdstories.yolasite.com/leonard -t-duval.php. Duval's story is derived from this website, which includes multiple variants of his experience.

3. Charles A. Lindbergh, *The Wartime Journals of Charles A. Lindbergh* (Harcourt, Brace, Jovanovich, 1970), 843.

4. Ibid., 852.

5. Ibid., 853.

6. Ibid., 856.

7. Ibid., 857.

8. Ibid., 858.

9. Ibid., 875.

10. Ibid., 865.

11. Ibid., 871–73.

CHAPTER 29: "HE CURSED AND SHOUTED"

1. Richard L. Dunn, Double Lucky?—The Campaigns of the 77th Hiko Sentai (Part 3), 2005. https://www.warbirdforum.com/lucky3.htm.

2. Kenney, 234.

EPILOGUE

1. "Historical Notes: Giving Them More Hell," *Time*, December 3, 1973. https://content.time.com/time/subscriber/article/0,33009,908217-1,00.html.

BIBLIOGRAPHY

Arnold, Henry Harley. *Global Mission*. Harper and Brothers, 1949.

Benson, James. *Prisoner's Base and Home Again: The Story of a Missionary P.O.W.* Spencer, 1959.

Bergerud, Eric M. *Fire in the Sky: The Air War in the South Pacific*. Basic Books, 2009.

Boyer, Allen D. *Rocky Boyer's War*. Naval Institute Press, 2017.

Claringbould, Michael John, Jim Laurier, and Gareth Hector. *P-39/P-400 Airacobra vs A6M2/3 Zero-Sen: New Guinea, 1942*. Osprey Publishing, 2018.

Crawford, William, and Ted Saucier. *Gore and Glory: A Story of American Heroism*. David McKay Co., 1944.

Crocker, Mel. *Black Cats and Dumbos: WWII's Fighting PBYs*. Crocker Media Expressions, 2002.

Duffy, James P. *War at the End of the World: Douglas MacArthur and the Forgotten Fight for New Guinea, 1942–1945*. Dutton Caliber, 2023.

Ewer, Peter. *Storm over Kokoda: The Air War for New Guinea, 1942*. Murdoch Books, 2011.

Ferguson, S. W., and William K. Pascalis. *Protect & Avenge: The 49th Fighter Group in World War II*. Schiffer Pub., 1996.

Galdorisi, George, and Thomas Phillips. *Leave No Man Behind: The Saga of Combat Search and Rescue*. Zenith Press, 2010.

Graham, Burton. *None Shall Survive: The Graphic Story of the Annihilation of the Japanese Armada in the Bismarck Sea Battle by the U.S. Fifth Air Force and the Royal Australian Air Force: The War against Japan, 1943*. F. H. Johnston Pub., 1946.

Gunn, Nathaniel. *Pappy Gunn*. AuthorHouse, 2004.

Hammel, Eric M. *Aces against Japan: The American Aces Speak*. Presidio, 1992.

Henebry, John P. *The Grim Reapers: At Work in the Pacific Theater: The Third Attack Group of the U.S. Fifth Air Force*. Pictorial History Pub, 2002.

Hess, William N. *Pacific Sweep: The 5th and 13th Fighter Commands in World War II*. Doubleday, 1974.

Hickey, Lawrence J. *Warpath across the Pacific: The Illustrated History of the 345th Bombardment Group during World War II*. International Historical Research Associates, 2008.

Kenney, George C. *General Kenney Reports: A Personal History of the Pacific War*. Air Force History and Museums Program, 1997.

Lindbergh, Charles Augustus. *The Wartime Journals of Charles A. Lindbergh*. Harcourt Brace Jovanovich, 1970.

Marquat, W. F. *On Target: With the American and Australian Anti-Aircraft Brigade in New Guinea*. Angus and Robertson Ltd., 1943.

McAulay, Lex. *The Battle of the Bismarck Sea*. Banner Books, 2008.

———. *Into the Dragon's Jaws: The US 5th Air Force at Rabaul October–November 1943*. Banner Books, 2012.

———. *MacArthur's Eagles: The U.S. Air War over New Guinea, 1943–1944*. Naval Institute Press, 2005.

Middlebrook, Garrett. *Air Combat at 20 Feet: Selected Missions from a Strafer Pilot's Diary*. The Global Group, 1989.

Millman, Nicholas, and Ronnie Olsthoorn. *Ki-61 and Ki-100 Aces*. Osprey Publishing, 2015.

Mortensen, Max. *Warpath: A Story of the 345th Bombardment Group (M) in World War II*. Schiffer Publishing, 2016.

Murphy, James T., and A. B. Feuer. *Skip Bombing*. Praeger, 1993.

Perrone, Stephen M. *World War II B-24 "Snoopers": Low Level Anti-Shipping Night Bombers in the Pacific Theater*. S. M. Perrone, 2001.

Reynolds, Quentin J. *70,000 to 1*. Random House, 1946.

Rothgeb, Wayne P. *New Guinea Skies: A Fighter Pilot's View of World War II*. Iowa State University Press, 1992.

Sakaida, Henry. *The Siege of Rabaul*. Phalanx, 1996.

Stanaway, John. *475th Fighter Group*. Osprey Publishing, 2013.

———. *Kearby's Thunderbolts: The 348th Fighter Group in World War II*. Schiffer Publishing, 1997.

Stout, Jay A. *Air Apaches: The True Story of the 345th Bomb Group and Its Low, Fast, and Deadly Missions in World War II*. Stackpole Books, 2023.

———. *Jayhawk: Love, Loss, Liberation, and Terror over the Pacific*. Casemate, 2020.

Sturzebecker, Russell L. *The Roarin' 20's: A History of the 312th Bombardment Group, U.S. Army Air Force, World War II*. Sturzebecker, 1976.

Wright, Jim. *The Flying Circus: Pacific War, 1943, As Seen through a Bombsight*. Lyons Press, 2005.

INDEX

A5M, 24

A6M. *See* Zeroes

A-20s, 87, 181, 215, 292; Kenney on, 88–89; of 3rd Attack Group's 8th Bomb Squadron, 139; of 3rd Bomb Group, 145, 263

A-24s, 17–18, 21–22, 23, 46, 69; Davies on, 73; of 3rd Attack Group's 8th Bomb Squadron, 59

ace pilots, 268

Adams, Richard, 250, 253

Adelaide Advertiser, 219–20

Adkins, Frank, 41

ADVON, 90

Africa, ix

Aichi 99, 179

Air Corps Tactical School, 110

AirSols, 244

Aitape, 268, 275

Aiyo Maru, 134

Akikaze, 155

Alexishafen, 260, 278

Alger, Martin, 161, 163

Allies, ix–x, 4–5

Allport, Lawrence, 174–75

ammunition, 123

Anacker, Lyle, 230–31

Anderson, Bruce, 10

Andres, Arthur, 37

Andrews, Buddy, 252

Andrews, Stanley, 145–46

Arashio, 134, 145, 150

Army Air Corps, 17, 41, 42, 87

Arnold, Henry, 76, 111, 158–59, 177; Kenney and, 189, 241–42

Asagumo, 134, 137, 154, 157

Asashio, 134, 151

Aso, Tetsuo, 224

Atabrine, 185

Australia: American pilots cooperating with, 44–45; American relations with Australians, 103, 259–60; New Guinea controlled by, 2. *See also specific topics*

Ayatosan Maru, 68

B-17s, 50, 70, 79, 137; B-24s replacing, 189; firepower of, 107; of 43rd Bomb Group, 113, 138, 171; Kenney on, 108; of 19th Bomb Group, 93–94; at Rabaul, 108; Walker, K. N., on, 112; at Wewak, 192

B-18s, 79

B-24s, 216; B-17s replaced by, 189; firepower of, 107; of 43rd Bomb Group, 272–73; at Hollandia, 275–76, 277; at Lakunai, 228–29;

of 19th Bomb Group, 136–37; of 90th Bomb Group, 251; of RAAF, 249; at Rabaul, 229; at Vunakanau, 225–26, 228–29; at Wewak, 191, 192

B-25s, 122, 223; at Dagua, 196; of Fifth Air Force, 100–101; in 405th Bomb Squadron, 192, 193; Gunn modifying, 100; at Kavieng, 264; Larner on, 142; modifications to, 198–99; of 90th Bomb Group, 144; origins of, 47; at Rabaul, 222, 230, 240–41; at Rapopo, 227; at Simpson Harbor, 237; of 3rd Attack Group's 8th Bomb Squadron, 47–48, 68; in 3rd Bomb Group, 193, 222; at Vunakanau, 227; Walker, B., on, 141–42; Webster on, 174; at Wewak, 201

B-26s, 23; fuel transfer systems of, 24; at Lae, 62; of 22nd Bomb Group, 170

Baird, Julian, 278–79

Ball, Ed, 146–47

Ball, William, 253

Barker, Ronald, 247–48; on Vultee Vengeance, 248–49

Barnes, Clay, 146–47

Barron, William, 282

Bataan Death March, 17, 155

Battle of Brisbane, 103

Battle of Midway, 134, 240

Bauhof, Arthur, 169; death of, 167–68

Bauman, Michael, 24; Kenney and, 162

Beaufighters, 80, 156; of 30 Squadron, 139; at Vunakanau, 224–25; Walker, B., on, 140

Bell Aircraft, 41, 42

Bellairs, William, 6

Bena Bena, 183–84

Benson, Eugene, 263–65, 267

Benson, James, 58, 67, 71, 304; survival of, 72–73

Bente, Frederick, 160

Bentson, William, 103

Berry, Jack, 84

Berry Field, 84

Best, Ezra, 150

Best, Robert, 277–78

Bevlock, James, 37

Biak, 297; seizure of, 289

Bishop, Billy, 268

Bismarck Sea, 133, 281

Bismarck Sea Battle, 158, 161–62, 214, 274

Black Sunday, 286

Blaney, Fred, 250–51

Bomber Mafia, 110–11

Bombs to Nip On, 98–99

Bong, Richard, 267, 268, 305

Boram, 181, 194–95, 198

Bosnek Beach, 289

Bossi, Fred, 237

Bougainville, 97, 221, 234

Boulton, Bill, 224–25

Bradley, Donald, 274

Brereton, John Le Gay, 8–9, 11

Brereton, Lewis, 46–47

Brett, George, 49, 77; as commander, 50, 52; MacArthur and, 75; Smith on, 52; Sutherland and, 50–51

Brewster Buffalos, 4

Brisbane, 5, 17, 90, 101–2, 297–98

British Register Corporation, 274

Brown, Paul, 37

Brown, Weslie, 277

Bulova, Arde, 159

Bulova Watch Company, 159

Buna, 58, 68, 157–58

Bundy, William, 252

Burley, Enoch, 187, 188

Burtnette, Claude S., 117

Busama, 20

Butler, Mick, 25

Byars, Donald, 166

Bybee, Donald, 201

C-47s, 79, 83, 101–2, 182, 183, 188, 215; at Port Moresby, 123, 125; at Wau, 122–27

CAC. *See* Commonwealth Aircraft Corporation

Cairnes, 160

camouflage, of Zeroes, 166

Campbell, Charles: aircraft of, 33; Greene and, 32

cannibalism, 211

Cape Boram, 273

Cape Gloucester, 136–37, 221, 256

Cape Grenville, 33

Cape Nelson, 163–64, 165

Cape Torokina, 234, 241

Cape Ward Hunt, 138, 149

Cape York Peninsula, 1; Greene on, 31

cargo vessels, 160

Carins, 31

Caroline Island, 3

Carroll, Joseph, 202, 282

Casale, Joe, 191

Casey, John, 32–33

Cassidy, Frederick, 140, 143, 156

Cater, 163

Cathcart, Charles, 188

Celebes, 301

Champlin, Fred, 242

Chance-Vought, 295

Chand, Nirpal, 210

Channon, Oswald, 25

Chapman, Charles, 39

Charters Towers, 85–86

Cheli, Ralph, 198–99, 200; memorialization of, 208; survival of, 208–9

Chennault, Claire, 111

chiggers, 185

Christmas, 256

Chudoba, Edward, 19, 144

colonization, 2

Colwell, Alfred, 282–83

Commonwealth Aircraft Corporation (CAC), 4

Cooktown, 32

Cooper, George, 229, 236

Coral Sea, 45, 67

Cowie, William, 93

Cox, Barry, 7; death of, 28

Crawford, Robert, 5–6, 15, 22, 25; on Milne Bay, 91; on American comrades, 45

Crawford, William, 93–94

Cresswell, Richard, 156; on sharks, 157

Curry, Robert, 304

Czarnecki, Edward, 255

Dagua, 181, 193; B-25s at, 196; Gay at, 195–96; Lackness at, 194–95; Middlebrook at, 195, 198

Daniels, M. E., 282

Danson, Warren, 272

Darwin, 53

Davidson, Charles, 284; rescue of, 285–86

Davies, John, 17–18; on A-24s, 73

Davis, Alfredo, 175

Davis, George, on Oro Bay, 163–65

DB-7, 87

DC-2s, 79

DC-3s, 79, 123

DC-5s, 79

DDT, 185–86

Dean, Claude, 59

Dean, Kenneth, 223

DeHaven, Robert, 180, 248–49

dengue fever, 185

dentistry, 187

diarrhea, 186

Dickinson, Wesley, 55, 56, 58–59, 72

Difilippo, John, 262, 263

Distinguished Flying Cross, 259

Dockery, Virgil, 187

Dobodura, 131, 147, 159, 215, 255; P-40 fighters at, 163

Donegan, John, 199; at Wewak, 201–3
Doolittle, James, 75
Douglas A-24 Banshee, 17
Drury, George, 142
Ducci, Ercoli, 184
Duigan, Terry, 137–38
Durand, Edward, 37, 84
Durand Airfield, 197–98
Duval, Leonard, 291–93; escape of,
    293–94
dysentery, 13, 185

Eason, Hoyt, 146
Eastern Front, 43
Efogi, 81
8th Bomb Squadron, 238
8th Fighter Group, 31, 167; aircraft
    of, 42–43; ground crews, 35; P-39s
    of, 35–36; at Port Moresby, 35; at
    7-Mile Drome, 37; Wagner in, 36
18th Pursuit Group, Walker, K. N.,
    at, 111
822nd Bomb Squadron, 276
823rd Bomb Squadron, 262
871st Airborne Engineer Aviation
    Battalion, 182
Eisenhower, Dwight D., 305
11 Squadron, 116
Ellerton, Montague David, 33; Tucker
    and, 34
Emirau, 295
Empress Augusta Bay, 221
English, Malcolm, 256
executions, 210

F4U, 65
F6F, 65
Falletta, Charles, 36th Pursuit
    Squadron led by, 34–35
Fall River, 91
Fanning (Lieutenant), 167
Fanning, Gordon, 228
Far East Air Forces, 46–47

Farley, Tom, 164
Fat Cat flights, 160
Faurot, Bob, 105
Felch, William, 262
Ferris, Richard, 257
Fifth Air Force, 47, 82, 89, 101,
    154–55, 215, 296–97; aircraft of,
    191–92, 257; B-25s of, 100–101;
    fighter protection of, 107; Kenney
    improving, 161–62; medical care in,
    185; Navy, U.S. and, 158; P-38s of,
    104; at Rabaul, 221–22, 228–29,
    240, 243, 244–45; in Wewak,
    181–82, 192
51st Division, Japanese Army, 134;
    destruction of, 153; at Lae, 153
Finschafen, 146, 248
1st Provisional Air Corps Regiment,
    17
5-Mile Drome, 84
Flying Aces, 268
Flying Tigers, 111, 299
food, 160, 284
Ford, Earnest, 101–2
Forster, Joe, 269
43rd Bomb Group, 108, 110, 131,
    149, 155; B-17s of, 113, 138, 171;
    B-24s of, 272–73
49th Fighter Group, 53, 289; aircraft
    of, 117–18; claims of, 169; Control
    Squadron, 163; losses of, 160; at
    Oro Bay, 164–66, 168; P-38s of,
    128–29, 145, 165–66; P-40s of,
    151–52, 165; at Wau, 128
405th Bomb Squadron, 194; B-25s in,
    192, 193
418th Night Fighter Squadron, 257
475th Fighter Group: creation of, 189;
    Lindbergh in, 296–97; P-38s of,
    258
498th Bomb Squadron, 273–74, 277
499th Bomb Squadron, 236
14-Mile Drome, 84

Fourth Air Army, Japanese, 181; at
    Wewak, 205
Fourth Air Force, 268
Foxworth, James, 292
Franklin, Obert, 160

G-8 and His Battle Aces, 268
Garbutt Field, 23
Garing, William: on sharks, 156;
    Walker, B., and, 156; Whitehead
    and, 136
Garoka, 183
Gasmata, 116, 221, 281
gastroenteritis, 13
Gato, 261
Gay, William, 194; combat experience
    of, 197; at Dagua, 195
Geelvink Bay, 300
Geer, Ray, 229
Giertsen, Owen, Manuel and, 242–43,
    253
Gilbert Island, 3
Gordon, Nathan, 264, 266, 267
Graham, Burton, 143–44
Great Britain, 2
Greene, George, 37; Campbell and,
    32; on Cape York Peninsula, 31;
    failures of, 34; on Horn Island,
    32–33
Green Island, 295
Griffith, John, 165
ground war, 213
Guadalcanal, 82, 91, 157
Guam, 2
Gully, John, 35
Gunn, Paul, 46–47, 139, 304–5; B-25s
    modified by, 100; Kenney and, 87,
    88–89, 100

Hall, Jack, 33
Halsey, William, 243–44
Haney, Bill, 166
Hangiri, 58

Hansa Bay, 271–72; seizure of, 274–
    75
Harbour, David, 129
Harris, Ernest, 118, 167
Hayman, May, 58, 67; death of, 72
Hayworth, Arnold, 290
Heckling Hare, 63
Hecox, Thane, 229
Heller, Robert, 187, 188
Henebry, John, 142, 259, 274, 288
Herman, B. F., 199
Hill, John, 69
Hollandia, 272, 274, 296; B-24s at,
    275–76, 277; destruction of, 286;
    Kenney on, 275, 277, 278; P-38s
    at, 277–78
Holloway, Bruce, 111
Hong Kong, 2
Honi Kuu Okole, 71
Hoppe, Franklyn, 71
Horii, Tomitaro, 82
Horn Island, 31; Greene on, 32–33
House, A. T., Jr., 117, 151–52
Howard, Robert, 167
Huhn, Robert, 281; at Saidor, 282–83
Huisman, William, 272
Humboldt Bay, 278, 300–301
Hungerpiller, James, 237–38
Huon Gulf, 154–55, 173
Huon Peninsula, 247, 271, 286
Hyland, Norman, 239

I-17, 157
I-26, 157
Induna, 173
Iron Range, 97; airfields at, 98
Isokaze, 95

Jackson, John F., 7–8, 10, 14–15, 84;
    death of, 27–28; solo missions of,
    19–20
Jackson, Les, 25, 28
Jackson Field, 84

Japan: aircraft of, 64–65, 107; war
    crimes of, 210–11
Java, 18
Jazbo of New Dubuque, 258–59
Jeffrey, Peter, 6–7
Johnson, Gerald, 258; on Rabaul,
    227–28
Johnson, Lyndon, at Port Moresby,
    62–63
Jones, Curran, at Lae, 61–62
jungle rot, 186
jungles, 20–21

Kanga Force, 121–22, 124, 125
Kavieng, 155, 262, 276; B-25s at, 264;
    rescues at, 265
Kawasaki Ki-61s, xii
Kearby, Neel, 177, 272, 305
Keel, Henry, 56; death of, 57;
    Murphy, L., on, 57
Keifuku Maru, 114
Keisho Maru, 226
Kembu Maru, 134
Kenney, George, 75, 135, 154–55,
    182, 262; on A-20s, 88–89;
    accolades of, 303; Arnold and,
    189, 241–42; arrival of, 76–77;
    on B-17s, 108; Bauman and, 162;
    Fifth Air Force improved by,
    161–62; Gunn and, 87, 88–89,
    100; on Hollandia, 275, 277, 278;
    on Japanese, 162–63; Kearby and,
    177–78; on Kokoda Track, 80–81;
    on Lae, 156; as leader, 76, 85;
    Lindbergh and, 297–98; MacArthur
    and, 77–78, 81–82, 86–87;
    McMahon on, 87; on 90th Bomb
    Group, 97, 100; on Operation 81,
    157–58; on P-38s, 106; on P-47s,
    177–78; performance of, 86; on
    Port Moresby, 81; publicity of, 268;
    on Rabaul, 227, 240; reorganization
    led by, 86; salvaging efforts of, 83;

staff fired by, 86; Sutherland and,
    76–77, 85; on Sverdrup, 130–31;
    True and, 233; Walker, B., on,
    85–86; Walker, K. N., and, 110,
    111–12, 113–14; on Wewak, 203;
    Whitehead and, 90
Ki-21s, 195–96, 224
Ki-43s, 65–66, 134, 173, 196, 199,
    268; at Wau, 128
Ki-45s, 262
Ki-46s, 161
Ki-48s, 187, 188–89
Ki-61s, 252; design of, 205; at Wewak,
    205
Kila Kila, 25, 83
Kimura, Masatomi, 133, 136–37,
    151; convoy of, 137, 138, 143; on
    Operation 81, 157; vessels of, 134
Kiriwina Island, 24, 220, 227, 242–43,
    288
Kittyhawks. See P-40 fighters
Klausner, John, 99
Knight, Frederick, 99–100
Knox, Frank, 158
Kokoda Track, 67, 68–69, 73, 213;
    aircraft maintenance on, 79;
    challenges on, 78–79; Kenney on,
    80–81; MacArthur and, 129; Seizo
    on, 82; 35th Fighter Group at, 80
Komachi, Sadamu, 64, 65
Korean War, MacArthur in, 304
Kotoku Maru, 69, 70
Krayenbuhl, Craigie, 263
Kudo, Shigetoshi, 171
Kyokusei Maru, 134, 137; sinking of,
    139, 153

Lackness, Berdines: combat experience
    of, 197; at Dagua, 194–96
LaCroix, Lucius, 180
Lae, 18–19, 36, 38, 39, 214–15; attacks
    on, 90, 109; B-26s at, 62; 51st
    Division, Japanese Army at, 153;

Jones on attack on, 61–62; Kenney on, 156; Tsunoda on, 109; Walker, K. N., on, 112–13

Lakunai, 114, 225; B-24s at, 228–29

Landing Craft Infantry (LCI), 176

Larner, Edward, 141; on B-25s, 142

Larronde, Felix, 144

Larson, Paul, 98

LCI. *See* Landing Craft Infantry

Lee, Donald, 179–80

Leighton, Leonard, 189

Leslie, George, 116–17

Lexington, 45–46

Lindbergh, Charles, 295; in 475th Fighter Group, 296–97; Kenney and, 297–98; P-38 piloted by, 297; Sutherland and, 298

Lindsay, Kenneth, 291, 292, 293

Lobo, 252

Lockheed Hudson, 7, 10

Long, John, 33

Los Negros Island, 271, 305

Love, Francis, 178–79, 239

Lovett, Joseph, 38, 39

Lowery, Herman, 55–56

loyalty, 41

Luftwaffe, 43

Lutton, Lowell, 239

Lynch, Thomas, 268, 305

MacArthur, Douglas, 50, 116, 303; Brett and, 75; Kenney and, 77–78, 81–82, 86–87; Kokoda Track and, 129; in Korean War, 304; as leader, 129; on Operation 81, 158; on Philippines, 220–21; public relations and, 158, 268; on Rabaul, 220–21, 226; strategies of, 214

MacAvoy, David, 256

Madang, 193, 248, 260, 283; capture of, 285–86

Maeda, Yoshimitsu, 37

Maffin Bay, 289

Mainwaring, John, 38

Malachick (Sergeant), 185

Malahang, 117

malaria, 13, 22, 185

Malay Peninsula, 2–3

Manila, 46

Manuel, Gordon, 256, 304; Giertsen and, 242–43, 253; natives and, 207–8; on New Britain Island, 261; rescue of, 207; survival of, 172–73

Manus, 271

Mapos, 21

March Field, 111

Marilinan, 182, 193

Marine Corps, 73, 244, 256

Markham Valley, 215

Marling, Milby, 228

marriage, 102–4

Marshall, George, 75, 86, 220

Marshall Island, 3

Martin, James, 151–52

Masuda, Reiji, 144

Matala plantation, 173

Mayo, Leo, 164, 238–39

McGhee, Donald, 38

McGovern, William, 33

McGuire, Thomas, 267, 305

McKenna, John, 284; rescue of, 285–86

McLaughlin, James, 272

McMahon, Robert, on Kenney, 87

McWhirt, Joseph, 149, 150

Me-109, 11

Meadows, Maureen, 102

Medal of Honor, of Walker, K. N., 115

Meehan, Arthur, 98

Melbourne, 4, 53

Meng, Louis, 37, 38

Mevelo River, 253

Middlebrook, Garrett, 194; combat experience of, 197; at Dagua, 195, 198

Midway, 119
Mills, Harold, 252
Milne Bay, 70; attack on, 91, 93, 213–14; conditions at, 91; Crawford, R., on, 91; as critical location, 90; Turnbull at, 92
mites, 185
Mitsubishi A6M Zero, 4
Mitsubishi G3M, 16, 39
Mitsubishi G4M, 7
Mokmer, 289, 290
Moluccas, 301
Moore, Woodrow, 146, 155
Morgan, Mostyn, 156
morphine, 202
Morris-Hadwell, Edward, 225
Mortensen, Max, 229
Mount Lawes, 28
Moye, Albert, 24
Munro, Keith, 188
Murphree, Clinton, 208, 209
Murphy, James, 108–9, 131
Murphy, Louis, on Keel, 57–58
Murray, Frances, 174–75
Musik, Island, 176
Myoko Maru, 117, 118
Myola Lake, 81

Nadzab, 19, 217, 266, 278; attack on, 215
Nassau Bay, 176
Navy, U.S., 45–46, 73, 154; Fifth Air Force and, 158; at Rabaul, 243
Nazis, 305
Nell. *See* Mitsubishi G3M
New Britain Island, 222, 256; Manuel on, 261
New Georgia Islands, 220
New Guinea: Australian control of, 2; colonization of, 2; conflict in, ix; geography of, ix, 1–2; jungles of, 20–21. *See also specific topics*

New Guinea Volunteer Rifles, 21, 22, 26
Nichiryu Maru, 117, 118
Nichols, Franklin, 117
Nimitz, Chester, 276, 278, 286
19th Bomb Group, 50; B-17s of, 93–94; B-24s of, 136–37
90th Bomb Group, 136, 141, 225, 291–92; B-24s of, 251; B-25s of, 144; Kenney on, 97, 100; mission reports, 144; at Wewak, 250
9th Fighter Squadron, 147–48, 228, 258, 272
Noemfoor Island, 297
Nojima, 134; sinking of, 145
Normanby Island, 95
North American NA-16, 4
Nutter, Frank, 166

OA-10, 119
O'Brien, William, 155
Oigawa Maru, 134
110th Reconnaissance Squadron, 260
O'Neill, Brian, 150
Operation 18, 116, 118–19
Operation 81, 134, 141, 147, 302; failure of, 153; Kenney on, 157–58; Kimura on, 157; MacArthur on, 158; ships destroyed in, 157
Operation Cartwheel, 220, 256, 271
Operation Mo, 45
Operation Persecution, 276
Operation Reckless, 276
Oro Bay: Davis, G., on, 163–65; 49th Fighter Group at, 164–66, 168; P-36s at, 165–66; records of, 168; Zeroes at, 164, 168–69
Orr, John, 237–38
Overson, Keith, 166
Owen Stanley Range, 19, 36, 37, 67, 108, 130, 250

P-36s, 11, 111

P-38s, 65, 122, 268, 269; design of, 104–5; of Fifth Air Force, 104; of 49th Fighter Group, 128–29, 145; of 475th Fighter Group, 258; at Hollandia, 277–78; Kenney on, 106; Lindbergh piloting, 297; at Rabaul, 240–41; at Simpson Harbor, 238–39; success of, 106; of 35th Fighter Group, 145; 39th Fighter Squadron, 105; Zeroes *vs.*, 105–6, 146

P-39s, xi, 31, 36–37, 38, 45, 51, 187, 268; design of, 41–42; of 8th Fighter Group, 35–36; potential of, 43; Soviet use of, 43; of 35th Fighter Group, 128–29; Wagner on, 41; Zero *vs.*, 39–40

P-40 fighters, 4, 5, 6, 9, 117, 122; Crawford on, 45; at Dodobura, 163; of 49th Fighter Group, 151–52, 165; light bulbs in, 13; maintenance of, 11, 16; Pettett on, 12; of 75 Squadron, 25; Zeroes and, 27–28

P-47 Thunderbolt, xi–xii, 65, 257, 272, 284, 287; design of, 177, 258; development of, 177; Kenney on, 177–78

P-51s, 65

P-70s, 257

P-400s, 42

Pacific Ocean Areas, 276

Papuans, 2, 20, 78, 183–84, 287; after war, 305

parachutes, 79, 89

parademolition bombs, 89–90

parafrags, 89, 278

Parker, Joseph, 71

Parkinson, Mavis, 58, 67; death of, 72

Payne, Robert, 276, 277

PBY Catalinas, 116–19, 133, 137, 169; accidents of, 266–67; rescues by, 264–66

Pearl Harbor, 2–3, 49, 155

Pearson, William, 263

Peaslee, Jesse, 166

Peebles, Charles, 201–2

Peters (Lieutenant), 185

Peterson, Harlan, 230

Peterson, James, 160

Pettett, John, 5, 10, 16; on P-40s, 12

Philippines, 17, 18, 87, 301–2; MacArthur on, 220–21

pinks, 102

Piper, John, 9, 15, 21, 35

Pistol Packin' Mama, 250–51

Pittman, William, 200

Planck, Carl, 255

Pomeroy (Sergeant), 175–76

Popondetta, 71–72

Porebada, 25

Port Moresby, 3–4, 5, 7, 14–15, 29, 34; attacks on, 90; C-47s at, 123, 125; 8th Fighter Group at, 35; Johnson at, 62–63; Kenney on, 81; makeup of, 83; 75 Squadron at, 10, 16, 25, 43–44; 22nd Bomb Group at, 23

Portugal, 2

Potts, Joe, xii

Poulsen, Bryant, 251

Pratt & Whitney, 88

Prentice, George, 177

Price, Theron, 228

Purzai, R. U., 211

Put Put, 173

Queensland, 5, 97

R1830, 88

RAAFs. *See* Royal Australian Air Force

Rabaul, 3, 23–24, 57–58, 78, 93, 113–14, 130, 300; airbase at, 219; aircraft at, 233–34; B-17s at, 108; B-24s at, 229; B-25s at, 222, 230, 240–41; enemy losses at, 240–41; fallout from, 244–45; Fifth Air Force at, 221–22, 228–29, 240, 243, 244–45; geography of, 219; Johnson, G., on, 227–28; Kenney on, 227, 240; MacArthur on, 220–21, 226; Navy at, 243; P-38s at, 240–41; success of attack on, 240; 38th Bomb Group at, 229; 345th Bomb Group at, 229; 22nd Bomb Group at, 170

radar, 16, 163

RAF. *See* Royal Air Force

Ramu Valley, 250

Rapopo, 221; B-25s at, 227; 3rd Bomb Group at, 224

Ratajski, Charles, 255

religion, 188

Renneisen, Bob, 150

Rich, Hampton, 226

Richards, Albert, 266

Richardson, Kenneth, 239–40

Richthofen, Manfred von, 268

Rickenbacker, Eddie, 268

Rippy, John, 304

Rizor, Quintin, 290

Roberts, Allan, 242, 254, 304

Rodgers, Fred, 281–82

Rogers, Arthur, 225

Rogers, Floyd, 59–60, 76; as commander, 69

Rogers Field, 84

Roosevelt, Franklin D., 116, 295

Roper, Clarence, 251

Rororna, 27

Royal Air Force (RAF), 42–43, 88

Royal Australian Air Force (RAAFs), 1–7, 10, 35, 42, 50, 247; B-24s of, 249; in Wewak, 303

Royal New Zealand Air Force, 244

Royce, Ralph, 51

Royce Mission, 51

Saidor, 249, 278; Huhn at, 282–83

Sakai, Saburo, 168

Salamaua, 18, 36–38, 170, 175–76, 214–15; attacks on, 90

Sam, Ralph, 70

San Antonio Rose, 113–16

SBD Dauntless, 17

SBDs, 73

Scammel, Victor, 202

Scandrett, P., 14

Schwab, Virgil, 21

Schwimmer, Charles, 84

scrub typhus, 185

SBD dive bombers, 244

Seizo, Okado, on Kokoda Track, 82

Sentai, Hiko, 299

7-Mile Drome, 7, 13, 25, 68, 215–16; construction of, 83–84; 8th Fighter Group at, 37

7th Fighter Squadron, 151, 179, 248

Sevene, Earl, 55–56

17-Mile Drome, 84

71st Bomb Squadron, 266

75 Squadron, 1, 5, 14–16; P-40s of, 25, 43; pilot casualties in, 44; at Port Moresby, 10, 16, 25, 43–44; reputation of, 44; struggles of, 28; undertrained pilots in, 43–44

71st Bomb Squadron, 150, 184, 193; at Wewak, 199–200

Sfarnas, James, 252

Shaggy Ridge, 248

sharks: Cresswell on, 157; Garing on, 156

Sheehan, Oliver, 251

Shelman, Jacob, 290

Shifflet, Fred, 146

Shikinami, 134, 154, 157

Shimura, 143

Shin-ai Maru, 134

Shirayuki, 134
Shōhō, 45–46
Silver Star, 63
Simpson Harbor, 23–24, 114, 295;
    attack on, 221–22, 234–35; B-25s
    at, 237; P-38s at, 238–39; 345th
    Bomb Group at, 234–35; Zeroes
    at, 236
Singapore, 210
Singh, Chint, 211
Skinner, William, 199
Sky Aces, 268
Small, Art, 149
Smith, Arthur, 72–73
Smith, Frederick, 52
Smith, Lawrence, 252
Smith, William, 263–64, 265
Smoots, William, 290
Sogaard, Folmer, 108
Soloc, John, 273
Solomon Islands, 45, 82
Solomon Sea, 135
Soviet Union, 305; P-39s used by, 43
Stimson, Henry, 75
Stokes, T. V., 116
Sutherland, Richard, 159; Brett and,
    50–51; Kenney and, 76–77, 85;
    Lindbergh and, 298
Sverdrup, Leif, 130–31
Swanson, Dustin, 191, 252–53
Swanson, Paul, 260
Swift, Raymond, 258
Sydney, 291

Tadji, 275
Taimei Maru, 134, 144
Taiyei Maru, 274
Takano (Colonel), 210, 211
Takar, 288
Talili Bay, 209
Tamura, Yoshikazu, 209
Tanikawa, Kazuo, 203–4
Teiyo Maru, 134

Ten Knights in a Bar Room, 251
test-hopping, 257
3rd Attack Group's 8th Bomb
    Squadron, 17–18, 44, 46, 69, 103,
    289; A-20s of, 139; A-24s flown
    by, 59; B-25s used by, 47–48, 68;
    mission reports, 144
3rd Attack Group's 89th Bomb
    Squadron, 55, 88
3rd Bomb Group, 155, 236–37, 273,
    288, 301; A-20s of, 145, 263; B-25s
    in, 193, 222, 224; at Rapopo, 224
3rd Destroyer Flotilla, 133
3rd Marine Division, 234
Thirteenth Air Force, 300
30-Mile Drome, 84
30 Squadron, 128, 140; Beaufighters
    of, 139
32nd Division, moving of, 81–82
32 Squadron, 7, 10
35th Fighter Group, xi, 159, 188; at
    Kokoda Track, 80; on medical
    care, 185; P-38s of, 145; P-39s of,
    128–29; at Wau, 128–29
35th Pursuit Squadron, 34, 308n1;
    aircraft of, 42–43
36th Fighter Squadron, 272
38th Bomb Group, 155, 184, 223,
    262, 281; at Rabaul, 229; at
    Wewak, 199
39th Fighter Squadron, 62, 145–46;
    P-38s of, 105
36th Pursuit Squadron, Falletta leading,
    34
Thompson, Jack, 93–94
Thompson, Paul, 196
3-Mile Drome, 83–84
3 Squadron, 7
312th Bomb Group, 284
321st Bomb Squadron, 252
345th Bomb Group, 223–24, 228, 265;
    at Rabaul, 229; at Simpson Harbor,
    234–35; at Wewak, 273–74

347th Troop Carrier Group, 186
348th Fighter Group, 177, 251
Tice, Clay, 147
Tobera, 221, 224–25, 228–29
Tokitsukaze, 134
Tony. *See* Ki-61s
Topolcany, Frank, 187
Townsville, 23, 62–63
Transport Command, 47
True, Clinton, 223, 229; Kenney and, 233
Truk, 241
Tsili Tsili, 182, 183, 186, 208
Tsunoda, Kazuo, 109
Tucker, Arthur, 1, 4–5, 8, 27; Ellerton and, 34; on pilot struggles, 28
Tufi, 154
Tulagi, 45
Tumleo Island, 276
Turnbull, Peter, 10, 16; at Milne Bay, 92
Tusunoda, Kazuo, 64
12-Mile Drome, 84
22nd Bomb Group, 62, 168; B-26s of, 170; at Port Moresby, 23; at Rabaul, 170
24 Squadron, 248–49
27th Bombardment Group, 17–18
2/33rd Infantry Battalion, 215

United States: Australian pilots cooperating with, 44–45; Australian relations with Americans, 103, 259–60
Uranami, 134, 157
U.S. Army Air Forces (USAAF), 4, 42–43, 44; fighter unit redesignations, 49

Val, 179–80
Vernon, David, 116
V Fighter Command, 169
Vitiaz Strait, 135, 138

Vodra, Dick, 164
Volk, Floyd, 169
Vukelic, Wade, 273–74
Vultee Vengeance, 247; Barker on, 248–49; 24 Squadron and, 248–49
Vunakanau, 114, 221; attack on, 222–23; B-24s at, 225–26, 228–29; B-25s at, 227; Beaufighters at, 224–25

Wabash Cannonball, 63
Wackett, Wilbur, 7, 10, 22
Wagner, Boyd, 40, 84; in 8th Fighter Group, 36; on P-39s, 41
Waigani, 84
Wakde, seizure of, 289
Walker, Brian, 91, 139; on B-25s, 141–42; on Beaufighters, 140; as commander, 111; Garing and, 156; on Kenney, 85–86
Walker, Dick, 236–37
Walker, Kenneth N.: on B-17s, 112; death of, 115–16; at 18th Pursuit Group, 111; Kenney and, 110, 111–12, 113–14; on Lae, 112–13; Medal of Honor of, 115
Wallace, Ralph, 230
Ward Field, 84
Waren, 291–92
Warren, Raymond, 208, 209
Watom Island, 209
Watut Valley, 182
Wau, 121; C-47s at, 122–27; as critical location, 122; 49th Fighter Group at, 128; Ki-43s at, 128; 35th Fighter Group at, 128–29
weather, 149, 228, 283
Webb, James, 56–57, 59
Webster, Bill, 173, 176; on B-25s, 174
Wesche, Fred, 110, 114
Wewak, 108, 188–89, 198, 268; aircrew reports from, 204; airfields

in, 181; B-17s at, 192; B-24s at, 191, 192; B-25s at, 201; death of, 274; destruction in, 204; Donegan at, 201–32; Fifth Air Force in, 181–82, 192; Fourth Air Army, Japanese at, 205; Kenney on, 203; Ki-61s at, 205; 90th Bomb Group at, 250; RAAF in, 303; seizure of, 303; 71st Bomb Squadron at, 199–200; Tanikawa on, 203–4; 38th Bomb Group at, 199; 345th Bomb Group at, 273–74
Whetters, Alan, 12, 25–26, 27
Whetters, William, 8
White, Alpheus, 290
Whitehead, Ennis, 87; Garing and, 136; Kenney and, 90
Widener, Robert, 173–74
Wilkins, Raymond, 70, 238
Williams, Paul, 161
Wirraway, 4, 6, 11, 43, 80

Wood, Howard, 216
Woodlark Island, 220
World War I, 49, 110, 268
Wuerpel, Theodore, 56

Yakumo Maru, 273
Yancey, John, 166
Yanks from Hell, 191
Yayoi, 94–95
Yoshihara, Masao, 169
Yukikaze, 134, 137, 154, 157

Zekes. *See* Zeroes
Zeroes, 9–11, 18–19, 25, 36–37, 134, 152; camouflage of, 166; design of, 64; destruction of, 168–69; at Oro Bay, 164, 168–69; P-38s *vs.*, 105–6, 146; P-39s *vs.*, 39–40; P-40 fighters and, 27–28; paint schemes of, 166; piloting, 64–65; at Simpson Harbor, 236